INDEPENDENT SCHOOL GUIDE

FOR WASHINGTON, D.C. AND SURROUNDING AREA

— 13th EDITION —

INDEPENDENT SCHOOL GUIDE

FOR WASHINGTON, D.C. AND SURROUNDING AREA

— 13th EDITION —

A COMPREHENSIVE GUIDE TO INDEPENDENT, PRIVATE, RELIGIOUS AND PAROCHIAL SCHOOLS IN AND AROUND WASHINGTON, D.C.

INCLUDES EDUCATIONAL SPECIALISTS

EDITED BY JILL ZACHARIE

Copyright ©   1971, 1973, 1977, 1980, 1983, 1987, 1989, 1991, 1993, 1995, 1998

Lois H. Coerper   Shirley W. Mersereau

Copyright ©   2001, 2004 by Jill Zacharie

Published by Lift Hill Press, Inc., Independent School Guides

Printed in the United States of America

ISBN: 0-9700022-1-1

Library of Congress Control Number: 2003098226

Cover design and typography by Victor Weaver

Additional copies may be ordered from:

Lift Hill Press, Inc.
4930-A Eisenhower Avenue
Alexandria, VA 22304

703-212-9113   FAX   703-212-9114   E-mail: jillwbd@prodigy.net

Lift Hill Press is distributed exclusively to the trade by
Washington Book Distributors
www.washingtonbk.com

Contents

Index to Schools by Location

Acknowledgments

Our thanks to the creators of this book, Lois Coerper and Shirley Mersereau, for their vision, guidance and vote of confidence.

Special thanks are due to Art Brown of Vandamere Press/ABI Associates who continues to share his time and expertise to help us in our publishing efforts.

We appreciate the continuing support of our colleagues at Washington Parent Magazine and Karen Toussaint of The Parent Pages.

Thanks to graphic designer/typographer Victor Weaver for taking us to the next level.

Thanks to our friend Merry Cavanaugh, author and publisher of *The Metropolitan Washington Preschool and Daycare Guide.*

Thanks are also due to Victor Zacharie, III, Victor Zacharie, Jr., Keegan Zacharie, Ellen Fetzner, Ann Wrigley, Terry Fenton and Theresa Nugent for the many and varied roles they played as database creator, envelope stuffer, information verifier, proofreader, administrative aid and general moral support.

Our thanks are given to the educational specialists whose listings and ads give us financial help to create this book.

And last, our thanks to all the schools who provide us with the information that is the core of this publication. While schools were not required to pay a fee to be included, there were many who gave us voluntary financial support, for which we are especially grateful. The names of these Supporting Schools follow.

Supporting Schools

The following schools generously gave financial support towards the publication of this guide:

Academy of Christian Education
Accotink Academy
Alexandria Country Day School
Ambleside School
Aquinas Montessori School
Beddow High School, Junior High School
   and Beddow Montessori Schools
Blessed Sacrament School Chevy Chase
Bowie Montessori Children's House
Brooksfield School
Burgundy Farm Country Day School
Chesapeake Academy of Northern Virginia
Christian Family Montessori School
Christian Fellowship School
Commonwealth Academy
Concord Hill School
The Congressional Schools of Virginia
Edlin School
Emerson Preparatory School
Episcopal High School
Flint Hill School
The Franklin Montessori School, Forest Hills
Grace Lutheran School
Green Acres School
Henson Valley Montessori School
Holton-Arms School
Kenwood School
The King's Christian Academy
The Kiski School
The Lab School of Washington
The Langley School
The Learning Community of Northern Virginia
The Madeira School
McLean School of Maryland
Mercersburg Academy

Miller School
Montrose Christian School
National Cathedral School
The Newport School
Norwood School
Nysmith School for the Gifted
Oak Hill Christian School Herndon
Oak Hill Christian School Reston
Oasis School
Olney Adventist Preparatory School
Parkmont School
Paul VI Catholic High School
Pinecrest School
Powhatan School
Randolph-Macon Academy
Reston Montessori School
The River School
Riverdale Baptist School
Seneca Academy/Circle School
Sheridan School
Sidwell Friends School
St. Andrew's Episcopal School
St. Charles Catholic School
St. Luke School
St. Patrick's Episcopal Day School
St. Stephen's & St. Agnes School
Sydenstricker School
Trinity Christian School
Washington Hebrew Congregation Rabbi Joseph Weinberg
    Early Childhood Center and
Washington Hebrew Congregation Primary School
Washington Hebrew Congregation Edlavitch-Tyser
    Early Childhood Center
Washington Waldorf School
The Woods Academy
Wyoming Seminary

Foreword

If you are holding this book in your hands, you are invested in the search for the best education possible for a child. Parents, schools and educational professionals alike have two women to thank for the existence of this guide.

In 1971, Lois Coerper and Shirley Mersereau realized in the course of making decisions about their own families' education that there was no single source for information about the many private schools in the Washington, D.C. Metropolitan area. So they created one. Through eleven editions it served thousands of families in their quest for the best school for their own unique needs. Its bright school bus-yellow cover has become familiar to the educational community here and the book has developed an excellent reputation for its comprehensiveness. In effect, it creates a portrait of the rich diversity of educational choices in our area. In compiling the 12th edition we followed in Lois' and Shirley's hard-to-fill footsteps and learned firsthand the challenges and rewards of an undertaking this size.

Now we have produced the 13th edition and it is the largest and most comprehensive yet. We actively sought out schools in a wider geographical area, responding to parents' requests for specific cities. We looked for more schools in religious denominations and approached more special needs schools. We scanned regional periodicals to learn of schools opening, relocating or closing. The happy result is almost 50 additional schools in this new edition.

The school listings were compiled after submitting questionnaires to over 600 schools. In addition, we spoke directly with many schools to obtain or clarify their listings in this book. Thus the information in our book is provided by the people who know it best- the schools themselves. The web is a helpful tool, but we feel it is no substitute for current information received directly from the school administration. A caveat arising from this is that parents will need to check the facts with the schools they are researching. We cannot be responsible for errors and omissions and have not independently verified the information that has been provided to us by the schools.

A very few schools, for reasons of their own, did not want to be included in this book and their wishes were respected. But the vast majority of educators we contacted provided us with information, answered our questions and wished us well. We ask parents contacting the schools to please let them know you learned about them in the *Independent School*

Guide. This will encourage even greater participation in future editions. If there are schools we missed, we would very much like to learn about them both for the 14th edition and for possible inclusion on our website, where we hope to keep updated information between editions.

The information herein is not a reflection of the personal views of the editor, but is intended as a collection of facts to help the reader focus on what is most important to them.

Our *Guide* does not indicate whether a school is accredited. All independent schools must receive state or local approval but they do not have to be accredited to operate. Parents concerned with a school's accreditation must research this for themselves. All information was as correct as we could make it at press time, but as change is inevitable, please contact the schools for the most current word. We would appreciate learning about changes as we strive to keep our database accurate between editions.

We wish you well in your search for quality education and hope this book helps you.

Jill Zacharie

Why Should I Consider an Independent School?

Far more than public schools, private schools are designed to meet the individual needs of each student. Smaller classes and personal attention assure a better learning environment and greater academic and social growth. Close student/teacher relationships are developed not only in the classroom but also on the playing fields, on the stage, and in a variety of extracurricular settings.

These schools emphasize values, self-confidence and responsible citizenship which serve as foundations for critical thinking and future achievement. Studies have shown that independent school students are far more likely to participate in sports and other extracurricular activities and in general will assume more active roles in the school community.

Due to the private school selection process, teachers are relieved from the burden of unruly, disruptive students and thus are free to devote their energy to communicating knowledge and ideas. Individual academic problems and potentials are more easily identified and addressed: students can be helped and encouraged to work to their highest capacity. Likewise, guidance counselors have time to spend with each student which means that each student's course selection and college applications will be carefully reviewed.

Private schools also allow parents to make clear choices about the basic direction of their child's education. Therefore, be sure to determine what is important to you. Is a specific religious emphasis desired? Do you seek greater opportunities in art, music, theater, dance- or want a particular second language? Does your child need the expertise of trained LD/ED teachers? Will you and your child be happier in a relatively free atmosphere which requires a great deal of self-motivation on your child's part to learn, or is a more highly structured, disciplined daily routine more compatible with your home lifestyle?

You do have a choice! Examine a school's philosophy and objectives to understand what is expected not only of each student but of each parent. Today, the single largest financial commitment you will ever make may be to the education of your children. Make the choice carefully and analyze at which level in school the expenditure will be the most valuable. Many educators believe that excitement for learning and the development of good study habits must happen in elementary and secondary school if students are to achieve at the college level and in later life.

When looking for a school for your child, here are some things to consider. First, know your child. If he or she is presently enrolled in a school, is it a happy and challenging situation? Are his work habits good? Are her extracurricular activities and friends constructive and satisfying? Confer with the teacher to determine if your child is progressing at an appropriate rate. For the younger child, an excellent analysis of school readiness is contained in *The Metropolitan Washington Preschool and Daycare Guide* by Merry Cavanaugh.

Second, decide on your basic requirements. That is, are you seeking religious, single-sex, boarding, special programs, LD/ED, extended day care, etc.? Then, with the aid of our geographically-keyed index, identify some appropriate schools. Visit their websites to learn more about them. Request catalogues and other pertinent information from the schools, and determine then which philosophy and program seems to meet your needs. All of this is best done by the fall of the year preceding the year of actual enrollment.

Third, plan to visit several schools and talk to the admission directors. Each school is a unique community. To find the right match between your child and a school is not an easy task but it is the most important goal in the admission process.

If you feel in need of additional advice from one who can realistically evaluate your child's potential and give an objective opinion, there are many educational counselors trained to do this very thing. These counselors will also have broad knowledge of the local school market and be able to guide you towards an appropriate school choice as well as identify ways of obtaining financial assistance should that be needed. A listing of some of these educational specialists is included in the last section of this book.

Will a private school insulate your child from the "real world"? Today's independent schools are committed to diversity as well as to the community. Indeed, many private schools have a much broader ethnic, cultural, and international mix than the neighborhood public school. Also, each student in the independent school is valued as an individual for his or her unique contribution to the group. Through school community service programs and other involvement the students are made aware of the needs of others not only on the local level but nationally and internationally as well.

How do independent schools assist working parents? Most schools today offer extended day or after school programs to allow parents flexibility with their work schedules. Some schools offer transportation or help with arranging car pools. Conference and meeting times are individually set to give parents the opportunity to be involved with their child's education. Many of the schools offer summer programs designed specifically to cover the same hours as the school year.

What is involved in the actual admissions process? Call, e-mail or write the schools you wish to know more about and ask for their literature to be sent to you, preferably in the fall of the year before your child will be applying. Arrange to visit the school and meet with the admissions director. At that time review with the director their admissions procedure. Also ask questions about financial arrangements and specific school programs. Quite often the school policy will require: an interview with your child, a transcript of grades, some standardized testing and personal and/or teacher recommendations. If you are applying to more that one school, inquire about the testing procedure because many of the local independent schools have agreed to share test results to keep the child from having to take the same intelligence, aptitude, and achievement tests more than once.

Application dates vary from school to school, but generally an application is made between September and January for the following fall. Acceptances are usually made in mid-March to April. However, many schools have "rolling admission" which means a child may apply and be accepted at any time during the year, space permitting.

Abbreviations and Acronyms

Following is a list of some of the abbreviations and acronyms used in this book:

ACE	Accelerated Christian Education Program
ACT	American College Testing
ADD	Attention Deficit Disorder
ADHD	Attention Deficit Hyperactivity Disorder
AMI	Association Montessori Internationale
AMS	American Montessori Society
AP	Advanced Placement
ACSI	Association of Christian Schools International
CYO	Catholic Youth Organization
ED	Emotionally Disturbed
ERB	Educational Records Bureau
ESL	English as a Second Language
ESY	Extended School Year
ETS	Educational Testing Service
FAFSA	Free Application for Federal Student Aid
GT	Gifted/Talented
IAC	Independent Athletic Conference
IB	International Baccalaureate
IEP	Individualized Education Program
ISEE	Independent School Entrance Exam
ISL	Independent School League
K	Kindergarten
LD	Learning Disability
LEA	Local Education Agency
MMR	Mildly Mentally Retarded
N	Nursery
NAEYC	National Association for the Education of Young Children
NHS	National Honor Society
NJHS	National Junior Honor Society
NILD	National Institute for Learning Disabilities
PE	Physical Education
PG	Post Graduate
PK	Pre-Kindergarten
SADD	Students Against Destructive Decisions
SAT	Scholastic Aptitude Test
SOL	Standards of Learning
SSS	School and Student Service for Financial Aid
SSAT	Secondary School Admission Test
TERI	The Education Resources Institute
TOEFL	Test of English as a Foreign Language
VAIS	Virginia Association of Independent Schools
WISC-III	Weschler Intelligence Scale for Children-Third Edition
WPPSI-R	Weschler Preschool and Primary Scale of Intelligence-Revised
WRAT	Wide Range Achievement Test

Information and Resources

Professional and Membership Organizations

Association of Independent Schools of Greater Washington (AISGW)
Executive Director, Elizabeth Downes
P.O. Box 9956
Washington, D.C. 20016   202-625-9223   FAX 202-625-9225
www.aisgw.org   Info@aisgw.org

A service organization and a network of nonprofit independent schools in the greater Washington, D.C. area

Association of Independent Schools of Maryland (AIMS)
890 Airport Park Road Suite 103
Glen Burnie, MD 21061   301-858-6311   or   410-761-3700
www.aimsmd.org

Private school membership association; professional development for teachers and administrators

National Association of Independent Schools (NAIS)
1620 L Street, N.W. Suite 1100
Washington, D.C. 20036-5605   202-973-9700   FAX 202-973-9790
www.nais.org

Membership organization representing approximately 1,200 independent schools and associations in the U.S. and abroad

Virginia Association of Independent Schools (VAIS)
6802 Paragon Place, Suite 525
Richmond, VA 23230   804-282-3592   FAX 804-282-3596
www.vais.org   info@vais.org

Service organization that promotes educational, ethical and professional excellence

Catholic Archdiocese Office of Education for D.C. and Maryland
5001 Eastern Avenue
Hyattsville, MD 20782
P.O. Box 29260
Washington, D.C. 20017   301-853-3800
www.adw.org

Office of Catholic Schools Diocese of Arlington
200 N. Glebe Road, Suite 503
Arlington, VA 22203   703-841-2519   FAX 703-524-8670
www.arlingtondiocese.org/schools   catholicschools@arlingtondiocese.org

Friends Council on Education
1507 Cherry Street
Philadelphia, PA 19102   215-241-7245   FAX 215-241-7299

www.friendscouncil.org   QuakerEd@aol.com

Serves Quaker education by advising and consulting with schools about their work as Friends institutions

Islamic Schools' League of America
P.O. Box 1265
Falls Church, VA 22041   571-278-0806
www.4islamicschools.org

Nonprofit organization supporting and improving Islamic education in America

Jewish Education Service of North America (JESNA)
111 8th Avenue
New York, NY 10011   212-284-6950   FAX 212-284-6951
www.jesna.org

Educational coordinating, planning and development agency

Lutheran Education Association
7400 Augusta Street
River Forest, IL 60305   708-209-3343   FAX 708-209-3458
www.lea.org

Professional organization linking, equipping, and affirming educators in Lutheran ministries

National Association of Episcopal Schools
815 Second Avenue, Suite 313
New York, NY 10017   800-334-7626 ext. 6134   FAX 212-286-9366
www.episcopalschools.org   Info@episcopalschools.org

An independently incorporated, voluntary membership organization

Council for American Private Education (CAPE)
PMB 457 13017 Wisteria Drive
Germantown, MD 20874   301-916-8460   FAX 301-916-8485
www.capenet.org   cape@capenet.org

A coalition of national organizations and state affiliates serving private elementary and secondary schools

American Montessori Society
281 Park Avenue South 6th floor
New York, NY 20010   212-358-1250   FAX 212-358-1256
www.americanmontessorisociety.org

Nonprofit service organization dedicated to stimulating the use of the Montessori teaching method in private and public schools

Council for Exceptional Children
1110 north Glebe Road Suite 300
Arlington, VA 22201   703-620-3660
www.cec.sped.org

Information on programs for gifted and/or learning disabled

Virginia Association of Independent Specialized Educational Facilities (VAISEF)
118 N. 8th Street

Richmond, VA 23219   804-780-2776   FAX 804-648-8036
www.vaisef.org   kids@vaisef.org

Association of Virginia providers of specialized education and services for children and youth with special needs, and their families

Council for Spiritual and Ethical Education (CSEE)
1465 Northside Drive # 220
Atlanta, GA 30318   800-298-4599   FAX 404-355-4435
www.csee.org   info@csee.org

A national resource for schools

Association of Christian Schools International (ACSI)
731 Chapel Hills Drive
Colorado Springs, CO 80920   800-367-0798
www.acsi.org   info@acsi.org

Provides an array of services and programs to its member schools

National Association of Private Schools for Exceptional Children
1522 K. Street, N.W. Suite 1032
Washington, D.C. 20005   202-408-3338   FAX 202-408-3340
www.napsec.com   napsec@aol.com

Nonprofit association representing private special education programs and affiliated state associations

The Association of Boarding Schools (TABS)
4455 Connecticut Avenue N.W. Suite A-200
Washington, D.C. 20008   202-966-8705   FAX: 202-966-8708
www.schools.com   tabs@schools.com

U.S.-based nonprofit educational organization exclusively serving boarding schools and students

Catholic Boarding Schools Association (CBSA)
1701 Hall Street
Hays, KS 67601   785-625-6577
www.cbsa.org

An affiliation of North American Catholic schools which share a residential component in their educational programs

Independent Educational Consultants Association (IECA)
3251 Old Lee Highway, Suite 510
Fairfax, VA 22030   703-591-4850   FAX 703-591-4860
www.IECAonline.com   Requests@IECAonline.com

Non-profit, international association representing full-time experienced independent educational advisors

Washington Independent Services for Educational Resources (WISER)
11140 Rockville Pike PMB 105
Rockville, MD 20852   301-816-0432   FAX 301-498-7559
www.wiser-dc.com

An organization for educational professionals in the Washington, D.C. metropolitan area.

Testing

Secondary School Admission Test (SSAT)
Box CN 5339
Princeton, NJ 08543   609-683-4440   FAX 609-683-4507
www.ssat.org   Info@ssat.org

The Independent School Entrance Exam (ISEE)
Educational Records Bureau
220 E. 42nd Street
New York, NY 10017   800-989-3721
www.erbtest.org   Info@erbtest.org

Accreditation

Middle States Association of Colleges and Schools
3624 Market Street
Philadelphia, PA 19104   215-662-5603   FAX 215-662-0957
www.middlestates.org
www.css-msa.org   Commission on Secondary Schools
www.ces-msa.org   Commission on Elementary Schools

One of six similar regional accrediting associations, covering DC, MD, PA and DE, among other states

Southern Association of Colleges and Schools
1866 Southern Lane
Decatur GA 30033   404-679-4500
www.sacs.org

Accredits public and private educational institutions from Pre-Kindergarten through university level in 11 states (including Virginia) of the Southeastern U.S. and Latin America

Virginia Council for Private Education (VCPE)
1901 Huguenot Road, Suite 301
Richmond, VA 23235   804-423-6435   FAX 804-423-6436
www.vcpe.org

Oversees accreditation of nonpublic preschool, elementary and secondary schools in the Commonwealth

Financial Aid

The Black Student Fund
3636 16th Street, N.W. Suite 500
Washington, D.C. 20036   202-387-1414
www.blackstudentfund.org   mail@blackstudentfund.org

Latino Student Fund
P.O. Box 5403
Washington, D.C. 20016   202-244-3438   FAX 202-244-3438
www.latinostudentfund.org   director@latinostudentfund.org

Washington Scholarship Fund
1133 15th Street, N.W. Suite 550
Washington, D.C. 20005   202-293-5560   FAX 202-293-7893
www.washingtonscholarshipfund.org

Homeschooling

Home Educators Association of Virginia
1900 Byrd Avenue Suite 201
Richmond, VA 23230   804-288-1608   FAX 804-288-6962
www.heav.org   info@heav.org

Maryland Home Education Association
Manfred Smith
9085 Flamepool Way
Columbia, MD 21045   410-730-0073 voice   FAX 410-964-5720
www.mhea.com   MSmith@mhea.com

National Homeschool Association
P.O. Box 327
Webster, NY 14580   513-772-9580
www.alumni.caltech.edu/~casner/nha/

Public School Information

Washington, D.C. Public Schools   202-724-4222
www.k12.dc.us

Virginia

Alexandria City Public Schools   703-824-6600
www.acps.k12.va.us

Arlington County Public Schools   703-228-7660
www.arlington.k12.va.us

Fairfax County Public Schools   703-246-2991
www.fcps.edu

Falls Church City Public Schools   703-248-5699
www.fccps.k12.va.us

Fauquier County Public Schools   540-428-1120
www.fcps1.org

Loudoun County Public Schools   703-771-6400
www.loudoun.k12.va.us

Manassas City Public Schools   703-257-8800
www.manassas.k12.va.us

Prince William County Public Schools   703-791-7200
www.pwcs.edu

Stafford County Public Schools   540-658-6000
www.staffordschools.net

Maryland

Anne Arundel County Public Schools   410-222-5000
www.aacps.org

Calvert County Public Schools   410-535-1700
www.calvertnet.k12.md.us

Charles County Public Schools   301-932-6610
www.ccboe.com

Frederick County Public Schools   301-644-5000
www.fcps.org

Howard County Public School System   410-313-6682
www.hcpss.org

Montgomery County Public Schools   301-279-3000
www.mcps.k12.md.us

Prince Georges County Public Schools   301-952-6001
www.pgcps.org

St. Mary's County Public Schools   301-475-5511
www.smcps.k12.md.us

Washington County Public Schools   301-766-2800
www.wcboe.k12.md.us

SCHOOLS

ACADEMY FOR IDEAL EDUCATION   202-726-0313   FAX 202-726-9265
1501 Gallatin Street, N.W., Washington, DC 20011
HEAD: Paulette Bell-Imani
WEBSITE: www.idealed.org   E-MAIL: mcarr@idealed.org
GRADES: Age 3–grade 5   ENROLLMENT: 50 Co-ed
SPECIAL COURSES: Special needs incorporated into the mainstream program.
Spanish, Super Learning Program in phonics and math. For older children, see
listing for Academy for Ideal Education Middle/High School.
EXTENDED DAY: 7:30 a.m.–7:00 p.m.
ATHLETICS: Athletic program
TUITION: $5,170 lower school; before and after care $50/week; before care only
$25/week; after care only $35/week
SUMMER PROGRAMS: LIFT (Learning is Fun Time) ages 4–14, June to early
August. Academics in the morning, camp time in the afternoon

ACADEMY FOR IDEAL EDUCATION MIDDLE/HIGH SCHOOL
202-723-6008   FAX 202-726-7406
5331 Colorado Avenue, N.W., Washington, DC 20011
HEAD: Paulette Bell-Imani
WEBSITE: www.idealed.org   E-MAIL: mcarr@idealed.org
GRADES: 6–12   ENROLLMENT: 52 Co-ed
SPECIAL COURSES: Super Learning, phonics and math; special needs
TUITION: $4,950 6–8; $4,730 9–12

ACADEMY OF CHRISTIAN EDUCATION   703-471-2132   FAX 703-471-5790
1808A Michael Faraday Court, Reston, VA 20190
Founded 1996
HEAD: Donna Strater
WEBSITE: www.ace-academy.com   E-MAIL: icanread@ace-academy.com
GRADES: K4–grade 6   ENROLLMENT: 185 Co-ed
FACULTY: 30 full- and 2 part-time
AVERAGE CLASS SIZE: 15
SPECIAL COURSES: Academically accelerated. Accelerated reading and math
program, science, social studies, technology program, history, geography, health,
art and music
EXTENDED DAY: 8:00 a.m.–5:45 p.m.
ADMISSION: Interview
TUITION: Call for information.
LUNCH: Bring   DRESS CODE: Uniform required
SUMMER PROGRAMS: Reading, math and Christian play camp

ACADEMY OF THE CHILD MONTESSORI   301-601-0991
19711 Waters Road, Germantown, MD 20872
Founded 1996
HEAD: Michele C. Hutchinson
DIRECTOR OF ADMISSIONS: Michele C. Hutchinson

WEBSITE: www.academyofthechild.com
E-MAIL: administrator@academyofthechild.com
GRADES: Ungraded 18 months–grade 6   **ENROLLMENT:** 65+ Co-ed
FACULTY: 4 full- and 5 part-time   **AVERAGE CLASS SIZE:** 22
MISSION STATEMENT: (Excerpted) Academy of the Child is dedicated to creating an environment where each child can maximize his unique potential. Children are guided individually according to their own developmental needs and abilities. Cooperative work with other children of various ages fosters expression of ideas and development of the whole personality enabling each to learn at his own pace, free from competition, understimulation and anxiety.
SPECIAL COURSES: Toddler (18 months–36 months), primary (ages 3–6), elementary (ages grades 1–6). Elaborate music and arts program. Annual spring stage performance. Italian language instruction for ages 5+. Extensive cooking, baking and food prep exercises increase concentration and independence while providing healthy snacks for younger students.
EXTENDED DAY: 8:00 a.m–5 p.m.
PLANT: Charming independent facility which looks like a large home but will soon be able to accommodate more than 125 students. The lovely classrooms are
equipped with furniture sized appropriately for the children and a full array of scientifically designed materials. The ambiance conveys the school's goals of warmth and nurturing while creating high standards of education.
ADMISSION: Application fee $50. Parent-only observation, parent interview, transcripts and student interview required for ages 4 1/2 and older. Rolling admission
TUITION: $4,500–$6,750
LUNCH: Milk provided
OTHER FEES: Before school program $500 annually. After school program $1000
annually
DRESS CODE: School shirts for spirit day and field trips
SUMMER PROGRAMS: Part-time, theme based
FUTURE PLANS: Plans for expansion of lower level of facility for new classrooms.

ACADEMY OF THE HOLY CROSS   301-942-2100   FAX 301-929-6440
4920 Strathmore Avenue, Kensington, MD 20895
Catholic 1868
HEAD: Sister Katherine Kase, CSC
WEBSITE: www.academyoftheholycross.org
E-MAIL: schooloffice@academyoftheholycross.org
GRADES: 9–12   **ENROLLMENT:** 565 girls
FACULTY: 56   **AVERAGE CLASS SIZE:** 19
SPECIAL COURSES: In the Holy Cross tradition, our mission is to develop women of courage, compassion and scholarship. Our college preparatory curriculum is designed with these goals in mind.
Languages: Latin I-IV, French I-V, Spanish I-V. Math through calculus. Science: physical science, biology, chemistry, physics, physiology, environ-

4

mental science, forensics, marine science, Global Ecology and independent study. Social science: World, Latin American, Asian, African and Middle Eastern Studies, U.S. history, U.S. government, U.S. economics and U.S. Ethnic Studies. English: English I-IV, expository, Southern Literature, Democratic Thought, Page to Screen and Creative Writing, Shakespeare and Women of Mystery. Theology. Health and P.E. Visual and performing arts: theatre, speech, vocal and instrumental music, dance, drawing, design, painting, photography, publication and web design, ceramics. Honors Programs. AP: English literature, English composition, French, Spanish, calculus BC, statistics, biology, chemistry, U.S. history, U.S. government and studio art.

ATHLETICS: P.E., field hockey, soccer, tennis, equestrian, crew, cross-country, lacrosse, cheerleading, basketball, volleyball, track and field, softball, swimming and diving

CLUBS: French, Spanish, Amnesty International, Black Awareness Society, equestrian, golf, drama, International Thespian Society, Model U.N., math, science, National Honor Society, peer support, Kaleidoscope, photography, Pro-Life, SADD, SAFE, speech and debate

PUBLICATIONS: Literary magazine, student newspaper, yearbook

COMMUNITY INVOLVEMENT: Students are involved in ongoing service projects through Christian Service Commitment. Senior Project provides students with fieldwork opportunities in a chosen profession.

PLANT: 28-acre campus, library 11,000 volumes, art studio, auditorium, gym, 3 playing fields, Chapel, cafeteria. New in 2003: 3 science labs, greenhouse, 3 art studios, kiln room, 400-seat state of the art theatre, additional classrooms, computer center and photography dark room.

ADMISSION: Shadow visit, interview, Washington Archdiocese Entrance Exam, transcript, recommendations

TUITION: $10,750   **FINANCIAL AID:** Available

BOOKS: Average $300   **OTHER FEES:** Activities fee $125

DRESS CODE: Uniform required

SUMMER PROGRAMS: Sports Camp including basketball, soccer, lacrosse, volleyball, field hockey and softball. Summer enrichment programs including writing, art, math, SAT prep, study skills and leadership courses.

ACCOTINK ACADEMY   703-451-8041   FAX 703-569-5365
8519 Tuttle Road, Springfield, VA 22152
Founded 1963
HEAD: Elaine McConnell
DIRECTOR OF ADMISSIONS: Julia Oaks
WEBSITE: www.accotink.com
GRADES: Ungraded ages 5–21 LD/ED
ENROLLMENT: 192 Co-ed
FACULTY: See Special Courses
AVERAGE CLASS SIZE: 9 (3:1 student/teacher)
SPECIAL COURSES: Faculty includes: 153 Full-time. 14 psychologists, 12 speech pathologists, 7 art therapists, 5 occupational therapists, physical education director, 4 job coaches.
One of the primary goals is the re-establishment of a good self-image. Program is structured but ungraded so each child may progress at own rate without undue

pressure. Reading, math and perceptual skills are developed through individualized programs, while language arts provides group work experience. A multisensory approach is used in all classroom instruction. Science, social studies and history are part of the classroom instruction. In addition to regular classroom, school offers intensive services: psychological services which include individual and group therapy and art therapy, intensive language therapy and occupational therapy and a socialization program. A strong behavior management program is an integral part of the student's daily educational plan. Pre-vocational training and on-the-job training are available for the older student.

ATHLETICS: Full-time program with special emphasis placed on perceptual motor activities. Consultation with occupational therapist is included.

PLANT: Library, 3 computer labs, offices for individual psychological, speech, art and occupational therapy services. Curriculum room and testing facilities

ADMISSION: Referral through local area school systems. Generally referred by local agencies

TUITION: County-funded; call for information.

TRANSPORTATION: Provided and funded by the counties

AD FONTES ACADEMY   703-266-8300   FAX 703-266-8499
P.O. Box 7518, Fairfax Station, VA 22039
Christian 1996
HEAD: Nancy Zins
WEBSITE: www.adfontes.com   **E-MAIL:** princeps@adfontes.com
GRADES: Kindergarten–grade 12   **ENROLLMENT:** 112 Co-ed
AVERAGE CLASS SIZE: Maximum 20
SPECIAL COURSES: A Christ-centered classical education.
PLANT: Two campuses: elementary school in Chantilly and high school in Centreville, Virginia. Elementary school phone is 703-263-2228.
ADMISSION: Application, interview, $100 application fee
TUITION: $4,300 K half day; $5,700 1–6; $6,600 7–8; $6,900 9–12
DRESS CODE: Uniforms elementary; certain guidelines grades 7–12

AGAPE CHRISTIAN ACADEMY   703-360-1996
5632 Mt. Vernon Memorial Highway, Alexandria, VA 22309
Founded 1999
HEAD: Mercedes S. Morison
WEBSITE: www.agapechristianacademy.org
GRADES: Nursery 3–grade 6   **ENROLLMENT:** Co-ed
SPECIAL COURSES: A Beka curriculum, Spanish, art, music, P.E.
EXTENDED DAY: 6:30 a.m.–6:00 p.m.
CLUBS: Instrumental lessons, computer club, dance, gymnastics
TUITION: Call for information.
LUNCH: Hot lunches   **TRANSPORTATION:** Available

AIDAN MONTESSORI SCHOOL   202-387-2700   FAX 202-387-0346
2700 27th Street, N.W., Washington, DC 20008-2601
Founded 1961
HEAD: Kathleen M. Minardi
DIRECTOR OF ADMISSIONS: Christine Kranz Smith

WEBSITE: www.aidanschool.org
GRADES: Toddler–grade 6   **ENROLLMENT:** 165 Co-ed (80 boys/85 girls)
FACULTY: 12 full- and 11 part-time
AVERAGE CLASS SIZE: 12, 25 Pre-K/K, 16 elementary
MISSION STATEMENT: (Excerpted) The mission of Aidan Montessori School is to create and sustain an optimum Montessori educational environment to enable each child to realize his or her richest potential for learning and to become an independent, self-motivated and contributing member of the world community.
SPECIAL COURSES: Montessori program, accredited by the Association Montessori Internationale, with integrated curriculum including art, Spanish, Mandarin Chinese, P.E., and music. Mixed-age classes: 18–35 months, 3–6 years, 6–9 years, 9–12 years
EXTENDED DAY: 8:00 a.m.–6:00 p.m.
CLUBS: Elementary after school Discovery Programs offer: athletics, language clubs, art, computer animation, calligraphy, crafts, etc.
PLANT: Spacious and well-lit classrooms, Montessori designed environment, library media center with internet access, and playground on its Woodley Park campus
ADMISSION: Applications due by January 31. Follow AISGW guidelines. Interview with parent and child required. Kindergarten and older require previous school records. Attendance at Open House recommended
TUITION: $8,420–$13,075
FINANCIAL AID: Limited available
BOOKS: Not included   **LUNCH:** Not available
OTHER FEES: $60 application fee. $500 Student Enrollment Fee (annually, per student). $1,800 Family Initial Enrollment Fee (one-time only, per family). Extended day fees $1,425–$7,000.
SUMMER PROGRAMS: Offerings vary annually but frequently include Montessori and arts programs for Toddlers and Preschool–K.

AL FATIH ACADEMY   703-437-9382   FAX 703-620-6567
730 Jackson Street, Herndon, VA 20170
HEAD: Afeefa Syeed and Pervin Divleli
WEBSITE: www.alfatih.org
GRADES: Pre-K–grade 4   **ENROLLMENT:** Co-ed
SPECIAL COURSES: Voice, art, P.E., Arabic
CLUBS: Peace Leaders Program, Kids Giving Salaam (Peace)
TUITION: Call for information.
SUMMER PROGRAMS: Summer Camp

AL-HUDA SCHOOL   301-982-2402   FAX 301-982-2325
5301 Edgewood Road, College Park, MD 20740
Islamic
WEBSITE: www.alhuda.org
GRADES: Kindergarten–8   **ENROLLMENT:** 300 Co-ed
SPECIAL COURSES: Boys and girls have separate classrooms. School also does home school supervision. Full-time Hifzh School.
EXTENDED DAY: After care until 6:00 p.m.
TUITION: Call for information.

ALEPH BET JEWISH DAY SCHOOL   410-263-9044   FAX 410-263-5740
1125 Spa Road, Annapolis, MD 21403
Multi-denominational Jewish
HEAD: Nan Jarashow
WEBSITE: www.alephbet.org   **E-MAIL:** info@alephbet.org
GRADES: Kindergarten–grade 5   **ENROLLMENT:** 61 Co-ed (30 boys/31 girls)
FACULTY: 6 full- and 5 part-time   **AVERAGE** CLASS SIZE: 10
MISSION STATEMENT: The mission of Aleph Bet Jewish Day School is to intro-
duce young children to the richness and variety of Jewish tradition; to challenge
students to think critically and reflectively; to nurture individual interests and tal-
ents; and to foster a sense of community within and beyond the school.
EXTENDED DAY: 8:00 a.m.–5:30 p.m.
ADMISSION: Call/write for packet. Application and $100 fee due Feb.1.
TUITION: $6,980
LUNCH: Students bring   **OTHER FEES:** $250 student activity fee
DRESS CODE: None
FUTURE PLANS: Expand physical plant

ALEXANDRIA COUNTRY DAY SCHOOL   703-548-4804   FAX 703-549-9022
2400 Russell Road, Alexandria, VA 22301
Founded 1983
HEAD: Alexander "Exie" Harvey IV
DIRECTOR OF ADMISSIONS: Julia Love
WEBSITE: www.acdsnet.org   **E-MAIL:** admissions@acdsnet.org
GRADES: K (full day)–grade 8   **ENROLLMENT:** 245 Co-ed (123 boys/122 girls)
FACULTY: 28 full- and 9 part-time   **AVERAGE CLASS SIZE:** 12
MISSION STATEMENT: Alexandria Country Day School engenders and nur-
tures enthusiasm, compassion, and self-confidence in its students by means of
developmentally appropriate academic and other programs, high behavioral
expectations, and an emphasis on citizenship.
SPECIAL COURSES: Algebra; Spanish K–8; art; music; computer instruction;
six-week rotations for middle school students in art, music, computers, yearbook,
and drama; exchange program to Mexico for eighth graders; integrated
History/Art/Music/Language Arts curriculum in middle school.
EXTENDED DAY: 7:00–8:00 a.m and 3:00–6:00 p.m.
ATHLETICS: Basketball, softball, soccer, and cross-country teams for grades 5–8
CLUBS: Drama program, Chess Club, German Club, band (beginner and
advanced), chorus, handbell choir, Student Council, Honor Council
PUBLICATIONS: Student-produced yearbook, literary magazine
COMMUNITY INVOLVEMENT: Community service in all grades with intensi-
fied middle school service program.
PLANT: Three levels of classrooms; gym/auditorium; science lab; library; music
room; fully equipped and staffed computer lab; art studio; playing field; two
playgrounds; parcours
ADMISSION: Application including recommendations and transcripts; parent
visit; class visit for students applying to grades 1–8; playgroup visit for applicants
to Kindergarten; testing: K–2 requires the WPPSI-III; 3–4 requires in-house testing; 5–8 requires ISEE.
TUITION: $13,100 K–3; $14,520 4–8

FINANCIAL AID: Available. Need-based
BOOKS: Included   **LUNCH:** Extra
TRANSPORTATION: Available. $790 one-way; $1,300 two-way
DRESS CODE: K: school attire. 1–8 khaki pants, shorts, skorts, skirts, or jumper; hunter green or white collared shirt
SUMMER PROGRAMS: All grades
FUTURE PLANS: Middle school science lab and classroom renovation (summer 2003); additional classroom renovations to take place summer 2004, with addition of middle school-size gym, additional classrooms, and workspaces within next three years.

ALL SAINTS CATHOLIC SCHOOL   703-368-4400
9294 Stonewall Road, Manassas, VA 20110
Catholic
HEAD: David E. Conroy
WEBSITE: www.rc.net/arlington/all_saints
GRADES: Kindergarten–grade 8   **ENROLLMENT:** Co-ed
EXTENDED DAY: 7:00 a.m.–6:30 p.m.
TUITION: Call for information.

AMBLESIDE SCHOOL   703-435-3300   FAX 703-435-8520
1700 Reston Parkway, Reston, VA 20194
Non-denominational 1999
HEAD: Kym Gardner
DIRECTOR OF ADMISSIONS: Sarah Bruce
WEBSITE: www.AMBLESIDE.org
GRADES: Kindergarten–grade 8
ENROLLMENT: 75+ Co-ed (50% boys/50% girls)
FACULTY: 7 full- and 3 part-time   **AVERAGE CLASS SIZE:** 16
MISSION STATEMENT: Ambleside is a Christ-centered school, providing students with a strong academic program, within the framework of a traditional, evangelical Christian worldview. Our goal is to join with our students' parents in laying the foundation for a life of serving God with excellence, no matter where He may call. One of our key tools is employing the philosophies of educator Charlotte Mason who advocated "nourish a child daily with loving, right and noble ideas . . . which may bear fruit in his or her life."
SPECIAL COURSES: Art, Spanish, music, P.E.
CLUBS: Field trips and observational learning very important. Silent auction
COMMUNITY INVOLVEMENT: All grades involved in community service
PLANT: Library, playground, large classrooms. Very commuter-friendly, near Dulles Toll Road, Route 7 and Reston Parkway
ADMISSION: Submit application with $50 application fee per student (maximum $100 per family). Student Recommendation form, standardized test results and/or most recent report card. Student assessment, parent interview. Once accepted, secure child's space with a $500 enrollment fee, to be applied to tuition. We accept students on an on-going basis, as spots are available. First round of applications accepted Oct. 1–Nov. 15, second round Jan. 1–Feb. 15.
TUITION: $4,900–$5,900
FINANCIAL AID: Available   **BOOKS:** Included

CH: Bring own lunch and snack daily
SS CODE: Uniforms purchased from Lands' End uniform catalog
MER PROGRAMS: Some tutoring available

ANACOSTIA BIBLE CHURCH CHRISTIAN SCHOOL
202-678-6555   FAX 202-678-7008
1610 T Street, S.E., Washington, DC 20020
WEBSITE: www.anacostiabible.org
GRADES: K3–6   **ENROLLMENT:** 27 Co-ed
SPECIAL COURSES: A Beka curriculum
EXTENDED DAY: 6:45–8:00 a.m. and 3:30–6:30 p.m.
TUITION: $3,300
LUNCH: Hot and cold lunches available   **DRESS CODE:** Uniforms
SUMMER PROGRAMS: Summer Camp

ANGELUS ACADEMY   703-924-3996   FAX 703-924-9683
6601 Springfield Center Drive, Springfield, VA 22150
Catholic 2000
HEAD: Jane Adkins
WEBSITE: www.angelusacademy.com   **E-MAIL:** angelusacademy@juno.com
GRADES: K–grade 8   **ENROLLMENT:** Co-ed
SPECIAL COURSES: Religion, music, drama, art, language arts, mathematics, science, P.E., history, geography, French, Latin, band
ADMISSION: Application, provide birth and baptismal certificates and reports from previous school, interview
TUITION: $3,750
FINANCIAL AID: Available   **BOOKS:** $100
DRESS CODE: Uniforms from Lands' End

ANNAPOLIS AREA CHRISTIAN SCHOOL   410-266-8251   FAX 410-573-6866
716 Bestgate Road, Annapolis, MD 21401
Founded 1971
HEAD: Larry Kooi
DIRECTOR OF ADMISSIONS: Cheryl Townshend
WEBSITE: www.aacsonline.org
GRADES: Age 4(K Readiness)–grade 12
ENROLLMENT: 820 Co-ed (410 boys/410 girls)
FACULTY: 63 full- and 7 part-time
AVERAGE CLASS SIZE: 25
MISSION STATEMENT: Annapolis Area Christian School in partnership with Christian parents, engages students in a rigorous program of learning from a Biblical worldview to serve Jesus Christ faithfully in the world.
SPECIAL COURSES: Primarily college preparatory curriculum. Spanish introduced at the elementary level, continuing to AP Spanish in high school. AP courses offered in English, calculus, U.S. history, government, economics, and studio art. Computer technology classes at high school level, with computer instruction beginning at the middle school level. French offered at the high school level. Biblical studies required. Marching and concert bands, plus Madrigals, art, music and drama. A learning disabilities program (DISCOVERY) is available for an

extra fee.

EXTENDED DAY: 7:00–8:00 a.m. and 3:00–6:00 p.m.

ATHLETICS: Required. Intramural and interscholastic. Soccer, softball, baseball, basketball, volleyball, cheerleading, wrestling, lacrosse, track and field, sailing, golf

CLUBS: Various clubs, drama productions, logic

PUBLICATIONS: Yearbook, newspaper, literary publications

COMMUNITY INVOLVEMENT: Service clubs

ADMISSION: Interview with parent and child, testing and transcript review. Required that at least one parent be of the Christian faith.

TUITION: $2,772 Kindergarten Readiness (age 4); $3,905 K half day; $6,039 K full; $6,765 1–5; $7,293 6–8; $8,030 9–12

FINANCIAL AID: Available

TRANSPORTATION: Available. $105/month

DRESS CODE: Uniform required

SUMMER PROGRAMS: Sports Camps

FUTURE PLANS: New high school to open in Severn, Maryland in August, 2004. Middle school will then relocate to the Bestgate Campus in Annapolis.

ANNUNCIATION SCHOOL   202-362-1408   FAX 202-363-4057

3825 Klingle Place, N.W., Washington, DC 20016

Catholic 1954

HEAD: K. Marguerite Conley

WEBSITE: www.annunciationschool.net   **E-MAIL:** aroberts@annunciationschool.net

GRADES: K–grade 8   **ENROLLMENT:** 202 Co-ed (89 boys/113 girls)

FACULTY: 11 full- and 8 part-time   **AVERAGE CLASS SIZE:** 26

MISSION STATEMENT: The mission of Annunciation School is the development of the whole child through a community experience in which exists a synthesis of culture and faith and a synthesis of faith and life.

SPECIAL COURSES: Daily religion classes required K–8. Weekly Mass attendance required grades 2–8, enrichment mathematics grade 4–7, pre-algebra or algebra in grade 8, computer. Art and music in grades K–8.

EXTENDED DAY: 3:00–6:00 p.m. Monday–Friday

ATHLETICS: CYO boys' and girls' basketball teams grade 5–8, CYO Co-ed track team grades K–8

CLUBS: Altar Servers grade 5–8; Annunciation/Roth youth choir grade 4–8; safety patrols grade 6–8; Student Council grade 3–8

PUBLICATIONS: Yearbook grade 8

COMMUNITY INVOLVEMENT: Outreach program serving Martha's Table

PLANT: Church and Parish Center, library/computer lab, math/science lab, resource room, art room, music room, gym and playground

ADMISSION: Application with $50 fee, academic records and standardized testing from the last two years, birth certificate, Baptismal Certificate (if Roman Catholic), 2 teacher recommendations, Pastor/Minister recommendation, entrance test with writing sample and school visit. Application deadline February 15

TUITION: $4,770

FINANCIAL AID: Available

BOOKS: $350

DRESS CODE: Uniform required

ANTIOCH CHRISTIAN SCHOOL   410-757-5000   FAX 410-757-7557
1535 Ritchie Highway, Arnold, MD 21012
HEAD: David Wright
WEBSITE: www.antiochchristianschool.com
GRADES: Kindergarten–grade 12   **ENROLLMENT:** 100 Co-ed
SPECIAL COURSES: Basic academic program. Religion required. Computers, music, art, home economics
ATHLETICS: P.E., basketball, baseball, soccer, volleyball
TUITION: $4,300 grades 1–12.

APPLE TREE SCHOOL FAIRFAX   703-281-7747   FAX 703-281-0278
9655 Blake Lane, Fairfax, VA 22031
HEAD: Beckii Pittman
E-MAIL: snrz.educ8tor@aol.com
GRADES: Nursery–grade 4   **ENROLLMENT:** 113 Co-ed
SPECIAL COURSES: Accelerated Christian curriculum, Spanish, computers, Character Education, small classroom size.
EXTENDED DAY: 7:00 a.m.–6:00 p.m.
ATHLETICS: Intramurals, gymnastics, karate, tumbling, ballet
CLUBS: After school activities, ballroom dance, piano
TUITION: $195 per week for preschool five full days; $216 per week for older grades (academy). Call for half day tuition fees.
SUMMER PROGRAMS: Full 10 week summer camp

APPLE TREE SCHOOL VIENNA   703-281-2626   FAX 703-281-9596
712 Tapawingo Road, S.E., Vienna, VA 22180
HEAD: Annely Meinen
GRADES: Age 3–Kindergarten   **ENROLLMENT:** Co-ed
SPECIAL COURSES: Higher grades located in Fairfax location.
EXTENDED DAY: 7:00 a.m.–6:00 p.m.
CLUBS: Ballet, computer classes
TUITION: $8,050 5 full days, 41 weeks

AQUINAS MONTESSORI SCHOOL   703-780-8484   FAX 703-360-2875
8334 Mount Vernon Highway, Alexandria, VA 22309
Founded 1965
HEAD: Kathleen H. Futrell
WEBSITE: www.aquinasmontessorischool.com
GRADES: Ungraded ages 2 1/2–12   **ENROLLMENT:** 175 Co-ed (84 boys/91 girls)
FACULTY: 12 full- and 15 part-time   **AVERAGE CLASS SIZE:** 25
MISSION STATEMENT: To provide a Montessori prepared environment for children ages 2 1/2 to 6, and an enriched curriculum for the children at the elementary level.
SPECIAL COURSES: Spanish K–6, Latin 3–6, art, music, science, geography, Great Books Discussion Program, drama.
EXTENDED DAY: 7:30–8:45 a.m. and 12:00–6:00 p.m.
ATHLETICS: P.E.   **COMMUNITY INVOLVEMENT:** Outreach program
ADMISSION: Application fee $50; evaluation visit and interview
TUITION: Call for information. Tuition includes books

LUNCH: Bring   **TRANSPORTATION:** Contracted
DRESS CODE: Uniform required
SUMMER PROGRAMS: Day Camp for ages 2 1/2 to 9

AQUINAS SCHOOL   703-491-4447   FAX 703-492-8828
13750 Mary's Way, Woodbridge, VA 22191
Catholic
HEAD: Sister Dominic Mary, OP
WEBSITE: www.aquinasschool.org
GRADES: Pre-K–grade 8   **ENROLLMENT:** Co-ed
EXTENDED DAY: 6:30–8:00 a.m. and 3:00–6:30 p.m.
TUITION: Call for information.

ARCHBISHOP CARROLL HIGH SCHOOL   202-529-0900   FAX 202-526-8879
4300 Harewood Road, N.E., Washington, DC 20017
Catholic 1951
HEAD: James Mumford
WEBSITE: archbishopcarroll.org
GRADES: 9–12   **ENROLLMENT:** Co-ed
SPECIAL COURSES: Primarily college preparatory curriculum. AP and honors courses available.
ATHLETICS: Football, basketball, baseball, cross-country, golf, soccer, lacrosse, softball, track and field, volleyball, fencing, and cheerleading
CLUBS: Art, audio-visual, Carroll Ambassadors, cheerleaders, drama, French Honor Society, Spanish Honor Society, hiking, Latino Student, Future Business Leaders of America, Mock Trial, National Honor Society, Pan-African Society, Pom Squad, science, Silhouette Modeling, Spirit and Pep
PUBLICATIONS: Newspaper, yearbook, literary magazine
COMMUNITY INVOLVEMENT: Christian/Community Service, walkathon, food drive
TUITION: $6,000 Catholic; $6,250 Non-Catholic
FINANCIAL AID: Available   **FEES:** Books and fees $700

ARCHBISHOP NEALE SCHOOL   301-934-9595   FAX 301-753-1717
104 Port Tobacco Road, LaPlata, MD 20646
Catholic 1927
HEAD: Sister Helene Fee, IHM
DIRECTOR OF ADMISSIONS: Sister Helene Fee, IHM
WEBSITE: www.myschoolonline.com/md/ans   **E-MAIL:** neale@erols.com
GRADES: Pre-K–grade 8   **ENROLLMENT:** 520 Co-ed (248 boys/272 girls)
FACULTY: 28 full- and 2 part-time   **AVERAGE CLASS SIZE:** 25
MISSION STATEMENT: (Excerpted) Archbishop Neale, a Catholic school, is a Christian community and an academic institution comprised of students, parents, priests, and staff drawn from a consolidation of parishes and the surrounding community. Within this Faith Community we work to transmit the Gospel message, to enhance the building of relationships and to render service. As an academic institution, we strive to create a climate in which knowledge is pursued in an organized and integrated manner.
SPECIAL COURSES: Spanish I, algebra I

EXTENDED DAY: School day 7:40 a.m.–2:00 p.m. Extended care 2:00–6:00 p.m.
ATHLETICS: Volleyball, basketball, cheerleading, track, softball
TUITION: $2,660 in parish
FINANCIAL AID: Available
LUNCH: Hot lunch available   **OTHER FEES:** Books and other fees $150
TRANSPORTATION: Available free from Charles County
DRESS CODE: Yes
FUTURE PLANS: We are rebuilding after a tornado.

ARCHBISHOP SPALDING HIGH SCHOOL   410-969-9105   FAX 410-969-1026
8080 New Cut Road, Severn, MD 21144
Catholic 1966
HEAD: Kathleen Mahar
DIRECTOR OF ADMISSIONS: Thomas Miller
WEBSITE: www.archbishopspalding.org
E-MAIL: millert@archbishopspalding.org
GRADES: 9–12   **ENROLLMENT:** 965 Co-ed (463 boys/502 girls)
FACULTY: 65 full- and 2 part-time   **AVERAGE CLASS SIZE:** 24
MISSION STATEMENT: As a Catholic college preparatory secondary school, Archbishop Spalding High School is committed to challenging our students to grow spiritually, academically, physically, and socially. The school community provides a caring environment that affirms the dignity of the individual and promotes learning.
SPECIAL COURSES: Advanced Placement, honors and college prep courses; Aquinas Program for students with language-based learning disabilities.
ATHLETICS: Thirty-three league sports include soccer, football, field hockey, cross-country, volleyball, basketball, track, boys' and girls' ice hockey, swimming, wresting, lacrosse, golf, baseball, tennis, softball, cheerleading and dance. Equestrian and rugby intramural teams
CLUBS: Award-winning band and choral music program. Seven honor societies. Forty additional extracurricular activities
PUBLICATIONS: Newspaper, literary magazine and yearbook
PLANT: Three story academic wing, gym, library/media center, fine arts wing, 1200-seat auditorium; on forty-seven acre campus with stadium and athletic fields.
ADMISSION: Open House October for all interested applicants. Admissions testing for all applicants to 9th grade December. $30 registration fee. Application deadline in January. Please call for exact dates and more information.
TUITION: $7,600
FINANCIAL AID: Yes. Applicants apply through School Scholarship Service of Princeton, New Jersey. $17 fee for application. Call for exact January application deadline.
BOOKS: Additional   **LUNCH:** Available
OTHER FEES: Aquinas program $2,000 additional. Books, uniforms, testing, class dues, retreats and Parents' Association membership are additional.
TRANSPORTATION: Available   **DRESS CODE:** Uniform required
SUMMER PROGRAMS: Summer Sports camps. Call ext. 246 for more information.
FUTURE PLANS: Expansion of athletic and academic facilities.

ARK ACADEMY   703-450-9135   FAX 703-450-9135
1439 Shepard Drive, Sterling, VA 20164
HEAD: Mrs. Snowdon
GRADES: Kindergarten–grade 8
ENROLLMENT: Co-ed
SPECIAL COURSES: Latin, music
EXTENDED DAY: 6:30 a.m.–6:30 p.m.
ATHLETICS: Interscholastic sports, cheerleading
PLANT: Preschool ages 2–4 offered at separate campus 21370 Potomac View Road, Sterling, VA 20164. Phone 703-450-5196, FAX 703-430-2989.
TUITION: Call for information.
SUMMER PROGRAMS: Summer travel abroad, Summer Camp

ARNOLD CHRISTIAN ACADEMY   410-544-1882   FAX 410-544-5765
365 Jones Station Road, Arnold, MD 21012
HEAD: Scott Connell
WEBSITE: www.arnoldchristianacademy.org
GRADES: Kindergarten–grade 8   **ENROLLMENT:** 91 Co-ed
SPECIAL COURSES: A Beka curriculum. School day ends at 2:30 p.m. Mondays and at 3:15 p.m. Tuesday through Friday.
EXTENDED DAY: 7:30 a.m.–6:00 p.m.
ADMISSION: Interview with Administrator, transcript, possible testing and evaluation.
TUITION: Call for information.
DRESS CODE: Uniform required

ASCENSION LUTHERAN SCHOOL   301-577-0500   FAX 301-577-9558
7415 Buchanan Street, Landover Hills, MD 20784
Lutheran 1952
HEAD: Jack D. Bartels
WEBSITE: www.ascensionschool.org
E-MAIL: ascenluth@aol.com
GRADES: Kindergarten–grade 8   **ENROLLMENT:** 200 Co-ed
AVERAGE CLASS SIZE: 25
SPECIAL COURSES: Music and art. Religious studies and P.E. required. After school programs: choir, computer, drama.
EXTENDED DAY: 7:00 a.m.–6:00 p.m.
TUITION: $5,190
DRESS CODE: Yes

ASSUMPTION SCHOOL   202-562-7070   FAX 202-574-5829
220 High View Place, S.E., Washington, DC 20032
Catholic
HEAD: Christopher Kelly
WEBSITE: www.adw.org
GRADES: Pre-Kindergarten–grade 8
ENROLLMENT: Co-ed
EXTENDED DAY: Before and after care
TUITION: $3,100 first child in parish

ATHOLTON ADVENTIST SCHOOL   301-596-5593   FAX 410-997-1297
6520 Martin Road, Columbia, MD 21044
HEAD: Marilyn Peeke
GRADES: Kindergarten–grade 8   **ENROLLMENT:** 130 Co-ed
AVERAGE CLASS SIZE: 20 maximum
SPECIAL COURSES: Computers, private piano lessons, school choir, beginner and advanced band, foreign language instruction.
EXTENDED DAY: 7:00 a.m.–6:00 p.m.
ADMISSION: Interview, testing, rolling admission as space admits.
TUITION: $5,400

THE AVALON SCHOOL   301-770-2800
6300 Tilden Lane, Rockville, MD 20852
Founded 2003
HEAD: Kevin Davern
DIRECTOR OF ADMISSIONS: Louise Fowler
WEBSITE: www.avalonschools.org   **E-MAIL:** rmcpherson@avalonschools.org
GRADES: 3–9; grades will be added   **ENROLLMENT:** 100 boys
FACULTY: 9 full-time   **AVERAGE CLASS SIZE:** 15
MISSION STATEMENT: The Avalon School, an independent school for boys, seeks to cultivate in its students intellectual freedom, personal responsibility, and a spirit of adventure in an atmosphere that allows boys to be boys. The distinctive learning characteristics of young men will be addressed both in and out of the classroom through a curriculum steeped in the humanities and sciences, the arts and athletics. A male faculty well-versed in the liberal arts will serve as both teachers and role models. The school desires to form boys into men of faith and purpose who will foster a more human, more vital society through their daily lives as husbands, fathers, professionals and citizens.
SPECIAL COURSES: Latin, Spanish, Saxon Mathematics, science, history, literature, poetry, grammar, religion (Catholic), music, art, Advanced Placement courses, P.E. daily.
EXTENDED DAY: 7:00 a.m.–6:00 p.m., no charge
ATHLETICS: Football, soccer, cross-country, basketball, baseball, lacrosse, tennis, golf
CLUBS: Chess and backgammon, computer, art, Mountaineers
PUBLICATIONS: Yearbook, school newspaper
PLANT: Leased Montgomery County middle school– classrooms, labs, gymnasium, auxiliary gymnasium, library, 3 playing fields, 4 tennis courts.
ADMISSION: Application form and $50 fee. One recommendation, transcript, family interview. A full-day visit by the applicant is strongly encouraged. Rolling admissions.
TUITION: $8,400 lower school (3–5); $9,600 middle school (6–8); $10,800 high school
FINANCIAL AID: Available. Fill out two page form, copy of tax returns.
BOOKS: Included   **LUNCH:** Students can buy hot lunch twice during week
OTHER FEES: None
TRANSPORTATION: Available. $1,000; free courtesy shuttle from Grosvenor Metro

DRESS CODE: Dress shirt, dress trousers, dress shoes, belt and tie. High school students are required to wear a sport coat.

SUMMER PROGRAMS: Undecided

FUTURE PLANS: Add grades 10, 11, and 12 in consecutive years. Looking for a permanent site in Germantown or surrounding area. Hope to open a coordinate girls' school.

—B

THE BANNER SCHOOL   301-695-9320   FAX 301-695-9336

1730 North Market Street, Frederick, MD 21701

Founded 1982

HEAD: Michael S. Mullin

DIRECTOR OF ADMISSIONS: Suzanne Roos

WEBSITE: www.bannerschool.org   **E-MAIL:** sroos@bannerschool.org

GRADES: full-day Kindergarten–grade 8

ENROLLMENT: 301 Co-ed(151 boys/150 girls)

FACULTY: 33 full- and 2 part-time   **AVERAGE CLASS SIZE:** 15

MISSION STATEMENT: The Banner School strives to motivate students to achieve to the best of their abilities while recognizing their individual talents and interests. The school encourages a strong school-family partnership, fosters self-esteem among students, and promotes respect for others. The Banner School is committed to creating an academically challenging curriculum in a secure environment, while instilling a love of learning that will last a lifetime.

SPECIAL COURSES: Offered to all students, K–8: French, Spanish, art, music, computers. Middle school students have additional opportunities in drama and band. Accelerated math is available to qualified middle school students.

EXTENDED DAY: 7:00–8:45 a.m. and 3:15–6 p.m.

ATHLETICS: Middle school three-season sports are available in basketball, soccer, volleyball and track and field. The Banner School is a member of the Maryland Junior Athletic Conference. Sports Academy is available to primary students (K–4) for six weeks during the fall and spring. Football

CLUBS: Reading, chess, American Sign Language, drama, art and other activities according to interest

PUBLICATIONS: Yearbook

COMMUNITY INVOLVEMENT: Community service

ADMISSION: The Banner School admits qualified students who are motivated to learn and who will benefit from and contribute to the school's goals. Applications are considered at any time of the year- provided there are openings. Acceptance is based on: review by faculty and principals of past academic performance (as indicated by test scores, transcripts and report cards); references from current and/or previous teachers; and observed behavior during the student's classroom visit to Banner. Applications are reviewed and given consideration in the order in which they are received. Kindergarten applicants must be 5 on or before October 31, 2004 to join the class of 2004–05, as mandated by the state of Maryland.

TUITION: $7,500

FINANCIAL AID: Financial aid is available and awarded with selection based on demonstrated need. Financial aid is awarded in May, with applications due no later than April 15.

LUNCH: Available

OTHER FEES: Tuition includes books, yearbook and individual/class photos. Three payment plans are available to finance the year's tuition. Contact the school for detailed information. Classroom activity fee: $30. Lunch payment is due monthly. Cost varies depending on number of days purchased.

DRESS CODE: Boys: solid color polo shirt or oxford cloth shirt. Navy or khaki dress slacks with belts. Navy or khaki shorts are permitted in warm weather. Girls: solid color polo shirts or oxford cloth shirts. Navy or khaki dress slacks with belts, skirts or skorts. Navy or khaki shorts are permitted in warm weather. Plaid jumpers and skirts may be purchased through Lands' End or Rose Uniform.

SUMMER PROGRAMS: Summer Discovery Camp for children ages 3 1/2 through grade 8. Four two-week sessions are available from June through mid-August. Contact the school for details.

THE BARNESVILLE SCHOOL   301-972-0341   FAX 301-972-4076

21830 Peach Tree Road (P.O. Box 404), Barnesville, MD 20838
Founded 1969
HEAD: Jaralyn L. Hough
DIRECTOR OF ADMISSIONS: Judy Marsh
WEBSITE: www.barnesville-school.com
E-MAIL: info@barnesville-school.com
GRADES: Pre-K–Grade 8   **ENROLLMENT:** 250 Co-ed (123 boys/127 girls)
FACULTY: 22 full- and 6 part-time   **AVERAGE CLASS SIZE:** 14
MISSION STATEMENT: The Barnesville School is dedicated to offering a joyful and supportive learning environment for the development of excellence in each of us.
SPECIAL COURSES: Strong basic skills program, hands-on science throughout. Music, art, drama, Spanish (5–8 grades). Community service
EXTENDED DAY: 7:00–8:00 a.m. and 3:00–6:00 p.m.
ATHLETICS: Competitive extracurricular sports program. 6–8 grades interscholastic athletic program
CLUBS: Mountain Biking Club
PLANT: Library (9,200 volumes). Performing arts/athletic center and science lab, 2 buildings, 2 playgrounds, 40 acres, soccer/lacrosse fields
ADMISSION: Application fee $50, testing, classroom visit, transcript, recommendations. Preference to siblings
TUITION: $9,480   K–5; $10,145   6–8
FINANCIAL AID: Available   **OTHER FEES:** Activity fee $375 6–8
TRANSPORTATION: Available $1,650   **DRESS CODE:** Yes
SUMMER PROGRAMS: Ages 4–14: sports, art, music, science camps. Adventure Travel and specialty camps.

THE BARRIE SCHOOL   301-871-6200   FAX 301-871-6706

13500 Layhill Road, Silver Spring, MD 20906
Founded 1932
HEAD: Julia Wall
DIRECTOR OF ADMISSIONS: Robyn Carstensen
WEBSITE: www.barrie.org
GRADES: N–grade 12   **ENROLLMENT:** 510 Co-ed

AVERAGE CLASS SIZE: student/teacher 13:1

MISSION STATEMENT: The Barrie School is dedicated to providing a challenging academic environment and frequent opportunities for hand-on experiences within a diverse community that offers support and values mutual respect. Barrie students acquire the knowledge and skills essential for independent thinking, resourceful problem solving, active citizenship, and lifelong learning.

SPECIAL COURSES: Comprehensive curriculum for students aged 24 months though grade 12. Lower school program follows the guiding principles and philosophy of Maria Montessori in experiential learning. The school provides students with rigorous academics in a diverse community to become global citizens.

EXTENDED DAY: 7 a.m.–6 p.m. through grade 8 $1,850–$2,950

ATHLETICS: P.E. required. Intramural and Interscholastic (Potomac Valley Athletic Conference). Basketball, soccer, volleyball, baseball, lacrosse, tennis, horseback riding

CLUBS: Student Government, drama, SADD, choral group, Clown Club, math club. Parent involvement: Barrie Community Association, Mustang Club (athletic program), Drama Mamas and Papas

PUBLICATIONS: Student newspaper, yearbook

COMMUNITY INVOLVEMENT: Year-round classroom activities through elementary school. Middle school Community Service Day one day a month. 9th and 10th graders complete community service project once a week for one trimester; 11th and 12th graders complete Internship Program one day a week for one trimester.

PLANT: 45-acre wooded campus, 3 libraries 20,000 volumes, computer technology (all levels), 3 art studios, 2 gyms including fitness center, 200-seat theater, playing field, swimming pool, outdoor amphitheater, 4 playgrounds, stables, Institute for Advanced Montessori Studies (teacher training) located on campus.

ADMISSION: Regular admission tours. Application fee $100. Interview, classroom visit, recommendations and transcripts. Elementary, middle, upper school testing

TUITION: $9,700 half day primary; $13,800 full day primary and K; $15,400 1–5; $17,200 6–8; $19,100 9–12

FINANCIAL AID: Need-based grants available but limited starting at Kindergarten.

OTHER FEES: Equestrian program, Capital Levy (new parents only)

TRANSPORTATION: one-way $1,820, two-way $2,520

SUMMER PROGRAMS: Day camp for ages 3 1/2–14. Swimming, horseback riding, camping, canoeing, arts and crafts, nature study, sports, etc. Specialty camps: horseback riding, computer, drama, studio arts, sports, Counselor Training (14 year-olds)

BAY MONTESSORI SCHOOL   301-737-2421
20525 Willows Road, Lexington Park, MD 20653
HEAD: Vicky Pool
WEBSITE: www.baymontessori.com
GRADES: Ungraded ages 2–12   **ENROLLMENT:** Co-ed
SPECIAL COURSES: Montessori program
EXTENDED DAY: 7:00 a.m.–5:00 p.m.
TUITION: Call for information.

BEAUVOIR   202-537-6493   FAX 202-537-5778
3500 Woodley Road, N.W., Washington, DC 20016
Episcopal 1933
HEAD: Paula J. Carreiro
WEBSITE: www.beauvoirschool.org
GRADES: Pre-Kindergarten–grade 3
ENROLLMENT: 388 Co-ed (194 boys/194 girls)
FACULTY: 51 full-time   **AVERAGE CLASS SIZE:** 20
MISSION STATEMENT: Beauvoir, The National Cathedral Elementary School, is a primary school dedicated to educating a diverse student body within a caring and creative environment designed to nurture children's intellectual, ethical, spiritual, physical, and social development. We seek to foster a spirit of inquiry and a joy in learning.
SPECIAL COURSES: Resources in: Spanish, science, art, P.E., technology, performing arts/music
EXTENDED DAY: 3:00–6:00 p.m. daily   **CLUBS:** Enrichment classes
COMMUNITY INVOLVEMENT: Community service
PLANT: Newly renovated physical plant on grounds of Washington National Cathedral in Washington, D.C. Nineteen new classrooms, interior courtyard, playground, fields, gymnasium, performance space
ADMISSION: Call admissions office 202-537-6493 to schedule a tour beginning in October.
TUITION: $18,583 includes books and lunch
FINANCIAL AID: Available   **BOOKS:** Included
LUNCH: Included   **TRANSPORTATION:** Available
DRESS CODE: None.
SUMMER PROGRAMS: Full summer program, pool

BEDDOW HIGH SCHOOL AND JUNIOR HIGH SCHOOL
301-292-1968   FAX 301-292-2095
501 Bryan Point Road, Accokeek, MD 20607
Founded 1993
HEAD: Trudy Beddow
WEBSITE: www.thebeddowschool.org   **E-MAIL:** beddow@erols.com
GRADES: 7–12   **ENROLLMENT:** 60 Co-ed
FACULTY: 9 full-time   **AVERAGE CLASS SIZE:** 10
SPECIAL COURSES: English literature, drama and writing. Math through calculus. Early American History, The Study of Ancient Civilizations and Western Civilization. Biology, earth science, chemistry, physics. Latin, French, Spanish. Computer skills, art, photography, silk screen. Full college preparatory program including SAT Prep Course.
EXTENDED DAY: Before and after school hours available for an additional fee.
ATHLETICS: Soccer team, P.E. is required; includes golf, volleyball, archery, biking
CLUBS: Chess club. Trips: Annual Wilderness Adventure Trip, includes rock climbing, caving, canoeing, high ropes, low ropes, hiking (3 days); Annual upper school trips have included New York City, Bermuda and Cancun, Mexico. Trip planned for 2004 to Italy and Greece.
PUBLICATIONS: Yearbook, newsletters
COMMUNITY INVOLVEMENT: 40 hours required to graduate

PLANT: Building located on a 7-acre campus, pond, greenhouse, large playing field, science lab, computer lab, darkroom, multipurpose room with portable stage

ADMISSION: Admission is based on receipt of an application and $50 application fee, entrance exam, transcripts, writing sample, two teacher recommendations, interview. Applications accepted September through March.

TUITION: $9,500 payable in monthly installments (price includes textbooks)

FINANCIAL AID: Limited availability

DRESS CODE: Neat and appropriate

SUMMER PROGRAMS: Various mini-camps offered

FUTURE PLANS: To increase Endowment and Financial Aid

BEDDOW MONTESSORI SCHOOL   301-567-0330   FAX 301-839-0396
8600 Loughran Road, Fort Washington, MD 20744
Founded 1974
HEAD: Trudy Beddow
WEBSITE: www.thebeddowschool.org   **E-MAIL:** beddow@erols.com
GRADES: Ungraded ages 2 1/2–12 years   **ENROLLMENT:** 175 Co-ed
FACULTY: 19 full-time   **AVERAGE CLASS SIZE:** 25
SPECIAL COURSES: The Beddow School provides an educational program for Primary and Elementary students based on the principles of Dr. Maria Montessori. It features individually paced instruction, self-initiated learning and an individualized curriculum. The program includes French for all ages and computers in classrooms.

EXTENDED DAY: Before and after school care is offered at an additional fee. Day care hours may vary (7:30 a.m.–6:00 p.m.)

PLANT: 5 acres, two playing fields, one with swings, climbing equipment, etc. Greenhouse and pond for student use, garden plots

ADMISSION: Admission is based on receipt of an application, $25 application fee and interview.

TUITION: $5,000–$6,500, payable in monthly installments. $ 500 deposit required

FINANCIAL AID: Limited availability

SUMMER PROGRAMS: Summer camp, including swimming lessons

FUTURE PLANS: To increase Endowment and Financial Aid

BEDDOW MONTESSORI SCHOOL   301-870-8660   FAX 301-870-7302
6008 Hampshire Circle, Waldorf, MD 20603
Founded 1974
HEAD: Trudy Beddow
WEBSITE: www.thebeddowschool.org   **E-MAIL:** beddow@erols.com
GRADES: Ungraded ages 2 1/2–9 years   **ENROLLMENT:** 65 Co-ed
FACULTY: 8 full-time   **AVERAGE CLASS SIZE:** 25
SPECIAL COURSES: The Beddow School provides an educational program for Primary and Elementary students based on the principles of Dr. Maria Montessori. It features individually paced instruction, self-initiated learning and an individualized curriculum. The program includes French for all ages and computers in classrooms.

EXTENDED DAY: Before and after school care is offered at an additional fee. Day care hours may vary (7:30 a.m.–6:00 p.m.)

PLANT: 2-acre campus, two play areas, one with state of the art climbing equipment, lake access, garden plots
ADMISSION: Admission is based on receipt of application, $25 application fee and interview.
TUITION: $5,000–$6,500, payable in monthly installments. $500 deposit required
FINANCIAL AID: Limited availability
FUTURE PLANS: To increase Endowment and financial aid

BELTSVILLE ADVENTIST SCHOOL   301-937-2933   FAX 301-595-2431
4230 Ammendale Road, Beltsville, MD 20705
Seventh-day Adventist
HEAD: Wendy Pega
WEBSITE: www.baschool.org   **E-MAIL:** baschool@erols.com
GRADES: Kindergarten–grade 8   **ENROLLMENT:** 213 Co-ed
FACULTY: 12   **AVERAGE CLASS SIZE:** 24
SPECIAL COURSES: Computer, chorus, bell choirs
EXTENDED DAY: 7:45 a.m–6:45 p.m.
ATHLETICS: Gymnastics, basketball, soccer
TUITION: Call for information. Reduction for church members
TRANSPORTATION: Available   **DRESS CODE:** Neat, modest attire

BERWYN BAPTIST SCHOOL   301-474-1561   FAX 301-441-3178
4720 Cherokee Street, College Park, MD 20740
Southern Baptist 1967
HEAD: Ann Elizabeth Zibrat
E-MAIL: bbscollegepark@hotmail.com
GRADES: N3–grade 6   **ENROLLMENT:** 115 Co-ed
FACULTY: 12 full- and 2 part-time   **AVERAGE CLASS SIZE:** 15
SPECIAL COURSES: Computer in each class and computer lab. Self-contained classes for each grade. Separate instructors for library, music and P.E.
CLUBS: Handbell choir   **PUBLICATIONS:** Yearbook
ADMISSION: Open enrollment begins March 1. Registration fee $75–$100 (before June 1); $125–$150 (after June 1)
TUITION: $1,300 Pre3; $1,929 Pre4; $2,558 K (a.m. only) $3837 K (all day); $4,404 1–6
OTHER FEES: Curriculum fees P3 $40 P4 $50 K $130 1-6 $170
DRESS CODE: Some guidelines

BETHEL CHRISTIAN ACADEMY   301-725-4673   FAX 301-617-9277
P.O. Box 406, Savage, MD 20763
Assembly of God 1984
HEAD: Alice Green
WEBSITE: www.bethelchristianacademy.com
GRADES: K4–grade 8   **ENROLLMENT:** 300 Co-ed
FACULTY: 26 full- and 15 part-time   **AVERAGE CLASS SIZE:** 20–22
SPECIAL COURSES: Chapel, library, music, art, media
EXTENDED DAY: 7:15 a.m.–6:00 p.m.
ATHLETICS: Soccer, basketball, lacrosse, running
CLUBS: Band, Praise Dance, chess club

PLANT: Gymnasium, state of the art computer lab, middle school science lab, music room.
ADMISSION: Test 1st grade and up. Interview
TUITION: $3,500–$4,300
FINANCIAL AID: Available   **OTHER FEES:** Registration fee $400
TRANSPORTATION: Available. Free of charge   **DRESS CODE:** Uniform required

BETHEL CHRISTIAN SCHOOL   703-590-5199   FAX 703-730-3342
3713 Pennington Lane, Woodbridge, VA 22192
Baptist
HEAD: Gaye Nobles
WEBSITE: www.BethelFWBaptist.com
E-MAIL: school office@BethelFWBaptist.com
GRADES: K4–grade 6   **ENROLLMENT:** Co-ed
SPECIAL COURSES: A Beka and ACE curriculums
EXTENDED DAY: Before and after care
TUITION: Call for information.
DRESS CODE: Uniforms

BISHOP DENIS J. O'CONNELL HIGH SCHOOL
703-237-1400   FAX 703-237-1465
6600 Little Falls Road, Arlington, VA 22213
Catholic 1957
HEAD: Alward V. Burch
WEBSITE: www.ee.cua.edu\~oconnell
GRADES: 9–12   **ENROLLMENT:** 1,450 Co-ed
FACULTY: 90 lay, 15 religious   **AVERAGE CLASS SIZE:** 19
SPECIAL COURSES: Religion, Latin, French, Spanish, German. Biology, chemistry, physics, World Culture, U.S. and Virginia history, trigonometry, calculus, economics, practical law, computer programming, studio art, public speaking, journalism, theater arts, creative writing, music. AP: English, Spanish, biology, chemistry, history, calculus, French, German, art, economics, U.S. government.
TUITION: Call for information.
FINANCIAL AID: Available
BOOKS: Extra   **LUNCH:** Cafeteria
TRANSPORTATION: Limited from East Falls Church Metro and some areas.
DRESS CODE: Uniform required
SUMMER PROGRAMS: Call for information.

BISHOP IRETON HIGH SCHOOL   703-751-7606   FAX 703-212-8173
201 Cambridge Road, Alexandria, VA 22314
Catholic 1964
HEAD: Rev. Matthew Hillyard, OSFS
WEBSITE: www.bishopireton.org   **E-MAIL:** phamer@bishopireton.org
GRADES: 9–12   **ENROLLMENT:** 800 Co-ed (390 boys/410 girls)
FACULTY: 58 full- and 6 part-time   **AVERAGE CLASS SIZE:** 20–25
SPECIAL COURSES: French, Spanish, German, Latin. Math includes calculus, Computer Introduction, Pascal, applications, programming, keyboarding. Science: biology, chemistry, physics, astronomy, organic chemistry, Introduction

to Psychology. History: World Cultures, Modern European, U.S. and Virginia Government and History. Religious studies required. Creative Writing, public speaking, journalism, publishing, art, wind ensemble, concert band, drama, theater, stage crafts. Honors and AP Program: English, U.S. history, government, chemistry, art I and II, computers, French, Spanish, biology, calculus AB, BC. Academic enrichment, study skills. 4 year technology curriculum: C++ programming, website development.

EXTENDED DAY: Proctored area until 6:00 p.m.

ATHLETICS: Required 9–10. Intramural basketball. Interscholastic: football, basketball, baseball, tennis, swimming and diving, lacrosse, soccer, golf, cross country, wrestling, track and field, softball, volleyball, cheerleading.

CLUBS: Chorus, competition math, drama, French, German, Spanish, Latin, "It's Academic", Key, Model U.N., National Honor Society, stage crew, Student Government, BI TV, ice hockey, bowling.

PUBLICATIONS: Newspaper, yearbook, literary journal

COMMUNITY INVOLVEMENT: Required. Key and Beta Clubs, St. Coletta's Best Buddies.

PLANT: Library 12,000 volumes, 250+ computers, computer labs, T-1 Internet connection, writing center, math center, newly renovated science labs, art room, 800-seat performance hall, gym, mat room, weight room, fields, use of tennis courts and pool.

ADMISSION: Application and transcripts required. Entrance test for incoming 9th graders. Interviews for transfers.

TUITION: $7,700–$11,800

FINANCIAL AID: Available

BOOKS: $350–$500 **LUNCH:** May be purchased

OTHER FEES: Registration fee $200

TRANSPORTATION: Shuttle to King Street Metro/VRE station

DRESS CODE: Uniform required

SUMMER PROGRAMS: Keyboarding, driver's ed, study skills

BISHOP MCNAMARA HIGH SCHOOL   301-735-8401   FAX 301-735-0934
6800 Marlboro Pike, Forestville, MD 20747
Catholic 1964
HEAD: Heather Gossart
WEBSITE: www.bmhs.org   **E-MAIL:** admit@bmhs.org
GRADES: 9–12   **ENROLLMENT:** 800 Co-ed
FACULTY: 60 full- and 10 part-time   **AVERAGE CLASS SIZE:** 24
SPECIAL COURSES: French, Spanish, Latin, all 9–12. Math: includes trigonometry and calculus, computer programming, literacy, applications, functions and statistics. Science: general science, biology, chemistry, physics, zoology, anatomy and physiology, psychology, environmental issues, genetics. History: U.S. and world, African American history, American government, economics. Sociology, religious studies required. Remedial reading and math. Dance, studio art. Music: 5 bands, Popular Music in the 20th Century, composition and theory. Special programs- peer ministry, internships, Model U.N. AP: chemistry, physics, English, calculus, psychology.
EXTENDED DAY: 7:00–8:00 a.m. and 3:15–5:30 p.m.
ATHLETICS: 19 varsity men's and women's sports

CLUBS: Over 30 clubs and organizations
PUBLICATIONS: Newspaper, yearbook, literary magazine
COMMUNITY INVOLVEMENT: Service requirement
PLANT: Library 13,000 volumes, language labs, 4 science labs, art studio, music room, auditorium, gym, 3 playing fields, weight room, synthetic track, updated computer labs. New fine arts and athletic center with state of the art auditorium.
ADMISSION: Application, test, essay
TUITION: $6,600
FINANCIAL AID: Available
BOOKS: $250   **DRESS CODE:** Uniform required
SUMMER PROGRAMS: Academic courses available. Athletic camps.

BLESSED SACRAMENT SCHOOL   703-998-4170   FAX 703-671-3219
1417 West Braddock Road, Alexandria, VA 22302
Catholic 1948-72/Reopened 1985
HEAD: Valerie Garcia
WEBSITE: www.blessedsacramentcc.org/school
E-MAIL: bsfrogs@eols.com
GRADES: Preschool–grade 8   **ENROLLMENT:** 365 Co-ed (175 boys/190 girls)
FACULTY: 13 full- and 21 part-time   **AVERAGE CLASS SIZE:** 30
MISSION STATEMENT: Creating an educated community to serve Christ and each other.
SPECIAL COURSES: French, Spanish, and writing workshops.
EXTENDED DAY: 7:00–8:45 a.m. and 12:00–6:00 p.m.
ATHLETICS: Basketball and tennis
CLUBS: Drama, chess, choir, Safety Patrols, band, Student Council, spelling and geography bees, Junior Great Books Program, Scouts.
PLANT: Two-level school attached to a Catholic Church. Twelve main class-rooms, library, computer lab, art room, cafeteria, gymnasium, 2 playgrounds and soccer field.
ADMISSION: Complete and submit registration application, workbook fee and technology fee in the spring before the school year.
TUITION: $3,460
FINANCIAL AID: Available
BOOKS: $100   **LUNCH:** None   **OTHER FEES:** Technology fee $50
DRESS CODE: Uniform required

BLESSED SACRAMENT SCHOOL   202-966-6682   FAX 202-966-4938
5841 Chevy Chase Parkway, N.W., Washington, DC 20015-2599
Catholic 1923
HEAD: Frances A. Scango
DIRECTOR OF ADMISSIONS: Eleanor T. Clark
WEBSITE: www.blessedsacramentdc.org
E-MAIL: fscango@blessedsacramentdc.org
GRADES: K–grade 8   **ENROLLMENT:** 497 Co-ed (205 boys/287 girls)
FACULTY: 31 full- and 16 part-time   **AVERAGE CLASS SIZE:** 20–27
MISSION STATEMENT: Blessed Sacrament is a parish, neighborhood school dedicated to excellence within an atmosphere of Christian love and concern. Our mission is to assist parents in the development of the whole child.

SPECIAL COURSES: AP Spanish and French, computers, resource, band, music, art; after school art, keyboarding.
EXTENDED DAY: 3:10–6:00 p.m.
ATHLETICS: CYO Athletics
CLUBS: Literary Club, Student Council, school play, Brownies/Girl Scouts, Boy Scouts.
PUBLICATIONS: Yearbook committee
COMMUNITY INVOLVEMENT: Social service opportunities
PLANT: Gym, media center, computer and science labs, art studio
ADMISSION: Open House beginning in December. Call for dates and brochure. Contact Director of Admissions at eclark@blessedsacramentdc.org.
TUITION: $5,155 parish, $8,400 non-parish
FINANCIAL AID: Available
BOOKS: $200 **DRESS CODE:** Uniform required
SUMMER PROGRAMS: K–1 only.
FUTURE PLANS: Celebrating Blessed Sacrament's 80th year.

BOOK OF LIFE ACADEMY   410-263-5377   FAX 410-263-5685
913 Cedar Park Road, Annapolis, MD 21401
Annapolis Assembly of God
HEAD: Kay Colbert
E-MAIL: kaycolbert@hotmail.com
GRADES: N3–grade 3   **ENROLLMENT:** 80 Co-ed
SPECIAL COURSES: Spanish. A Beka curriculum. P.E., music, art, computers
EXTENDED DAY: 7:30 a.m.–5:00 p.m.   **ATHLETICS:** Athletic teams
ADMISSION: Open enrollment preschool fall/spring semester. Transfers accepted.
TUITION: $2,780
OTHER FEES: Maintenance fee, book fee   **DRESS CODE:** Uniforms
SUMMER PROGRAMS: Available   **FUTURE PLANS:** Add grades

BOWIE MONTESSORI CHILDREN'S HOUSE
301-262-3566   FAX 301-262-3566
5004 Randonstone Lane, Bowie, MD 20715
Founded 1967
HEAD: Anne T. Riley
DIRECTOR OF ADMISSIONS: Anne T. Riley
WEBSITE: www.BMCH.net
GRADES: Ungraded Pre-K–Jr. High
ENROLLMENT: 270 Co-ed (135 boys/135 girls)
FACULTY: 27 full- and 5 part-time   **AVERAGE CLASS SIZE:** 28
SPECIAL COURSES: Montessori Method used. Exposure to Latin, computers, art and music.
EXTENDED DAY: 7:00–9:00 a.m. and 3:00–6:00 p.m.
CLUBS: Spanish, music
PLANT: Library, rustic 22-acre campus, computer lab, playing fields
ADMISSION: Tour campus, child interviewed, registration.
TUITION: $6,900 primary; $7,100 elementary
BOOKS: Workbooks extra
SUMMER PROGRAMS: Rustic Woods Summer Day Camp

THE BOYD SCHOOL BROADLANDS/ASHBURN

703-723-3364   FAX 703-723-5761
42945 Waxpool Road, Ashburn, VA 20148
Founded 1994
HEAD: Jack Quigley
DIRECTOR OF ADMISSIONS: Tony A. Wilkinson
WEBSITE: www.theboydschool.com
E-MAIL: broadlandsadmin@theboydschool.com
GRADES: 18 months–grade 6   **ENROLLMENT:** 290 (boys 50%/girls 50%)
FACULTY: Soon to be 30 full-time
AVERAGE CLASS SIZE: 26 (teacher & assistant)
MISSION STATEMENT: See The Boyd School Reston/Great Falls.
SPECIAL COURSES: Spanish, P.E., art
EXTENDED DAY: 7:00–8:30 a.m. and 3:15–6:00 p.m.
PLANT: New campus built to suit. Soccer field, 10,000-square foot playground, aquatic learning center, basketball court, paved track
ADMISSION: Continuous enrollment. First come, first served. $50 application fee
TUITION: $3,089–$9,394 depending on age of child and number of days attending
BOOKS: Provided   **LUNCH:** Provided   **DRESS CODE:** Uniforms
SUMMER PROGRAMS: Large summer camp planned for 2004.

THE BOYD SCHOOL CENTREVILLE/CLIFTON

703-631-8476   FAX 703-631-8596
6001 Centreville Crest Lane, Centreville, VA 20121
Founded 1994
HEAD: Nancy Studds
DIRECTOR OF ADMISSIONS: Michelle Austin
WEBSITE: www.theboydschool.com
E-MAIL: centrevilleadmin@theboydschool.com
GRADES: 18 months–grade 6   **ENROLLMENT:** 205 Co-ed (boys 50%/girls 50%)
FACULTY: 22 full-time   **AVERAGE CLASS SIZE:** 26 (teacher & assistant)
MISSION STATEMENT: See The Boyd School Reston/Great Falls.
SPECIAL COURSES: Spanish, P.E., art
EXTENDED DAY: 7:00–8:30 a.m. and 3:15–6:00 p.m.
PLANT: New campus location under construction. Expect to occupy in school year 2003-2004. New campus will have 13 classrooms, soccer field, track, 10,000-square foot playground, aquatic learning center.
ADMISSION: Continuous enrollment. First come, first served. $50 application fee
TUITION: $2,863–$8,776
BOOKS: Included   **LUNCH:** Included   **DRESS CODE:** Uniforms
SUMMER PROGRAMS: Yes

THE BOYD SCHOOL FAIRFAX/FAIRFAX STATION

703-934-0920   FAX 703-934-1340
3909 Oak Street, Fairfax, VA 22030
Founded 1994
HEAD: Gail Moore
DIRECTOR OF ADMISSIONS: Gail Moore
WEBSITE: www.theboydschool.com

E-MAIL: fairfaxadmin@theboydschool.com
GRADES: Age 3–Kindergarten   **ENROLLMENT:** 52 Co-ed (boys 50%/girls 50%)
FACULTY: 7 full-time   **AVERAGE CLASS SIZE:** 26 (teacher & assistant)
MISSION STATEMENT: See The Boyd School Reston/Great Falls.
SPECIAL COURSES: Spanish, P.E., art
EXTENDED DAY: 7:00–8:30 a.m. and 3:15–6:00 p.m.
PLANT: Remodeled building. Looking for location to build a new, larger campus
ADMISSION: Continuous enrollment. First come, first served. $50 application fee
TUITION: $2,863–$8,776 depending on age of child and number of days attending
BOOKS: Included   **LUNCH:** Yes

THE BOYD SCHOOL HERNDON/OAK HILL

571-203-8686   FAX 571-203-9882
13251 Woodland Park Road, Herndon, VA 20170
Founded 1994
HEAD: Sonya Baker
DIRECTOR OF ADMISSIONS: Nicole Lewis
WEBSITE: www.theboydschool.com
E-MAIL: herndonadmin@theboydschool.com
GRADES: 18 months–Kindergarten
ENROLLMENT: 145 Co-ed (boys 50%/girls 50%)
FACULTY: 15 full-time   **AVERAGE CLASS SIZE:** 26 (teacher & assistant)
MISSION STATEMENT: See The Boyd School Reston/Great Falls.
SPECIAL COURSES: Spanish, P.E., art
EXTENDED DAY: 7:00–8:30 a.m. and 3:15–6:00 p.m.
PLANT: Campus located in a build to suit building which is 18 months old.
ADMISSION: Continuous enrollment. First come, first served. $50 application fee.
TUITION: $2,982–$8,317 depending on age of child and number of days attending
BOOKS: Included   **LUNCH:** Included
SUMMER PROGRAMS: Yes

THE BOYD SCHOOL RESTON/GREAT FALLS

703-404-9733   FAX 703-404-9734
11579 Cedar Chase Road, Herndon, VA 20170
Founded 1994
HEAD: Tamara Balis
DIRECTOR OF ADMISSIONS: Tamara Benotti
WEBSITE: www.theboydschool.com
E-MAIL: restonadmin@theboydschool.com
GRADES: 18 months–Kindergarten   **ENROLLMENT:** 171 (boys 50%/girls 50%)
FACULTY: 20 full-time   **AVERAGE CLASS SIZE:** 26 (teacher & assistant)
MISSION STATEMENT: (Excerpted) To provide a solid academic foundation in education employing the philosophy and materials developed by Dr. Maria Montessori. To provide a child-centered environment which emphasizes the social, emotional, cognitive, and physical development of the child.
SPECIAL COURSES: Spanish, P.E., art
EXTENDED DAY: 7:00–8:30 a.m. and 3:15–6:00 p.m.
PLANT: New building 2 years old built as a school. 10,000-square foot playground
ADMISSION: Continuous enrollment. First come, first served. $50 application fee

TUITION: $2,982–$8,317 depending on age of child and number of days attending
BOOKS: Provided   LUNCH: Provided
DRESS CODE: Uniforms mandatory for Kindergarten, optional for others
SUMMER PROGRAMS: Yes

BRENTWOOD ACADEMY   703-780-5750   FAX 703-683-2006

3725 Nalls Road, Alexandria, VA 22309
Founded 1981
HEAD: Susan Pnevmatikatos
WEBSITE: www.brentwoodacademy.org
GRADES: 16 months–grade 2   ENROLLMENT: 85 Co-ed
AVERAGE CLASS SIZE: 10
SPECIAL COURSES: Phonics based for reading
EXTENDED DAY: 6:30 a.m.–6:30 p.m.
CLUBS: Trips during school term for students 4 and up. Entertainers for all students monthly
ADMISSION: Interview, one day in a class, then acceptance if these have gone well
TUITION: $670–$1,999
LUNCH: No fee   OTHER FEES: Registration and summer camp activity
DRESS CODE: Uniforms
SUMMER PROGRAMS: Available June–August

BRIDGES ACADEMY   202-829-1901   FAX 202-829-2429

6119 Georgia Avenue, N.W., Washington, DC 20011
Founded 1979
HEAD: C. Lillette Green-Campbell
GRADES: Preschool–grade 8   ENROLLMENT: 170 Co-ed
AVERAGE CLASS SIZE: 15 maximum
SPECIAL COURSES: Music, art, computer, Spanish
EXTENDED DAY: 6:30 a.m.–6:30 p.m.
ATHLETICS: Soccer, t-ball, basketball   CLUBS: Band
TUITION: Call for information.
LUNCH: Breakfast, lunch and snack available
DRESS CODE: Uniforms K–8
SUMMER PROGRAMS: Summer Camp and Summer School

BRITISH SCHOOL OF WASHINGTON   202-829-3700   FAX 202-829-6522

4715 16th Street, N.W., Washington, DC 20016
Founded 1998
HEAD: Jenny Arwas, OBE
DIRECTOR OF ADMISSIONS: Pia Bernardini
WEBSITE: www.britishschool.org   E-MAIL: admissionsbsw@britishschool.org
GRADES: Nursery to Year 12 (ages 3–17)
ENROLLMENT: 300 Co-ed (175 boys/125 girls)
FACULTY: 35 full- and 3 part-time   AVERAGE CLASS SIZE: 16
MISSION STATEMENT: The British School of Washington provides high quality education in a structured, positive and caring environment, which meets the individual needs of pupils. The school community draws strength from its British identity and its American home. It welcomes all nationalities, engenders respect

for all cultures and a sense of discipline is naturally achieved. The British School of Washington offers a challenging, broad curriculum based on the National Curriculum (England) and focuses on the whole development of the child, aiming to equip every pupil with the essential skills for lifelong learning.

SPECIAL COURSES: French beginning at age 4, Latin at age 8, Spanish at age 10. GCSE (General Certificate of Secondary Education) in Years 10 and 11. International Baccalaureate Diploma in Years 12 and 13.

EXTENDED DAY: 3:30–6:00 p.m.   **ATHLETICS:** Sports

CLUBS: After school clubs in arts, drama, languages, geography.

ADMISSION: Applicants are asked to submit: registration form, $150 registration fee, most recent school report/report card, photograph.   After registration, prospective students are invited for an evaluation visit and asked to submit an applicant statement and teacher evaluation forms. We operate a rolling admissions programme. Our main intake is at the beginning of the academic year, but we are able to admit children as and when a space becomes available throughout the year.

TUITION: $7,400 half day nursery; $13,400 nursery–Year 6; $14,900 Year 7–11; $16,900 Years 12–13

TRANSPORTATION: Available $2,500–$2,900   **DRESS CODE:** Uniform

SUMMER PROGRAMS: Summer adventure camp

BROADFORDING CHRISTIAN ACADEMY   301-797-8886   FAX 301-797-3155

13535 Broadfording Church Road, Hagerstown, MD 21740

Bible Brethren 1973

HEAD: William Wyand

WEBSITE: www.broadfording.com   **E-MAIL:** bca@broadfording.com

GRADES: N (age 2)–grade 12   **ENROLLMENT:** 400 Co-ed

AVERAGE CLASS SIZE: 22

SPECIAL COURSES: French, Spanish. Math includes calculus, computer, basic programming, word processing, literacy, general business math. Science: general science, biology, chemistry, physics. History: world and U.S., American government, world geography. Religious studies required. Bible Class daily. Remedial reading and math; individualized program for students with special needs in any subject. Art, music, vocal, instrumental and handbell choir.

EXTENDED DAY: 7:00 a.m.–6:00 p.m.

TUITION: $3,100 Preschool–6; $3,200   7–12

FINANCIAL AID: Some available

LUNCH: Purchase   **DRESS CODE:** Modest, conservative

SUMMER PROGRAMS: Summer Day Care

BROOKSFIELD SCHOOL   703-356-5437   FAX 703-356-6620

1830 Kirby Road, McLean, VA 22101

Founded 1987

HEAD: Anita Labetti

DIRECTOR OF ADMISSIONS: Sandi Metro

WEBSITE: www.brooksfieldschool.org   **E-MAIL:** brksfield@aol.com

GRADES: Preschool ungraded/K–3 graded   **ENROLLMENT:** 84 Co-ed

FACULTY: 7 full-/6 part-/6 specs   **AVERAGE CLASS SIZE:** 1:10 ratio or lower

MISSION STATEMENT: The Brooksfield School is founded upon the belief that learning happens through the joys of friendship, shared experience, and self-discovery.

SPECIAL COURSES: Spanish, art, dance/movement, P.E., digital photography, yoga, theatre, computers, outdoor education.

EXTENDED DAY: 7:30 a.m.–5:30 p.m.

CLUBS: Many programs are offered after school at various times during the school year, such as: science, sing-a-long, Culture Club, theater, etc.

PLANT: 5 beautiful, wooded acres in McLean, Virginia

ADMISSION: Ages 2 1/2–K: Tour, interview, recommendation form. Ages 6–9: Tour, interview, transcripts, recommendations

TUITION: $6,677 ages 2 1/2–6 lower school 9–12; $9,654 9–3; $12,500 extended day; $10,900 grades 1–3 upper school 8:30–3; $13,500 extended day

FINANCIAL AID: Scholarships offered if available.

LUNCH: Included for lower school   **OTHER FEES:** Small activity fee

SUMMER PROGRAMS: Summer day camp

FUTURE PLANS: To expand and grow to 6th grade

BROWNE ACADEMY   703-960-3000   FAX 703-960-7325

5917 Telegraph Road, Alexandria, VA 22310

Founded 1941

HEAD: Mort Dukeheart

DIRECTOR OF ADMISSIONS: Kerri Harris

WEBSITE: www.browneacademy.org

GRADES: Preschool (age 3)–grade 8   **ENROLLMENT:** 300 Co-ed

FACULTY: 40 full- and 1 part-time   **AVERAGE CLASS SIZE:** 15

MISSION STATEMENT: (Excerpted) Browne Academy is dedicated to developing independent, passionate, lifelong learners who will actively participate as responsible, caring citizens in a global community. The curriculum is individualized and interdisciplinary with a focus on multicultural and global perspectives. The school promotes direct experience and cooperative learning as well as a healthy body through physical education, athletics and outdoor activities.

SPECIAL COURSES: Spanish, French, critical thinking skills program, technology, art, music

EXTENDED DAY: 7:00–8:00 a.m. and 3:30–6:00 p.m.

ATHLETICS: Soccer, softball, basketball teams. Tae kwon do and dance also offered.

CLUBS: Scouts, drama, Student Council

PUBLICATIONS: Newspaper, yearbook, literary magazine

COMMUNITY INVOLVEMENT: Community service

PLANT: 11 acres, stream, playing fields, swimming pool, basketball court, outdoor amphitheater, computer lab, library–9,000 volumes.

ADMISSION: Application, $50 application fee, teacher recommendation, transcript, testing, visit and interview. Deadline: February 1.

TUITION: $6,395–$15,380 includes lunch

FINANCIAL AID: Available   **LUNCH:** Included   **DRESS CODE:** Neat

SUMMER PROGRAMS: ACA Camp, 8 weeks ages 3-13. Includes swimming, drama, arts & crafts, sports. Summer study program provides academic enrichment and tutoring.

FUTURE PLANS: Multipurpose building: gym/fine arts

THE BULLIS SCHOOL   301-299-8500   FAX 301-299-9050

10601 Falls Road, Potomac, MD 20854
Founded 1930
HEAD: Thomas B. Farquhar
DIRECTOR OF ADMISSIONS: Nancy L. Spencer
WEBSITE: www.bullis.org   **E-MAIL:** info@bullis.org
GRADES: 3–grade 12   **ENROLLMENT:** 604 Co-ed (324 boys/280 girls)
FACULTY: 90 full- and 5 part-time   **AVERAGE CLASS SIZE:** 15
MISSION STATEMENT: The Bullis School is an independent, co-educational college preparatory day school offering boys and girls in grades 3 through 12 an educational program of excellence in a community that values integrity, respect, responsibility, diversity and service. A caring and supportive faculty fosters a positive attitude about learning and challenges our students to achieve their highest potential in academics, the arts, and athletics.
SPECIAL COURSES: The lower and middle schools emphasize strong preparation in English, mathematics, science, history, art, music, classical and modern languages, computer literacy, skill development, study techniques, effective use of the library, critical thinking and oral skills. The upper school provides a supportive and challenging program for college-bound students with both traditional and innovative courses. The four years of required English emphasize writing and literary analysis. Students must take three years of math (courses range from algebra to AP calculus), three years of laboratory sciences (biology, chemistry and physics) and three years of social studies (one of which must be U.S. history). Upper school students are required to complete at least two years of one language at the high school level and must study that language through a Level III course. Students may choose from a variety of art courses and from technology courses ranging from fundamentals to AP programming. Honors and Advanced Placement courses and tests are offered in 16 subject areas. Upper school students meet Bullis' full credit fine arts requirement through studio work and history survey courses in art, music and theatre.
EXTENDED DAY: 3:30–6:00 p.m.
ATHLETICS: Beginning in grade 6, students can choose from approximately 20 teams for sports similar to those offered for upper school. Upper school participates in IAC (boys) and ISL (girls). Football, cheerleading, soccer, tennis, field hockey and cross-country, aerobics, basketball, wrestling, ice hockey, swimming and fitness training, softball, baseball, lacrosse, golf, equestrian team.
CLUBS: SADD, Outing Club, Tour Guides and Multicultural Student Union, Science Club, "It's Academic" team.
PUBLICATIONS: Newspaper, yearbook, literary magazine
COMMUNITY INVOLVEMENT: Projects sponsored by the Key Club and individual classes. Peer leadership, Adopt-a-Grandparent Program, Freshman/Sophomore Senior Citizen Prom and Peer Tutoring Program.
PLANT: Blair Family Center for the Arts includes teaching spaces, multimedia computer lab and 750-seat theatre. The Marriott Family Library is a 15,000 square foot on-line digital library with additional classroom space and computers. Administrative offices, dining hall, school book store, science labs, student commons, guidance and counseling offices, art studio, computer lab. Bullis Athletic Center features a 1,000-seat gym, three basketball courts, wrestling facility, cardiovascular fitness and weight center and locker facilities. 2,000-seat stadium,

football field, all-weather track, outdoor and indoor tennis courts, outdoor basketball courts, baseball diamonds, soccer fields, field hockey and lacrosse field, softball diamond and football practice field.

ADMISSION: Applicants take either the SSAT/ISEE (grade 4 ERB, grade 3 WISC and Bullis' own test), interview or group visit, three recommendations, essays and $60 application fee.

TUITION: $18,880 grades 3–5; $20,350 grades 6-8; $21,200 grades 9–12

FINANCIAL AID: Need-based financial aid is available.

BOOKS: Deposit required   **LUNCH:** Included in tuition

OTHER FEES: Extended day program

TRANSPORTATION: Available. One way $1,250, round trip $2,100.

SUMMER PROGRAMS: Academic: 6 week program, make-up, enrichment, full credit courses, grades 7–PG. Camps: 1–6 weeks, baseball/softball, basketball, lacrosse, soccer, wrestling, tennis, plus computer art/writing workshop and drama program. Bulldog Day Camp for children.

BURGUNDY FARM COUNTRY DAY SCHOOL

703-960-3431   FAX 703-960-5056
3700 Burgundy Road, Alexandria, VA 22303
Founded 1946
HEAD: Richmond Abbe
DIRECTOR OF ADMISSIONS: Patricia Harden
WEBSITE: www.burgundyfarm.org   **E-MAIL:** info@burgundyfarm.org
GRADES: Junior K–grade 8   **ENROLLMENT:** 277 Co-ed (139 boys/138 girls)
AVERAGE CLASS SIZE: 8–16

MISSION STATEMENT: (Excerpted) Burgundy Farm Country Day School seeks to empower its students to become thinking, informed, committed, creative individuals who will contribute to all levels of society, from their family and school class, to their community and nation. Burgundy nurtures the natural enthusiasm of children, so that learning will remain a joyful, lifelong process. The school's cooperative philosophy is based in the belief that education is intrinsically a cooperative enterprise in which a community of parents, teachers and students work together to benefit the educational process.

SPECIAL COURSES: Spanish, French from age 6, computers, general science, biology, art, music, drama. Interdisciplinary, experiential approach. Transition (K1) class, grades 1, 2/3, 4/5, middle school 6,7,8 departmental focus. Fine arts electives in middle school (pottery, mural painting, photography, architecture, Shakespearean Drama, drums)

EXTENDED DAY: 3:00–6:00 p.m.

ATHLETICS: Co-ed, boys' and girls' soccer teams. Boys' and girls' basketball teams. Co-ed track and field.

PLANT: New classroom buildings 1–8. Newly renovated early childhood barns. New gymnasium. 300-acre wilderness campus in West Virginia.

ADMISSION: Individual testing school-referred testers. References, school visit, parent interviews. School seeks diverse student body.

TUITION: $15,696–$16,475

FINANCIAL AID: Available   **BOOKS:** Provided   **LUNCH:** Not provided

OTHER FEES: $500 maintenance fee   **TRANSPORTATION:** Available. $1,450–$2,170

SUMMER PROGRAMS: Summer Day Camp, Cooper's Cove Center for Wildlife Studies

BUTLER SCHOOL   301-977-6600   FAX 301-977-2419
15951 Germantown Road, Darnestown, MD 20874
Founded 1971
HEAD: Cheryl Rowe
WEBSITE: www.butlerschool.org
GRADES: Preschool–grade 8   **ENROLLMENT:** 175 Co-ed (84 boys/91 girls)
AVERAGE CLASS SIZE: 24
MISSION STATEMENT: Butler School aspires to create a peaceful community of learners. Our school is built on the principles of Maria Montessori. We trust and respect our students, and we believe in the power of our students to make a difference in the world.
SPECIAL COURSES: Butler School is a Montessori school which embodies the educational principles established by Dr. Maria Montessori. In addition to language arts, mathematics, science, history and cultural subjects, the curriculum also includes art, music, drama, P.E., foreign languages and a challenging ropes course.
EXTENDED DAY: 8:00 a.m.–5:15 p.m.
ATHLETICS: Equestrian program   **CLUBS:** Piano lessons
PLANT: Beautiful 22-acre campus, stables, swimming pool, tennis court, ropes course, playing fields, library, organic garden, creek and pond
ADMISSION: Application fee $25. Parent interview and classroom observation
TUITION: $5,675–$9,335
FINANCIAL AID: Available   **TRANSPORTATION:** Available $1,800
DRESS CODE: For 7th and 8th grades. Uniform for elementary
SUMMER PROGRAMS: Summer Camp for ages 3–13. Horseback riding, fishing and canoeing, ropes course, swimming, art

—C

CALVARY BAPTIST CHURCH ACADEMY   410-768-5324
407 Marley Station Road, Glen Burnie, MD 21060
Independent Baptist 1973
HEAD: John Bandy
GRADES: K3–grade 12   **ENROLLMENT:** 500 Co-ed
FACULTY: 20 full- and 5 part-time   **AVERAGE CLASS SIZE:** 25
SPECIAL COURSES: Spanish, algebra, general science, biology, chemistry, physics, history, U.S. government, world geography. Religious studies required. Art, music, typing, computer science.
EXTENDED DAY: 6:00 a.m.–6:00 p.m.
TUITION: Call for information.
TRANSPORTATION: Available   **DRESS CODE:** Rules stated in student handbook

CALVARY CHRISTIAN ACADEMY   202-526-5176   FAX 202-526-2672
806 Rhode Island Avenue, N.E., Washington, DC 20018
HEAD: Bernard Perry
GRADES: Infants–grade 8   **ENROLLMENT:** Co-ed
EXTENDED DAY: 6:30–8:15 a.m and 3:30–6:00 p.m.
ATHLETICS: Cheerleader team   **CLUBS:** Choir, tutoring service
TUITION: $160/week infants; $135/week toddler; $3,750/year ages 2(trained)–4 $4,400 K–8
SUMMER PROGRAMS: Summer Camp

CALVARY CHRISTIAN SCHOOL   703-221-2016
4345 Inn Street, Triangle, VA 22172
HEAD: John Wallace
WEBSITE: www.calvary-christianschool.com
GRADES: K4–grade 12   **ENROLLMENT:** Co-ed
EXTENDED DAY: Before and after care
TUITION: Call for information.
LUNCH: Available   **DRESS CODE:** Uniforms
SUMMER PROGRAMS: Summer Camp

CALVARY LUTHERAN SCHOOL   301-589-4001   FAX 301-589-0931
9545 Georgia Avenue, Silver Spring, MD 20910
Lutheran 1951
HEAD: Marlys-Jean Natonick
WEBSITE: www.celcs.org
E-MAIL: schoolsecretary@genesis.celcs.org
GRADES: K–grade 8   **ENROLLMENT:** 125 Co-ed
FACULTY: 13 full- and 1 part-time
AVERAGE CLASS SIZE: 25 or less
MISSION STATEMENT: (Excerpted) Calvary Lutheran School is dedicated to providing Christian education to children from Kindergarten through Grade Eight as they praise in joy, grow in faith, and reach in love. During these important years, a child grows in knowledge, attitudes, and skills that will greatly determine the course of his or her life. Responding to God's call in their lives and trusting Him for guidance, our teachers help their students develop a personal philosophy of life based upon the Christian faith.
SPECIAL COURSES: Remedial reading and math, study skills, art, music. Religious studies, Spanish, computers, library, religion, reading, phonics, Chapel, hymn sing, primary choir, intermediate choir, middle school choir, chime choir, Christmas Program, Spring Arts Festival, Easter Drama, Art Fair, poetry contest, field trips, MCAP-Maryland Children Assault Prevention program, Kindergarten 100th Day Celebration, 1st Grade Authors Tea, 3–6 spelling bee, K–5 math backpack, 5th science JASON project, 5th grade Colonial Restaurant, 6th grade history day, 6th grade outdoor education, middle school Science Fair, Presidential Fitness program.
EXTENDED DAY: 7:00–8:00 a.m. and 3:00–6:00 p.m.
ATHLETICS: 4–8 volleyball and flag football; 3–8 track and field, 5–8 girls' basketball and boys' basketball
CLUBS: Boy Scouts, patrols, dance troupe, piano
COMMUNITY INVOLVEMENT: Servant and Community activities and projects, Walk for the Homeless, St. Jude's Math-a-Thon, Muscular Dystrophy Read-a-Thon, American Heart Association Jump Rope for Heart
PLANT: Library 9,000 volumes, playing field, multi-purpose room
ADMISSION: Parent visitation, informal student interview and testing, admissions committee.
TUITION: $5,200–$6,100
FINANCIAL AID: Available
BOOKS: $575–$675   **LUNCH:** K–5 by ticket only
DRESS CODE: Yes

CALVARY ROAD CHRISTIAN SCHOOL   703-971-8004   FAX 703-971-0130

6811 Beulah Street, Alexandria, VA 22310
Baptist 1976
HEAD: Harold Jones
DIRECTOR OF ADMISSIONS: Bridget Tice
WEBSITE: www.crcs.org   **E-MAIL:** Tice@crcs.org
GRADES: Preschool 3 year old–grade 8   **ENROLLMENT:** 320 Co-ed
FACULTY: 40 full- and 3 part-time   **AVERAGE CLASS SIZE:** 20
SPECIAL COURSES: Computer, Spanish, music, private music lessons available,
Religious Studies
EXTENDED DAY: 6:45–6:00 p.m.
ATHLETICS: Soccer, volleyball, basketball, cheerleading
PUBLICATIONS: Yearbook
PLANT: Library, computer lab, gym, auditorium, kitchen
ADMISSION: Grade placement test. Interview with Administrator. Registration
fee $260.
TUITION: $ 6,520 Pre-K; $3,900 K–8
LUNCH: Fee   **DRESS CODE:** Uniform required
SUMMER PROGRAMS: Day camp 2 1/2 to 12 years (entering 7th grade).
Weekly themes–crafts, field trips.
FUTURE PLANS: Building expansion

THE CALVERTON SCHOOL   410-535-0216   FAX 410-535-6934

300 Calverton School Road, Huntingtown, MD 20639
Founded 1967
HEAD: Dr. Elizabeth Cataldi, M.Ed., Ed.D.
DIRECTOR OF ADMISSIONS: Erna Casalino
WEBSITE: www.calvertonschool.org   **E-MAIL:** ecasalino@calvertonshool.org
GRADES: Pre-Kindergarten–grade 12   **ENROLLMENT:** 420 Co-ed
AVERAGE CLASS SIZE: 11
MISSION STATEMENT: To teach young people to seek truth, virtue and beauty
through mental, physical, artistic, and moral pursuits to prepare them for higher
education and responsible citizenship. The goal of The Calverton School is to pro-
duce well-balanced and well-educated students.
SPECIAL COURSES: AP courses: biology, chemistry, physics, U.S. history,
English, calculus, French and Spanish. Language: French grades 2–5 and 9–12,
Latin grades 6–8, and Spanish grades 9–12. Math includes calculus. Science: general science, chemistry, physics, Chesapeake Bay Studies, Environmental Studies,
and engineering. History: American Studies, American government, and eco-
nomics. Electives: theater, art, music, computer, health, P.E., instrumental music,
and chorus.
EXTENDED DAY: 7:00 a.m.–6:00 p.m.
ATHLETICS: Basketball, cross-country, golf, field hockey, lacrosse, tennis, and
soccer.
CLUBS: Photography, chess, chorus, Japanese Club, International Thespian
Society, Math Counts, Bantam Lacrosse, strings ensemble, National Honor
Society, Student Council, basketball club and lacrosse club.
PUBLICATIONS: Yearbook, literary magazine, newspaper
COMMUNITY INVOLVEMENT: All levels involved in community service

PLANT: 150 acres, four buildings, state of the art science labs, black box theater
ADMISSION: (Excerpted) Admission is based on academic ability, achievement, and character. Campus visit, Open house. While applications may be submitted at any time, families are urged to apply by February 1 for entrance in the fall. Evaluation, current school transcript, teacher recommendation.
TUITION: $6,366–$13,260
FINANCIAL AID: Available
TRANSPORTATION: Available. $1,060–$2,100   **DRESS CODE:** Uniform required
SUMMER PROGRAMS: Summer Activities Program for children ages 5–18
FUTURE PLANS: Hundred Acre Expansion: Athletic Complex and Environmental Facility.

CAPITOL CHRISTIAN ACADEMY   301-336-2200   FAX 301-336-6704
610 Largo Road, Upper Marlboro, MD 20774
Baptist 1961
HEAD: Gary O'Neill
WEBSITE: www.ccacad.org   **E-MAIL:** info@ccacad.org
GRADES: K4–grade 12   **ENROLLMENT:** 330 Co-ed
FACULTY: 20 full- and 1 part-time   **AVERAGE CLASS SIZE:** 25
MISSION STATEMENT: To train young people to walk with God and live in this world.
SPECIAL COURSES: Spanish K4–12. Algebra I and II, geometry, computer. Science: general science, biology, chemistry, physics. Religious studies required. Art, music, band, choir, computer.
EXTENDED DAY: 6:30–8:00 a.m. and 3:30–6:00 p.m.
ATHLETICS: Volleyball, soccer, basketball
CLUBS: Fine arts   **PUBLICATIONS:** Newspaper, yearbook
PLANT: Gym, library, science lab, computer lab
ADMISSION: File enrollment application with fee. Interview and testing. References.
TUITION: $5,630–$6,020, depending on age and grade
FINANCIAL AID: Available
TRANSPORTATION: Available, call for information.   **DRESS CODE:** Uniforms
SUMMER PROGRAMS: Day Camp

CAPITOL HILL DAY SCHOOL   202-547-2244   FAX 202-547-0510
210 South Carolina Avenue, S.E., Washington, DC 20003-1998
Founded 1968
HEAD: Catherine Peterson
WEBSITE: www.chds.org   **E-MAIL:** admissions@chds.org
GRADES: Pre-K–grade 8   **ENROLLMENT:** 230 Co-ed (115 boys/115 girls)
FACULTY: 32 full- and 12 part-time   **AVERAGE CLASS SIZE:** 24
MISSION STATEMENT: To provide an educational program that engages students in the process of learning with the aim of helping them become thoughtful, caring young people.
SPECIAL COURSES: French and Spanish, field education, community service, computer lab, art, music, drama, library, P.E., augment studies of science, mathematics, literature, language, history and culture. Foreign language studies culminate with an opportunity to participate in home-stay trip to foreign country.

EXTENDED DAY: 3:00–6:00 p.m.

ATHLETICS: Competitive sports for upper grades include basketball, soccer, softball and track. Also available are squash, skating, rollerblading, bowling, bicycling and games.

CLUBS: Music lessons, website development   **PUBLICATIONS:** Yearbook

COMMUNITY INVOLVEMENT: Community service programs are available

PLANT: Expansive library, art and computer facilities. Resources include adjunct educational facilities used for field education throughout the region. Main building and neighboring townhouse are across the street from 7-acre park with playing fields.

ADMISSION: Parent visit, application between October and February 1. Requires assessment test, school visit, recommendation, transcript and $50 fee

TUITION: $14,450–$15,750

FINANCIAL AID: Available

LUNCH: Bring   **OTHER FEES:** Security deposit $1,000

TRANSPORTATION: Available, $925 one way, $1,400 round trip.

DRESS CODE: Neat and clean appearance

SUMMER PROGRAMS: Day Camp 1 week sessions June–July, ages 4–14. Swimming, field trips, camping, sailing included

FUTURE PLANS: Ongoing improvements to facility and curriculum enhancement

CARDINAL HICKEY ACADEMY   410-286-0404   FAX 410-286-6334
1601 West Mount Harmony Road, Owings, MD 20736
Catholic 1997
HEAD: Sister Christine Born, OP
DIRECTOR OF ADMISSIONS: Peggy Ball
E-MAIL: cardinal.hickey.academy@comcast.net
GRADES: Preschool–grade 8   **ENROLLMENT:** 300 Co-ed
FACULTY: 12 full- and 9 part-time   **AVERAGE CLASS SIZE:** 28
MISSION STATEMENT: The Cardinal Hickey Academy is a Catholic School of the Archdiocese of Washington, D.C. It functions under the authority of the Pastor of Jesus the Good Shepherd and adheres to the policies of the Covenant Community and those of the Catholic Schools Office. The Academy recognizes that human dignity requires that each person act out of conscious and free choice, as moved and drawn in a personal way from within. The Academy embraces a sacred respect for this process and individual conscience. The Academy serves the educational needs of the Catholic families in northern Calvert County and southern Anne Arundel County.

SPECIAL COURSES: Algebra, chorus, computer, Latin, Religion and Spanish

EXTENDED DAY: 6:30–8:30 a.m. and 3:30–6:30 p.m.

ATHLETICS: Basketball, cheerleading, soccer

CLUBS: Band, chess and checkers, drama, Girl Scouts, handbells, Hands-on-Science

PLANT: Multi-level school attached to Jesus the Good Shepherd Catholic Church. Nine main classrooms, science and computer labs, art/music studio, primary grades library, gymnasium, athletic field, sports pavilion, dining hall, basketball/tennis court and playground.

ADMISSION: Submit completed application, including registration fee (call for rates), standardized test results and most recent report card in early February (prior to fall enrollment).

TUITION: $4,725 Catholic student; $5,075 Non-Catholic student; $3,590 Kindergarten
FINANCIAL AID: Limited financial aid is available.
BOOKS: Included   **DRESS CODE:** School uniform required
FUTURE PLANS: Addition of Media Center in 2005

CARDINAL MONTESSORI SCHOOL   703-491-3810   FAX 703-499-9994
1424 G Street, Woodbridge, VA 22191
1992 (AMS Affiliated)
HEAD: Erick Gallegos
WEBSITE: www.CardinalMontessori.com   **E-MAIL:** CMSmontessori@aol.com
GRADES: Ungraded 3–12 years   **ENROLLMENT:** 120 Co-ed (60 boys/60 girls)
FACULTY: 5 full-time   **AVERAGE CLASS SIZE:** Varies; 15:1 ratio
MISSION STATEMENT: Cardinal Montessori School is the oldest AMS affiliated Montessori School in Prince William County. Our school is committed to assist each child to reach his or her full potential in the areas of child development.
SPECIAL COURSES: Spanish, music, art. Music/dance/piano (extra).
EXTENDED DAY: 6:00 a.m.–6:30 p.m. EDC over 5 $1,643; under 5 $2,961
PUBLICATIONS: Yearbook, newspaper
ADMISSION: Application fee $250/ $150 deposit
TUITION: $3,000 Under 5; $4,500 Over 5
BOOKS: $100   **LUNCH:** Bring   **DRESS CODE:** Uniform required
SUMMER PROGRAMS: Available for enrolled students only

CHARLES E. SMITH JEWISH DAY SCHOOL
301-881-1400   FAX 301-984-7834
1901 East Jefferson Street, Rockville, MD 20852
Jewish 1965
HEAD: Gerry Nussbaum
WEBSITE: www.cesjds.org **E-MAIL:** cesjds@cesjds.org
GRADES: Kindergarten–grade 6   **ENROLLMENT:** 1,515 Co-ed both campuses
FACULTY: 70 full-and 100 part-time   **AVERAGE CLASS SIZE:** 20
SPECIAL COURSES: Apply to both locations: French 7–12, Spanish 7–12; Hebrew Language and Literature required K–12. Math: through calculus, computer. Science: general science, biology, chemistry, physics. History: geography, U.S., Modern European, Jewish; Senior Seminars: Vietnam and the 60's; Human Growth and Development. Religious studies required. Remedial reading and math. Art and music, photography K–9, Choir 4–6, drama. Business management, computer keyboarding. Israel Work/Study Program Senior year.
ATHLETICS: Intramural and interscholastic. Soccer, softball, basketball, tennis, baseball, volleyball, cross-country
CLUBS: Social Action, Student Council, cooking
PUBLICATIONS: Newspaper, literary magazine (in Hebrew and English), yearbook
COMMUNITY INVOLVEMENT: Service program required in upper school; intergenerational programs with senior citizens, clothing and food drives for the homeless, and other programs.
PLANT: 2 libraries– 27,500 volumes, 3 science labs, art studio, 3 gyms, 2 auditoriums, playing fields, 2 chapels.
ADMISSION: Interview, screening tests, transcript, teacher recommendation

TUITION: $12,530 K–6; $15,840 7–11; $7,920 grade 12 1st semester; 2nd semester work/study program in Poland and Israel.
FINANCIAL AID: Available
BOOKS: Extra 7–12 only   LUNCH: Cafeteria
OTHER FEES: Activity fee $60–$380   TRANSPORTATION: Available
DRESS CODE: Neat and clean; no cut-offs, halter tops, short shorts grades 7–12

CHARLES E. SMITH JEWISH DAY SCHOOL   301-881-1400
11710 Hunters Lane, Rockville, MD 20852
Jewish 1965
HEAD: Roslyn Siegel Landy
WEBSITE: www.cesjds.org   E-MAIL: cesjds@cesjds.org
GRADES: 7–grade 12 this campus
SPECIAL COURSES: See listings under lower school address at 1901 East Jefferson Street.

CHATHAM HALL   434-432-2941   FAX 434-432-2405
800 Chatham Hall Circle, Chatham, VA 24531-3085
Episcopal 1894
HEAD: Dr. Gary Fountain
DIRECTOR OF ADMISSIONS: Alexis A. Weiner
WEBSITE: www.chathamhall.org   E-MAIL: admission@chathamhall.com
GRADES: 9–12   ENROLLMENT: 143 girls (120 boarding)
FACULTY: 31 full- and 8 part-time   AVERAGE CLASS SIZE: 8
MISSION STATEMENT: Chatham Hall prepares young women for college and productive, fulfilled lives. We esteem equally the intellect and character of each student. A community of honor and trust, we value our Episcopal heritage and welcome students from diverse backgrounds. Our rigorous educational program encourages intellectual growth, creative development, and personal responsibility.
SPECIAL COURSES: AP courses: biology, calculus AB, calculus BC, chemistry, English, European history, French language, French literature, Human Geography, Latin, Latin literature, music theory, physics, Spanish language, studio art, U.S. history. Trimester electives include Model U.N. economics, DNA Science, journalism, music history, art history, veterinary science.
ATHLETICS: Varsity basketball, cross-country, field hockey, soccer, swimming, tennis, volleyball. Junior varsity basketball. Also intramural lacrosse and softball.
CLUBS: Clubs include art, Athletic Council, dance committee, French, Latin, photography, Spanish, Student Council, Student Senate, and more.
PUBLICATIONS: Literary magazine, newspaper, yearbook
COMMUNITY INVOLVEMENT: Service League, Habitat for Humanity, Appalachian Service Project
PLANT: Library 20,000 volumes, science and technology building, greenhouse, 4 computer labs, art studio, stables and indoor arena, 3 playing fields, 6 tennis courts, 2 dorms, health care center, Chapel, black box theater, gym.
ADMISSION: Application and fee, essay, parent questionnaire, math and English teacher recommendations, transcripts, interview, SSAT. Application deadline in February; notification in March. Call for specific dates.
TUITION: $28,500
FINANCIAL AID: Available. Need-based only

BOOKS: $600   LUNCH: No cost   DRESS CODE: Neat appearance
SUMMER PROGRAMS: Equestrian

CHELSEA SCHOOL   301-585-1430   FAX 301-585-5865
711 Pershing Drive, Silver Spring, MD 20910
Founded 1976
HEAD: Dr. Linda Handy
WEBSITE: www.chelseaschool.edu   E-MAIL: information@chelseaschool.edu
GRADES: 5–12   ENROLLMENT: 113 Co-ed (79 boys/34 girls)
FACULTY: 33 full- and 3 part-time   AVERAGE CLASS SIZE: 8
MISSION STATEMENT: To educate average to gifted students with language-based learning differences in a college preparatory setting.
SPECIAL COURSES: All classes are taught by special education teachers. Grades 5–8: reading, writer's workshop, math, science, and social studies. Electives in Physical Education, art, music, drama, media, community service and careers. Grades 9–12: English: Introduction to Literature, American Literature, British Literature, 20th Century African-American Literature, business English, World Literature. Math: algebra I and II, geometry, trigonometry, pre-calculus, calculus. History: U.S. history, government, world history, AP world history. Other high school courses: media, technology education, fine arts, music, P.E., careers. All grades: Related Services include speech-language therapy, counseling, occupational therapy, and physical therapy. Tutorials are also provided in reading, written language, and math. Reading programs include Orton-Gillingham, Lindamood Bell, Wilson, Stevenson, Scottish Rite, Kurzweil 3000 reading technology. All students participate in Social Skills/Outdoor Education classes.
ATHLETICS: Interscholastic athletic competition in soccer, basketball, softball
CLUBS: Student Government, chess club   PUBLICATIONS: Yearbook
COMMUNITY INVOLVEMENT: Community service projects
PLANT: Library 10,000 volumes, science lab, art studios, music studio, pottery studio, media lab, computers in all classrooms, full-size gymnasium.
ADMISSION: Application is submitted with current psycho-educational testing. Appropriate candidates are interviewed and visit school for 2–3 days.
TUITION: $31,098
FINANCIAL AID: Available
DRESS CODE: None
SUMMER PROGRAMS: 5-week summer school program for academic remediation in reading, written language and mathematics
FUTURE PLANS: Renovating classrooms

CHESAPEAKE ACADEMY   410-647-9612   FAX 410-647-6088
1185 Baltimore Annapolis Boulevard, Arnold, MD 21012
1980
HEAD: David Michelman
WEBSITE: www.chesapeakeacademy.com
E-MAIL: nsabold@chesapeakeacademy.com
GRADES: Preschool age 3–grade 5
ENROLLMENT: 319 co-ed (175 boys/142 girls)
FACULTY: 46 full-time   AVERAGE CLASS SIZE: 17
MISSION STATEMENT: Chesapeake Academy is dedicated to serving the best

interests of its children while opening doors to a life of learning.

SPECIAL COURSES: Spanish, computer, art, music, library, Renaissance Program, drama

EXTENDED DAY: 7:15 a.m. to 6:00 p.m.

ATHLETICS: P.E. requirements. Volleyball, basketball, soccer, field hockey.

CLUBS: Drama, crafts, Brownies

COMMUNITY INVOLVEMENT: Children perform community service

PLANT: Library has 8,000 volumes, science lab, auditorium, playing fields, computer lab, music/dance studio

ADMISSION: Application fee $55.00. Tour, interview, testing. Elementary grades outside testing WISC III, one day visit.

TUITION: $4,805–$9,810

FINANCIAL AID: Available   **BOOKS:** $350

OTHER FEES: Field Trip/activity fee $190   **DRESS CODE:** Uniform required

CHESAPEAKE ACADEMY OF NORTHERN VIRGINIA

703-256-1900   FAX 703-256-1923

5533 Industrial Drive, Springfield, VA 22151

Founded 1978

HEAD: Carolynn Shomo

DIRECTOR OF ADMISSIONS: Cynthia McIver

WEBSITE: www.qualitygraduates.org

E-MAIL: chesapeakeacad@mindspring.com

GRADES: K–12; parent/adult education   **ENROLLMENT:** 70 Co-ed

FACULTY: 10 full- and 3 part-time   **AVERAGE CLASS SIZE:** 15

MISSION STATEMENT: (Excerpted) To help all students gain the knowledge they need to succeed in life and have the self-confidence to think for themselves so that they are able to accomplish their goals and be productive members of society. To ensure students are competent in the basic academic subjects and in knowing how to study and learn. To assist students to learn through the study methodologies and reference works on children and education written by L. Ron Hubbard. To create an environment where children are treated with respect and are taught to respect the rights of others.

SPECIAL COURSES: Individualized instruction, "how to learn", study and communication courses for students at elementary through high school ages. Licensed by Applied Scholastics International to use the study methods developed by L. Ron Hubbard. Emphasis on 100% comprehension and practical application in all subjects. Innovative Reading Program raises student literacy level to new heights through individual instruction. Emphasis is on having the child read lots of good books that gradiently increase in difficulty so child meets many of the important and valuable individuals of his society, culture and heritage through reading. Job experience considered a priority for high school students. College bound program available. Foreign languages: French, Spanish, and German. Math: advanced geometry, trigonometry, calculus. Science: physical science, biology, chemistry, physics. Some electives are: typing, home skills, art, computer, word processing, basic programming, economics, photography. Adult education component includes how to read effectively, study and communication courses, and parent workshops. Tutoring service available year round.

EXTENDED DAY: Available in summer session only. 7:30 a.m.–5:30 p.m.

ATHLETICS: P.E. daily

PUBLICATIONS: Quarterly newsletter and student magazine

COMMUNITY INVOLVEMENT: Participation in environmental clean-ups; visit senior citizen homes; volunteer service at homeless/community centers; other Way to Happiness projects

PLANT: 4.5-acre campus, soccer field, outdoor basketball courts (half court), library, film room, darkroom

ADMISSION: Interview with student and parents; $100 Registration/Testing fee; student's own interests and goals for education important. Year round enrollment

TUITION: $7,000 K–5; $7,250 6–12

FINANCIAL AID: Limited number of partial scholarships available

BOOKS: $500 K–5 $525   **LUNCH:** Bring own lunch

OTHER FEES: $100 Registration/testing fee

TRANSPORTATION: Available. $110-$150 charged by zone

DRESS CODE: Casual/neat. Monday is Dress Up Day.

SUMMER PROGRAMS: 8 weeks (4 week min.); Morning academics: how to study, communication courses. Afternoon fun: bowling, ice skating, swimming, field trips, arts and crafts, outings. Students can catch up.

FUTURE PLANS: Parent workshops develop into Institute of Parent Education; Teacher/Tutor Training Institute.

CHESAPEAKE MONTESSORI SCHOOL   410-757-4750   FAX 410-757-8770

30 Old Mill Bottom Road North, Annapolis, MD 21401

Founded 1977

HEAD: Anne H. Locke

WEBSITE: www.chesapeake-montessori.com

E-MAIL: cms@chesapeake-montessori.com

GRADES: age 18 months–grade 5   **ENROLLMENT:** 125 Co-ed

FACULTY: 5 full- and 2 part-time   **AVERAGE CLASS SIZE:** 25

MISSION STATEMENT: (Excerpted) We at Chesapeake Montessori School are dedicated to helping children become confident, independent individuals with well-developed powers of reasoning and with enthusiasm for learning. We believe that as children develop these qualities, they become increasingly able to take advantage of the strong academic program that we offer.

SPECIAL COURSES: Montessori Method; French for ages 18 months–11; music and P.E. for K–5

EXTENDED DAY: 7 a.m.–6 p.m.   **PUBLICATIONS:** Yearbook, newsletter

COMMUNITY INVOLVEMENT: American Heart Association's Jump Rope for Heart

PLANT: Central library, library in classes, sports court and playing fields, swimming pool, multipurpose room, playground

ADMISSION: Observation of classes, interview with parent and child. Test age 6 and over. $25 application fee. Registration fee equals 2 monthly tuition payments.

TUITION: $5,760 toddler (18 months–2 1/2) and half day primary; $8,080 full day K; $8,560   elementary

FINANCIAL AID: Available   **DRESS CODE:** None

SUMMER PROGRAMS: Three 2-week sessions in late June through July for ages 3–8; includes swimming, arts and crafts, field trips, singing, drama. Morning or full day programs. (No before or after care in summer.)

CHESAPEAKE MONTESSORI SCHOOL   410-257-0535
4190 Hunting Creek Road, Huntingtown, MD 20639
HEAD: Lynda Hampshire
WEBSITE: www.cmc@mymontessori.com
GRADES: 18 months–age 12   **ENROLLMENT:** Co-ed
SPECIAL COURSES: Spanish to all age groups, music program with instruments elementary, library program, P.E.
EXTENDED DAY: Before and after care
ADMISSION: Admissions beginning in March for following school year
TUITION: Call for information.
SUMMER PROGRAMS: Summer Camp

CHESTERBROOK ACADEMY ELEMENTARY   703-397-0555   FAX 703-397-0565
3753 Centerview Drive, Chantilly, VA 20151
Founded 1999
HEAD: Laura Ravenstahl
DIRECTOR OF ADMISSIONS: Lori Grebner
WEBSITE: www.nobellearning.com   **E-MAIL:** laura.ravenstahl@nlcinc.com
GRADES: Pre-Kindergarten–6   **ENROLLMENT:** 213 Co-ed (123 boys/90 girls)
AVERAGE CLASS SIZE: 15
MISSION STATEMENT: To create a unique educational environment built on sound research, qualified instruction, and local communities of learning that foster academic excellence, instill a love of active learning, and provide experiences that enable all students to acquire a foundation of skills for lifelong achievement.
SPECIAL COURSES: Our elementary guidelines outline an educational program that is built upon national standards and guarantees that students will acquire basic skills and knowledge in reading, math, social studies, science, Spanish, visual and performing arts, computer technology and physical education.
EXTENDED DAY: 6:30 a.m.–6:30 p.m.
ATHLETICS: After school sports/activities (soccer, basketball, ballet)
CLUBS: Student Government, PTO   **PUBLICATIONS:** Yearbook, newsletter
PLANT: 5-acre campus includes preschool building, elementary school building, soccer field, outdoor basketball court, playground, gymnasium, computer lab and library.
ADMISSION: Family/parent tour and student visit to begin the enrollment process.
TUITION: $9,200 JrK–2; $9,350 3–6
FINANCIAL AID: Available
BOOKS: $250   **LUNCH:** Available $3.00 a day
OTHER FEES: Registration/deposit   **DRESS CODE:** Uniform required
SUMMER PROGRAMS: CAMP ZONE 10 week basic and enrichment camps available

CHESTERBROOK ACADEMY ELEMENTARY SCHOOL
703-404-0202   FAX 703-421-7874
46100 Woodshire Drive, Sterling, VA 20166
Founded 1996
HEAD: MarySue Lindsay, Ed.M.
DIRECTOR OF ADMISSIONS: Lydia Soto
WEBSITE: www.nobellearning.com   **E-MAIL:** marysue.lindsay@nlcinc.com

GRADES: Junior K–grade 8   **ENROLLMENT:** 150 Co-ed (70 boys/80 girls)
FACULTY: 22 full- and 8 part-time   **AVERAGE CLASS SIZE:** 15
MISSION STATEMENT: Our mission is to create unique educational environments built on sound research, qualified instruction, and local communities of learning that foster academic excellence, instill a love of active learning, and provide experiences that enable all students to acquire a foundation of skills for lifelong achievement.
SPECIAL COURSES: We believe in: Nurturing creativity and a love of learning; Promoting collaboration among our community of learners; Fostering respect among children, parents, employees, and the community; Meeting the needs of children and the expectations of parents; Providing educational programs that consistently meet quality assurance criteria; Demonstrating accountability and effectiveness to our constituencies; Developing and improving instructional delivery of our programs; Building and maintaining our learning communities on a foundation of integrity and high standards. All students also receive Spanish instruction, P.E., and computer instruction. Our Creative Arts Program involves all students and integrates art, music, dance and drama.
EXTENDED DAY: 6:30 a.m.–6:30 p.m.
ATHLETICS: Football clinics, soccer clinics, cheerleading clinics, ballet, karate, tennis clinics, golf clinics
CLUBS: Drama club, Genius Jones Science, Parents' Book Club, active PTO. Family outings to Wizards games, etc. Middle school students spend every Thursday involved in a hands-on field trip related to the curriculum.
PUBLICATIONS: Newspaper club, yearbook
PLANT: Beautiful brick school. Auditorium/gym, well-equipped playground, library, computer lab, computers in each classroom
ADMISSION: Parent/child interview and tour, transcript review, testing may be recommended
TUITION: $8,050–$8,600
BOOKS: $150   **LUNCH:** $3.00
OTHER FEES: Registration $75, application $100, activity fee $150, deposit (one time) $300
DRESS CODE: Uniform
SUMMER PROGRAMS: Summer Camp, Winter Camp, Spring Break Camp

THE CHILDREN'S GUILD   410-444-3800   FAX 410-444-5764
6802 McClean Boulevard, Baltimore, MD 21234
Founded 1953
HEAD: Dr. Andrew L. Ross
DIRECTOR OF ADMISSIONS: LaMar Williams
WEBSITE: www.childrensguild.org   **E-MAIL:** williaml@childrensguild.org
GRADES: 1–8   **ENROLLMENT:** 128 Co-ed (116 boys/12 girls)
FACULTY: 92 full- and 5 part-time   **AVERAGE CLASS SIZE:** 9–10
MISSION STATEMENT: Our mission is to teach children the values and life skills necessary for a successful life, one filled with caring, contribution and commitment. We seek to empower each student with the vision to see opportunity with diversity and the value of setting goals; the courage to try and the value of accepting obstacles as challenges to meet; and the will to succeed and the value of making the commitment to persevere.

SPECIAL COURSES: ED/LD

CLUBS: Girls club

PLANT: Brand new libraries, outdoor math and science adventure classroom designed by the Longwood Gardens landscape architect. The Children's Guild has three schools- one in Baltimore city, one in Anne Arundel County located at Annapolis Middle School and one in Prince George's County located in Chillum, Maryland.

ADMISSION: Receive referral materials usually from a school system. Materials are reviewed by admissions department/director of education and school psychiatrist to determine appropriateness. Interviews are then scheduled. Applications accepted year-round.

TUITION: Tuition is paid by the school system.

BOOKS: Included   **LUNCH:** Included

TRANSPORTATION: Transportation available at no cost

SUMMER PROGRAMS: Yes

FUTURE PLANS: Add/develop high school program at the Chillum campus

THE CHILDREN'S LEARNING CENTER   301-871-6600   FAX 301-871-6015

4511 Bestor Drive, Rockville, MD 20853

Jewish 1978

HEAD: Renee Popkin

DIRECTOR OF ADMISSIONS: Dorothy Harris

WEBSITE: www.clcmd.org   **E-MAIL:** info@clcmd.org

GRADES: Nursery–grade 4   **ENROLLMENT:** 300 Co-ed

FACULTY: 40 full- and 30 part-time   **AVERAGE CLASS SIZE:** 12

MISSION STATEMENT: The Children's Learning Center, Inc. (CLC), an inclusive educational community, is dedicated to stimulating the imagination, instilling confidence and promoting each child's self-esteem through warm and nurturing Jewish Education.

SPECIAL COURSES: CTY accessible. Hebrew/Judaic Studies instruction

EXTENDED DAY: 7:00 a.m.–6:00 p.m.

ATHLETICS: Karate, soccer

CLUBS: Art, chess, cooking, dance, drama, gardening

PLANT: Expansive 50,000-square foot facility with 1,000-square feet classroom space. Large diversely-stocked media center, computers in every elementary school classroom, multiple acres of playground equipment with ball fields and basketball courts

ADMISSION: E-mail info@clcmd.org for electronic applications. Contact CLC office for paper applications and for generalized information on programs and availability. Open door policy: feel free to stop by CLC at any time for a tour.

TUITION: $2,500–$12,000

FINANCIAL AID: Applications for financial aid must be submitted to the Financial Committee of the Board of Directors, in writing.

BOOKS: $140   **LUNCH:** $3.25/meal

OTHER FEES: Activity fee (variable)

TRANSPORTATION: Available. $100/month

SUMMER PROGRAMS: Camp CLC ages 2–6 with before and after camp care available

FUTURE PLANS: Please see website.

CHILDREN'S MANOR MONTESSORI SCHOOL   410-461-6070
4465 Montgomery Road, Ellicott City, MD 21043
HEAD: Dr. Ghosh
GRADES: 2 years–grade 5   **ENROLLMENT:** Co-ed
EXTENDED DAY: Before and after care
TUITION: Call for information.

CHRIST EPISCOPAL SCHOOL   301-424-6550   FAX 301-424-0494
109 South Washington Street, Rockville, MD 20850
Episcopal 1966
HEAD: Jane M. Pontius
DIRECTOR OF ADMISSIONS: Carol Lechner
WEBSITE: www.ces-rockville.org   **E-MAIL:** clechner@cesstaff.org
GRADES: Preschool–grade 8   **ENROLLMENT:** 205 Co-ed (90 boys/115 girls)
FACULTY: 18 full- and 22 part-time   **AVERAGE CLASS SIZE:** 18
MISSION STATEMENT: Christ Episcopal School prepares talented girls and boys for the rigors of secondary education. Our students are members of a Christian community of learners, one which teaches them to use their minds well. A CES education instills a work ethic, a commitment to service, and an appreciation for the differences in others. We build confidence, integrity, and create an enduring sense of belonging.
SPECIAL COURSES: Spanish K–8, daily P.E., computer skills, art, music, drama, algebra, Great Books program K–4, Shakespeare, daily chapel program, library skills, and community service. Learning resource teachers on staff.
EXTENDED DAY: 7:30–6:00 p.m.
CLUBS: Enrichment classes in art, cooking, science, sports and chess
PLANT: Main building with a church, computer lab, library; preschool in a cozy house on campus, and playgrounds
ADMISSION: Christ Episcopal School seeks religious, racial, ethnic, cultural and economic diversity. Application, parent interview, tour, testing, class visit, teacher recommendations and transcripts. Application and testing fees.
TUITION: $8,830 K–8
FINANCIAL AID: Yes
BOOKS: Extra fee   **LUNCH:** Bring
OTHER FEES: Preschool tuition up to $5,260, depending on the numbers of days attending. Extended day fees additional
DRESS CODE: Uniform required K–8

CHRISTCHURCH SCHOOL   800-296-2306   FAX 804-758-0721
Rt. 33 Christchurch School, Christchurch, VA 23031
Episcopal 1921
HEAD: John E. Byers
DIRECTOR OF ADMISSIONS: Nancy M. Nolan
WEBSITE: www.christchurchschool.org
E-MAIL: admission@christchurchschool.org
GRADES: 8–Postgraduate   **ENROLLMENT:** 235 Co-ed (190 boys/45 girls)
FACULTY: 35 full-time   **AVERAGE CLASS SIZE:** 12
MISSION STATEMENT: (Excerpted) Christchurch School, as one of the Church Schools in the Episcopal Diocese of Virginia, believes that each student has infinite

value. Christchurch provides a caring, structured environment so that students can develop a sense of confidence, purpose, and identity by which they can be guided. Christchurch offers a sound college preparatory education which recognizes that, although all students are endowed with gifts, some students also have special strengths and weaknesses that the School seeks to address.

SPECIAL COURSES: School is co-ed for day school only. Boarding for boys begins in grade 8. Limited 5 day boarding available for families within a 40 mile radius of school. AP: English literature, Latin, French, Spanish; trigonometry, calculus (AB), computer science A, biology, chemistry, environmental science, United States history, comparative government and politics, United States government and politics. Science: Introduction to physical science, biology, chemistry, physics, marine science I and II. History: World, U.S., U.S. government, 20th century, world geography, Comparative Ideologies, economics, Old and New Testament, art, music theory and harmony, drama, marine science. ESL. Learning Skills Program (LSP) for students diagnosed with learning difficulties. Serving 20% of the student body with diagnosed LD.

ATHLETICS: Required. Football, basketball, baseball, lacrosse, tennis, golf, sailing, crew, cross-country, soccer, girls' field hockey, indoor track, wrestling

CLUBS: Student Government, FOCUS, Student Vestry, Student Ambassadors, social activities, drama, chorus, Honor Society

PUBLICATIONS: Newsletter ("Currents"), yearbook

COMMUNITY INVOLVEMENT: Participation with local civic clubs and organizations, recycling efforts, river clean-up projects, Habitat for Humanity, peer tutoring, food bank donations

PLANT: 2-story library 10,800 volumes, 3 science labs, 2 gyms, art studio, 5 playing fields, outdoor swimming pool, 6 tennis courts with lighting. Campus is located on 124 acres; Rappahannock Riverfront campus in Chesapeake Bay area of Tidewater Virginia. All students and faculty have e-mail and internet access, campus-wide computer network online. Fine arts center with studios and stage, field house with 3 basketball and volleyball courts.

ADMISSION: Common Application accepted. Interviews conducted Monday through Friday. Timeline: first round acceptance notifications March 10, then on space-available basis.

TUITION: $29,100 boarding; $26,100 5-day boarding; $12,200 day Includes lunch.

FINANCIAL AID: Available. Based on demonstrated need

TRANSPORTATION: Available

DRESS CODE: No jeans, t-shirts or tennis shoes in classroom

SUMMER PROGRAMS: Enrichment courses in marine science I and II, math skills, writing skills, study skills. Crew, sailing

CHRISTIAN ASSEMBLY ACADEMY   703-698-7458   FAX 703-698-9860

8200 Bell Lane, Vienna, VA 22182-5299

Founded 1984

HEAD: Daniel Johannes

WEBSITE: www.christianassembly.net   **E-MAIL:** caa@christianassembly.net

GRADES: Kindergarten–grade 8   **ENROLLMENT:** 88 Co-ed

FACULTY: 10 full- and 4 part-time   **AVERAGE CLASS SIZE:** 11

SPECIAL COURSES: Algebra, earth science, music, art, health

ATHLETICS: P.E., basketball, soccer, softball (5–8)

PLANT: 7 classrooms, art/health room, cafeteria, library, soccer field, blacktop basketball court
ADMISSION: Application and interview
TUITION: Call for information.

CHRISTIAN CENTER SCHOOL   703-971-0558   FAX 703-971-4264
5411 Franconia Road, Alexandria, VA 22310
Independent Reformed 1976
HEAD: Kathy J. Sens
GRADES: K3–grade 6   **ENROLLMENT:** 220 Co-ed
FACULTY: 30 full- and 10 part-time   **AVERAGE CLASS SIZE:** 20
SPECIAL COURSES: Computer, Spanish, music, P.E.
EXTENDED DAY: 6:30 a.m.–6:00 p.m.
TUITION: Call for information.
TRANSPORTATION: Available depending on distance

CHRISTIAN FAMILY MONTESSORI SCHOOL
301-927-7122   FAX 301-927-2980
3628 Rhode Island Avenue, Mt. Rainier, MD 20712
Christian 1981
HEAD: Robert N. Soley
DIRECTOR OF ADMISSIONS: Judy Walsh-Mellett
WEBSITE: www.cfmschool.org
GRADES: Ungraded ages 2 1/2–12   **ENROLLMENT:** 78 Co-ed
FACULTY: 4 full- and 5 part-time   **AVERAGE CLASS SIZE:** 26
MISSION STATEMENT: CFMS is a diverse community of parents, children and staff working together to provide an affordable Montessori school where children will be prepared to meet the academic, social and moral challenges ahead of them, and grow in a loving relationship to God through the catechesis of the Good Shepherd.
SPECIAL COURSES: Spanish, music, art, creative movement, tumbling for elementary
EXTENDED DAY: Until 6:00 p.m.
PUBLICATIONS: School newspaper
PLANT: Rent space in St. James Catholic Church
ADMISSION: Call for information followed by a tour of the school, application and interview
TUITION: $4,190 elementary; $3,860 5 year old full day; $3,090 3 and 4 year old half day
FINANCIAL AID: Available   **OTHER FEES:** $150 materials
FUTURE PLANS: Expanding to 6th grade by fall 2004

CHRISTIAN FELLOWSHIP SCHOOL   703-729-5968   FAX 703-729-6635
21673 Beaumeade Circle, Ashburn, VA 20147
Non-denominational 1980
HEAD: Renee Phillips
WEBSITE: www.cfellowships.org
GRADES: Preschool–grade 10   **ENROLLMENT:** 400 Co-ed
FACULTY: 34 full- and 12 part-time

MISSION STATEMENT: The mission of Christian Fellowship School is to have a positive influence on our world by developing students whose actions authentically reveal the character of Christ– by partnering with Christian families– to spiritually, academically, physically, and socially educate their students in a program of intentional excellence.

SPECIAL COURSES: Computer lab, Spanish program (preschool–high school), art, ceramics, music, P.E.; ACSI competitions. Bible. Preschool (fully ACSI accredited)

EXTENDED DAY: 6:00 a.m.–6:00 p.m.

ATHLETICS: Middle and high school interscholastic athletics

PLANT: Baseball, soccer fields, playground, large gym

ADMISSION: Tour, apply, pastor's recommendation, parent testimony, birth certificate, transcripts, testing, family interview.

TUITION: Call for information.

BOOKS: $325   **LUNCH:** Optional 3 days/week $3 a meal

OTHER FEES: Application fee $100, registration fee $150

DRESS CODE: Uniform

SUMMER PROGRAMS: Summer camp option

FUTURE PLANS: Continue through 12th grade

CHURCH OF THE REDEEMER CHRISTIAN ACADEMY   301-330-3389

19425 Woodfield Road, Gaithersburg, MD 20879

WEBSITE: www.church-redeemer.org

GRADES: Nursery 3–grade 7   **ENROLLMENT:** Co-ed

ADMISSION: Registration opens to the community March 1 for following school year.

TUITION: Call for information.

DRESS CODE: Uniforms elementary and middle school

FUTURE PLANS: Will add grade 8

CITY LIGHTS SCHOOL   202-832-4366   FAX 202-832-3654

62 T Street, N.E., Washington, DC 20002

Founded 1982

HEAD: Kathleen Curtin

DIRECTOR OF ADMISSIONS: Leslie Carter

WEBSITE: www.citylightsschool.org

GRADES: 8–12   **ENROLLMENT:** 45 Co-ed (34 boys/11 girls)

FACULTY: 15 full-time   **AVERAGE CLASS SIZE:** 12

MISSION STATEMENT: City Lights School (CLS) helps the District of Columbia's emotionally disturbed and/or mildly mentally retarded (MMR) youth learn to lead healthy, independent lives. Students age 12 to 22 are acquiring the academic, vocational and social skills needed to realize their greatest level of self-sufficiency in our supportive, therapeutic environment.

SPECIAL COURSES: City Lights School operates the following programs: 1) High school and IEP (Individual Educational Plan) diploma academic courses for 45–60 youth in conjunction with D.C. Public Schools; 2) Individual, group therapy and parent outreach with licensed clinical social workers, on-site; 3) job training and employment development program for at-risk youth; 4) after school program for 25–45 full-time and mainstream community students, offering mentor-

ing and arts enrichment; and 5) summer camp for area youth, featuring a rotating schedule of academic enrichment, field trips, computer technology and reading labs (nearly 1,000 youth, ages 5 to 16, were successfully served in 2002).
EXTENDED DAY: 3:00–6:00 p.m.
CLUBS: September through May, the City Lights After School Program (CLASP) meets five days a week, from 3:00 p.m. until 6:00 p.m. at City Lights School. The program offers a daily rotation of vocational, entrepreneurial, recreational, artistic, and academic activities to keep youngsters in a safe, trouble-free environment where tutorial and non-direct learning can take place. Our selected services supplement day program objectives but do not duplicate them in content or form, as studies show as most beneficial.
ADMISSION: Ongoing admissions. All students must be approved by DCPS, Office of Special Education for placement.
TUITION: Call for information.
LUNCH: Lunch and breakfast free   **TRANSPORTATION:** Provided by DCPS
DRESS CODE: DCPS standards
SUMMER PROGRAMS: Extended School Year (ESY) for Special Education population and Summer Camp–community wide recreation program.

CLARA MUHAMMAD SCHOOL   202-610-1090   FAX 202-610-1092
2313 Martin Luther King, Jr. Avenue, S.E, Washington, DC 20020
Islamic 1978
HEAD: Samuel A. Shareef
E-MAIL: cmschooldc@aol.com
GRADES: Pre-K–grade 8   **ENROLLMENT:** 53 Co-ed
FACULTY: 8 full- 3 part-time   **AVERAGE CLASS SIZE:** 9
MISSION STATEMENT: The mission of Clara Muhammad School (CMS) is to provide an Islamic education, foundation, and structure for students with which they can grow as morally conscientious, intelligent, upright human beings who are prepared to lead, contribute and compete on a global level, guided by ALLAH (G'D), through HIS creation, the Holy Qur'an, and the Life Example of Prophet Muhammad (Peace and Blessings be Upon Him).
SPECIAL COURSES: Qur'an centered curriculum, Arabic language, discipline and moral conduct integrated into the program.
EXTENDED DAY: 7:00 a.m.–6:00 p.m.   **PUBLICATIONS:** Quarterly newsletter
COMMUNITY INVOLVEMENT: CMS and Urban Oasis Community Garden Project.
ADMISSION: Application fee $25, interview
TUITION: $4,500   Reduction for siblings
BOOKS: $50
OTHER FEES: Activity fee $50; PTA $40; Tuition Management $50; Registration fee $25
SUMMER PROGRAMS: Islamic Summer Camp.

CLINTON CHRISTIAN SCHOOL   301-599-9600   FAX 301-599-9603
6707 Woodyard Road, Upper Marlboro, MD 20772
Baptist 1966
HEAD: Lisa S. Duey
WEBSITE: www.clintonchristian.org

GRADES: K4–grade 12   **ENROLLMENT:** 650 Co-ed
FACULTY: 50   **AVERAGE CLASS SIZE:** 25
SPECIAL COURSES: Foreign language, computer instruction grade 10–12, Religious studies required, Bible, piano, chorus, drama, college prep, resource/help classes.
EXTENDED DAY: 6:30 a.m.–6:30 p.m.
ATHLETICS: Required 1–12. Volleyball, basketball, soccer
PUBLICATIONS: Yearbook
COMMUNITY INVOLVEMENT: MS Read-a-thon, Thanksgiving basket project, community service
PLANT: Auditorium, playing fields, gym
ADMISSION: Registration and fee, conference, testing
TUITION: $5,000
TRANSPORTATION: Available depending on zone
DRESS CODE: Specific regulations
SUMMER PROGRAMS: Summer school and summer camp available

COLONIAL ACADEMY   540-659-1810   FAX 540-720-7187
2726 Jefferson Davis Highway, Stafford, VA 22554
HEAD: Mickey Creed
WEBSITE: www.cbcca.com
GRADES: K4–grade 7   **ENROLLMENT:** 80 Co-ed
TUITION: Call for information.

COLUMBIA ACADEMY   410-312-7413   FAX 410-312-7416
10350 Old Columbia Road, Columbia, MD 21046
Founded 1991
HEAD: Colleen Bakhsh
WEBSITE: www.columbiaacademy.com
GRADES: Kindergarten–grade 8   **ENROLLMENT:** 250 Co-ed
AVERAGE CLASS SIZE: 16
SPECIAL COURSES: Spanish, music, computers. Enrichment and remedial program. Comprehensive curriculum, resource program. Individualized instruction.
EXTENDED DAY: 6:30 a.m.–6:30 p.m.
ATHLETICS: P.E.   **CLUBS:** Scouts, Science Encounters
PLANT: Library, computer lab, music room, playground, science lab. Preschools located on separate campuses on Route 108, Deepage Dr. and Old Columbia Road in Columbia. New location: 6000 University Blvd., Ellicott City, MD.
ADMISSION: Parent tour, child visits, interview
TUITION: $7,500–$8,300
DRESS CODE: Uniform required
SUMMER PROGRAMS: Camp: swimming and field trips

COMMONWEALTH ACADEMY   703-548-6912   FAX 703-548-6914
1321 Leslie Avenue, Alexandria, VA 22301
Founded 1997
HEAD: Susan J. Johnson, Ph.D.
WEBSITE: www.commonwealthacademy.org
E-MAIL: Susan_Johnson@commonwealthacademy.org

GRADES: 6–12   **ENROLLMENT:** 55 Co-ed
FACULTY: 10 full- and 4 part-time   **AVERAGE CLASS SIZE:** 7–10
MISSION STATEMENT: Commonwealth Academy is a high school and college preparatory program for average to superior students in grades 6 through 12 who have organizational, attention, or learning differences, along with those who benefit from small classes and individualized instruction. Personal responsibility for learning, behavior, use of technology, and compensatory strategies are embedded in the curriculum, as well as directly taught, to help students reach their highest achievement levels reflective of their true potential.
SPECIAL COURSES: The middle and high school programs emphasize college preparatory classes. Math includes algebra, geometry, pre-calculus, and calculus. Science: physical science, biology, chemistry, physics, astronomy/oceanography, geology. English: British literature, American literature, Literary Genres, Universal Themes. Writing is taught as a separate subject through 11th grade. Spanish is offered in high school as well as U.S. history, world history, government, geography, electives. SAT/ACT practice and preparation course is required for upper high school. Art, music and drama are fine arts electives. Computer graphics, photography, and web design are also offered as electives. Study skills incorporated into curriculum. Homework monitoring and assistance incorporated for all. Flexible pace and schedule designed to meet individual needs. Full-time counselor on staff. Outdoor team building and field trips held monthly.
EXTENDED DAY: 7:00 a.m.–4:00 p.m.
ATHLETICS: Participation in small school sports league
CLUBS: Chess club   **PUBLICATIONS:** Yearbook
PLANT: Newly renovated, 15,000-square foot facility in a primarily residential area. Spacious classrooms, multiple computer labs, science lab, project room, art and drama rooms
ADMISSION: Application including transcript, recommendations, interview. Rolling admission
TUITION: $21,800
FINANCIAL AID: Available. Minimal
BOOKS: Approx $500   **OTHER FEES:** P.E. fee, graduation fee

CONCORD HILL SCHOOL   301-654-2626   FAX 301-654-1374
6050 Wisconsin Avenue, Chevy Chase, MD 20815
Founded 1965
HEAD: Denise Gershowitz
DIRECTOR OF ADMISSIONS: Debra Duff
WEBSITE: www.concordhill.org   **E-MAIL:** dgershowitz@concordhill.org
GRADES: Nursery–grade 3   **ENROLLMENT:** 100 Co-ed
FACULTY: 12 full- and 6 part-time   **AVERAGE CLASS SIZE:** 18
MISSION STATEMENT: Concord Hill School, a coeducational school for children in preschool through third grade, emphasizes both the academic and the developmental growth of the young child. We strongly believe in educating the whole child by promoting intellectual, social, emotional, physical and character development. During these important and formative years, Concord Hill demonstrates to its students that acquiring knowledge can be both challenging and fun. We celebrate each child's unique strengths and seek to build self-confidence through achievement. By maintaining small student-to-teacher ratios, we are able

to respond to each student's ideas, needs and learning styles. Concord Hill instills in its students a strong sense of caring and respect for others. Children experience the responsibilities and benefits of being positive, contributing members of their community and our diverse world.

SPECIAL COURSES: P.E., art, music, computer (all levels), science. Note: small classes allow much individual attention- a ratio of 1:4 teacher/pupil.

EXTENDED DAY: 8:00–8:25 a.m.

CLUBS: Kindergarten Clubs on Monday and Wednesday afternoon (Tuesday and Thursday are full day programs). Early bird 8:00–8:25 a.m.

PLANT: Library, computer at all levels, science lab, playground. Spacious class-rooms with indoor play/assembly facilities

ADMISSION: $55 application fee, transcripts, teacher recommendation. Parent interview then child visits. Interviews begin October 1st. Application deadline January 31

TUITION: $9,400 pre-primary and primary; $12,300 K; $13,970 1–3

FINANCIAL AID: Available

LUNCH: Brown bag. Milk provided

SUMMER PROGRAMS: Summer camp for 3–5 year olds

CONCORDIA LUTHERAN SCHOOL   301-927-0266   FAX 301-699-0071

3799 East-West Highway, Hyattsville, MD 20782

Lutheran 1946

HEAD: Dr. David Falkner

GRADES: Preschool–grade 8   **ENROLLMENT:** 250 Co-ed (125 boys/125 girls)

FACULTY: 12 full- 5 part-time   **AVERAGE CLASS SIZE:** 27

SPECIAL COURSES: Algebra, computer, general science, world and U.S. histo-ry, world and U.S. geography, religious studies. Language arts and math grouped according to performance. Music, chorus, band.

EXTENDED DAY: 7:00 a.m–6:00 p.m.

ATHLETICS: P.E. required grades 1–8. Interscholastic basketball

PUBLICATIONS: Yearbook

COMMUNITY INVOLVEMENT: Students participate in various charity drives, Hyattsville Clean-Up, canned good for "Help by Phone", "Jump for Heart", and annual mission projects

PLANT: Library, science labs, computer lab, gym, playing fields. Second campus located at 3705 Longfellow Street, Hyattsville, MD 20782 houses 4th–8th grades.

ADMISSION: Application, report card, birth certificate, fee $240, testing, interview

TUITION: $4,600

FINANCIAL AID: Available

TRANSPORTATION: Available. $850 round trip/ $500 one way

DRESS CODE: Yes (grades 4–8 only)

SUMMER PROGRAMS: Available for Preschool–3rd grade

THE CONGRESSIONAL SCHOOLS OF VIRGINIA

703-533-9711   FAX 703-532-5467

3229 Sleepy Hollow Road, Falls Church, VA 22042

Founded 1939

HEAD: Shirley K. Fegan

DIRECTOR OF ADMISSIONS: Karen H. Weinberger
WEBSITE: www.congressionalschools.org
E-MAIL: admissions@csov.org or info@csov.org
GRADES: Infants (6 weeks)–grade 8
ENROLLMENT: 389 Co-ed (194 boys/195 girls)
FACULTY: 51 full- and 4 part-time   **AVERAGE CLASS SIZE:** 18 maximum
MISSION STATEMENT: (Excerpted) The mission of the Congressional Schools of Virginia is to develop and encourage the personal and intellectual growth of each child entrusted to its care. To that end, we seek to: Provide a safe and stimulating environment in which children can develop academically, physically, creatively, socially, and emotionally; Foster a climate which emphasizes traditional values of citizenship, service, personal responsibility, self-discipline, and respect and compassion for others; Challenge students with an accelerated, interactive, and age-appropriate curriculum.
SPECIAL COURSES: French K–8; Spanish 5–8; accelerated curriculum, integrated technology Full time registered nurse and full-time guidance counselor on staff.
EXTENDED DAY: 7:00–8:00 a.m. and 3:10–6:00 p.m.
ATHLETICS: Extensive after-school athletic program. Intra- and intermural sports
CLUBS: Parent Organization, Boosters Club, choir, band
PUBLICATIONS: Literary magazine, yearbook, weekly school newspaper
COMMUNITY INVOLVEMENT: 6–8 graders involved in tutoring program at ESL Tutoring Center in community, 8th graders prepare and serve lunch once a month at a homeless shelter, various other community projects for all grades
PLANT: 2 science labs, 2 Technology Centers, 2 libraries, art studio, music studio, gymnasium/auditorium, 2 swimming pools, 4 age-appropriate playgrounds, extensive athletic fields, amphitheater, ropes course, climbing wall. 40-acre campus.
ADMISSION: Application, transcripts, teacher recommendations, testing, student visit
TUITION: $11,815–$14,960 Bright Beginnings $260 per week year-round.
BOOKS: $250–$650   **LUNCH:** $620–$800
OTHER FEES: $25–$400   **TRANSPORTATION:** Available $2,830–$3,990
DRESS CODE: Uniform required grades 1–8
SUMMER PROGRAMS: Great Adventures for Children (ages 3–5), Summer Camp (ages 6–14), also   specialty camps including: cheerleading, computers, culinary, studio art, scrapbook, circus, puppeteering, robotics, golf, basketball, soccer

CONNELLY SCHOOL OF THE HOLY CHILD   301-365-0955   FAX 301-365-0981
9029 Bradley Boulevard, Potomac, MD 20854
Catholic 1961
HEAD: Maureen K. Appel
DIRECTOR OF ADMISSIONS: Sheri M. Mural
WEBSITE: www.holychild.org   **E-MAIL:** admissions@holychild.org
GRADES: 6–12   **ENROLLMENT:** 450 girls
AVERAGE CLASS SIZE: 16
MISSION STATEMENT: Schools of the Holy Child Jesus share in the mission of the Society of the Holy Child Jesus which is "to help others to believe that God

lives and acts in them and in our world, and to rejoice in the divine presence." The Schools, committed by heritage to the educational mission of the Catholic Church through the philosophy and spirituality of Cornelia Connelly, endeavor to develop mature persons capable of making choices which enrich their own lives and contribute to the lives of others.

SPECIAL COURSES: Members of the faculty and administration at Holy Child are committed to enabling each student to realize her greatest academic and personal potential. The following AP courses are offered: English language, English literature, French, Spanish, calculus, statistics, biology, chemistry, and United States history. Honors courses are available. Year-long seminar classes are offered in conjunction with area schools.

ATHLETICS: Upper school athletic teams: baseball, cross-country, dance, diving, equestrian, field hockey, lacrosse, soccer, softball, swimming, tennis, track and volleyball. Middle school athletic teams: basketball, cross-country, field hockey, lacrosse, soccer, softball, swimming, track and volleyball

CLUBS: Art Club, Best Buddies, Black Student Union, Cancer Awareness Club, Drama Club, Educated Teen Consumers, International Club, Latinas con Fuerza, MOAS, National Honor Society, Step Club, Teenage Democrats, Teenage Republicans, Trial Lawyers.

PUBLICATIONS: School newspaper and yearbook

ADMISSION: $50 application fee; 9th grade applicants take the Archdiocese Entrance Test and middle school applicants take the SSAT. Letters of recommendation; transcript; essay and interview. Applications are due in mid-December for 9th grade applicants, early February for middle school applicants, and are considered on a rolling basis for upper school transfer applicants.

TUITION: $14,450 middle school; $15,450 upper school

FINANCIAL AID: Financial aid is distributed upon demonstrated need.

BOOKS: $400 upper school

OTHER FEES: Technology fee $200, graduation fee $250, middle school books and materials fee $250

DRESS CODE: Uniform required

CORNERSTONE CHRISTIAN ACADEMY   301-262-7683   FAX 301-262-5200
16010 Annapolis Road, Bowie, MD 20715
HEAD: Millie Lauffer
GRADES: Pre-K 4–grade 8   **ENROLLMENT:** 165 Co-ed
FACULTY: 17 full-time   **AVERAGE CLASS SIZE:** 14
SPECIAL COURSES: A Beka, Bob Jones 7 and 8; small classes, individual attention
EXTENDED DAY: 3:00–6:00 p.m.
TUITION: $3,890

CORNERSTONE COMMUNITY SCHOOL   202-543-2881   FAX 202-543-7884
907 Maryland Avenue, N.E., Washington, DC 20002
Founded 1998
HEAD: Heather Smith
WEBSITE: www.cornerstone-schools.org   **E-MAIL:** contact@cornerstone-schools.org
GRADES: Kindergarten–grade 6   **ENROLLMENT:** 70 Co-ed
TUITION: Sliding scale based on family income produces affordable tuition. Call for information.

CORPUS CHRISTI SCHOOL 703-820-7450 FAX 703-820-9635

3301 Glen Carlyn Road, Falls Church, VA 22041
Catholic 1990
HEAD: George E. Chiplock, Jr.
DIRECTOR OF ADMISSIONS: Marie Merle
WEBSITE: www.corpuschristischool.org **E-MAIL:** info@copuschristischool.org
GRADES: Preschool age 3–grade 8
ENROLLMENT: 650 Co-ed
FACULTY: 30 full- and 5 part-time
AVERAGE CLASS SIZE: 24
MISSION STATEMENT: (Excerpted) Corpus Christi School provides a quality Catholic education at an affordable price. It is committed to providing the best scholastic programs, geared to meet individual needs, in an environment which fosters Christian values and stimulates students to reach their fullest potential spiritually, intellectually, socially and physically. By uniquely integrating sound Catholic principles of faith and action into a strong academic curriculum, we prepare students to become responsible, dedicated adults, competent to meet the challenging demands of a complex society.
SPECIAL COURSES: Languages: French and Spanish (7th and 8th). For students in grades 1–6, after school foreign language classes are available for a fee. Algebra and pre-algebra offered. Science classes grades 6–8 have regular labs; grades 3–5 participate in quarterly science labs. Science: general, biology, chemistry, physics, and environmental. Mandatory science fair grades 6–8. Weekly music teacher for preschool students. Weekly music and P.E. classes K–8. Weekly art, library and computer classes 1–8. Special services are offered for students with academic needs. Resource teacher available. First graders are paired with sixth graders as reading buddies. Eighth graders volunteer as tutors for students in grades 1–3.
EXTENDED DAY: 7:00 a.m.–6:00 p.m. for both campuses
ATHLETICS: Catholic Youth Organization (CYO): basketball, track and tennis
CLUBS: Young Astronauts, Jason Project, Student Council, 8th Grade Tutors, band, choir, Christmas Pageant and Spring Play
PUBLICATIONS: Yearbook, student newspaper and quarterly school newsletter
COMMUNITY INVOLVEMENT: Food drives and baskets for various organizations, Toys for Tots, cards for senior citizens on holidays, Pennies for Patients, Jump Rope for Heart, St. Jude Math-a-Thon, and 8th graders complete a designated number of hours of community service as part of 8th grade religion curriculum.
PLANT: Two campuses- Pre-3–K and grades 1–8. Both campuses have been renovated over the past two years with new windows and air conditioning. The Early Childhood Center classrooms have new carpeted and tiled areas for art projects. The elementary campus has a new multipurpose hall/gym for school assemblies, P.E. and sporting events. It includes a stage and sound system. Classrooms are networked with internet/e-mail access, a computer lab with the most current hardware and software. Upgraded science lab with sinks/running water at each lab station. School library with an automated catalog system. Both campuses have safe and secure playground areas. Art room with a kiln for art classes.
ADMISSION: School visit/tour. Submit application packet including school records to the Main Office. After acceptance, $125 registration and computer fee for K–8 and $80 registration fee for preschool. Principal will review information

and meet with the family.

TUITION: $3,212 for one child in parish

FINANCIAL AID: Available for qualified parishioners and Catholic families.

BOOKS: Included   **LUNCH:** Not included

OTHER FEES: There are in-parish, out-of-parish, and non-Catholic rates. Visit website for all rates. Students bring lunch.

TRANSPORTATION: The bus transportation is limited within parish boundaries. There is also a campus-to-campus shuttle available.

DRESS CODE: Uniform for grades 1–8

SUMMER PROGRAMS: Summer Camp for Pre–3 through rising 1st grade at the Early Childhood Center

THE COUNTRY DAY SCHOOL   304-725-1438   FAX 304-728-8394

P.O. Box 659 Route 51, West Charles Town, WV 25414

Founded 1982

HEAD: Irene Bauer

DIRECTOR OF ADMISSIONS: Keith Biser

WEBSITE: www.thecountrydayschool.com

E-MAIL: cds.com@citynet.net

GRADES: Junior Kindergarten– 9

ENROLLMENT: 140 Co-ed (70 boys/70 girls)

AVERAGE CLASS SIZE: 18

MISSION STATEMENT: (Excerpted) The Country Day School was established in 1982 to provide a thorough, well-rounded education for students in grades Junior Kindergarten through ninth in a closely-knit, nurturing environment. Academics, individual attention, development of strong character and traditional values are emphasized. Thus, each student is presented with the opportunity to rise to his or her own level of excellence.

SPECIAL COURSES: Curriculum is enriched with French starting in Kindergarten, "Classics", current events and Latin. Computer is also offered to all students.

EXTENDED DAY: 7:00– 8:15 a.m. and 3:30–6:00 p.m.

ATHLETICS: Co-ed soccer team, track, softball

CLUBS: Student Senate

PUBLICATIONS: School newspaper

PLANT: 30-acre campus, 2 professional soccer fields, cross-country course, playground, outdoor basketball court, picnic/lunch area

ADMISSION: Family visit and interview with Director of Admissions, academic assessment, application and reservations fee with enrollment contract on file

TUITION: $4,800–$6,300

FINANCIAL AID: Available

BOOKS: $300

LUNCH: Available

OTHER FEES: Bus, lunch, corporate dues, "Pay or Play" program

TRANSPORTATION: Available $775–$970

DRESS CODE: Yes- modified

SUMMER PROGRAMS: Summer program open to the public

FUTURE PLANS: Finish multipurpose building (gymnasium) 2004. Add additional grade section each year. Adding additional 2nd grade 2003/2004

COVENANT LIFE SCHOOL   301-590-3982   FAX 301-948-4920
7503 Muncaster Mill Road, Gaithersburg, MD 20877
Non-denominational 1979
HEAD: Greg Somerville
WEBSITE: www.covlife.org
GRADES: Kindergarten–grade 12   ENROLLMENT: 314 Co-ed
AVERAGE CLASS SIZE: 25
TUITION: Call for information.
DRESS CODE: Uniforms

—D

DEMATHA CATHOLIC HIGH SCHOOL   301-864-3666   FAX 301-864-0248
4313 Madison Street, Hyattsville, MD 20781
Catholic
HEAD: Daniel J. McMahon; Rev. William Sullivan, Rector
WEBSITE: www.dematha.org   E-MAIL: admissions@dematha.org
GRADES: 9–12   ENROLLMENT: 950 boys
FACULTY: 65 full- and 5 part-time   AVERAGE CLASS SIZE: 22
SPECIAL COURSES: German, Latin, French, Spanish. Math through calculus BC, computer survey, biology, chemistry, geology, anatomy and physiology, astronomy, business law, accounting, journalism, art history, extensive music program. Religious studies required. AP: English, French, Spanish, German, government, history, biology, chemistry, physics, calculus, Pascal. Regular and Honors courses also offered in these areas. Strong counseling program. Some students attend university classes.
ATHLETICS: Not required. Intramural and interscholastic. Football, basketball, baseball, cross-country, track, ice hockey, softball, soccer, swimming, wrestling, lacrosse, tennis, golf
CLUBS: National Honor Society, science, Black Student Union, among others
PUBLICATIONS: Yearbook, newspaper, literary magazine
COMMUNITY INVOLVEMENT: Social action groups and campus ministry program
PLANT: Library 14,000 volumes, 5 science labs, art studio, gym. Use of public parks for playing fields.
ADMISSION: 9–10: Students in Catholic Elementary schools apply through the schools. Those in public school take high school entrance exam. School records, standard test scores and character references. 11–12: Students must submit transcript, references, high school entrance exam. $225 registration fee upon acceptance.
TUITION: $7,050 Reduced rate for siblings
FINANCIAL AID: Available
BOOKS: $200–$350   LUNCH: Cafeteria
DRESS CODE: Uniform blazer and gray dress or khaki trousers

DIFFERENT DRUM, INC.   703-802-2866   FAX 703-802-2196
4451 Brookfield Corporate Drive Ste. 201, Chantilly, VA 20151
Founded 1973
HEAD: Stephen E. Brown
GRADES: grades 9–12, ages 14–21   ENROLLMENT: 25 Co-ed

LTY: 8 full- and 1 part-time   **AVERAGE CLASS SIZE:** 6
CIAL COURSES: Counseling based program for students with learning, havioral or emotional disabilities. Each student is taught at his/her own level in a therapeutic learning environment. All required courses for Virginia high school diploma. Elective courses. Individualized curriculum for students who have been unsuccessful in public schools. Additional services include individual, group and parent counseling, speech and language therapy.
ATHLETICS: P.E. program in all grades
ADMISSION: Prior to on-site interview with parents and student, complete educational, psychological and medical evaluation reports, social history, transcript, and anecdotal records must be provided.
TUITION: Tuition paid by student's local county or city public school division

THE DISCOVERY SCHOOL   410-721-5525   FAX 410-721-9353
1041 Route 3 North, Gambrills, MD 21054
Founded 1997
HEAD: Amy Weaver
WEBSITE: www.thediscoveryschool.com
E-MAIL: mail@thediscoveryschool.com
GRADES: Pre-K–grade 5   **ENROLLMENT:** Co-ed
AVERAGE CLASS SIZE: 14 maximum
SPECIAL COURSES: Spanish, computer, library, music, P.E., cooking
EXTENDED DAY: 6:30 a.m.–6:30 p.m.
PLANT: Extensive computer lab and library
ADMISSION: Rolling admissions, registration fee $55
TUITION: $6,235–$7,145
OTHER FEES: Materials fee $325–$750
DRESS CODE: Uniforms
SUMMER PROGRAMS: Summer Camp

DIVINE PEACE LUTHERAN SCHOOL   301-350-4522   FAX 301-350-2420
1500 Brown Station Road, Largo, MD 20774
Lutheran 1981
HEAD: Jonathan Roux
GRADES: 1–8   **ENROLLMENT:** 42 Co-ed
FACULTY: 3 full-time   **AVERAGE CLASS SIZE:** 6
TUITION: $4,600
FINANCIAL AID: Some available
DRESS CODE: Uniforms

DOMINION ACADEMY   703-737-0157   FAX 703-771-9512
835 Lee Avenue SW, Leesburg, VA 20175
Baptist 1997
HEAD: Keith Currivean
DIRECTOR OF ADMISSIONS: Darlene Baldwin
WEBSITE: www.dominion academy.com   **E-MAIL:** info@dominionacademy.net
GRADES: Kindergarten–grade 8   **ENROLLMENT:** 290 Co-ed
FACULTY: 26 full- and 2 part-time   **AVERAGE CLASS SIZE:** 16
MISSION STATEMENT: The mission of Dominion Academy is to train and edu-

cate young students in partnership with their parents and church, to become spiritually, academically, socially and physically mature to the glory of God. Emphasis is placed on developing student strengths, fostering respect for others, understanding the individual's importance to the community and world, building confidence and success in problem solving skills and understanding the God who created them.

SPECIAL COURSES: Elementary: The language arts, science, social studies, health and mathematics curriculum for Kindergarten through grade 5 will follow the scope and sequence of the Λ Beka textbook series. The language arts program focuses primarily on the phonics approach to teaching reading. All students receive instruction by a qualified teacher in art, music, Spanish, computer and P.E. Health is taught by the classroom teacher. Bible class is taught Monday through Friday using the ACSI Bible curriculum. Chapel meets one day each week. Middle school: We have adapted and accelerated the state of Virginia's recommended curriculum and SOL's (Standards of Learning).

EXTENDED DAY: 6:45 a.m.–6:00 p.m.

ATHLETICS: Fellowship of Christian Athletes, bowling leagues, tennis (upper/lower sections).

CLUBS: Student Council, safety patrols, Boy Scouts, Girl Scouts, drama club, chess club, Odyssey of the Mind, Praise Band, spelling bee, Math Olympics, science fair

PUBLICATIONS: Yearbook

ADMISSION: Complete application with $100 fee. Admission testing is scheduled for all new applicants. Accepting applications ongoing.

TUITION: $4,978 K–5; $5,926 6–8

FINANCIAL AID: Available

BOOKS: $300 a year

LUNCH: Hot lunch program $3.00

DRESS CODE: Uniforms

SUMMER PROGRAMS: Sports camp

DOMINION CHRISTIAN SCHOOL   703-758-1055
10922 Vale Road, Oakton, VA 22124
HEAD: Jan Pierce
WEBSITE: www.dominionschool.com
E-MAIL: info@dominionschool.com
GRADES: Kindergarten–grade 7   **ENROLLMENT:** 99 Co-ed
SPECIAL COURSES: A Classical Christian School
TUITION: Call for information.
FUTURE PLANS: Add grade 8.

DOMINION SCHOOL   703-321-9091   FAX 703-321-9017
5410 Port Royal Road, Springfield, VA 22151
HEAD: Debbie Pell
WEBSITE: www.thedominionschool.com
GRADES: 7–12
ENROLLMENT: Co-ed
TUITION: Call for information.
SUMMER PROGRAMS: Summer program

DUPONT PARK SCHOOL   202-583-8500   FAX 202-583-0650
3942 Alabama Avenue, S.E., Washington, DC 20020
Seventh-day Adventist 1914
HEAD: Lafese Quinnonez
WEBSITE: www.dupontpark.org/school
GRADES: Pre-K–grade 10   **ENROLLMENT:** 300 Co-ed
FACULTY: 30 full-time   **AVERAGE CLASS SIZE:** 20
SPECIAL COURSES: Biology, general science, America: Its People and Values, history, Bible required K–10. Classroom worship service. Choir, computer, keyboarding, home economics.
EXTENDED DAY: 7:00 a.m.–6:00 p.m.
TUITION: Call for information.
DRESS CODE: Uniform required
SUMMER PROGRAMS: Summer Camp

—E

EARLY YEARS MONTESSORI SCHOOL   703-237-0264   FAX 703-734-6819
3241 Brush Drive, Falls Church, VA 22042
Founded 1990
HEAD: Jayanthi Bogollagama
GRADES: Ungraded ages 2–6 years   **ENROLLMENT:** 60 Co-ed
FACULTY: 6 full- and 1 part-time   **AVERAGE CLASS SIZE:** 20
MISSION STATEMENT: Montessori Method of education
SPECIAL COURSES: Spanish language, gymnastics, painting, music
EXTENDED DAY: 7:00 a.m.–6:00 p.m.
ATHLETICS: Dance/exercise   **CLUBS:** Computer, music
PLANT: Beautiful environment and large classrooms
ADMISSION: Visit school, pay registration fee of $100 and enroll
TUITION: $595–$704 per month, depending on age of child. Part-time programs available
OTHER FEES: $150 activity fee
SUMMER PROGRAMS: July and August

EDLIN SCHOOL   703-438-3990   FAX 703-438-3958
10742 Sunset Hills Road, Reston, VA 20190
Founded 1989
HEAD: Linda Schreibstein K–4/ Elaine Mellman 5–8
DIRECTORS OF ADMISSIONS: Linda Schreibstein and Elaine Mellman
GRADES: K4–grade 8   **ENROLLMENT:** 250 Co-ed
FACULTY: 28 full- and 2 part-time   **AVERAGE CLASS SIZE:** 15
MISSION STATEMENT: Edlin School provides an enriched, challenging curriculum for academically talented and gifted students in an environment that teaches respect, responsibility and kindness.
SPECIAL COURSES: All classes are G & T. There is no limit to academic placement.
EXTENDED DAY: Extended learning: 7:30–8:30 a.m. and 3:45–6:00 p.m.
ATHLETICS: Soccer, lacrosse, wrestling   **CLUBS:** Chess club
PUBLICATIONS: Yearbook, newspaper
PLANT: Edlin School is located on a 5-acre sylvan setting.

ADMISSION: Application, school visit. I.Q. test for 6 and above.
TUITION: $13,000
OTHER FEES: Books- consumables extra. After school activity fee
TRANSPORTATION: Available. Cost varies according to use
DRESS CODE: Yes   **SUMMER PROGRAMS:** Camp Eagle
FUTURE PLANS: We are currently adding a library and a computer lab. We want to remain a small school under 300 students.

EDMUND BURKE SCHOOL   202-362-8882   FAX 202-362-1914
2955 Upton Street, N.W., Washington, DC 20008
Founded 1968
HEAD: David Shapiro
DIRECTOR OF ADMISSIONS: Jean Marchildon
WEBSITE: www.eburke.org   **E-MAIL:** admissions@eburke.org
GRADES: 6–12 grade   **ENROLLMENT:** 290 Co-ed (155 boys/135 girls)
FACULTY: 43 full- and 5 part-time   **AVERAGE CLASS SIZE:** 12
MISSION STATEMENT: Edmund Burke School consciously brings together students who are different from each other in many ways, actively engages them in their own education, has high expectations for them, gives them power and responsibility, and supports and advances their growth as skilled an independent thinkers who step forward to make positive contributions to the world in which they live.
SPECIAL COURSES: In addition to the required college preparatory courses, Burke offers the Senior Seminars, electives which vary from year to year. Course offerings for 2003–04 include 21st Century Economics, World Religions, The Comic Tradition in American Literature, Decisive Battles, The United Kingdom and Leviathan: The Individual and the State in Democratic Society. AP courses are offered in biology, chemistry, physics, calculus, statistics, Latin, French, Spanish, studio art, English and history. General electives include painting, drawing, ceramics, photography, sculpture, theater arts, music, computer graphics, mixed media, creative writing and journalism.
ATHLETICS: Intramural and interscholastic: 24 varsity, junior varsity and middle school teams in 9 sports (member of the Potomac Valley Athletic Conference)
CLUBS: Academic Integrity Club, British Film Club, chess club, French club, Imani, martial arts club, Save the Bengal, Web Writers, Model UN, " It's Academic", Spanish club and others
PUBLICATIONS: Student publications include the Cageliner, the newspaper, the Lit, the literary magazine, and the yearbook
COMMUNITY INVOLVEMENT: Burke has an annual Community Service Day for all students. Each grade also has a service learning program, and each individual student must complete 60 hours of community service as a graduation requirement.
PLANT: Burke is an urban school, located in the northwest quadrant of the District of Columbia near the Van Ness Metro stop. At the center of the school building is an architecturally attractive atrium that is used for assemblies, meetings and performances. The building has classrooms and offices, four science labs, a computer lab, art and ceramic rooms, a darkroom, gym, music and drama room, and a library.
ADMISSION: Request admissions materials by phone at 202-362-8882, by mail

or by e-mail at admissions@eburke.org. Application form, parent letter, student essay (if applicable), application fee, visit, interview, testing (SSAT or ISEE), transcripts and recommendations
TUITION: $20,050
FINANCIAL AID: Available
OTHER FEES: Activity/trip fee: middle school $250, high school $115, senior fee $300
SUMMER PROGRAMS: Summer programs include courses in math and science, study skills, video and creative writing. A course in sailing, trips abroad and a rock and jazz band camp are also offered. Camps are available in volleyball and basketball.

ELIZABETH SETON HIGH SCHOOL   301-864-4532   FAX 301-864-8946
5715 Emerson Street, Bladensburg, MD 20710
Catholic 1959
HEAD: Sharon Pasterick
DIRECTOR OF ADMISSIONS: Leanna Burke
WEBSITE: www.setonhs.org
GRADES: 9–12   **ENROLLMENT:** 530 girls
FACULTY: 50 full-time   **AVERAGE CLASS SIZE:** 20
MISSION STATEMENT: Elizabeth Seton High School strives to provide an outstanding college preparatory program for all young women who seek a community that celebrates diversity and creativity, fosters moral, spiritual, academic and physical growth, and promotes the Gospel values through service to others.
SPECIAL COURSES: In addition to general college preparatory offerings, we offer: AP courses in English, math, social studies, foreign language, and art.
EXTENDED DAY: 7:00 a.m.–5:00 p.m.
ATHLETICS: Sports include basketball, cross-country, softball, track, cheerleading, lacrosse, swimming, crew, soccer, tennis and volleyball
CLUBS: Over 27 clubs available
COMMUNITY INVOLVEMENT: Community service required
ADMISSION: Applications due by December 15th
TUITION: $6,800
FINANCIAL AID: Available
BOOKS: $400
OTHER FEES: Uniforms
DRESS CODE: Uniforms required

EMBASSY SCHOOL   703-476-8667   FAX 703-476-8328
3013 West Ox Road, Herndon, VA 20171
HEAD: Sepi Aghili
E-MAIL: theembassyschool@yahoo.com
GRADES: N (age 3)–grade 2   **ENROLLMENT:** Co-ed
SPECIAL COURSES: Spanish, music, computer science, dance program
EXTENDED DAY: 7:00 a.m.–6:00 p.m.
PLANT: 5 acres of land, playgrounds
TUITION: Call for information.
LUNCH: Available
SUMMER PROGRAMS: Summer Camp

EMERSON PREPARATORY SCHOOL   202-785-2877   FAX 202-785-2228

1324 18th Street, N.W., Washington, DC 20036
Founded as Emerson Institute in 1852
HEAD: Margot Ann Walsh
WEBSITE: www.emersonprep.net   **E-MAIL:** info@emersonprep.net
GRADES: 9–12 and post-graduate
ENROLLMENT: 100 Co-ed (50 boys/50 girls)
FACULTY: 6 full- and 7 part-time   **AVERAGE CLASS SIZE:** 10
MISSION STATEMENT: Emerson Preparatory School provides a challenging academic curriculum and educational community that encourages the development of the attitudes, habits and thought processes requisite to a meaningful life.
SPECIAL COURSES: Concentrated academic program, ages 13–19; opportunity to complete high school in fewer than 4 years. Small, 90-minute classes per day, per class. Foreign languages, math, English, social studies, science, ESL workshop for international students.
CLUBS: Enriching field trips   **PUBLICATIONS:** Yearbook
COMMUNITY INVOLVEMENT: Community service projects
PLANT: 10 classrooms, science lab, computer lab/library, conference room, student lounge, courtyard/recreational area, bookstore
ADMISSION: Personal interview, 3 recommendations required, transcript, placement exams-ETS in math and English
TUITION: $16,000
FINANCIAL AID: Available
BOOKS: $475   **OTHER FEES:** Application fee $50, graduation fee $150
TRANSPORTATION: School is one block from Dupont Circle Metro
DRESS CODE: Good taste
SUMMER PROGRAMS: 6-week session, academic subjects
FUTURE PLANS: To continue the Emerson tradition for another 152 years.

EMMANUEL CHRISTIAN SCHOOL   703-369-3950   FAX 703-330-9285

8302 Spruce Street, Manassas, VA 20111-2196
Southern Baptist 1979
HEAD: Stanford D. Stone
DIRECTOR OF ADMISSIONS: Julie Edgar
WEBSITE: www.ECSFlames.org   **E-MAIL:** EmmanuelCS@aol.com
GRADES: K3–grade 12   **ENROLLMENT:** 510 Co-ed (248 boys/262 girls)
FACULTY: 39 full- and 3 part-time   **AVERAGE CLASS SIZE:** 18
SPECIAL COURSES: AP courses: English Literature, biology, chemistry, French, Spanish, U.S. history, calculus AB, art portfolio
EXTENDED DAY: 6:30 a.m.–6:00 p.m.
ATHLETICS: FCA (Fellowship of Christian Athletes); 23 athletic teams- soccer, tennis, swimming, volleyball, baseball, golf, softball, cross-country, cheerleading
CLUBS: NHS, NJHS, Student Council, SADD
PLANT: Classrooms, auditorium, gymnasium, library, 3 computer labs, science lab, kitchen, ball fields
TUITION: $4,100–$5,000
FINANCIAL AID: Available
LUNCH: Full lunch $3.00–$3.50   **OTHER FEES:** $150 registration
DRESS CODE: Coordinated uniform

ENGLESIDE CHRISTIAN SCHOOL   703-780-4332   FAX 703-780-3947
8428 Highland Lane, Alexandria, VA 22309
Independent Baptist 1970
HEAD: Keith Paddock
DIRECTOR OF ADMISSIONS: Keith Paddock
WEBSITE: www.ebc-ecs.org   **E-MAIL:** kpaddock@ebc-ecs.org
GRADES: K4–grade 12   **ENROLLMENT:** 130 Co-ed
FACULTY: 11 full- and 5 part-time   **AVERAGE CLASS SIZE:** 10
MISSION STATEMENT: Our purpose is to develop students into the image of
Christ in order to prepare and equip them for a lifetime of service to the Lord in
whatever vocation God directs their lives. Our primary goal is to develop the
whole child by promoting his spiritual and moral growth, his intellectual and aca-
demic progress, his physical development, and his social development. Our sec-
ondary goal is to prepare the student for further education at a Christian college,
university, or vocational school.
EXTENDED DAY: 7:00 a.m.–6:00 p.m.
ATHLETICS: Volleyball, basketball, track   **CLUBS:** Band, handbells
ADMISSION: Contact school office for informational packet.
TUITION: Up to $3,650
BOOKS: Up to $315   **OTHER FEES:** Additional fee for extended care program
DRESS CODE: Conservative, uniform required on secondary level

EPIPHANY SCHOOL   540-825-8982   FAX 540-825-8987
114 East Edmondson Street, Culpeper, VA 22701
Catholic
HEAD: Barbara Terry
WEBSITE: www.epiphanycatholicschool.org   **E-MAIL:** pbcc@erols.com
GRADES: Preschool–grade 5   **ENROLLMENT:** 152 Co-ed (92 K–5, 60 preschool)
SPECIAL COURSES: Art, music, Spanish, P.E., sign language grades 4 and 5
EXTENDED DAY: 7:00–9:00 a.m. and 12:00–6:00 p.m.
TUITION: Call for information

EPISCOPAL HIGH SCHOOL   703-933-4062   FAX 703-933-3016
1200 North Quaker Lane, Alexandria, VA 22302
Episcopal 1839
HEAD: F. Robertson Hershey
DIRECTOR OF ADMISSIONS: Douglas C. Price
WEBSITE: www.episcopalhighschool.org
E-MAIL: admissions@episcopalhighschool.org
GRADES: 9–12   **ENROLLMENT:** 415 Co-ed (240 boys/175 girls)board
FACULTY: 70 full and 5 part-time   **AVERAGE CLASS SIZE:** 12
MISSION STATEMENT: Episcopal High School is dedicated to the student's
pursuit of excellence and to the joy of learning and self-discovery in a caring and
supportive community. Enriched by the educational and cultural resources of the
nation's capital, Episcopal's dynamic academic program encourages students to
develop individual talents and prepares them to attend selective colleges and universities. Students from diverse backgrounds live and learn together in a residential community based on a foundation of honor, spiritual growth, responsibility, and mutual respect. They develop enduring relationships at EHS and grow

as discerning, self-reliant, creative, and compassionate individuals. The Episcopal High School community prepares young people to lead principled and fulfilling lives of leadership and service to others.

SPECIAL COURSES: 40 AP and Honors classes; Washington Program with Senior Internships; School Year Abroad and other summer programs to Spain, France, Italy and Germany. Laptop program.

ATHLETICS: 42 teams in 15 sports; boys compete in IAC, girls in ISL.

CLUBS: Choir, three a capella groups, orchestra. Multiple clubs including Model U.N., fishing, academic teams

PLANT: 135-acre campus; 9 dorms; athletic complex with indoor and outdoor track; library with over 35,000 volumes; fully networked campus

ADMISSION: January 31 deadline for March decisions; late applicants on rolling basis; SSAT, campus visit and interview

TUITION: $29,300

FINANCIAL AID: Available

BOOKS: $600   **OTHER FEES:** Laptop computer

SUMMER PROGRAMS: Sports Camp: ages 7–14

FUTURE PLANS: New Art Center opened in September 2003.

ETS CHAIYIM SCHOOL   301-216-9592   FAX 301-216-9594
20300 Pleasant Ridge Drive, Montgomery Village, MD 20886
Founded 1980
HEAD: Dr. Daniel L. Switzer
GRADES: Kindergarten–12
MISSION STATEMENT: "Established by God to raise up youth who are mighty in spirit."
ATHLETICS: Soccer, volleyball, basketball   **CLUBS:** Chess club
TUITION: Call for information.

EVANGEL CHRISTIAN SCHOOL   703-670-7127
14836 Ashdale Avenue, Dale City, VA 22193
HEAD: Charles Weinberg
WEBSITE: www.evangelbaptistchurch.org
GRADES: K4–grade 12   **ENROLLMENT:** 300 Co-ed
FACULTY: 33   **AVERAGE CLASS SIZE:** 20
SPECIAL COURSES: Traditional college preparatory in High School
EXTENDED DAY: 6:00 a.m.–6:00 p.m. for enrolled students
ATHLETICS: Soccer, volleyball, baseball, basketball, softball
TUITION: Call for information.
DRESS CODE: Uniforms

EVERGREEN SCHOOL   301-942-5979   FAX 301-946-0311
10700 Georgia Avenue, Wheaton, MD 20902
Founded 1964
HEAD: Marcia Jacques
WEBSITE: www.evergreenschool.com
E-MAIL: admissions@evergreenschool.com
GRADES: Ungraded ages 2 1/2–grade 6   **ENROLLMENT:** 95 Co-ed
FACULTY: 12 full- and 3 part-time   **AVERAGE CLASS SIZE:** 18

SPECIAL COURSES: Integrated curriculum taught using the Montessori method, including (on the primary level): language arts, geography, science, music, art, math, motor development and exercises in daily living. Curriculum at the elementary level includes computers, history, drama, language arts, including Spanish, geography, math, science, music, and art.

EXTENDED DAY: 7:30 a.m.–6:00 p.m. Holiday Care, Winter and Spring Breaks

ATHLETICS: P.E. required for all levels- includes: motor development, soccer, gymnastics. Elementary students also study health and participate in the Presidential Physical Fitness Program.

COMMUNITY INVOLVEMENT: Older children spend time with younger children as part of the Reading Buddy Program. Community Outreach includes intergenerational and environmental activities.

PLANT: Library, computer lab, gym, 7 classrooms, playground

ADMISSION: $75 application fee, interview, parents visit school, elementary age children visit. Preference given to siblings and children with Montessori experience.

TUITION: $6,570–$9,760 ages 2 1/2–6+ depending on half or full day; $10,180 elementary

FINANCIAL AID: Some available

LUNCH: Bring

SUMMER PROGRAMS: 10 week summer camp program: ages 2 1/2–grade 6; field trips, swimming, sports, art, crafts, special events and fun

FUTURE PLANS: New site with expanded facilities, middle school

—F

FAIR OAKS ACADEMY   703-631-1467   FAX 703-631-3007
4601 West Ox Road, Fairfax, VA 22030
Independent Baptist 1973
HEAD: Janice Iddins
WEBSITE: www.fairoaksacademy.org
GRADES: K3–grade 12   **ENROLLMENT:** 455 Co-ed
FACULTY: 55 full-time   **AVERAGE CLASS SIZE:** 20
MISSION STATEMENT: Our mission is to fully develop passionate followers of Jesus Christ for local and global impact.

SPECIAL COURSES: Spanish I-IV. Math: algebra-calculus, business math, computer. Science: physical science, biology, chemistry, physics. History: world geography and world history, U.S./Virginia history, U.S./Virginia government, political science/economics. Religious studies required. Remedial reading and math. Art, music, speech, typing, accounting, choir, band, drama, journalism.

EXTENDED DAY: 7:00–8:00 a.m. and 3:15–6:00 p.m.

ATHLETICS: Required to grade 10. Interscholastic: soccer, baseball, cheerleading, volleyball, softball

CLUBS: American Christian Honor Society, Student Council

PUBLICATIONS: Yearbook, newspaper

PLANT: Library, science lab, art studio, gym, playing fields

ADMISSION: Parent/child interview, $150 registration fee, principal/student interview, entrance testing

TUITION: $5,500 K3–K5 depending on number of full or half days; $4,950 1–6 $5,200 7–12

OTHER FEES: Additional fees for technology/art/P.E. uniforms, etc. Call for information.
SUMMER PROGRAMS: Recreational camp K4–grade 8.

FAIRFAX BAPTIST TEMPLE ACADEMY   703-323-8100   FAX 703-250-8660
6401 Missionary Lane, Fairfax Station, VA 22039
Baptist 1976
HEAD: Gil Hansen
WEBSITE: www.fbtministries.org   **E-MAIL:** academyoffice@fbtministries.org
GRADES: Kindergarten–grade 12   **ENROLLMENT:** 280 Co-ed   **FACULTY:** 41
SPECIAL COURSES: Strong phonics program. Grades K–6 A Beka; grades 7–12 combination of A Beka, Saxon and Bob Jones curriculums. Higher math and science. Piano and instrumental instruction available. French, Spanish. Independent study option available through ACE. Purpose of the Academy is to give academic training throughout and develop strong character based on Biblical principles.
EXTENDED DAY: Until 5:00 p.m.
TUITION: $4,340–$4,700; Reduction for siblings
LUNCH: Available   **DRESS CODE:** Uniform required

FAIRFAX BREWSTER SCHOOL   703-820-2680   FAX 703-820-8437
5860 Glen Forest Drive, Falls Church, VA 22041
Founded 1954
HEAD: Victoria Londergan
DIRECTOR OF ADMISSIONS: Victoria Londergan
WEBSITE: www.chancellorbeacon.com
GRADES: K–grade 6
MISSION STATEMENT: (Excerpted) The Fairfax Brewster School is a small K–6 community of learners where instruction is responsive to the needs of children. We believe that children want to learn, create and discover themselves and their world. We appreciate that learning happens within the context of relationships, whether student to student, student to faculty or faculty to faculty. Being understood by the important people in your world is a vital component of a student's social/emotional life. The expectations and principles that guide our daily activities and interactions hold a critical role in the teaching and learning process.
SPECIAL COURSES: Computers, P.E., Spanish, art
EXTENDED DAY: 6:30 a.m.–6:00 p.m.
ATHLETICS: Sports   **CLUBS:** Student Council, after school clubs
PUBLICATIONS: Yearbook
PLANT: School sits on 2.2 acres. Formal colonial mansion. Quaint, family-like atmosphere.
ADMISSION: Admissions decisions are based on: academic record and recommendation(s), admission testing, interview, school visit and/or group observation, demonstrated talent, interest, and experience in activities that enhance the class and school; school readiness, behavioral maturity and motivation, and comparison with others in the applicant pool.
TUITION: $5,950 base tuition
FINANCIAL AID: Available
LUNCH: Available   **TRANSPORTATION:** Available   **DRESS CODE:** Uniform required
SUMMER PROGRAMS: Available. Call for information.

FAIRFAX CHRISTIAN SCHOOL   703-759-5100   FAX 703-759-2143

1624 Hunter Mill Road, Vienna, VA 22182
Founded 1961
HEAD: Jo A.S. Thoburn
DIRECTOR OF ADMISSIONS: Jo A.S. Thoburn
WEBSITE: www.FairfaxChristianSchool.com
E-MAIL: jast@fairfaxchristianschool.com
GRADES: K3–grade 12   **ENROLLMENT:** 280 Co-ed (135 boys/125 girls)
FACULTY: 18 full- and 10 part-time   **AVERAGE CLASS SIZE:** 15
MISSION STATEMENT: Founded in 1961, Fairfax Christian School is a non-denominational, private school offering a college preparatory curriculum for students from four-year-old Kindergarten through High School. Fairfax Christian School offers a challenging classical curriculum in a traditional, Christian atmosphere. Our mission is to provide an education with a Christian worldview so that our students may know and pursue the truth. Students receive personal attention from an experienced faculty and administration. Discipline and order are maintained and are seen as essential to progress in education.
SPECIAL COURSES: AP courses, English for international students
EXTENDED DAY: 7:15 a.m.–6:00 p.m.
CLUBS: International trips during summer vacation   **PUBLICATIONS:** Yearbook
PLANT: 4 buildings, 15 classrooms, 28 acre campus with volleyball court, basketball court, soccer fields and playground
ADMISSION: Submit an application of consideration
TUITION: $5,500–$7,200 Includes books
BOOKS: Included   **LUNCH:** Students bring
OTHER FEES: $250 registration fee. Students pay for their own uniform, lunch (school provides milk), and school pictures. All other fees are included in tuition. The school does no fund raising.
TRANSPORTATION: Available $2,100 per year   **DRESS CODE:** Uniforms
SUMMER PROGRAMS: Summer Camps, high school math program and ESL program

FAIRFAX COLLEGIATE SCHOOL   703-256-9380   FAX 703-256-9384

4300 Evergreen Lane, Annandale, VA 22003
Founded 1993
HEAD: Steven Nossal, President and Founder
DIRECTOR OF ADMISSIONS: Jennifer Nossal
WEBSITE: www.fairfaxcollegiate.org
GRADES: 4-9   **ENROLLMENT:** Co-ed
AVERAGE CLASS SIZE: 12
MISSION STATEMENT: The mission of the Fairfax Collegiate School is to provide students with a challenging and engaging summer enrichment program as well as other educational services such as tutoring and small classes.
SPECIAL COURSES: Formerly a day school. Now offering summer programs and tutoring services.
EXTENDED DAY: 7:30–8:15 a.m. and 4:15–6:00 p.m.
ADMISSION: $100 deposit
TUITION: $540 for full day and $360 for half day
SUMMER PROGRAMS: Four 2-week sessions for rising 4th–9th graders in math, computers, writing, video film making and test taking

FAIRFAX SCITECH ACADEMY　　703-437-3333　FAX 703-318-8741
620 Herndon Parkway, Herndon, VA 20171
Founded 2003
WEBSITE: www.fairfaxscitech.com　**E-MAIL:** info@fairfaxscitech.com
GRADES: Pre-Kindergarten–grade 6　**ENROLLMENT:** Co-ed
AVERAGE CLASS SIZE: Maximum 15
TUITION: Call for information.
FUTURE PLANS: Add grades 7 and 8

FAIRHAVEN SCHOOL　　301-249-8060　FAX 301-218-3549
17900 Queen Anne Road, Upper Marlboro, MD 20774
Non-denominational 1998
HEAD: Administered by democratically elected Clerks
DIRECTORS OF ADMISSIONS: Linda Jackson and Gayle Friedman
WEBSITE: www.fairhavenschool.com　**E-MAIL:** staff@fairhavenschool.com
GRADES: Ungraded K–grade 12　**ENROLLMENT:** 60 Co-ed (37 boys/23 girls)
FACULTY: 1 full- and 7 part-time　**AVERAGE CLASS SIZE:** 3
MISSION STATEMENT: Fairhaven School, a democratically governed community, provides a vibrant, respectful environment in which students hold exclusive responsibility for their own education.
SPECIAL COURSES: Fairhaven School is a Sudbury-model school. It is democratically run by students, staff, and (for major policies and budget) by parents. The curriculum is entirely self-directed, allowing students to play, converse, work and learn according to their own priorities and individual styles. Students are treated with the same respect as adults and learn to handle freedom and its accompanying responsibilities through direct experience. Program is appropriate for a wide range of students- gifted, learning disabled, shy students, high energy students, students with different learning styles, etc. All learning is individualized. Staff are available on request for classes, tutorials, informal individual instruction and collaboration as well as for casual conversations and play.
EXTENDED DAY: School is open 8:00 a.m.–5:00 p.m., with a minimum of 5 hours/day attendance required
PLANT: Two buildings: a community-built post-and-beam building put up in 1998, and a two-story building with extensive porches put up this year. Both comfortably furnished. 12 acres of woods, fields and stream. All-day access to all school facilities including computer network/internet, kitchen, audio-visual equipment, library, sports equipment, art, music, science equipment, etc.
ADMISSION: Open admissions throughout the year. $35 application fee. Interview and visiting week required. $75 waitlist fee. Students must be able to take responsibility for their own behavior. Parents must become familiar and comfortable with the Sudbury model. Fairhaven School welcomes racial, ethnic, and religious diversity and families of every composition.
TUITION: $6,050 for first child in family. Reduced for siblings. Set by majority vote each year.
FINANCIAL AID: Available
LUNCH: Bring own lunch, kitchens available
OTHER FEES: Occasional materials and field trips
SUMMER PROGRAMS: Summer camp available for enrolled students in July
FUTURE PLANS: Enrollment will be gradually increased to 100–125

FAIRMONT CHRISTIAN PREPARATORY SCHOOL

703-361-5593   FAX 703-361-5593
8225 Barrett Drive, Manassas, VA 20109-3536
Seventh-day Adventist 1965
HEAD: Brian Arner
GRADES: Kindergarten–8   **ENROLLMENT:** 60 Co-ed
FACULTY: 4 full-time   **AVERAGE CLASS SIZE:** 15
SPECIAL COURSES: Bible class, music, P.E., Hands-on learning
ADMISSION: Kindergarten readiness test, rolling admission
TUITION: Call for information.
LUNCH: Available M–Th; dismissed at noon on Friday
OTHER FEES: $250 registration fee includes books

FAITH ARTS ACADEMY   301-438-2012

13618 Layhill Road, Silver Spring, MD 20906
GRADES: Pre-K3–grade 3   **ENROLLMENT:** Co-ed
SPECIAL COURSES: A Beka curriculum
EXTENDED DAY: 7:00 a.m.–6:00 p.m.
TUITION: Call for information.
DRESS CODE: Uniforms 4 days a week

FAITH BAPTIST SCHOOLS   540-786-4953

4105 Plank Road, Fredericksburg, VA 22407
Independent Fundamental Baptist 1979
HEAD: Wayne Scott
WEBSITE: www.fbsnet.org   **E-MAIL:** mail@fbsnet.org
GRADES: Preschool–grade 12   **ENROLLMENT:** 370 Co-ed
FACULTY: 35 full- and 25 part-time   **AVERAGE CLASS SIZE:** 25
MISSION STATEMENT: As an educational ministry of Faith Baptist Church, Faith Baptist Schools works in cooperation with Christian families for the purpose of training for life young men and women to be academically equipped and spiritually prepared for Christian service and leadership beyond their school years.
SPECIAL COURSES: The school receives materials from such publishers as A Beka Book Publications, Bob Jones University Press, Saxon Math and Positive Action for Christ. Bible, art, computer, English, algebra, calculus, business math, consumer math, biology, chemistry, physics, physical science, Creation Science, Spanish, U.S. government, U.S. history, Virginia history, world history, P.E., health/first aid, SAT prep, band, choir
EXTENDED DAY: 7:00 a.m.–6:00 p.m.
ATHLETICS: Competitive athletics begin in grade 7: soccer, basketball, boys' baseball, girls' volleyball
CLUBS: Graded piano lessons offered, instrumental band begins grade 5, American Christian Honor Society, Ministry Team (a traveling music/drama team)
PUBLICATIONS: Yearbook
PLANT: Classroom building, library, activity field, playground, gymnasium, locker rooms, offices, staff housing
ADMISSION: Interview, records from previous school, placement/diagnostic tests
TUITION: $2,110–$3,250 Reduced rates for siblings Tuition Management System
BOOKS: $125–$275   **LUNCH:** $1.75 full lunch

OTHER FEES: Registration fee $125
DRESS CODE: Men: conservative haircut, long trousers. Ladies: dresses to the knee.
SUMMER PROGRAMS: Summer tutoring and day camp program
FUTURE PLANS: 20 year site plan to accommodate 800 to 1,000 students

FAITH CHRISTIAN SCHOOL   703-430-0499   FAX 703-430-4235
21393 Potomac View Road, Suite 100, Sterling, VA 20164-3559
Independent Bible Church 1980
HEAD: Kathryn M. Teston
DIRECTOR OF ADMISSIONS: Barbara S. Pyles
WEBSITE: Website in development   **E-MAIL:** fcschool@hotmail.com
GRADES: Pre-K–grade 12   **ENROLLMENT:** 240 Co-ed
FACULTY: 30 full- and 8 part-time   **AVERAGE CLASS SIZE:** 15-20
MISSION STATEMENT: Education in Cooperation with the Creator through our four hallmarks: teaching a Biblical world view, challenging academics, affordability, nurturing environment.
SPECIAL COURSES: Enhanced, Choice, and Honors activities; Christ-centered curriculum; Bible classes required; cross-cultural studies; Discovery (Learning Differences Program)- NILD accredited; band, art, computer, drama, music, Spanish, online courses and dual enrollment for high school students; home school partnership.
EXTENDED DAY: 7:00–8:00 a.m.; 11:15–3:00 p.m.; 3:00–6:00 p.m.
ATHLETICS: Sports: basketball, soccer, volleyball
CLUBS: Drama, art, Faithful Singers
PLANT: Permanent and modular classrooms, computer lab
ADMISSION: Contact school office; testing and interview required
TUITION: $2,300 Pre-K 3 half days; $3,350 Pre-K 5 half days; $3,350 K5 half days $4,525 1–6; $4,825 7–8; $5,225 9–12
BOOKS: $125–$250   **LUNCH:** Hot lunch program available
OTHER FEES: Athletics: $90/sport; Faithful Singers, $25/year; Discovery Program: $500/initial testing, $500/Wechsler test, $3,200/year educational therapy; extended care $8/hour; monthly rates available.
DRESS CODE: Uniform required
SUMMER PROGRAMS: Vacation Stations, 1–6; Summer Reading Program, 7–12.
FUTURE PLANS: Summer Camps

FALLS CHURCH CHILDREN'S HOUSE OF MONTESSORI
703-573-7599   FAX 703-573-2807
3335 Annandale Road, Falls Church, VA 22042
Founded 1973
HEAD: Judith W. Clarke
WEBSITE: www.vamontessori.com   **E-MAIL:** mshr_fcch@hotmail.com
GRADES: Ungraded Pre-K–K   **ENROLLMENT:** 150 Co-ed with MSHR
FACULTY: 12 full- and 10 part-time   **AVERAGE CLASS SIZE:** 20
MISSION STATEMENT: Parental involvement is actively encouraged. College preparatory, with emphasis on independence and self-motivation.
SPECIAL COURSES: Great Books for Kindergarten. Elementary grades continued in Montessori School of Holmes Run

EXTENDED DAY: 7:30 a.m.–6:00 p.m. at this location

PLANT: Two campuses- one on Gallows Road, one on Annandale Road

ADMISSION: Call for information and to schedule an observation, apply for enrollment and schedule a visit to the school by your child

TUITION: $3,800–$6,900

OTHER FEES: Application fee $75, activity fee, acceptance fee

TRANSPORTATION: Available. Call for details.

SUMMER PROGRAMS: Available to those enrolled at the schools, June–August

FATHER ANDREW WHITE SCHOOL   301-475-9795   FAX 301-475-3537

P.O. Box 1756, Leonardtown, MD 20650

Catholic

HEAD: Linda Maloney

WEBSITE: www.fatherandrewwhite.org   **E-MAIL:** frandwh@erols.com

GRADES: Pre-K–grade 8   **ENROLLMENT:** Co-ed

TUITION: $2,790 one child in parish

DRESS CODE: Uniforms

THE FIELD SCHOOL   202-295-5800   FAX 202-295-5858

2301 Foxhall Road, NW, Washington, DC 20007

Founded 1972

HEAD: Elizabeth C. Ely

DIRECTOR OF ADMISSIONS: Clay Kaufman

WEBSITE: www.fieldschool.org   **E-MAIL:** admissions@fieldschool.org

GRADES: 7–grade 12   **ENROLLMENT:** 278 Co-ed

FACULTY: 37 full- and 3 part-time   **AVERAGE CLASS SIZE:** 11

MISSION STATEMENT: The Field School values the individual and inspires creativity, compassion for others, and passion for learning. We select students with a variety of challenges, abilities and backgrounds. Through dialogue among students and teachers, we encourage students to seek knowledge and join in community. Field connects the various realms of knowledge to help students understand their world and lead full lives.

SPECIAL COURSES: Languages: French, Latin, Spanish (Exchange programs to French- and Spanish-speaking countries). Science: general science, biology, chemistry, physics, environmental. History: European, American, ancient and medieval, modern. Art history taught with history classes one day a week. Curriculum is integrated (literature/history/history of art/music history) by historical period for each grade. Language and math are ability-grouped. Studio arts: art, graphic art, digital art, music, drama, photography, ceramics, theater presentations, chorus. AP: American history, calculus, art, French, Spanish, literature. Peer tutoring is available in writing and math, computer and study skills are incorporated into the humanities curriculum.

ATHLETICS: Required. Intramural and interscholastic. Member PVAC. Soccer, cross-country, basketball, swimming, tennis, baseball, track and field, lacrosse (girls), volleyball, ultimate frisbee, yoga, aerobics, bowling.

CLUBS: Jazz band, drama, Model U.N. and others

PUBLICATIONS: Yearbook, newspaper

COMMUNITY INVOLVEMENT: Annual 2-week internship program for all students. Each student must complete at least one community service internship.

HEAD: Lt. General John E. Jackson, Jr.(ret)
DIRECTOR OF ADMISSIONS: Lt. Col. Jim Akers
WEBSITE: www.forkunion.com   **E-MAIL:** akersj@fuma.org
GRADES: 6–12 grades, postgraduate   **ENROLLMENT:** 655 boys (625 boarding)
FACULTY: 45 full-time   **AVERAGE CLASS SIZE:** 17
MISSION STATEMENT: To provide young men a college preparatory education in a residential Christian environment. Using the best aspects of the military system, the Academy teaches its cadets responsibility, leadership, discipline and pride by providing an atmosphere in which spiritual, mental, and physical growth can flourish.
SPECIAL COURSES: ESL, Spanish, French, German. Science: general science, biology, chemistry, physics, astronomy. History: world, U.S., economics, world geography, Asian studies, U.S. Government, sociology. Religious studies required of all 11th graders or new 12th graders. Band, chorale, computer science, health, P.E., Driver's Ed. AP program: U.S. History, calculus, English, biology.
ATHLETICS: Required. Intramural, interscholastic. Football, basketball, baseball, lacrosse, wrestling, track, cross-country, orienteering, swimming and diving, tennis, golf, soccer, riflery
CLUBS: Boy Scouts, Explorers, bicycling, canoeing, computer, Civil Air Patrol, Flight Training, bayonet, military history, debate, fishing, weight lifting, Fellowship of Christian Athletes, National Rifle Association, model building, community service organization, chess, science, Quadrille
PUBLICATIONS: Yearbook, school newspaper
COMMUNITY INVOLVEMENT: Cadets participate in community activities for various churches and charities
PLANT: 19,000+ volume library, multiple science labs, 3 gyms, 6 playing fields, 4 tennis courts, state of the art weight training room, racquetball courts, internet-wired campus, all on over 1,000 acres
ADMISSION: Interview recommended. $50 application fee. Two letters of recommendation required. Applicants accepted on basis of character and ability.
TUITION: $18,540
FINANCIAL AID: Available. Please inquire.
LUNCH: All meals included
OTHER FEES: Midyear enrollment tuition: October $15,682, January $12,915, February $10,148. Estimated additional cost for uniforms: $2,700
DRESS CODE: Uniforms are required
SUMMER PROGRAMS: Summer session, non-military, grades 7-12 for enrichment, remediation, and review. Also a one week basketball camp for boys

FOUNDATION INTERMEDIATE SCHOOL   301-772-1200   FAX 301-772-8442
1835 Brightseat Road, Landover, MD 20785
Founded 1975
HEAD: Ruth Nolan, M.S.
GRADES: 1–8   **ENROLLMENT:** 90 Co-ed
FACULTY: 34 full- and 3 part-time   **AVERAGE CLASS SIZE:** 8
SPECIAL COURSES: ED as primary disability. Secondary issues addressed are LD, ADD, speech and language.
CLUBS: Chess, media, movement, crafts, music
PLANT: Library, computer lab, use of nearby recreational facility for P.E. and

sports programming

ADMISSION: Referrals come through local educational agencies, mental health professionals, schools, agencies or families

TUITION: Provided by school system with a referral

OTHER FEES: Related services extra

TRANSPORTATION: Provided by public school systems

DRESS CODE: School appropriate standards

SUMMER PROGRAMS: Extended school year (July)

FOUNDATION SCHOOL OF ALEXANDRIA   703-212-2090   FAX 703-212-0465

25 South Quaker Lane, Alexandria, VA 22314

Founded 1995

HEAD: Denise Lombardi, M.A.

WEBSITE: www.foundationschools.org

GRADES: 6–12   **ENROLLMENT:** 75 Co-ed

FACULTY: 28 full- and 1 part-time

AVERAGE CLASS SIZE: 8

SPECIAL COURSES: All ED courses required for High School diploma in Maryland, Virginia and D.C. Vocational component including job placement. Remedial reading emphasis.

ATHLETICS: Intramurals in basketball, volleyball. Member of Small Schools League

CLUBS: Chess   **PUBLICATIONS:** Yearbook, newsletter

PLANT: Gymnasium, library, computer lab, art studios

ADMISSION: Referrals through local educational agencies, mental health professionals, schools, agencies or families

TUITION: Tuition is paid by the school system, with a referral

TRANSPORTATION: Provided by public school system

DRESS CODE: School appropriate standards

SUMMER PROGRAMS: Extended school year (July)

FOUNDATION SCHOOL OF MONTGOMERY COUNTY

301-468-9700   FAX 301-468-3466

5320 Marinelli Road, Rockville, MD 20852

HEAD: Dr. Sheila Kaler

WEBSITE: www.foundationschools.org

GRADES: 7–12   **ENROLLMENT:** 80 Co-ed

SPECIAL COURSES: Program is designed to meet the academic needs of Emotionally Disturbed and Learning Disabled students.

FOUNDATION SCHOOL OF PRINCE GEORGES COUNTY

301-773-3500   FAX 301-773-1170

1845 Brightseat Road, Landover, MD 20785

HEAD: Dr. Addys Karunaratne

WEBSITE: www.foundationschools.org

GRADES: 7–12

ENROLLMENT: 80 Co-ed

SPECIAL COURSES: Individualized classes for students with emotional and learning disabilities.

FOURTH PRESBYTERIAN SCHOOL   301-765-8133   FAX 301-765-8138
10701 South Glen Road, Potomac, MD 20854
Presbyterian 1999
WEBSITE: www.fourthschool.org   **E-MAIL:** alaw@fourthschool.org
GRADES: Pre-K–grade 5   **ENROLLMENT:** 100 Co-ed
FACULTY: 10 full- and 3 part-time   **AVERAGE CLASS SIZE:** 10–16
MISSION STATEMENT: The Fourth Presbyterian School has as its mission to pass on the best of our cultural inheritance to our covenant children in the light of a Reformed Christian world view so that all students may know and pursue what is good, true, and beautiful. Through this pursuit, our graduates will be able to understand, evaluate, and transform their world under the Lordship of Christ by contributing thoughtfully and responsibly to family life, to the church's life and mission, and to the political and cultural life of the general society, all to the glory of God.
SPECIAL COURSES: Literature-based interdisciplinary curriculum; integrated art/music curriculum, Spanish beginning in Kindergarten, Latin beginning in grade 3. Chapel on MWF.
PLANT: 30-acre rural campus, library featuring classic children's literature
ADMISSION: Application fee $75. Interview; parent and teacher assessments, transcripts. Regular decision March 31.
TUITION: $3,770 Pre-K; $4,520 K; $8,270 grades 1–5
FINANCIAL AID: Available
DRESS CODE: Uniform required
SUMMER PROGRAMS: Summer Camp and swim lessons offered on campus
FUTURE PLANS: The school will add a grade each year through grade 8

FOXCROFT SCHOOL   540-687-5555   FAX 540-687-3627
P.O. Box 5555, Middleburg, VA 20118-5555
Founded 1914
HEAD: Mary Louise Leipheimer
DIRECTOR OF ADMISSIONS: Rebecca B. Gilmore
WEBSITE: www.foxcroft.org   **E-MAIL:** admissions@foxcroft.org
GRADES: 9–12 boarding begins 9th grade   **ENROLLMENT:** 182 girls (133 board)
FACULTY: 52 full- and 5 part-time   **AVERAGE CLASS SIZE:** 10
MISSION STATEMENT: Foxcroft provides a residential learning experience for girls in which academic excellence, leadership, responsibility, and integrity are our highest values.
SPECIAL COURSES: AP courses: English language, English literature, French, Spanish, U.S. history, macroeconomics, calculus AB, calculus BC, biology, chemistry, physics. Writing lab, math lab, learning center, 19th Century Women, classical drama, writing poetry, contemporary world fiction, The Mirrors of Our Lives, writing short fiction, senior thesis, international relations, Lie, Myths and Legends: An Introduction to Australian History and Culture, Roman history, architecture: history, theory and design, constitutional law, The Forgotten Memories: A Survey of American Culture in the 20th Century, discrete mathematics, probability and statistics, astronomy I and II, ecology, pharmacology, anatomy and physiology, environmental science: energy, resources and environment, forensics, digital graphic design I and II, advanced art studio: independent study, Bach, Beethoven and the Boyz, advanced music theory: independent

study, chorale, It's Only Rock and Roll- The History of Rock music, ensemble, vocal/instrumental lessons, dance company, theater, public speaking and presentation.

ATHLETICS: Dance, riding, combined training, showing, field hockey, soccer, volleyball, P.E. conditioning, basketball, rock climbing, swimming, yoga, lacrosse, softball, tennis

CLUBS: Afternoon Delights, art club, athletic association, astronomy club, Blue Planet Society, CAPS, Christmas pageant, current events/debate, Day Students, drama club, Flag, float committee, Foxcroft Reaching Out, horse show, International Club, Lab Rats, Octet, Old Girl/New Girl, Rhythm Nation, riding club, Riding Monitor, Soggy Cheerios, Whippers In

PUBLICATIONS: Annual literary arts magazine (Chimera), yearbook (Tally-Ho)

COMMUNITY INVOLVEMENT: Middleburg Humane Foundation, Special Friends/Adopt a Grandparent, Therapeutic Riding, Windy Hill Tutoring

PLANT: Library 50,000 volumes, science labs, math lab, computer labs, 4 playing fields, 5 dormitories, dance studio, pool, art studio, gym, stables (trails and rings), 8 tennis courts, indoor riding ring, fields, observatory, 500 acres, auditorium, faculty housing for more than 80% of the faculty, dining hall, gardens, guest house.

ADMISSION: SSAT required. Transcript and personal information required. Fee $50 and $100 International. Interview at school required of U.S. students, recommended for overseas students.

TUITION: $22,000 day; $32,000 boarding; Day students stay on campus three days a week.

FINANCIAL AID: Available. Parents seeking financial aid must complete SSS form. There is the MARS Scholarship available for incoming 9th graders.

BOOKS: $500 **LUNCH:** Included in tuition

OTHER FEES: Student activity fee **TRANSPORTATION:** Available. Cost varies.

DRESS CODE: Neat and orderly in appearance. Khaki or black pants/skirts/collared shirts

SUMMER PROGRAMS: Co-ed, 5 day residential camp for ages 9–13; Adventure Program for ages 11–13; Day Camp for ages 5–13: riding, swimming, canoeing, arts and crafts, sports, music, hiking and camping

FUTURE PLANS: Renovation of dorms

THE FRANKLIN MONTESSORI SCHOOL, FOREST HILLS

202-966-7747   FAX 202-966-8508
4473 Connecticut Avenue, N.W., Washington, DC 20008-2302
Founded 1977
HEAD: Randy Crowley and Todd Grindal
DIRECTOR OF ADMISSIONS: Randy Crowley
WEBSITE: www.metromontessori.com   **E-MAIL:** FMSchool@covad.net
GRADES: Ungraded 2 1/2–6 year olds
ENROLLMENT: 60 Co-ed (30 boys/30 girls)
FACULTY: 10 full- and 2 part-time   **AVERAGE CLASS SIZE:** 20
MISSION STATEMENT: The Franklin Montessori School's early childhood program provides a quality early learning environment for children ages 2 1/2–6 years old. Our program is based on the Montessori approach to education. Our main objective is to provide developmentally appropriate experiences that cultivate each child's natural desire to learn. We use a variety of multi-disciplinary

materials and activities to develop academics, independence, leadership, and self confidence.

SPECIAL COURSES: Spanish program
EXTENDED DAY: Call for hours
CLUBS: Creative movement and Spanish classes are given on a weekly basis, drama classes weekly
PLANT: New facility, Montessori environment with a library/computer area and an indoor and outdoor playground
ADMISSION: Visit the school and then submit an application. If space is available, we will set up a visiting day with you and your child. After the visiting day, the acceptance notification will be mailed to your home.
TUITION: $7,075   9:30–12:30; $9,450   9:30–3:30
FINANCIAL AID: Available
SUMMER PROGRAMS: Summer camp
FUTURE PLANS: We will be opening two new classrooms

THE FRANKLIN SCHOOLS   301-279-2799   FAX 301-762-4544
10500 Darnestown Road, Rockville, MD 20850
Founded 1977
HEAD: Pamela W. Trumble
DIRECTOR OF ADMISSIONS: Melanie Celenza
WEBSITE: www.montessori-mmi.com   **E-MAIL:** montessori@hers.com
GRADES: Ungraded. 2 year olds–grade 3   **ENROLLMENT:** 250 Co-ed
FACULTY: 20 full- and 40 part-time   **AVERAGE CLASS SIZE:** 24
SPECIAL COURSES: Montessori method
EXTENDED DAY: 7:30–9:00 a.m. and 3:00–6:00 pm
TUITION: Call for information.

FREDERICK ACADEMY OF THE VISITATION
301-662-2814   FAX 301-695-8549
200 East Second Street, Frederick, MD 21701
Catholic 1856
HEAD: Dr. Bernadette Emerson
WEBSITE: www.frederickvisitation.com   **E-MAIL:** info@frederickvisitation.com
GRADES: Pre-K(four year olds)–grade 8
ENROLLMENT: 245 girls (12 boarding 6–8 grades)
FACULTY: 17 full- and 4 part-time   **AVERAGE CLASS SIZE:** 15–19
MISSION STATEMENT: The Visitation Academy, a private Catholic school for girls, strives to perpetuate, in the spirit of Saint Francis de Sales, a great reverence toward God and a gentle strength in its young ladies. In its pursuit of academic excellence in a Catholic atmosphere, it concentrates on establishing Christian ideas in an environment where the spiritual, academic, physical, emotional, and social needs of each child receive first consideration. It encourages each student to reach her highest potential of academic and personal success by developing each student's particular individual gifts, that, when developed, enrich not only her community but also the world.
SPECIAL COURSES: French, Spanish, ESL, computer ed, music, chorus, band
EXTENDED DAY: 7:00–8:00 a.m. and 3:00–6:00 p.m.
ATHLETICS: P.E. after school for boarders

PLANT: Located on 3 acres in the heart of Frederick. Library, computer lab, dormitories
ADMISSION: Kindergarten: EPSF testing in mid-May; grades 1–7: 3R's testing in mid-May.
TUITION: $4,000 day; $17,000 boarding
LUNCH: Catered lunch program
OTHER FEES: Registration fee $200 day students/ $250 boarding
DRESS CODE: Spring and winter uniforms
SUMMER PROGRAMS: Summer camp

FREDERICK ADVENTIST SCHOOL   301-663-0363   FAX 301-663-0363
6437 Jefferson Pike, Frederick, MD 21703
Seventh-day Adventist 1951
HEAD: Robin Correia
GRADES: Kindergarten–grade 8   **ENROLLMENT:** 68 Co-ed
FACULTY: 6 full-time   **AVERAGE CLASS SIZE:** 15–18
MISSION STATEMENT: FAS emphasizes spiritual ideals, service to God and humanity, academic excellence, physical achievements and Christian social development. FAS has been established to provide a Christian atmosphere conducive to academic and spiritual development.
SPECIAL COURSES: Religious studies required, art, music, bell choir, vocal choir, computer, Spanish
EXTENDED DAY: M–F 7:30–8:15 a.m.   M–Th 3:45–6:00 p.m.
ATHLETICS: Basketball team, cheerleaders, Pep Squad, soccer
CLUBS: Student Council   **PUBLICATIONS:** Yearbook
PLANT: The facility was built in 1997. Features 5 classrooms, gymnasium, lunchroom, library, computer lab and Chapel
ADMISSION: Iowa Test of Basic Skills. Registration fee $280.
TUITION: Call for information.
DRESS CODE: Dress code specified in Handbook.

FREDERICK CHRISTIAN ACADEMY   301-473-8990   FAX 301-473-5701
6642 Carpenter Road, Frederick, MD 21703
Founded 1974
HEAD: Brad Fleming
GRADES: K3–grade 12   **ENROLLMENT:** 350 Co-ed
FACULTY: 30   **AVERAGE CLASS SIZE:** 20
SPECIAL COURSES: Foreign languages, English, history, government, geography, science, math, computer, accounting, business law, business procedures, drama, speech, drafting, photography, fine arts
EXTENDED DAY: 6:30 a.m.–6:00 p.m.
TUITION: $3,800 Reduction for siblings.
LUNCH: Available.
DRESS CODE: Uniform required

THE FREDERICK MONTESSORI SCHOOL   301-371-9639   FAX 301-371-0003
Box 210, Braddock Heights, MD 21714
Founded 1994
HEAD: Dr. Pamela O'Brien

DIRECTOR OF ADMISSIONS: Martina Bannasch
GRADES: Ungraded ages 4–10   **ENROLLMENT:** 50 Co-ed (29 boys/21 girls)
FACULTY: 5 full- and 3 part-time   **AVERAGE CLASS SIZE:** 7–10
ATHLETICS: Swimming, P.E., karate, ballet, tai chi, soccer, basketball
CLUBS: Piano, yoga
TUITION: $4,430–$7,000
FINANCIAL AID: Available
LUNCH: Sack lunches
OTHER FEES: $500
DRESS CODE: Uniforms
SUMMER PROGRAMS: Enrichment programs
FUTURE PLANS: Extension to grade 8

FREDERICKSBURG ACADEMY   540-898-0020
132 Falcon Drive, Fredericksburg, VA 22408
Founded 1992
HEAD: Donald A. Reed
DIRECTOR OF ADMISSIONS: Susan Reed
WEBSITE: www.fredericksburgacademy.org
E-MAIL: s.reed@fredericksburgacademy.org
GRADES: Pre-K–grade 12   **ENROLLMENT:** 410 Co-ed
SPECIAL COURSES: Full range of AP courses
EXTENDED DAY: Before and after care
ATHLETICS: Middle and upper school sports, swim team
PLANT: 12 acres, 2 academic buildings, sports center, 25-meter swimming pool, NCAA basketball court, 2 playgrounds, 4 tennis courts, 2 game fields, 3 practice fields
ADMISSION: Rolling admissions, Open Houses begin in November
TUITION: Call for information.
FINANCIAL AID: Available
LUNCH: Available for an extra fee
SUMMER PROGRAMS: Enrichment programs with special topics, SAT prep
FUTURE PLANS: New Arts and Science building planned for fall 2004.

FREE GOSPEL CHRISTIAN ACADEMY   301-420-2461   FAX 301-516-9717
4703 Marlboro Pike, Coral Hills, MD 20743
Apostolic 1994
HEAD: Dr. Lorraine M. Driggers
WEBSITE: www.freegospel.org
E-MAIL: fgmail@freegospel.org
GRADES: Kindergarten–grade 6   **ENROLLMENT:** Co-ed
AVERAGE CLASS SIZE: 12–16
MISSION STATEMENT: The mission of the Free Gospel Christian Academy is to provide a nurturing environment to educate and assist your child in achieving his or her highest potential spiritually, socially and academically.
SPECIAL COURSES: Computer, music, P.E.
EXTENDED DAY: 6:30 a.m.–6:30 p.m.
CLUBS: Holy Hands, Interpretive Dance, Step Team, Student Government, piano
PLANT: Computer/resource room with the latest technology including internet,

music room, Chapel area, TV/VCR for each class, 3-classroom facility located adjacent to the school for additional activities

ADMISSION: Admission fee $10, schedule appointment for interview along with immunization, report card and standardized test records. Registration fee $75. Schedule an evaluation test.

TUITION: $3,700

BOOKS: $200   **LUNCH:** $3.25 per day

OTHER FEES: Early care, $90 per month. Extended care $90 per month. Early and extended care $150 per month

SUMMER PROGRAMS: Varies

FUTURE PLANS: Implementation for the new site of F.G.C.A. for grades K–12, including a day care facility

FRENCH INTERNATIONAL SCHOOL   301-530-8260   FAX 301-564-5779

9600 Forest Road, Bethesda, MD 20814

Founded 1967

HEAD: Martine Quelen

WEBSITE: www.rochambeau.org

GRADES: N–grade 12   **ENROLLMENT:** 1,100 Co-ed

FACULTY: 80 full-time   **AVERAGE CLASS SIZE:** 20–25

MISSION STATEMENT: To offer students a French educational curriculum conforming to the standards and guidelines in effect in France in order to prepare students for the French Baccalaureate examination. To prepare students for admission to colleges and universities in the United States by offering a curriculum including courses focusing on the English language, American history and civilization.

SPECIAL COURSES: Latin 8–12, French K–12, Spanish 8–12, German 8–12, remedial reading, art, music, biology, chemistry, physics, general science, economics, American history, French History and Geography, computer learning, videotape. All classes are taught in French. The academic program follows the French school system except for additional English.

ATHLETICS: Required. Intramural: soccer. Interscholastic: volleyball, basketball.

PUBLICATIONS: Yearbook

PLANT: Library 10,000 volumes, art studio, gym, playing fields, media center

ADMISSION: Interview, Tests. Registration fee $250. Students must be fluent in French except in nursery school. Student body represents 49 nationalities.

TUITION: $7,880–$10,218

FINANCIAL AID: Available

TRANSPORTATION: Available   **SUMMER PROGRAMS:** Two sessions–ages 4–14

FRIENDS COMMUNITY SCHOOL   301-699-6086   FAX 301-779-4595

4601 Calvert Road, College Park, MD 20740

Quaker 1986

HEAD: Tom Goss

GRADES: K–grade 6   **ENROLLMENT:** 140 Co-ed

FACULTY: 12 full- and 3 part-time   **AVERAGE CLASS SIZE:** 16

MISSION STATEMENT: Quaker values and beliefs taught in a Progressive mode to develop lifelong, self-directed learners.

SPECIAL COURSES: Multi-grade classes, Conflict Resolution Program, whole

language and writers workshop, community service, art, music, Spanish, P.E.
EXTENDED DAY: 8 a.m.–6 p.m.
CLUBS: Significant field experiences including numerous overnights for all ages
PLANT: 10 classrooms, library, multipurpose room, excellent field and play-ground
ADMISSION: Application, parent interview, student screening–February 1 deadline. Open House monthly during school October and January Thursdays
TUITION: $6,900
FINANCIAL AID: Available
OTHER FEES: $ 100 activity fee
DRESS CODE: No.
SUMMER PROGRAMS: Summer Fun Day Camp- soccer, swimming, field trips
FUTURE PLANS: New building, expansion to grades 7 and 8

FRIENDS MEETING SCHOOL   301-798-0288   FAX 301-798-0299
3232 Green Valley Road, Ijamsville, MD 21754
Quaker 1995
HEAD: Annette Breiling
WEBSITE: www.friendsmeetingschool.org
E-MAIL: info@friendsmeetingschool.org
GRADES: 3 years–grade 8   **ENROLLMENT:** 109 Co-ed (54 boys/55 girls)
FACULTY: 11 full- and 7 part-time   **AVERAGE CLASS SIZE:** 14
MISSION STATEMENT: Our mission at Friends Meeting School is to provide an outstanding educational experience in the context of Quaker values by nurturing academic and human excellence in mind, body and spirit. We practice Truth and Love within a diverse community and encourage our students to "let their lives speak," at school, at home, in their community, and in the world.
SPECIAL COURSES: Spanish, peace skills, music & drama, art, computers, and weekly meeting for worship for all ages. Outdoor school program for grades 5–8. Hands-on science program including establishment of certified National Schoolyard Habitat.
EXTENDED DAY: 7:30–8:15 a.m. and 3:20–6:15 p.m.
CLUBS: Artisans Club
COMMUNITY INVOLVEMENT: Nursing home visitation, collections for the homeless
PLANT: 54-acre campus, 3 school buildings plus a residence, grade 5–8 science lab, computer lab, art room, and library
ADMISSION: Application, $50 fee, recommendations and information from student's current school required, informal testing, meeting with parents and child, optional school tour. Students may enroll during the school year if a vacancy exists.
TUITION: $5,100 PK morning only; $8,600 PK full day–grade 4; $8,800 5–8
FINANCIAL AID: Available
BOOKS: $400–$700
LUNCH: Bring
OTHER FEES: 5% discount for younger siblings
DRESS CODE: Clean, neat and simple
SUMMER PROGRAMS: Summer Friends Camp
FUTURE PLANS: Soccer field, high school

—G

GARRISON FOREST SCHOOL   410-363-1500   FAX 410-363-8441
300 Garrison Forest Road, Owings Mills, MD 21117
Founded 1910
HEAD: G. Peter O'Neill, Jr.
DIRECTOR OF ADMISSIONS: A. Randol Benedict
WEBSITE: www.gfs.org   **E-MAIL:** gfs_info@gfs.org
GRADES: Preschool 3 (co-ed)–grade 12
ENROLLMENT: 630 (590 girls/40 boys preschool)
FACULTY: 79 full- and 18 part-time   **AVERAGE CLASS SIZE:** 11–14
MISSION STATEMENT: (Excerpted) An independent day and boarding school for girls with a coeducational preschool, Garrison Forest School is dedicated to the intellectual, aesthetic, emotional, moral, physical, and spiritual growth of its students. The school seeks to develop within each student a strong sense of integrity, identity and self-esteem, reflecting its motto "Esse Quam Videri": "To be and not to seem."
SPECIAL COURSES: Latin 7–12, French and Spanish 1–12, Math: algebra, calculus, computer practical and programming, finite math. Science: biology, chemistry, physics, physical science, field studies in ecology, Current Issues in Science, animal behavior, geology. History: world, U.S., Contemporary World Issues, Ethnicity in 20th Century America, major religions, modern China, Russian/Soviet history, America since 1945. Economics, child development, art, music, theater arts, dance. AP: English, French, Spanish, Latin, U.S. history, calculus, biology, studio art, art history, chemistry. Boarding begins for girls in 8th grade. 60 board.
EXTENDED DAY: After school. Varies by division.
ATHLETICS: Required. Interscholastic. Riding, polo, field hockey, basketball, lacrosse, tennis, cross-country, badminton, soccer, softball.
CLUBS: Activities, Black Student Union, Cultural Awareness Explorations, singing groups, foreign language clubs, drama, outing, riding, tour guides, Model U.N.
PUBLICATIONS: Yearbook, newspaper, literary magazine
COMMUNITY INVOLVEMENT: Comprehensive community service program run by students with a faculty advisor
PLANT: 115-acre campus. Library 16,000 volumes, 5 science labs, 2 art studios, 400-seat auditorium, gym, campus center including three basketball courts, fitness center, dance studio, indoor running suspended track, and a new dining facility. Music practice rooms, 3 dorms, tennis courts, Chapel, stables, 2 outdoor riding rings and 2 indoor arenas, playing fields, photo lab, recital hall.
ADMISSION: Apply by January 10. Testing: SSAT, ISEE. Interview on campus required, transcript, teacher recommendations
TUITION: $3,900–$17,300 day; $31,650 boarding
FINANCIAL AID: Available
BOOKS: $300   **LUNCH:** $4.00. Included for boarders
TRANSPORTATION: Available. Future plans to expand transportation are in the works.
DRESS CODE: Uniform
SUMMER PROGRAMS: Pony Club, various other athletic camps
FUTURE PLANS: Continuing update of technology and campus network. Expand middle school and enhance science labs in middle and upper school

GEORGE E. PETERS SDA SCHOOL   301-559-6710   FAX 301-559-
6303 Riggs Road, Hyattsville, MD 20783
Seventh-day Adventist
HEAD: Delvin Chatham
WEBSITE: www.gepeters.org   **E-MAIL:** principal @members.virtualed.org
GRADES: Pre-K–grade 8   **ENROLLMENT:** 200 Co-ed
SPECIAL COURSES: Spanish, computer, music, keyboarding
EXTENDED DAY: 3:30–6:00 M–Th, 3:30–5:00 F
COMMUNITY INVOLVEMENT: Christian Service
TUITION: Call for information.
DRESS CODE: Uniforms

GEORGE SCHOOL   215-579-6547   FAX 215-579-6549
P.O. Box 4460, Rte. 413, Newtown, PA 18940
Quaker 1893
HEAD: Nancy Starmer
DIRECTOR OF ADMISSIONS: Karen S. Hallowell
WEBSITE: www.georgeschool.org   **E-MAIL:** admissions@georgeschool.org
GRADES: 9–12   **ENROLLMENT:** 540 (265 boys/275 girls) 300 board
FACULTY: 75 full- and 12 part-time   **AVERAGE CLASS SIZE:** 14
MISSION STATEMENT: Founded in 1893 as a Friends coeducational school,
George School offers an unusually broad curriculum including AP, ESL, and the
International Baccalaureate Program. World renowned, the IB Diploma is a rigor-
ous two-year course of study. A yearlong course in fine or performing arts is
required of all students each year. See financial aid section for scholarship informa-
tion. Quaker values such as tolerance, equality, and social justice create a diverse
community where academics, sports, arts and service learning share emphasis.
SPECIAL COURSES: Advanced Placement, International Baccalaureate, English
as a Second Language, International Work Camps/Service Projects, Cooperative
Work Program
TUITION: $30,370
FINANCIAL AID: Yes. 4.0 million dollars, nearly 40% of students on financial
aid. Four $10,000 Merit-based Anderson Scholarships awarded annually to
boarding students.
LUNCH: Included   **DRESS CODE:** Proper and appropriate

GEORGETOWN DAY SCHOOL HIGH SCHOOL
202-274-3200   FAX 202-364-9603
4200 Davenport Street, N.W., Washington, DC 20016
Founded 1945
HEAD: Peter M. Branch
WEBSITE: www.gds.org   **E-MAIL:** info@gds.org
GRADES: Pre-K–grade 12; two campuses
ENROLLMENT: 1,025 Co-ed (510 boys/515 girls)
FACULTY: 140 full-and 12 part-time
AVERAGE CLASS SIZE: 16 (high school)–18 (lower/middle schools)
MISSION STATEMENT: Georgetown Day School honors the integrity and
worth of each individual within a diverse school community. GDS is dedicated to
providing a supportive educational atmosphere in which teachers challenge the

lectual, creative, and physical abilities of our students and foster strength of
aracter and concern for others. From the earliest grades, we encourage our students to wonder, to inquire, and to be self-reliant, laying the foundation for a lifelong love of learning.

SPECIAL COURSES: French and Spanish 3–12, Latin 7–12. AP: art, studio, biology, chemistry, economics, environmental science, European history, French language, French literature, government and politics: U.S. government and politics: comparative, Latin: Virgil, Horace/Catullus, calculus AB, BC, physics C, psychology, Spanish language, Spanish literature, statistics, U.S. history. Advanced math students may take linear algebra/multivariable calculus and advanced math topics.

EXTENDED DAY: Until 6:00 p.m.

ATHLETICS: Interscholastic athletic teams for boys and girls. Soccer, golf, cross-country, basketball, wrestling, crew, track, baseball, softball, tennis, lacrosse

CLUBS: The high school offers more than 25 clubs and discussion groups, including debate, drama, Student Government, Amnesty International, women's issues, SADD, multicultural issues, "It's Academic", jazz ensemble, AIDS awareness, community service, Model Congress, Gay/Straight Alliance, a capella music, Model U.N., math, French, Spanish and science

PUBLICATIONS: Newspaper, literary magazines, art magazine, yearbook

COMMUNITY INVOLVEMENT: Students at all levels perform community service. High school students are required to perform 60 hours of community service outside of school.

PLANT: Two campuses- each with library, science labs, computer labs, gymnasium, theater, athletic field

ADMISSION: Open Houses. Interview and tour, student visit. Application deadline January 15. Fee $60. Standardized testing required for PK–5/ SSAT required for 6–12.

TUITION: $18,619–$21,472

FINANCIAL AID: Available. 2 million dollars of financial aid.

LUNCH: Bring   **OTHER FEES:** $500 replacement reserve fee for first 3 years

DRESS CODE: No

SUMMER PROGRAMS: Sports camp, technology camp, Spanish and French classes

GEORGETOWN DAY SCHOOL LOWER/MIDDLE SCHOOL
202-295-6200   FAX 202-295-6151
4530 MacArthur Boulevard, N.W., Washington, DC 20007
WEBSITE: www.gds.org   **E-MAIL:** info@gds.org
SPECIAL COURSES: See Listing for Georgetown Day School High School.

GEORGETOWN HILL EARLY SCHOOL POTOMAC
301-299-7360 option #3   FAX 301-299-0165
8311 Bells Mill Road, Potomac, MD 20854
Founded 1980
HEAD: Ellen S. Cromwell
DIRECTOR OF ADMISSIONS: Joyce Zier
WEBSITE: www.georgetownhill.org   **E-MAIL:** jzier@belmontcc.com
GRADES: 2–4's program, Pre-K 4 and 5   **ENROLLMENT:** Co-ed
FACULTY: 22 full- and 7 part-time

AVERAGE CLASS SIZE: 12–18, with two teachers
MISSION STATEMENT: Georgetown Hill's mission is to provide for children a high quality program incorporating developmentally-appropriate learning objectives, play and the arts in a warm and nurturing environment. We believe that dedicated teachers using a proven and exciting curriculum can foster joy, wonder and learning in children.
SPECIAL COURSES: Spanish age 4 and up, music age 2 and up
EXTENDED DAY: 7:30 a.m.–6:30 p.m.
ATHLETICS: Sports beginning at age 2
PLANT: Media center
ADMISSION: Rolling admissions, call for tours. Application fee $75 and $400 which applies towards tuition.
TUITION: Call for information.
FINANCIAL AID: Available
LUNCH: Bring   **TRANSPORTATION:** Available between campuses
SUMMER PROGRAMS: Summer Camp ages 2 and up open admission

GEORGETOWN HILL EARLY SCHOOL DARNESTOWN
301-527-1377 option #2
15120 Turkey Foot Road, Darnestown, MD 20878-3960
Founded 1980
HEAD: Ellen S. Cromwell
DIRECTOR OF ADMISSIONS: Joyce Zier
WEBSITE: www.georgetownhill.org   **E-MAIL:** jzier@belmontcc.com
GRADES: age 2–Pre-K   **ENROLLMENT:** Co-ed
FACULTY: 8 full- and 3 part-time
AVERAGE CLASS SIZE: 12–18 with two teachers
MISSION STATEMENT: See listing for Potomac campus.
SPECIAL COURSES: Spanish age 4 and up, music age 2 and up
EXTENDED DAY: 7:30 a.m.–6:30 p.m.
ATHLETICS: Sports ages 2 and up   **PLANT:** Media center
ADMISSION: Rolling admissions, call for tour information. Application fee $75 and $400 which applies towards tuition.
TUITION: Call for information.
FINANCIAL AID: Available
LUNCH: Bring   **TRANSPORTATION:** Available between campuses
SUMMER PROGRAMS: Summer Camp age 2 and up open admissions

GEORGETOWN HILL EARLY SCHOOL ROCKVILLE   240-453-9047 option #2
850 Nelson Street, Rockville, MD 20850-2051
Founded 1980
HEAD: Ellen S. Cromwell
DIRECTOR OF ADMISSIONS: Joyce Zier
WEBSITE: www.georgetownhill.org
E-MAIL: jzier@belmontcc.com
GRADES: 4 years–grade 2   **ENROLLMENT:** Co-ed
FACULTY: 4 full- and 1 part-time
AVERAGE CLASS SIZE: 12–18 with two teachers
MISSION STATEMENT: See listing for Potomac location.

SPECIAL COURSES: Spanish age 4 and up, music
EXTENDED DAY: 7:30 a.m.–6:30 p.m.
ATHLETICS: Sports   PLANT: Media center
ADMISSION: Rolling admissions, call for tour information. Application fee $75 and $400 which applies towards tuition.
TUITION: Call for information.
FINANCIAL AID: Available
LUNCH: Bring   TRANSPORTATION: Available between campuses.
SUMMER PROGRAMS: Summer Camp

GEORGETOWN PREPARATORY SCHOOL

301-493-5000   FAX 301-493-5905
10900 Rockville Pike, North Bethesda, MD 20852
Catholic 1789
HEAD: Dr. Peter D. Relic
WEBSITE: www.gprep.org   E-MAIL: admissions@gprep.org
GRADES: 9–12   ENROLLMENT: 440 boys (100 boarding)
FACULTY: 53   AVERAGE CLASS SIZE: 17
SPECIAL COURSES: Latin, French, Spanish, German, Greek. Math through calculus, computer, biology, chemistry, physics, American history, Western Civilization, economics, religious studies required. Art, music. ESL program. AP: 18 courses in most of the above disciplines including computer science, modern European history, art history, studio art.
ATHLETICS: Not required. Intramural and interscholastic. Football, track, basketball, cross-country, swimming, tennis, golf, lacrosse, soccer, wrestling, baseball
CLUBS: Forensics, German, French, Russian, international relations, math team, chess team, drama, fencing, computer, photography, Student Council
PUBLICATIONS: Yearbook, newspaper
COMMUNITY INVOLVEMENT: Required service projects for all students
PLANT: Library 15,000 volumes, language lab, 3 science labs, 3 computer science labs, theater, art studio, gym, playing fields, swimming pool, indoor tennis courts, Chapel, golf course, synthetic track
ADMISSION: Application deadline January 15. SSAT, interview, transcripts, recommendations from two teachers, autobiographical essay. Reply date March 1.
TUITION: $17,650 day includes lunch; $31,270 boarding
FINANCIAL AID: Available
BOOKS: $400   LUNCH: Included
TRANSPORTATION: Free shuttle bus from Grosvenor Metro stop a.m. only
DRESS CODE: Jacket and tie required
SUMMER PROGRAMS: Co-ed summer day camp ages 6–13. Summer school for foreign students, Co-ed, ages 14–18. Day and boarding. Intense English language instruction.

GEORGETOWN VISITATION PREPARATORY SCHOOL

202-337-3350   FAX 202-342-5733
1524 35th Street, N.W., Washington, DC 20007
Catholic 1799
HEAD: Daniel M. Kerns, Jr.
WEBSITE: www.visi.org   E-MAIL: quirk@visi.org

GRADES: 9–12   **ENROLLMENT:** 475 Girls
FACULTY: 40 full- and 15 part-time   **AVERAGE CLASS SIZE:** 15–18
SPECIAL COURSES: AP: English, modern European history, U.S. history, comparative politics, calculus, biology, chemistry. Electives in creative writing, anthropology, psychology, among others. Bridge Program with Georgetown University enables selected students to take courses for college credit. Language Consortium with area high schools.
ATHLETICS: P.E. required. Interscholastic athletic teams. Crew, volleyball, basketball, soccer, field hockey, cross-country, track, swimming, diving, softball, lacrosse, tennis
CLUBS: Co-curricular activities include over 35 clubs: Model U.N., Prism Multicultural, photography, forensics team, madrigal choir, environmental awareness, chorus, drama, dance, Great Books, service, Black Women's Society, language, Speakers Forum
PUBLICATIONS: Yearbook, newspaper, art and literary magazine
PLANT: 24-acre campus includes four-story main academic building, library 10,000 volumes, computer lab with campus-wide network and Internet access, 4 science labs, art studio, auditorium, gym, 4 tennis courts, 3 playing fields, lodge and cabin.
ADMISSION: Application deadline is December 5. Process includes a personal statement, student interview, recommendations from math and English teachers, transcript, Archdiocesan Entrance Exam
TUITION: $14,300
FINANCIAL AID: Available
BOOKS: $350   **LUNCH:** $3.50/day
DRESS CODE: Uniform required
SUMMER PROGRAMS: Academic, sports and performing arts camps

GERMAN SCHOOL   301-365-4400   FAX 301-365-3905
8617 Chateau Drive, Potomac, MD 20854
Founded 1961
HEAD: Klaus-Dieter Bloch
WEBSITE: www.dswashington.org   **E-MAIL:** mail@dswash.org
GRADES: N, K–grade 13   **ENROLLMENT:** 600 Co-ed
FACULTY: 37 full- and 28 part-time   **AVERAGE CLASS SIZE:** 18–21
SPECIAL COURSES: Art, music, Latin, French, German 1–13, English, math, computer science, general science, biology, chemistry, physics, world and American history, social science. Religious studies. Drama, choir, orchestra. AP: English, French, German, and math. Grades 5–13 are taught in preparation for admittance to universities and courses are equivalent to the curriculum taught in high schools in Germany in preparation for admittance to a university.
ATHLETICS: Required. Swimming, basketball, soccer, volleyball.
PUBLICATIONS: Yearbook
PLANT: Library 25,000 volumes, science lab, art studio, auditorium, 2 gyms, playing fields, and sports field, swimming pool, photography lab, music room
ADMISSION: Rolling admission, interview, test (if appropriate), transcript. Must be German speaking.
TUITION: Call for information.
BOOKS: Extra   **TRANSPORTATION:** Rates according to distance

GESHER JEWISH DAY SCHOOL   703-978-9789   FAX 703-978-2668
8900 Little River Turnpike, Fairfax, VA 22031
Jewish 1982
HEAD: Dr. Richard Wagner
DIRECTOR OF ADMISSIONS: Ellen Katz
WEBSITE: www.gesher-jds.org
GRADES: Kindergarten– grade 8   **ENROLLMENT:** 160 Co-ed (69 boys/75 girls)
FACULTY: 37 full-time   **AVERAGE CLASS SIZE:** 12
MISSION STATEMENT: (Excerpted) "Building a Bridge of Knowledge, Character, and Wisdom to the Future." Gesher Jewish Day School of Northern Virginia prepares its students to become knowledgeable and committed Jews, informed and responsible American citizens living in a pluralistic society, and morally sensitive human beings. Our educational program is dedicated to academic excellence and creative expression in both General and Judaic studies. Gesher promotes the intellectual, social, physical, and spiritual growth of each student by responding to each one's learning style, ability, and potential with a caring, supportive, and disciplined environment.
SPECIAL COURSES: General and Judaic studies include Hebrew language, resource program, enrichment courses, art, music, science, computers, Spanish
EXTENDED DAY: Morning and evening
CLUBS: Drama club, computer club, middle school activities
PUBLICATIONS: Yearbook
ADMISSION: Call for information.
TUITION: $9,450
FINANCIAL AID: Available
OTHER FEES: Building fund $500 per family.
TRANSPORTATION: Available. $1,550
FUTURE PLANS: New facility to open January 2005

GIBSON ISLAND COUNTRY SCHOOL   410-255-5370   FAX 410-255-0416
5191 Mountain Road, Pasadena, MD 21122
Founded 1947
HEAD: Charles H. Toll
WEBSITE: www.gics.org   **E-MAIL:** schoolsecretary@gics.org
GRADES: Pre-K–grade 5   **ENROLLMENT:** 92 Co-ed
FACULTY: 12 full- and 4 part-time   **AVERAGE CLASS SIZE:** 15
SPECIAL COURSES: French (Pre-K–5), art, music, science, environmental studies
EXTENDED DAY: Until 6:00 p.m.
TUITION: Call for information.
DRESS CODE: Uniform

GLENELG COUNTRY SCHOOL   410-531-8600   FAX 410-531-7363
P.O. Box 190, Glenelg, MD 21737
Founded 1954
HEAD: Ryland O. Chapman, III
DIRECTOR OF ADMISSIONS: Karen Wootton
WEBSITE: www.glenelg.org   **E-MAIL:** wootton@glenelg.org
GRADES: Pre-K–grade 12   **ENROLLMENT:** 715 Co-ed (354 boys/356 girls)
FACULTY: 92 full- and 12 part-time   **AVERAGE CLASS SIZE:** 16

MISSION STATEMENT: The mission of the Glenelg Country Schoo. duct a challenging academic curriculum, a vigorous athletic program, ai courses in graphic and performing arts such that each student will Intellectual curiosity and love for learning; Skills for effective communicai calculation; Athleticism and sportsmanship; Ecological and aesthetic awa Personal Integrity, respect and compassion for others, so that each graduate is qualified for admission to colleges and universities of high quality and prepared to contribute to the greater good.

SPECIAL COURSES: Humanities grades 9–12 (Integrative Seminar in grade 12). French, Spanish offered in all grades. Latin in grades 6–12. Astronomy. AP courses–French, Spanish, Latin, biology, chemistry, physics, calculus, statistics, environmental science, studio art, economics.

EXTENDED DAY: 7:30 a.m.–6:00 p.m.

ATHLETICS: Interscholastic sports for grades 6–8: soccer, field hockey, basketball, cross-country, track, ice hockey, lacrosse, tennis, baseball, golf

CLUBS: Drama, chorus, honor society

PUBLICATIONS: Yearbook, newspaper, literary magazine

COMMUNITY INVOLVEMENT: Community service projects

PLANT: 87-acre campus includes four academic buildings, gymnasium, outdoor pool, observatory, tennis courts, and playing fields

ADMISSION: Open House in October–call for date. Application deadline early February with rolling admission thereafter. Admission testing and a visit date/interview are required.

TUITION: $7,800 Pre-K; $13,600 K–4; $14,420 5–8; $15,360 9; $15,835 10–12

FINANCIAL AID: Available

BOOKS: $600   **LUNCH:** Catered lunch extra

OTHER FEES: $700 includes books through grade 8

TRANSPORTATION: Available. $2,000 per year, round trip

DRESS CODE: Yes

SUMMER PROGRAMS: Day camp, summer school, sports camps

FUTURE PLANS: Upper school expansion including new athletic facility, science labs, library and technology center

GONZAGA COLLEGE HIGH SCHOOL   202-336-7100   FAX 202-454-1188

19 Eye Street, N.W., Washington, DC 20001
Catholic 1821
HEAD: Michael Pakenham
WEBSITE: www.gonzaga.org   **E-MAIL:** cjoncas@gonzaga.org
GRADES: 9–12   **ENROLLMENT:** 900 boys
FACULTY: 66 full- and 8 part-time   **AVERAGE CLASS SIZE:** 28
SPECIAL COURSES: Latin, French, Spanish, German (9–12), Greek 3 years. Math through calculus, computer science, math analysis and statistics. Science: biology, chemistry, physics, psychology, marine biology, anatomy, earth systems science. History: world cultures, European and American. Politics, Economics and Social Justice. Religious studies required. Art, music, choral arts program, band. Learning development, Driver's Ed, drama, TV, communications. Extensive Retreat program. AP: languages, science, math, history, English, computer science, studio art.
ATHLETICS: Not required. Intramural and interscholastic. Football, soccer,

_y, ice hockey, basketball, baseball, softball, cross-country, track and field, tennis, golf, swimming, diving, crew

CLUBS: Languages, science, math, history, English, computer science, studio art

PUBLICATIONS: Newspaper, yearbook, literary magazine

COMMUNITY INVOLVEMENT: Mandatory Social Justice Program for all Seniors. Enrichment program for neighborhood children. Appalachian project and other projects.

PLANT: Library 15,000 volumes, language lab, science lab, art studio, gym, auditorium, playing fields, tennis courts, track

ADMISSION: Grade 9: application, achievement test, transcript, recommendations. Apply by December 15. For other grades, contact Director of Admissions.

TUITION: $10,850

FINANCIAL AID: Available.

BOOKS: Extra   **LUNCH:** Extra

DRESS CODE: Dress pants, shirts with collar, dress shoes

SUMMER PROGRAMS: Academic: remedial and enrichment. Purple Eagle Basketball Camp, football camp

GOOD SHEPHERD MONTESSORI SCHOOL   301-762-2524
1605 Veirs Mill Road, Rockville, MD 20851

Founded 1999

HEAD: Lili Hishmeh

WEBSITE: www.hometown.aol.com/gsmontessori

E-MAIL: GSMontessori@aol.com

GRADES: Preschool–grade 1   **ENROLLMENT:** 40 Co-ed

FACULTY: 3 full- and 2 part-time   **AVERAGE CLASS SIZE:** 15

MISSION STATEMENT: Dedicated to meeting the young child's needs for physical, cultural, intellectual and spiritual growth and development.

SPECIAL COURSES: Full Montessori curriculum, including mathematics, language, (reading and writing), science, music, geography, history. Also French, Monart (drawing) and Christian Life.

EXTENDED DAY: 7:30 a.m.–6:00 p.m.

PLANT: 2-acre campus in Rockville.

ADMISSION: Tour, application, parent/child interview.

TUITION: $4,000–$5,000

SUMMER PROGRAMS: Summer Camp

GRACE BRETHREN CHRISTIAN SCHOOL   301-868-1600   FAX 301-868-9475
6501 Surratts Road, Clinton, MD 20735

Grace Brethren 1965

HEAD: George Hornickel

DIRECTOR OF ADMISSIONS: Terrell Elam

WEBSITE: www.gbcseagles.org   **E-MAIL:** info@gbcseagles.org

GRADES: K4–grade 12   **ENROLLMENT:** 760 Co-ed

FACULTY: 45 full- and 10 part-time   **AVERAGE CLASS SIZE:** low 20's

MISSION STATEMENT: To provide an environment of academic excellence conducive to developing educated citizens with a Biblical worldview who are prepared to represent our Lord, Jesus Christ in all walks of life.

SPECIAL COURSES: AP and honors U.S. history; AP and honors calculus; honors chemistry; honors English 9–11. Advanced courses: trigonometry, anatomy/physiology; applied science and physics. LD Discovery Program for elementary and secondary students. Elementary: P.E., music, computers, art. PG Community College classes on campus for seniors (minimum number–12 seniors).

EXTENDED DAY: 6:30–8:00 a.m. and 3:00–6:00 p.m.

ATHLETICS: Boys: JV and varsity soccer, middle school, JV and varsity basketball, JV and varsity track, JV and varsity baseball, wrestling and swimming. Girls: JV and varsity cheerleading, volleyball, soccer, basketball and track, tennis

CLUBS: Chorus (JAM and WOG), band, National Honor Society, drama, Student Government, Young Writers

PUBLICATIONS: Yearbook (elementary and secondary)

COMMUNITY INVOLVEMENT: 75 community service hours

PLANT: Full size cafeteria, library, playing fields, Chapel, elementary gym, secondary gym, science lab, computer labs, music room

ADMISSION: Complete application, parent-child interview, recommendations, testing. Deadline–first-come, first-served basis after January 31 each year

TUITION: $5,500 K4–5; $5,700 6–8; $6,000 9–12

FINANCIAL AID: Available. Limited

LUNCH: $ 3.75

OTHER FEES: Academic fees: K4 $100; K5 $150; 1–5 $160; 6–8 $175; 9–12 $195 Registration fee $100

TRANSPORTATION: Van pools and car pools

SUMMER PROGRAMS: Summer School; Summer Camp K4–8

FUTURE PLANS: A few additional classrooms

GRACE CHRISTIAN SCHOOL   301-262-0158   FAX 301-262-4516

7210 Race Track Road, Bowie, MD 20715

Baptist 1975

HEAD: Don Jillson

DIRECTOR OF ADMISSIONS: Mrs. Ritter

WEBSITE: www.gracechristianbowie.com

GRADES: Kindergarten–grade 8   **ENROLLMENT:** 400 Co-ed

FACULTY: 35 full-time   **AVERAGE CLASS SIZE:** 24 maximum

SPECIAL COURSES: Spanish 7–8, algebra 8, computer science and lab all grades, P.E., art, music (vocal and instrumental). Religious studies required.

ATHLETICS: Not required. Soccer, volleyball, basketball, softball, baseball, track

PUBLICATIONS: Yearbook

COMMUNITY INVOLVEMENT: MS Readathon competition, Jump Rope for Heart, Math-a-thon

TUITION: $4,050

LUNCH: Bring   **TRANSPORTATION:** Privately contracted

DRESS CODE: Uniform required

GRACE EPISCOPAL DAY SCHOOL   301-585-3513   FAX 301-585-5240

9115 Georgia Avenue, Silver Spring, MD 20910

Episcopal 1960

HEAD: Carol H. Franek

DIRECTOR OF ADMISSIONS: Lisa Hollaender

WEBSITE: www.GEDS.ORG   **E-MAIL:** lhollaender@geds.org

GRADES: Pre-K–grade 6 two campuses   **ENROLLMENT:** 280 Co-ed
FACULTY: 22 full- 11 part-time   **AVERAGE CLASS SIZE:** N, K 8–15 1–6 15–18
MISSION STATEMENT: Grace Episcopal Day School will provide every student the opportunity for academic excellence in a caring, nurturing, moral environment that embraces diversity and promotes creativity, self confidence and service to others.
SPECIAL COURSES: Spanish, Latin, science, computer, music, art, P.E., health, Reading Recovery Program. Grades 1–6 are located at Kensington, Maryland campus. Nursery, Pre-K, Kindergarten are located in Silver Spring, Maryland.
EXTENDED DAY: 7:35 a.m.–6:00 p.m.
ATHLETICS: P.E. required, soccer
CLUBS: Chess club, Literary Lizards, art club, science club, drama club, Spanish and computer, Student Council
PUBLICATIONS: Yearbook, literary magazine of children's work
COMMUNITY INVOLVEMENT: Community outreach programs
PLANT: 2 campuses: Kensington has 11-acre campus with playing fields surrounded by woodlands; all-purpose room with stage, library, science room, art room, music room, computer lab
ADMISSION: Parents tour school and have interview with the administration. Testing K–6 and child visits for a day. Teacher recommendations and transcripts.
TUITION: $4,215–$11,865 depending on grade
FINANCIAL AID: Available. Awarded on need basis.
OTHER FEES: $100   **DRESS CODE:** Uniform required
SUMMER PROGRAMS: Drama production, music, art, Summer Scientist, computer, sports, academic enrichment, field trips

GRACE EPISCOPAL DAY SCHOOL KENSINGTON
301-585-3513   FAX 301-585-5240
9411 Connecticut Avenue, Kensington, MD 20895
SPECIAL COURSES: Contact school campus at Silver Spring for further information.

GRACE EPISCOPAL SCHOOL   703-549-5067   FAX 703-549-9545
3601 Russell Road, Alexandria, VA 22305
Episcopal 1959
HEAD: Connie Engelhardt
DIRECTOR OF ADMISSIONS: Debra Busker
WEBSITE: www.graceschoolalex.org
E-MAIL: admissions@graceschoolalex.org
GRADES: N–grade 5   **ENROLLMENT:** 110 Co-ed (47 boys/63 girls)
FACULTY: 22 full-time   **AVERAGE CLASS SIZE:** 13
MISSION STATEMENT: (Excerpted) Founded in 1959, Grace Episcopal School is charged by the Vestry of Grace Episcopal Church to provide a Christ-centered environment where children can obtain an excellent, developmentally appropriate educational foundation. Further, the School shall instill in its students a sense of responsible service to humankind, foster the development of spiritual and moral values, and integrate the teaching of religious principles throughout its programs. The Vestry encourages a diverse student body and staff representative of the community.

SPECIAL COURSES: Accreditation- VAIS; NAEYC. Phonics-based language program beginning in Nursery. Strong individualized academic program (Sr.K–grade 5) with studio art, Orff music program, computer, library, religion and P.E. Developmental Preschool program. Small instructional groups. Low pupil/teacher ratio (7/1).
EXTENDED DAY: 7:30 a.m.–6:00 p.m.
ATHLETICS: P.E. 3 times a week   **CLUBS:** Chorus
PUBLICATIONS: Monthly newsletter, weekly bulletins, yearbook, web page
COMMUNITY INVOLVEMENT: Outreach activities and community service projects
PLANT: Library 5,000+ volumes, auditorium/gym (shared), multipurpose rooms, new playground, athletic field, basketball, semi-wooded area for nature study
ADMISSION: Feb. 1 application deadline, $50 application fee. Testing: Jr.K and Sr.K- WPPSI; grades 1–5 WISC III.
TUITION: $5,440 N, Jr.K; $10,880 Sr.K–grade 5
FINANCIAL AID: Available
LUNCH: Sr.K–5 bring; N & Jr.K in extended care provided
OTHER FEES: Combines books and other fees: N–Jr.K $680; Sr.K $805; grades 1–5 $825
DRESS CODE: Yes, for grades 1–5

GRACE LUTHERAN SCHOOL   703-534-5517   FAX 703-534-1394
3233 Annandale Road, Falls Church, VA 22042
Lutheran 1973
HEAD: Robert Rebers
DIRECTOR OF ADMISSIONS: Robert Rebers
WEBSITE: www.gles.org   **E-MAIL:** grace@gles.vacoxmail.com
GRADES: K–grade 8   **ENROLLMENT:** 54 Co-ed
FACULTY: 3 full- and 2 part-time   **AVERAGE CLASS SIZE:** 12–15 multi-grade
MISSION STATEMENT: Our primary goal is to provide a Christian education for children to prepare them to be Christian citizens on earth and to live forever in heaven.
SPECIAL COURSES: Bible Studies, religion (required), Chapel once a month. Algebra, computer literacy, geography, general science, art, music, singing
EXTENDED DAY: 3:00–6:00 p.m.
ATHLETICS: P.E., sports on limited basis
CLUBS: Word Power, Geography Bee, Math-a-thon
PUBLICATIONS: Children's monthly newsletter
COMMUNITY INVOLVEMENT: Annual community festival, nursing home visits, sandwiches for the homeless
PLANT: 5-acre wooded campus, computer and science lab, playing field and playground
ADMISSION: Application, registration fee $120, parent/child interview, transcript, testing as necessary
TUITION: $4,100
BOOKS: $150   **LUNCH:** Bring; hot lunch offered twice a month
OTHER FEES: Activity fee $150, computer fee $30
TRANSPORTATION: Available on a limited basis $120 per month
DRESS CODE: Yes
SUMMER PROGRAMS: Vacation Bible School

GRACE LUTHERAN SCHOOL   301-932-0963   FAX 301-934-3435

1200 Charles Street, LaPlata, MD 20646
Lutheran Missouri Synod 1974
HEAD: Ruth Blackwell
WEBSITE: www.glcslaplata.org   **E-MAIL:** ruthblackwell@hotmail.com
GRADES: Nursery, Pre-K, K–grade 8   **ENROLLMENT:** 220 Co-ed
FACULTY: 14 full-and 10 part-time   **AVERAGE CLASS SIZE:** 20
EXTENDED DAY: Care available all day for preschool students, before (6:30–9:00 a.m.) and after (3:30–6:00 p.m.) for elementary students
CLUBS: Art club, sign language club, chorus, band, Mom & Me Book Club, Student Congress
ADMISSION: Parent and child visit, screening for all children entering Kindergarten–8th grade.
TUITION: $3,784
FINANCIAL AID: Available.
BOOKS: $100 N/$150 K–8
OTHER FEES: $50 non-refundable registration fee, $250 facilities fee (we just moved into a brand new school building in December 2002)
DRESS CODE: Neat and clean, all students K–8 required to purchase one school polo shirt
SUMMER PROGRAMS: Full-time summer daycare (6:30 a.m.–6:00 p.m.) and Summer Camp (one week each month for children age 3–12)

GRANITE BAPTIST CHURCH SCHOOL   410-761-1118   FAX 410-761-6983

7823 Oakwood Road, Glen Burnie, MD 21601
Baptist 1975
HEAD: Pastor William Townsend
WEBSITE: www.granitebaptistchurchschool.org
E-MAIL: gbcs@granitebaptist.org
GRADES: K4–grade 12   **ENROLLMENT:** 282 Co-ed
FACULTY: 3 full- and 20 part-time   **AVERAGE CLASS SIZE:** 25
MISSION STATEMENT: Granite Baptist Church School exists to glorify God through a Bible-centered educational ministry dedicated to assisting parents and the local Bible believing church in the task of training their children to reach their fullest potential, both academically and spiritually.
SPECIAL COURSES: We offer Bob Jones LINC (satellite courses) and Passport Learning (internet reading course)
EXTENDED DAY: 7:00 a.m.–5:30 p.m.
ATHLETICS: Volleyball, soccer, basketball, baseball and cheerleading
CLUBS: Individual instrument lessons
ADMISSION: Call the school for an enrollment packet
TUITION: $2,384–$3,554
BOOKS: $100–$175
LUNCH: Menu options daily
OTHER FEES: Discounts for referrals, Pastor's families, and multiple children. Other small fees apply (i.e., choir, art, sports, graduation, etc.)
DRESS CODE: Girls: knee-length dresses/skirts, no worldly expressions. Boys: jeans/slacks, belts, no t-shirts
SUMMER PROGRAMS: Tutoring

GREEN ACRES SCHOOL   301-881-4100   FAX 301-881-3319
11701 Danville Drive, Rockville, MD 20852
Founded 1934
HEAD: Louis Silvano
DIRECTOR OF ADMISSIONS: Marge Dimond
WEBSITE: www.greenacres.org   **E-MAIL:** info@greenacres.org
GRADES: Pre-K–grade 8   **ENROLLMENT:** 320 Co-ed (157 boys/163 girls)
FACULTY: 41 full- and 12 part-time   **AVERAGE CLASS SIZE:** 12
MISSION STATEMENT: Green Acres is a coeducational, progressive school for grades Pre-Kindergarten through eight, dedicated to fostering the natural curiosity of students, engaging them actively in the joy of learning, and facilitating problem solving. Based on an understanding of child development, the Green Acres program is cognitively, physically, and creatively challenging. Valuing acceptance of a variety of viewpoints, this community promotes socio-economic and cultural diversity. An environment of trust, cooperation, and mutual respect encourages students to become increasingly independent thinkers and responsible contributors to an ever-changing, multicultural world.
SPECIAL COURSES: A strong academic program, including courses in language arts, mathematics, social studies and science for all grade levels. Additional courses offered include fine arts (photography, music, drama, ceramics, creative movement, studio art), Spanish, algebra, computers, Family Life Education, advisory, library, outdoor education, P.E., and research and study skills. Progressive philosophy with child-centered approach.
EXTENDED DAY: 3:00–6:00 p.m.
ATHLETICS: After school sports program (soccer, basketball, softball, lacrosse)
CLUBS: After school enrichment program   **PUBLICATIONS:** Yearbook
COMMUNITY INVOLVEMENT: Forty hours of community service for grades 7 and 8. Other grades participate in community service projects of various sorts.
PLANT: Fifteen wooded acres with stream and amphitheater, main building, additional outlying classroom buildings, computer labs, art studio, photo lab, performing arts center/gymnasium, music studio, library (20,000 volumes), athletic field, playgrounds
ADMISSION: Parent tour/interview and student visit. Child must be age 4 by June 1 for Pre-K and age 5 by June 1 for Kindergarten. Applications due by January 15th.
TUITION: $18,390
FINANCIAL AID: Available
BOOKS: $60 grade 4; $750 5–8   **LUNCH:** Children bring own
OTHER FEES: Activity fee $45
TRANSPORTATION: Available. $780–$2,440 depending on type of service.
SUMMER PROGRAMS: Six week summer camp program
FUTURE PLANS: Completion of final phase of classroom building project

GREEN HEDGES SCHOOL   703-938-8323   FAX 703-938-1485
415 Windover Avenue, Vienna, VA 22180
Founded 1942
HEAD: Frederick Williams
DIRECTOR OF ADMISSIONS: Leslie Dixon
WEBSITE: www.GreenHedgesSchool.org   **E-MAIL:** ldixon@greenhedges.org

GRADES: Nursery–grade 8 **ENROLLMENT:** 190 Co-ed (88 boys/102 girls)
FACULTY: 28 full- and 3 part-time **AVERAGE CLASS SIZE:** 16–22 11:1 ratio
MISSION STATEMENT: Green Hedges School is committed to providing a classical education to a socially and culturally diverse group of children. Believing that happy, relaxed students learn best, we provide a safe, intimate environment and caring teachers. We inspire each child to master academic skills, to develop clear values, to experience joy, and to appreciate all human endeavors which broaden the mind and enlighten the spirit.
SPECIAL COURSES: French NK–8, Latin 5–8, Spanish 5–8, technology 1–8, drama, art, music, P.E. Individualized reading and phonics. Montessori preschool program for ages 3–5 years.
EXTENDED DAY: Until 6:00 p.m.
ATHLETICS: After school sports **CLUBS:** After school clubs
PUBLICATIONS: Yearbook, monthly newsletter for school community
PLANT: 3.5 acres, 4 buildings, library 14,000 volumes, science lab, computer lab, TVS and VCRs in each classroom, wired for Internet, fine arts building for music and art, playgrounds and playing fields
TUITION: $15,100 K–8 Includes books; $8,900 N half day
FINANCIAL AID: Available
LUNCH: Sack lunch
OTHER FEES: Activity fee for books, field trips and supplies $50 N $200 K–8
DRESS CODE: Uniform for special occasions
SUMMER PROGRAMS: Summer Camp grades 1–5

GUNSTON DAY SCHOOL   410-758-0620   FAX 410-758-0628
P.O. Box 200, Centreville, MD 21617
Founded 1911
HEAD: Jeffrey C. Woodworth
WEBSITE: www.gunstondayschool.org
GRADES: 9–12 **ENROLLMENT:** 130 Co-ed
FACULTY: 30 **AVERAGE CLASS SIZE:** 12
SPECIAL COURSES: College preparatory and Chesapeake Bay Studies.
TUITION: $15,800
FINANCIAL AID: Available
DRESS CODE: Yes
SUMMER PROGRAMS: Call for information.

THE GW COMMUNITY SCHOOL   703-978-7208
9001 Braddock Road Suite 111, Springfield, VA 22151
Founded 1999
HEAD: Alexa Warden
WEBSITE: www.gwcommunityschool.com
E-MAIL: info@gwcommunityschool.com
GRADES: 9–12 **ENROLLMENT:** 58 Co-ed   **AVERAGE CLASS SIZE:** 6
MISSION STATEMENT: The GW Community School mixes the best possible teachers with the most advanced technology and the most sophisticated educational philosophy to create a truly unique learning experience. Attitudes soar, grades improve, dreams are realized, lives are saved. There is not another school like this, anywhere. The future is under construction!

SPECIAL COURSES: AP courses, standard and advanced diplomas. College preparatory curriculum. Small class sizes allow for individual attention.
COMMUNITY INVOLVEMENT: 30 hours of community service per year. Cook meals for Ronald McDonald House, Write to Read program, therapeutic riding
PLANT: School has wireless network. Students use laptops.
ADMISSION: Call for information.
TUITION: $16,900
LUNCH: Bring   **TRANSPORTATION:** Carpools
SUMMER PROGRAMS: Writing workshops

—H

THE HARBOR SCHOOL   301-365-1100   FAX 301-365-7491
7701 Bradley Boulevard, Bethesda, MD 20817
Founded 1973
HEAD: Linda Perry
DIRECTOR OF ADMISSIONS: Marti Jacobs
WEBSITE: www.theharborschool.org   **E-MAIL:** harborsL72@aol.com
GRADES: Preschool–grade 2   **ENROLLMENT:** 100 Co-ed
FACULTY: 12 full- and 10 part-time   **AVERAGE CLASS SIZE:** 14
MISSION STATEMENT: The Harbor School prepares children for life's journey while fostering the child's continuing love of learning while respecting the uniqueness of each individual.
SPECIAL COURSES: Computer, library, art, music, movement, science, story-teller, dance, P.E. Preschool 9:00–12:00 M–Th. Full day option 9:00–3:00 M–Th. Junior K–2 8:45–3:00 M–Th; 8:45–12:00 F
EXTENDED DAY: Early morning drop-off Preschool–2 8:00 a.m. Extended day Junior K–2 M–Th 3:00–5:30 p.m. After school enrichment for ages 5 and over.
PLANT: Gym, playground, library, art/science room
ADMISSION: Call for information. Parent visits and then receives application. Open House. Visit with Director. Application fee $50.
TUITION: $6,840 Preschool; $13,213; Junior K–grade 2
FINANCIAL AID: Available
SUMMER PROGRAMS: For 3 to 5 year olds

HARBOUR SCHOOL   410-974-4248   FAX 410-757-3722
1277 Green Holly Drive, Annapolis, MD 21401
Founded 1982
HEAD: Dr. Linda J. Jacobs
DIRECTOR OF ADMISSIONS: Yvonne Callaway
WEBSITE: www.harbourschool.org   **E-MAIL:** ljacobs@harbourschool.org
GRADES: 1–12   **ENROLLMENT:** 147 Co-ed (94 boys/53 girls)
FACULTY: 83 full- and 7 part-time
AVERAGE CLASS SIZE: 7 1:4 teacher/pupil ratio
MISSION STATEMENT: Our mission is to provide a supportive, caring and individualized education to learning disabled and multi-disabled children. The program is tailored to meet the individual needs of the child rather than asking the child to adapt to an existing program. The child's learning style dictates our program. It is our mission to assist each child to attain a feeling of academic and personal achievement and success commensurate with the child's abilities.

Personal achievement includes success in social and vocational skills.

SPECIAL COURSES: Algebra, computer, general science, biology, chemistry, physics, American history, government, world history, economics, art, drama, remedial reading and math. A wide variety of individual abilities is served in our individualized program, from cognitively delayed to gifted. In each case, the child's strengths are emphasized while needs are addressed.

ATHLETICS: Not required. Basketball, volleyball, softball

CLUBS: Drama, computer, crafts, Student Council

PUBLICATIONS: Yearbook, newspaper

COMMUNITY INVOLVEMENT: Seniors complete community service project.

PLANT: Library 5,000 volumes, career center with extensive technology

ADMISSION: Application fee, submit all previous test records, interview and school visit for half day. Student should have some type of learning problem.

TUITION: Call for information.

FINANCIAL AID: Partial   **DRESS CODE:** Yes

SUMMER PROGRAMS: Tutoring and recreation

HEBREW DAY INSTITUTE   301-649-5808   FAX 301-649-5701
1840 University Boulevard West, Silver Spring, MD 20902
Jewish 1973
HEAD: Rabbi Moshe Isaacs
DIRECTOR OF ADMISSIONS: Elie Zarem
WEBSITE: www.hdionline.org   **E-MAIL:** hdischool@aol.com
GRADES: K–grade 6   **ENROLLMENT:** 79 Co-ed (43 boys/36 girls)
FACULTY: 7 full- and 8 part-time   **AVERAGE CLASS SIZE:** 10–15
MISSION STATEMENT: The Hebrew Day Institute is a community Jewish day school dedicated to providing quality education which integrates traditional Judaic studies and a secular curriculum in a nurturing and enriching environment. Small class size and a family atmosphere provide ample opportunity for attention to individual student needs and for the development of independent learning and critical thinking skills.
SPECIAL COURSES: Dual curriculum- secular and Judaic/Hebrew studies. Art, music, math and science enrichment
EXTENDED DAY: 3:15–6:15 p.m. except Fridays in winter, when day ends earlier
ATHLETICS: P.E., roller hockey, basketball, Tae Kwon Do, movement
CLUBS: Torah club
PLANT: Library and media center, computer lab, auditorium, eight classrooms, playground
ADMISSION: Interview with Educational Specialist
TUITION: $9,075 K–1 $10,150 2–6
FINANCIAL AID: Available
BOOKS: $200   **LUNCH:** $4.50   **TRANSPORTATION:** Available
FUTURE PLANS: HDI is adding a seventh and an eighth grade in 2004 and 2005 respectively.

HEBREW DAY SCHOOL OF MONTGOMERY COUNTY
301-649-5400   FAX 301-649-1274
1401 Arcola Avenue, Silver Spring, MD 20902
Jewish

HEAD: Rabbi Jeffrey Aftel
E-MAIL: hdsmc.office@verizon.net
GRADES: Kindergarten–grade 6 **ENROLLMENT:** 100 Co-ed
FACULTY: 6 full- and 8 part-time
MISSION STATEMENT: Hebrew Day School of Montgomery County is an Orthodox K–6 community day school located in the Kemp Mill neighborhood of Silver Spring, Maryland. HDS focuses on the needs of the whole child and the child's individual learning style. We provide a nurturing environment in which graduates are prepared for the most rigorous academic programs in both Judaic and secular studies. Our strong academic program, emphasis on Derech Eretz, character development, and the teaching of Jewish values, combined with a love for Am Yisrael (the people of Israel) and Medinat Yisrael (the state of Israel), encourage creative and critical thinking skills in every student. Teachers, administrators, parents and students work together to put Torah values and Derech Eretz into daily practice.
SPECIAL COURSES: Hebrew. Religious studies required. Full curriculum of Judaic Studies. Remedial math and reading. Art, music, choir, drama. Individualized instruction in all areas- child progresses at own rate.
EXTENDED DAY: 3:45–6:00 p.m. (M–Th)
TUITION: Call for information.
FINANCIAL AID: Available

THE HEIGHTS SCHOOL   301-365-4300   FAX 301-365-4303
10400 Seven Locks Road, Potomac, MD 20854
Catholic 1969
HEAD: Alvaro de Vicente
WEBSITE: www.heights.edu
GRADES: 3–12 **ENROLLMENT:** 420 boys
FACULTY: 50 full- and 5 part-time
AVERAGE CLASS SIZE: 18
SPECIAL COURSES: 18 AP courses, honors classes, college advisory
EXTENDED DAY: 8:20 a.m.–3:00 p.m.
ATHLETICS: Basketball, baseball, lacrosse, soccer, tennis, golf, track, squash and swimming
CLUBS: Chess club, debate team, mountaineers club, 2 a capella groups, 3 bands
PUBLICATIONS: The Heights Herald (newspaper), Cavalier (yearbook)
PLANT: 5 classroom buildings, 2 playing fields, gym, outdoor courts, library and assembly room
ADMISSION: Application and interview deadline January 31st.
TUITION: $10,250 lower school; $11,800 middle school; $12,800 high school
FINANCIAL AID: Available
BOOKS: $150–$250
OTHER FEES: Graduation fee $50, activities fee
TRANSPORTATION: Available
DRESS CODE: Grades 3–7 dress shirts, ties, slacks, sweaters. Grades 8–12 jackets, ties, slacks.
SUMMER PROGRAMS: Summer Math Program, basketball camp, soccer camp, Civil War and Leadership Camp, natural history camp, science camp, baseball camp, study skills seminar, history travel seminars

HENSON VALLEY MONTESSORI SCHOOL
301-449-4442   FAX 301-449-6695
7007 Allentown Road, Temple Hills, MD 20748
Founded 1965
HEAD: Valaida Wise
WEBSITE: www.hvms.org   **E-MAIL:** vwise@hvms.org
GRADES: Ungraded ages 3–14   **ENROLLMENT:** 214 Co-ed
FACULTY: 11 full- and 7 part-time
MISSION STATEMENT: To foster the healthy growth and development of the whole child by providing a high-quality Montessori program in partnership with a community committed to excellence in education.
SPECIAL COURSES: Montessori primary, elementary and middle school programs. Computers in all classes. Spanish all ages. Art, music, P.E. Comprehensive integrated program in math, science. LD specialist on staff. OWL Program (global learning)
EXTENDED DAY: 7:00–8:45 a.m and 3:00–6:00 p.m.
ATHLETICS: Tae Kwon Do
CLUBS: Chorus, chess, Girl Scouts, Daisies, dance, Step
PLANT: Currently on 3.8 acres of land. Building and facilities are built for a Montessori school.
ADMISSION: Rolling admissions
TUITION: $8,855 primary and elementary; $11,055 middle school
FINANCIAL AID: Available after one year
LUNCH: Catered lunches can be bought or bring own.
DRESS CODE: Neat attire
SUMMER PROGRAMS: Summer in the Valley is our traditional day camp.
FUTURE PLANS: Expanding the facility to larger acreage in 2005

HERITAGE ACADEMY CHRISTIAN SCHOOL
301-582-2600   FAX 301-582-2603
12215 Walnut Point West, Hagerstown, MD 21740
Founded 1965
HEAD: Harold Miles
GRADES: K4–grade 12   **ENROLLMENT:** 245 Co-ed
AVERAGE CLASS SIZE: 15:1 ratio
SPECIAL COURSES: Spanish 9–10, science through physics, computer science. Math includes advanced math, calculus, and business math. Typing, music, art, journalism
EXTENDED DAY: After care until 5:35 p.m.
TUITION: $3,685 Reduction for siblings.
FINANCIAL AID: Some available
BOOKS: Extra   **LUNCH:** Cafeteria   **DRESS CODE:** Uniform required

THE HIGH ROAD SCHOOL OF NORTHERN VIRGINIA
703-961-1567   FAX 703-961-1570
14102 Sullyfield Circle, Suite 350, Chantilly, VA 20151
Founded 2001
HEAD: Jane M. Fowler, M.A.
DIRECTOR OF ADMISSIONS: Jane M. Fowler, M.A.

WEBSITE: www.kids1inc.com   E-MAIL: jfowler@kids1inc.com
GRADES: 2–12   ENROLLMENT: 28 Co-ed (25 boys/3 girls)
FACULTY: 11 full- and 1 part-time   AVERAGE CLASS SIZE: 7–9
MISSION STATEMENT: The High Road School of Northern Virginia is committed to impacting the most challenging student populations, especially those who have never experienced success or confidence in the traditional school system. "Building Confidence and Competence through Personalized Academic Interventions."
SPECIAL COURSES: All curriculum meets the current Virginia Standards as well as those of the referring school districts. In addition, we offer Life Skills Curriculum, Transitional Services, and online academic courses as a supplement to a student's academics, as well as offering secondary courses for credit. Our curriculum is geared to students impacted by both emotional disabilities, as well as learning disabilities. All related services are provided as deemed by each student's IEP.
CLUBS: Book club and drama club beginning
PLANT: 4,100 square feet. Five classrooms, library, main kitchen, transitional work area, related services offices, and conference room space
ADMISSION: Students are referred for possible admission by their LEA, each referral is reviewed by the admissions team and an interview with parent and student is scheduled. Admission is based on the outcome of the records review, interview and the appropriate needs of the particular student.
TUITION: All tuition and associated school costs are paid for by the referring school district(s). Private pay is not available.
BOOKS: Provided   LUNCH: Student provided
TRANSPORTATION: LEA provided
DRESS CODE: Appropriate school wear following the current FCPS dress code.
SUMMER PROGRAMS: Extended school year (ESY) is available on a student to student IEP team decision.
FUTURE PLANS: Possible expansion as population grows

HIGHLAND SCHOOL   540-347-1221   FAX 540-347-5860
597 Broadview Avenue, Warrenton, VA 20186
Founded 1928
HEAD: David P. Plank
WEBSITE: www.highlandschool.org   E-MAIL: admin@highlandschool.org
GRADES: Pre-Kindergarten–grade 12   ENROLLMENT: 460 Co-ed
FACULTY: 75 full- and 2 part-time   AVERAGE CLASS SIZE: 18
MISSION STATEMENT: To provide a demanding academic program to develop the skills and character essential for its students to meet the challenges of college and leadership in the twenty-first century.
SPECIAL COURSES: 11 AP offerings (upper school), summer programs, marine biology, 6 Honors courses, Greek 1–4, SAT Prep, journalism, photography, speech and debate, world diplomacy, and human biology
EXTENDED DAY: 1:00–5 :45 p.m.
ATHLETICS: Intramural/interscholastic. Soccer, field hockey, lacrosse, cross-country, golf, tennis, swimming, volleyball, cheerleading and dance
CLUBS: Field trips   PUBLICATIONS: Yearbook, student newspaper
COMMUNITY INVOLVEMENT: Community service required

PLANT: 35 acres, 2 libraries, 2 science labs (Pre-K to 8), 3 science labs (9–12), air-conditioned classrooms, Internet/network, music and art studios. New Center for the Arts
ADMISSION: Application, fee, parent and student questionnaires, recommendation forms, visit/interview, test scores, grades
TUITION: $5,550–$12,300
FINANCIAL AID: Available
BOOKS: Included   **LUNCH:** Available- extra fees
OTHER FEES: Transportation, extended day
TRANSPORTATION: Available. Fees range from $475–$1,050
DRESS CODE: All grades have a dress code
SUMMER PROGRAMS: Available

HILL SCHOOL   540-687-5897   FAX 540-687-3132
130 South Madison Street (P.O. Box 65), Middleburg, VA 20118
Founded 1926
HEAD: Thomas Northrup
GRADES: Kindergarten–grade 8   **ENROLLMENT:** 225 Co-ed
FACULTY: 35 full- and 12 part-time   **AVERAGE CLASS SIZE:** 12
SPECIAL COURSES: Latin 7–8, algebra 8, computer 1–8, general science 1–8, art, drama, music K–8
ATHLETICS: Required. Intramural K–8. Interscholastic 4–8. Soccer, girls' field hockey, basketball, gymnastics, lacrosse, track and field
CLUBS: Outing club, camping, hiking, skiing
PUBLICATIONS: Yearbook, literary magazines
PLANT: Library 12,000 volumes, science lab, art studio, gym, playing fields, auditorium, 50 computers, outdoor science center, the Peard Music Lunchroom
ADMISSION: Interview, achievement testing, $25 fee
TUITION: $11,000 K; $14,600 1–8
FINANCIAL AID: Available
DRESS CODE: No blue jeans, T shirts or sweatshirts

HOLTON-ARMS SCHOOL   301-365-5300   FAX 301-365-6071
7303 River Road, Bethesda, MD 20817
Founded 1901
HEAD: Diana Coulton Beebe
DIRECTOR OF ADMISSIONS: Sharron Rodgers
WEBSITE: www.holton-arms.edu   **E-MAIL:** admit@holton-arms.edu
GRADES: 3–grade 12   **ENROLLMENT:** 650 girls
FACULTY: 73 full- and 12 part-time   **AVERAGE CLASS SIZE:** 15
MISSION STATEMENT: In the words of its founder, the Holton-Arms School is dedicated "to the education not only of the mind, but of the soul and spirit." Our goals are to build the confidence, integrity, and love of learning that will prepare young women for a changing world and to endow each with a profound sense of respect and responsibility for herself and the community. An accomplished and committed faculty encourages girls from diverse backgrounds to cultivate that which is unique in each of them. Rigorous programs in academics, the arts, and athletics, and significant opportunities for leadership allow students to develop their full potential.

SPECIAL COURSES: Latin and French 7–12, Spanish- lower school through 12. Math: through calculus and computer, statistics, discrete math. Science: general science, biology, chemistry, physics, botany, environmental, earth science. History and Social Science: western civilization, history of U.S. and Europe, Asian history, anthropology, western philosophy, contemporary history, geography, government and economics, art, art history, art and music. AP: English, U.S. history, biology, calculus, computer science, French literature, Spanish, Latin.

EXTENDED DAY: 4:00–6:00 p.m.

ATHLETICS: Required. Intramural and interscholastic. Crew team, field hockey, soccer, tennis, softball, track, volleyball, cross-country, basketball, swimming, lacrosse

CLUBS: Amnesty International, Boosters, community service, cultural awareness, debate, environmental awareness, Model U.N., peer counseling, "It's Academic", drama, chorus, swing choir, orchestra

PUBLICATIONS: Literary, newspaper, yearbook

COMMUNITY INVOLVEMENT: Long tradition of service by graduation requirement for 50 hours of voluntary service during one 12 month period of four years of high school.

PLANT: Library: upper school 22,000 volumes; lower school 6,000 volumes. Language lab, 2 computer centers, science labs, 3 art studios, 2 gyms, playing fields, tennis courts, dance studio, swimming pool, track, theater, amphitheater, black box theater, lecture hall

ADMISSION: ISEE or SSAT required 7–12. Individual aptitude and achievement testing 3–6; tour and interview. Application fee $60. January 15 deadline.

TUITION: $20,220

FINANCIAL AID: Available

BOOKS: $500   **LUNCH:** Included in tuition

TRANSPORTATION: Limited availability   **DRESS CODE:** Uniform required

SUMMER PROGRAMS: Creative Summer- programs for boys and girls ages 7–14: Art, music, dance, drama, tennis, swimming, computer, science. Creative Sixes: day program for age 6. Creative Morning: half day program for ages 4–6.

HOLY ANGELS–SACRED HEART   301-769-3389   FAX 301-769-4948

21335 Colton Point Road, Avenue, MD 20609
Catholic
HEAD: Dr. Carol Weber
E-MAIL: holyangelssacredheartschool@erols.com
GRADES: Preschool–grade 8   **ENROLLMENT:** Co-ed
TUITION: $2,200 one child in parish; $2,600 one child out of parish
DRESS CODE: Uniforms

HOLY COMFORTER–ST. CYPRIAN SCHOOL

202-547-7556   FAX 202-547-5686
1503 East Capitol Street, S.E., Washington, DC 20003
Catholic Schools merged 1965
HEAD: Valerie L. Swain
GRADES: Pre-K–grade 8   **ENROLLMENT:** 225 Co-ed
AVERAGE CLASS SIZE: 20
SPECIAL COURSES: Saxon Math, Open Court Reading, basic science, language

arts, computer classes, music, art and P.E.

EXTENDED DAY: 7:00–7:45 a.m. and 3:00–6:00 for grades PK–6

ADMISSION: Application fee $50 April 1–June 30; $75 July 1–September. Registration form, last standardized test scores, last report cards, updated medical records, grade assessment test

TUITION: $3,100 one child $4,875 two children; $6,100 three children; $7,050 four or more children; Fees are broken down into 10 month payments July–April.

FINANCIAL AID: Available. Inquire at school office.

BOOKS: $200   **LUNCH:** $2.75/day PK–4, $3.00/day 5–8

DRESS CODE: Uniforms for all students PK–8. Campus Outfitters in College Park, Maryland are the school's uniform distributors.

HOLY CROSS ACADEMY   540-286-1600   FAX 540-286-1625

250 Stafford Lakes Parkway, Fredericksburg, VA 22406
Catholic 1998
HEAD: Sister Susan Louise Eder, OSFS
DIRECTOR OF ADMISSIONS: Sister Susan Louise Eder, OSFS
WEBSITE: www.rc.net/arlington/hca   **E-MAIL:** holycrossacademy@erols.com
GRADES: Preschool–grade 8   **ENROLLMENT:** 506 Co-ed (244 boys/262 girls)
FACULTY: 21 full- and 4 part-time   **AVERAGE CLASS SIZE:** 30
MISSION STATEMENT: At Holy Cross Academy, we are guided by the spirit of Saint Francis de Sales as we dedicate ourselves to: Develop the whole child: spiritually, emotionally, academically and physically; Promote academic excellence by challenging all our students to recognize their gifts and fulfill their God-given potential.
SPECIAL COURSES: Spanish: enrichment in grades 1–5; classes for credit in grades 6–8. Reading Resource Program, algebra I
EXTENDED DAY: 7:00–8:00 a.m. and 3:00–6:00 p.m.
ATHLETICS: Basketball, field hockey, soccer, running club
CLUBS: Cub Scouts, Brownies, Student Council, Odyssey of the Mind, Junior Master Gardeners, band & strings
COMMUNITY INVOLVEMENT: Young Catholics for Change service group
PLANT: New building (1998) in a lovely, wooded setting. Library, computer lab, science lab, gymnasium and cafeteria, playground, softball field, soccer field
ADMISSION: Applications accepted at any time. Priority of admission: siblings of current students, St. Mary parishioners, Catholics, non-Catholics
TUITION: $3,400
FINANCIAL AID: Available
LUNCH: $2.00 a day   **DRESS CODE:** Uniforms
SUMMER PROGRAMS: Art enrichment; basketball camp
FUTURE PLANS: Expand according to need

HOLY CROSS ELEMENTARY   301-949-1699   FAX 301-949-5074

4900 Strathmore Avenue, Garrett Park, MD 20896
Catholic
HEAD: Sister Sharon Ann Mihm, CSC
WEBSITE: www.hcross.org   **E-MAIL:** smihm@hcross.org
GRADES: Pre-K–grade 8   **ENROLLMENT:** Co-ed
EXTENDED DAY: Before and after care
TUITION: $6,250 Pre-K; $4,000 Pre-K 1/2 day; $5,100 elementary

HOLY FAMILY CATHOLIC SCHOOL   703-670-8161   FAX 703-670-8323
14160 Ferndale Road, Dale City, VA 22193
Catholic 1989
HEAD: Barbara Mertens
GRADES: Preschool–grade 7   **ENROLLMENT:** 250 Co-ed
FACULTY: 15 full- and 15 part-time   **AVERAGE CLASS SIZE:** 29
MISSION STATEMENT: To provide a Christ-centered learning environment dedicated to building a vital Faith Community where each person is valued as a unique child of God.
SPECIAL COURSES: Great Books
EXTENDED DAY: 3:00–6:30 p.m.
ATHLETICS: NVJCYO- track and basketball
CLUBS: Girl Scouts, safety patrol, science fair, choir
PUBLICATIONS: Yearbook
PLANT: Two-level school attached to a Catholic Church, library, computer lab, art room, music room, gymnasium
ADMISSION: Complete and submit registration application and fee
TUITION: Call for information.
FINANCIAL AID: Available. Applications are accepted through the Archdiocese of Arlington.
OTHER FEES: Book fee and technology fee in the Spring
DRESS CODE: Uniform required
FUTURE PLANS: Adding an 8th grade, playground and adding on to the building

HOLY FAMILY SCHOOL   301-894-2323   FAX 301-894-7100
2200 Callaway Street, Hillcrest Heights, MD 20748
Catholic 1957
HEAD: Mary A. Hawkins
E-MAIL: holy.fmly@erols.com
GRADES: Pre-Kindergarten–grade 8
ENROLLMENT: 290 Co-ed
FACULTY: 20 full- and 5 part-time   **AVERAGE CLASS SIZE:** 27
MISSION STATEMENT: Rooted in the love and faith of Jesus Christ, Holy Family Catholic School strives for academic excellence, racial dignity and respect for self, others and the world.
SPECIAL COURSES: Spanish Pre-Kindergarten–grade 8
EXTENDED DAY: 7:00 a.m.–6:00 p.m.
ATHLETICS: P.E.
CLUBS: Art, music, computer, library, Spanish, chess club
PLANT: Science lab, library, reference library, art/music room, gym, cafeteria, computer lab. Campus wired for Internet
ADMISSION: Application fee $50, testing, transcripts, interview
TUITION: $3,490 one child in parish
FINANCIAL AID: Available
LUNCH: $3.00 per lunch
DRESS CODE: Uniform required
SUMMER PROGRAMS: Available
FUTURE PLANS: Air-conditioning

HOLY NAME CATHOLIC SCHOOL   202-397-1614   FAX 202-398-4832
1217 West Virginia Avenue, N. E., Washington, DC 20002
Catholic
HEAD: Sister Patricia Ralph, SSJ
E-MAIL: ralphp@centercityconsortium.org
GRADES: Pre-K–grade 8   **ENROLLMENT:** 210 Co-ed
EXTENDED DAY: 7:00 a.m.–6:00 p.m.
TUITION: $3,100 one child in parish
DRESS CODE: Uniform
SUMMER PROGRAMS: Summer Camp

HOLY REDEEMER SCHOOL   301-474-3993   FAX 301-441-8137
49th Avenue and Berwyn Road, College Park, MD 20740
Catholic
HEAD: Gregory Jones
WEBSITE: www.holy-redeemer.org
E-MAIL: school@holy-redeemer.org
GRADES: Kindergarten–grade 8   **ENROLLMENT:** Co-ed
EXTENDED DAY: After care
TUITION: $3,146 one child in parish

HOLY REDEEMER SCHOOL   202-638-5789   FAX 202-628-0401
1135 New Jersey Avenue, N.W., Washington, DC 20001
Catholic
HEAD: Mildred Tyler
WEBSITE: www.holyredeemer.homestead.com
E-MAIL: mbef@msn.com
GRADES: Pre-K–grade 8
EXTENDED DAY: Before and after care
TUITION: $3,900 one child in parish
DRESS CODE: Uniforms

HOLY REDEEMER SCHOOL   301-942-3701   FAX 301-942-4981
9715 Summit Avenue, Kensington, MD 20895
Catholic
HEAD: Harriann Walker
E-MAIL: hrkofc@erols.com
GRADES: Nursery–grade 8   **ENROLLMENT:** Co-ed
EXTENDED DAY: Before and after care
TUITION: Call for information.

HOLY SPIRIT SCHOOL   703-978-7117   FAX 703-978-7438
8800 Braddock Road, Annandale, VA 22003
Catholic
HEAD: Deborah S. Mohney
GRADES: Pre-K–grade 8   **ENROLLMENT:** Co-ed
EXTENDED DAY: 3:30–6:30 p.m.
TUITION: Call for information.
DRESS CODE: Uniforms

HOLY TRINITY EPISCOPAL DAY SCHOOL

301-262-5355   FAX 301-262-9609
13106 Annapolis Road, Bowie, MD 20720
Episcopal 1963
HEAD: Margaret C. Reiber
DIRECTOR OF ADMISSIONS: Susanne Anderson
WEBSITE: www.htrinity.org
GRADES: 1–4 this campus
ENROLLMENT: 600 Co-ed
FACULTY: 45 full- and 6 part-time
AVERAGE CLASS SIZE: 20 maximum
MISSION STATEMENT: To provide a comprehensive educational foundation within a setting where self-confidence, moral development and an acceptance of personal differences among individuals in the school are fostered.
SPECIAL COURSES: French, Spanish, Latin, computer, art, music, sacred studies, outdoor education, band
EXTENDED DAY: 7:00 a.m.–6:00 p.m.
ATHLETICS: P.E. Intramural and interscholastic sports, cheerleading
CLUBS: Drama, chess club
PLANT: Two campuses–preschool/Kindergarten and grades 5–8 on Daisey Lane, and lower school grades 1–4 on Annapolis Road. Both campuses are fully equipped with computer labs, multipurpose rooms, libraries and playing fields.
ADMISSION: Rolling admission, application fee is $50, includes testing. Priority extended to parish members, siblings, faculty/staff.
TUITION: $6,200–$7,850
FINANCIAL AID: Available. Limited
BOOKS: Included
LUNCH: Available for a fee
DRESS CODE: Uniform
SUMMER PROGRAMS: Available K–8

HOLY TRINITY SCHOOL   202-337-2339   FAX 202-337-0368

1325 36th Street, N.W., Washington, DC 20007
Catholic
HEAD: Ann Marie Crowley
WEBSITE: www.htsdc.org
E-MAIL: acrowley@htsdc.org
GRADES: Nursery–grade 8
ENROLLMENT: 335 Co-ed
EXTENDED DAY: 7:40 a.m.–6:00 p.m.
TUITION: Call for information.
DRESS CODE: Uniforms

HOPE MONTESSORI SCHOOL   703-941-6836

4614 Ravensworth Road, Annandale, VA 22003
GRADES: Ungraded ages 3–7
ENROLLMENT: 80 Co-ed
TUITION: Call for information.

I

IMMACULATE CONCEPTION SCHOOL   202-234-1093   FAX 202-462-6875
711 N Street, N.W., Washington, DC 20001
Catholic
HEAD: Gillian Pratt
E-MAIL: prattg@centercityconsortium.org
GRADES: Pre-K–grade 5   **ENROLLMENT:** 130 Co-ed
FACULTY: 10 full-time   **AVERAGE CLASS SIZE:** 18
EXTENDED DAY: 7:00–8:00 a.m. and end of day–6:00 p.m.
TUITION: $3,000 one child
FINANCIAL AID: Available
OTHER FEES: All questions about finances to Ms. K. Burton 202-234-4611. Fundraising fee; service hours
DRESS CODE: Uniforms: winter, spring and P.E.
SUMMER PROGRAMS: In summer 2004, program will be added.
FUTURE PLANS: Grades to be added: 6th grade (2004–2005) 7th (2005–2006) 8th (2006–2007)

IMMANUEL CHRISTIAN SCHOOL   703-941-1220   FAX 703-813-1945
6915 Braddock Road, Springfield, VA 22151
Non-denominational 1976
HEAD: Stephen Danish
DIRECTOR OF ADMISSIONS: Diane Carnahan
WEBSITE: www.immanuelchristian.net   **E-MAIL:** info@immanuelchristian.net
GRADES: Pre-K–grade 8   **ENROLLMENT:** 470 Co-ed
FACULTY: 40 full- and 30 part-time   **AVERAGE CLASS SIZE:** PK–12; K–20; 1–8 25
MISSION STATEMENT: Our purpose is to assist Christian parents in providing a sound education for their children through the integration of faith and learning.
SPECIAL COURSES: Music, art, Spanish, P.E., technology, Bible and Chapel. Well-rounded academic program. Discovery Center services through National Institute of Learning Disabilities.
ATHLETICS: After-school sports for middle school
CLUBS: Band/Orchestra, Student Government. High parent involvement.
PUBLICATIONS: Yearbook for 8th grade
COMMUNITY INVOLVEMENT: Community service and outreach
PLANT: Gym, library 11,000 volumes, computer lab, science lab, playground
ADMISSION: Application, testing, parent interview, tours available, Open House in February.
TUITION: $1,080–$2005 PK; $2,440 K; $4,665 1–5; $4925 6–8
FINANCIAL AID: Available. Maximum 50%
DRESS CODE: Uniform required

IMMANUEL LUTHERAN SCHOOL   703-549-7323   FAX 703-549-7323
109 Belleaire Road, Alexandria, VA 22301
Lutheran 1945
HEAD: Margaret Zensinger
WEBSITE: www.ilsalex.org
GRADES: Kindergarten–grade 8   **ENROLLMENT:** 100 Co-ed
FACULTY: 5 full- and 1 part-time   **AVERAGE CLASS SIZE:** 15–20

SPECIAL COURSES: French, general science, art program. Religious studies required. Strong academic and religious programs
EXTENDED DAY: 7:00 a.m.–6:00 p.m.
CLUBS: Drama club, choir   **PLANT:** Computer lab
TUITION: Call for information. Reduction for siblings and church members
FINANCIAL AID: Some available
DRESS CODE: Uniform required
FUTURE PLANS: Summer programs

INDEPENDENT BAPTIST ACADEMY   301-856-1616   FAX 301-856-8234
9255 Piscataway Road (P.O. Box 206), Clinton, MD 20735
Independent Baptist 1972
HEAD: Frank Burton
WEBSITE: www.independentbaptist.ws   **E-MAIL:** ibc9255@erols.com
GRADES: K4–grade 12   **ENROLLMENT:** 300 Co-ed
SPECIAL COURSES: Spanish, French, math through algebra, physical science, world geography, literature, typing, religious studies, computer
EXTENDED DAY: 7:00 a.m.–6:00 p.m.
ADMISSION: K4–grade 5 open enrollment; grades 6–12 closed enrollment
TUITION: Call for information. Reduced rate for siblings

INDIAN CREEK SCHOOL   410-987-0342   FAX 410-923-3884
680 Evergreen Road, Crownsville, MD 21032
Founded 1973
HEAD: Anne Chambers
DIRECTOR OF ADMISSIONS: Elizabeth Barclay
WEBSITE: www.indiancreekschool.com
E-MAIL: icsadm@indiancreekschool.com
GRADES: Pre-K–grade 8   **ENROLLMENT:** 475 Co-ed
FACULTY: 52 full- and 4 part-time   **AVERAGE CLASS SIZE:** 12–15
MISSION STATEMENT: Academic Excellence in a Nurturing Environment.
SPECIAL COURSES: Spanish Pre-K–grade 8
EXTENDED DAY: 7:10 a.m.–6:00 p.m.
ATHLETICS: Intramural sports, clinics
CLUBS: Friday clubs, jazz band, winter musical, model airplane club, Shakespeare troupe
PUBLICATIONS: Yearbook, school newspaper
COMMUNITY INVOLVEMENT: "Make a Difference" Days
PLANT: 2 computer labs, cafeteria, gymnasium, auditorium, 3 art rooms, music practice rooms
ADMISSION: Applications accepted year round; first-come, first-served; January and spring testing
TUITION: $8,900–$13,240
FINANCIAL AID: Available
BOOKS: Middle school only   **LUNCH:** Hot lunch $2.75 each
OTHER FEES: Activity fee   **TRANSPORTATION:** Available $925 per year
DRESS CODE: Uniforms
SUMMER PROGRAMS: 6 weeks of summer camp (Pre-K–8)
FUTURE PLANS: High School planned for 2006

ISLAMIC SAUDI ACADEMY   703-780-0606   FAX 703-780-8639
8333 Richmond Highway, Alexandria, VA 22309
Islamic 1984
HEAD: Ibrahim Al-Gosair
WEBSITE: www.saudiacademy.net
GRADES: 2–12   **ENROLLMENT:** Co-ed
SPECIAL COURSES: Advanced academic program all grades. Arabic language, Islamic Studies Program required for graduation. Boys and girls have separate schools within one facility structure.
ATHLETICS: Sports
CLUBS: Model U.N., Student Government, activity period including yearbook, tutoring, chess, ping pong
TUITION: $2,500

ISLAMIC SAUDI ACADEMY   703-691-0000   FAX 703-691-0454
11121 Popes Head Road, Fairfax, VA 22309
Islamic
HEAD: Nancy Wallace
WEBSITE: www.saudiacademy.net
GRADES: Pre-K–grade 1   **ENROLLMENT:** Co-ed
SPECIAL COURSES: Arabic language, Islamic Studies Program. Grades continue in Alexandria campus.
TUITION: $5,000

IVYMOUNT SCHOOL   301-469-0223   FAX 301-469-0778
11614 Seven Locks Road, Rockville, MD 20854
Founded 1961
HEAD: Janet L. Wintrol
DIRECTOR OF ADMISSIONS: Stephanie deSibour
WEBSITE: www.ivymount.org   **E-MAIL:** sdesibour@ivymount.org
GRADES: Ungraded ages 4–21   **ENROLLMENT:** 230 Co-ed
FACULTY: 112 full-time   **AVERAGE CLASS SIZE:** 10
MISSION STATEMENT: (Excerpted) The Ivymount School seeks to provide the best possible educational and therapeutic services for children with disabilities. Ivymount especially seeks to serve those children whose needs are not being met in the community. By identifying, consolidating, and building upon each child's unique needs and potential, the school promotes development and growth.
SPECIAL COURSES: The Ivymount School is a non-profit, non-public, coeducational, special education program which serves students ages 4 through age 21, who may be identified as learning disabled, mentally retarded, multiply handicapped, other health impaired, speech or language impaired or autistic. Most of the students have multiple learning needs and require a program that includes and integrates academic/functional programming and intensive related services in classrooms with low student/teacher ratios. Contact school for detailed descriptions of the Basic Program Services and the Autism Program.
ADMISSION: Ivymount accepts student application packets from the following sources: local education agencies' Special Education Units, parents/guardians, educational advocates, attorneys. Applications are reviewed, generally within ten days of receipt, to determine appropriateness of Ivymount's program to meet the stu-

dent's needs. Contact school to learn what must be included in the referral packet.
TUITION: $35,461 for Basic Program (10 months) $52,752 for Autism Program (11 months)
SUMMER PROGRAMS: Extended School Year Services are provided for current students as designated on their IEP.

JEFFERSON SCHOOL
301-840-8448   FAX 301-840-1619
8507 Emory Grove Road, Gaithersburg, MD 20877
HEAD: Dona Allen
WEBSITE: www.thejeffersonschool.com   **E-MAIL:** thejeffersonschool@erols.com
GRADES: N–grade 5   **ENROLLMENT:** 250 Co-ed
FACULTY: 12 full- and 4 part-time   **AVERAGE CLASS SIZE:** 25
SPECIAL COURSES: Montessori Preschool (N, K). Elementary: Spanish, German, French, music, art
EXTENDED DAY: 7:15 a.m.–6:15 p.m.   **PLANT:** 4-acre site
ADMISSION: Rolling admission for N and K. Testing and half day visit for 1–4
TUITION: $5,250 N & K half day; $7,350 full day N & K; $8,000–$9,000 1–4

JERICHO CHRISTIAN ACADEMY   301-333-9400
8501 Jericho City Drive, Landover, MD 20785
WEBSITE: www.jerichocop.org
GRADES: Kindergarten age 5–grade 12
TUITION: Call for information.

JEWISH PRIMARY DAY SCHOOL OF THE NATION'S CAPITAL   202-291-5737
6045 16th Street, N.W., Washington, DC 20011
Jewish 1988
HEAD: Susan Koss
WEBSITE: www.jpds.org   **E-MAIL:** info@jpds.org
GRADES: Pre-K–grade 6   **ENROLLMENT:** 155 Co-ed
FACULTY: 22 full- and 7 part-time   **AVERAGE CLASS SIZE:** 14
SPECIAL COURSES: A developmentally based education with hands-on, experiential learning at all grade levels. Small classes give each child the attention necessary for academic excellence as well as emotional and social growth. Focus is on positive self image, social awareness and cultural identity, strong emphasis on ethical values and actions. Integrated curriculum combining General and Judaic studies reinforcing concepts and skills. Learner-centered teaching develops students' ability to reason, question and communicate at a very high level. Teacher's classroom activities reinforced by specialists in science, art, music, library and P.E. Hebrew as a modern spoken language as well as language of prayer. Students with Hebrew background have been successfully integrated into upper grades. School serves families with wide spectrum of religious practice and affiliation.
EXTENDED DAY: Provided on site. Monday–Thursday until 6:30 p.m. Friday until 6:00 p.m. Also available for special programs, school holidays and vacations.
ATHLETICS: P.E. twice weekly, basketball, gymnastics
CLUBS: Student Council in upper grades, French, art, ballet, drama, science, model rocketry, after school enrichment classes

PUBLICATIONS: Yearbook, newspaper
COMMUNITY INVOLVEMENT: Activities within both metropolitan D.C. and Jewish communities
PLANT: Science lab, two or more computers in each classroom, two libraries, auditorium, multipurpose rooms. Two outdoor play areas
ADMISSION: Applications accepted September–January (later if space permits.) Parents visit at Open Houses November–January. Application fee $50. Pre-K and Kindergarten child visits for a play session and developmental screening. Teacher recommendations. For grades 1–5, call for application requirements.
TUITION: $8,000 Pre-K; $11,850 other grades
FINANCIAL AID: Some available
OTHER FEES: Activities fee $250 Pre-K; $450 other grades

JOHN NEVINS ANDREWS SCHOOL   301-270-1400   FAX 301-270-1403
117 Elm Avenue, Takoma Park, MD 20912
Seventh-day Adventist 1907
HEAD: David L. Waller
WEBSITE: www.jna.org   E-MAIL: principal@jna.org
GRADES: Pre-Kindergarten–grade 8   ENROLLMENT: 300 Co-ed
FACULTY: 25 full- and 5 part-time   AVERAGE CLASS SIZE: 25–30
MISSION STATEMENT: (Excerpted) JNA is a Christ-centered Seventh-day Adventist school that cooperates with the home and church to provide a well-balanced learning experience where Christ and academic excellence are the emphasis.
SPECIAL COURSES: Learning Center, large computer lab, Bible
EXTENDED DAY: 6:30 a.m.–6:00 p.m.
ATHLETICS: Boys' and girls' basketball teams
CLUBS: English handbell choir, chime choir, treble choir, steel band, robots
PLANT: Library 10,000 volumes, gym, playing fields, hot lunch program
ADMISSION: Application, interview, transcripts, achievement/readiness tests required of all new students. Gesell testing for admission to K. Metropolitan testing for grade 1. WRAT testing for all new students. Additional testing may be given to identify children with learning problems.
TUITION: $2,830–$5,780
FINANCIAL AID: Some available
BOOKS: Included in registration fee   LUNCH: $40/10 meals
OTHER FEES: Registration $200
TRANSPORTATION: Available. $83–$272 per month
DRESS CODE: Uniforms required. No jewelry, no heavy make-up.
SUMMER PROGRAMS: Only in Development Center (Pre-K)
FUTURE PLANS: Continue to expand the integration level of technology with the curriculum

THE JULIA BROWN MONTESSORI SCHOOLS COLUMBIA   410-730-5056
9760 Owen Brown Road, Columbia, MD 21045
Founded 1967
HEAD: Julia Brown
WEBSITE: www.juliabrownmontessorischools.com   E-MAIL: ebkjbms@aol.com
GRADES: Pre-K–grade 3 ages 2 1/2- 9   AVERAGE CLASS SIZE: 25–27
MISSION STATEMENT: At the Julia Brown Montessori Schools, we work with

nature, not against it, in helping your child achieve their goal. Our program accepts the endless energies, the creative impulses, and insatiable curiosities of the children and gradually directs their efforts into rewarding channels.

SPECIAL COURSES: Foreign language or other extracurricular activity offered each year at no additional cost.

EXTENDED DAY: Before and after care 7:00 a.m.–6:00 p.m.

PLANT: Our buildings are a culmination of years of experience in the care and education of young children. Each location has beautiful classrooms and large playgrounds.

ADMISSION: Call Administrator for information packet, set up a tour, complete and sign application, submit yearly registration fee of $90

TUITION: Ranges from $362–$725 per month

LUNCH: Included   **OTHER FEES:** Yearly registration fee $90

SUMMER PROGRAMS: Yes

THE JULIA BROWN MONTESSORI SCHOOLS LAUREL   301-498-0604

9450 Madison Avenue, Laurel, MD 20723
Founded 1967
HEAD: Julia Brown
WEBSITE: www.juliabrownmontessorischools.com
E-MAIL: ebkjbms@aol.com
GRADES: Pre-K–grade 3 ages 2 1/2 - 9   **AVERAGE CLASS SIZE:** 25-27
MISSION STATEMENT: At the Julia Brown Montessori Schools, we work with nature, not against it, in helping your child achieve their goal. Our program accepts the endless energies, the creative impulses, and insatiable curiosities of the children and gradually directs their efforts into rewarding channels.

SPECIAL COURSES: Foreign language or other extracurricular activity offered each year at no additional cost.

EXTENDED DAY: Before and after care 7:00 a.m.–6:00 p.m.

PLANT: Our buildings are a culmination of 36 years of experience in the care and education of young children. Each location has beautiful classrooms and large playgrounds.

ADMISSION: Call Administrator for information packet, set up a tour, complete and sign application, submit yearly fee of $90

TUITION: Ranges from $333–$693 per month

LUNCH: Included   **OTHER FEES:** Yearly registration fee $90

SUMMER PROGRAMS: Yes

THE JULIA BROWN MONTESSORI SCHOOLS OLNEY   301-774-5700

3400 Queen Mary Drive, Olney, MD 20832
Founded 1967
HEAD: Julia Brown
WEBSITE: www.juliabrownmontessorischools.com   **E-MAIL:** ebkjbms@aol.com
GRADES: Pre-K–grade 3 ages 2 1/2- 9   **ENROLLMENT:** Co-ed
AVERAGE CLASS SIZE: 25–27
MISSION STATEMENT: At the Julia Brown Montessori Schools, we work with nature, not against it, in helping your child achieve their goal. Our program accepts the endless energies, the creative impulses, and insatiable curiosities of the children and gradually directs their efforts into rewarding channels.

SPECIAL COURSES: Foreign language or other extracurricular activity offered each year at no additional cost.

EXTENDED DAY: Before and after care 7:00 a.m.–6:00 p.m.

PLANT: Our buildings are a culmination of years of experience in the care and education of young children. Each location has beautiful classrooms and large playgrounds.

ADMISSION: Call Administrator for information packet, set up a tour, complete and sign application, submit yearly registration fee of $90

TUITION: Ranges from $352–$704 per month

LUNCH: Included   **OTHER FEES:** Yearly registration fee $90

SUMMER PROGRAMS: Yes

THE JULIA BROWN MONTESSORI SCHOOLS SILVER SPRING
301-622-7808
1300 Milestone Drive, Silver Spring, MD 20904
Founded 1967
HEAD: Julia Brown
WEBSITE: www.juliabrownmontessorischools.com   **E-MAIL:** ebkjbms@aol.com
GRADES: Pre-K–grade 3 ages 2 1/2–9   **ENROLLMENT:** Co-ed
AVERAGE CLASS SIZE: 25–27
MISSION STATEMENT: At the Julia Brown Montessori Schools, we work with nature, not against it, in helping your child achieve their goal. Our program accepts the endless energies, the creative impulses, and insatiable curiosities of the children and gradually directs their efforts into rewarding channels.

SPECIAL COURSES: Foreign language or other extracurricular activity offered each year at no additional cost.

EXTENDED DAY: Before and after care 7:00 a.m.–6:00 p.m.

PLANT: Our buildings are a culmination of years of experience in the care and education of young children. Each location has beautiful classrooms and large playgrounds.

ADMISSION: Call Administrator for information packet, set up a tour, complete and sign application, submit yearly registration fee of $90

TUITION: Ranges from $368–$756 per month

LUNCH: Included   **OTHER FEES:** Yearly registration fee $90

SUMMER PROGRAMS: Yes

KATHERINE G. THOMAS SCHOOL   301-424-5200   FAX 301-738-8897
9975 Medical Center Drive, Rockville, MD 20850
Founded 1995
HEAD: Theresa Petrungaro
WEBSITE: www.ttlc.org
GRADES: Pre-K–grade 8   **ENROLLMENT:** 100 Co-ed
FACULTY: 10 full-time   **AVERAGE CLASS SIZE:** 10
SPECIAL COURSES: 10 full-time special educators. Part-time art, P.E., science, music and drama teachers. Program for Preschool, elementary and middle school students of average or above average intellectual potential who have Learning and/or Language Disabilities. Speech/Language Therapy and Occupational Therapy are available on site and integrated with classroom learning. Curriculum

is implemented through the study of themes which revolve around social studies topics and integrate activities in language arts, math, science, art, music.
EXTENDED DAY: 8:15 a.m.–5:30 p.m.
ATHLETICS: P.E.
ADMISSION: Rolling admission. Applicants should apply as early as possible and submit psycho-educational and other test reports. Interview, school visit
TUITION: $19,368; $12,219 preschool
FINANCIAL AID: Tuition may be funded through a public school system, following due process procedures, if public school has no appropriate program for the child. AMS and TERI programs available for tuition assistance.
SUMMER PROGRAMS: Academic enrichment and therapeutic language camp programs for children ages 3–12 with language and learning disabilities.

KEMP HILL MONTESSORI   KEHILAT MONTESSORI   301-593-4343
120 Claybrook Drive, Silver Spring, MD 20902
HEAD: Karen Gejdensen
WEBSITE: www.kehilatmontessori.org
GRADES: Ages 2 1/2–12   **ENROLLMENT:** Co-ed
SPECIAL COURSES: Judaic and secular studies
EXTENDED DAY: After care
TUITION: Call for information.

KENWOOD SCHOOL   703-256-4711   FAX 703-256-0659
4955 Sunset Lane, Annandale, VA 22003
Founded 1957
HEAD: Alison Zoby
DIRECTOR OF ADMISSIONS: Alison Zoby
WEBSITE: www.kenwoodschool.com   **E-MAIL:** office@kenwoodschool.com
GRADES: Nursery (2 years)–grade 6   **ENROLLMENT:** 183 Co-ed
AVERAGE CLASS SIZE: 12
MISSION STATEMENT: All school experiences at Kenwood are challenging and exciting. Small classes provide opportunities for students to work at their highest potential. Individual progress is carefully guided to stimulate curiosity and creativity. Our strong academic environment fosters a solid foundation of skills and study habits necessary for future success. Each student's intellectual growth, personal self-discipline, social values and emotional maturity are the result of a school philosophy that emphasizes a joy and love of learning.
SPECIAL COURSES: Specialized instructors in Spanish, computers, music and P.E.
EXTENDED DAY: 7:00 a.m.–6:00 p.m. M–F
CLUBS: After school clubs
PUBLICATIONS: Newspaper
PLANT: Multi-building campus, gym, computer lab, large spacious play area
ADMISSION: $50 registration fee
TUITION: $670 per month (school day only)
BOOKS: Extra   **LUNCH:** Extra
OTHER FEES: Activity fee
DRESS CODE: Neat
SUMMER PROGRAMS: Summer Day Camp program available June–August completed Kindergarten–grade 8

KEY SCHOOL   410-263-9231   FAX 410-280-5516
534 Hillsmere Drive, Annapolis, MD 21403
Founded 1958
HEAD: Marcella M. Yedid
WEBSITE: www.keyschool.org
GRADES: Pre-K–grade 12   **ENROLLMENT:** 720 Co-ed
FACULTY: 88 full- and 19 part-time   **AVERAGE CLASS SIZE:** 16–18
SPECIAL COURSES: Curriculum includes extensive programs in music, art, modern and classical languages–French 1–12, Latin and Spanish 9–12. Electives in Non-Western literature, dance, estuarine biology and music theory. Interdisciplinary courses include Ancient Civilization and American Civilization. Extensive field trips including outdoor education are integral to the program. AP: French, Spanish, Latin, English composition and literature, calculus, biology, physics, American history and studio art
EXTENDED DAY: Until 5:30 p.m.
ATHLETICS: Required through grade 11. Middle and upper school participate in Varsity, JV and middle school levels in interscholastic sports (26 teams). Soccer, field hockey, basketball, tennis, sailing, lacrosse, golf and cross-country
CLUBS: Activities include theater, chorus, instrumental and jazz ensemble, debate, Model Congress
PUBLICATIONS: Yearbook, literary magazine
COMMUNITY INVOLVEMENT: School sponsors community service activities
PLANT: 15 acres with 16 buildings, 3 libraries, 6 science labs, 3 art studios, 4 playing fields, language labs, gym, auditorium, amphitheater, 3 computer labs
ADMISSION: Rolling admissions, $45 application fee, testing
TUITION: $8,600 Pre-K, K; $15,075 1–4; $15,970 5–8; $17,150 9–12
FINANCIAL AID: Available
LUNCH: Bring or buy   **TRANSPORTATION:** Available
SUMMER PROGRAMS: Pre-K–grade 5 day camp

KHADIJAH ACADEMY FOR GIRLS   703-824-0044
3431-C Carlin Springs Road Suite 200, Falls Church, VA 22041
Muslim
GRADES: 5–9   **ENROLLMENT:** Girls
TUITION: Call for information.

THE KING'S CHRISTIAN ACADEMY   301-862-4355   FAX 301-862-9081
46855 Shangri-la Drive Suite 200, Lexington Park, MD 20653
Founded 1980
HEAD: Sarah T. Patterson
DIRECTOR OF ADMISSIONS: Joey Brown
GRADES: Kindergarten–12   **ENROLLMENT:** 275 Co-ed (140 boys/135 girls)
FACULTY: 15 full- and 5 part-time   **AVERAGE CLASS SIZE:** 25
MISSION STATEMENT: The King's Christian Academy exists to help parents and churches educate their children in Truth and Righteousness with academic excellence based on a Biblical worldview for Christian character development.
SPECIAL COURSES: Advanced placement: trigonometry-calculus, physics, advanced biology, Spanish. Computer program- University of Richmond, Virginia
ATHLETICS: Soccer, basketball, track and field   **CLUBS:** Junior Achievement

PUBLICATIONS: "The Eagle" newsletter, "Seeds" poetry anthology
COMMUNITY INVOLVEMENT: Serv-a-thon
PLANT: A new facility is to be completed at Callaway, Maryland in the fall of 2004.
ADMISSION: Contact the Admissions Director for testing schedule.
TUITION: $4,552 first child; tuition credits for other siblings
FINANCIAL AID: Available. Write for further information.
BOOKS: Included
TRANSPORTATION: Available. Free in St. Mary's County, $680 per year in Calvert County
SUMMER PROGRAMS: Tutoring   **FUTURE PLANS:** Building program

KINGSBURY DAY SCHOOL   202-722-5555   FAX 202-722-5533
5000 14th Street, N.W., Washington, DC 20011
Founded 1938
HEAD: Marlene S. Gustafson
DIRECTOR OF ADMISSIONS: Karen Soltes
WEBSITE: www.Kingsbury.org   **E-MAIL:** admissions@kingsbury.org
GRADES: Ungraded ages 5–16   **ENROLLMENT:** 215 Co-ed
FACULTY: 65 full-time   **AVERAGE CLASS SIZE:** 8–10
SPECIAL COURSES: Originally founded in 1938 as Kingsbury Center. Social studies, science, art, music; academic skill development in reading, math; extensive use of computer technology in all subjects. School offers intensive intervention for students of average or above cognitive abilities with learning disabilities. Occupational therapy, speech/language therapy, and psychotherapy are available on site and integrated with classroom learning. The Kingsbury Center offers assessment and tutoring for all ages.
EXTENDED DAY: 3:00–6:00 p.m.   **ATHLETICS:** P.E., non-competitive games
CLUBS: Arts, music, clubs, chorus, after school enrichment classes
PUBLICATIONS: Literary publications
PLANT: Library, arts studio, music studio, 2 computer labs, computer and resource rooms for all classes, athletic field
ADMISSION: Comprehensive testing required. Child must visit school. The school seeks students with average or above average intelligence who have diagnosed learning disabilities and who would benefit from intervention. Parent tours throughout the fall. Application deadline in February. $75 fee
TUITION: $22,900–$25,700 plus fees
FINANCIAL AID: Limited financial aid available. Tuition funded by local school system, if approved
SUMMER PROGRAMS: Extended school year. Financial aid available
FUTURE PLANS: Will add 11th and 12th grades in 2004 and 2005

THE KISKI SCHOOL   877-547-5448   FAX 724-639-8596
1888 Brett Lane, Saltsburg, PA 15681
Founded 1888
HEAD: Christopher A. Brueningsen
DIRECTOR OF ADMISSIONS: Lawrence J. Jensen
WEBSITE: www.kiski.org   **E-MAIL:** admissions@kiski.org
GRADES: 9–12 and postgraduate   **ENROLLMENT:** 210 boys, all boarding
FACULTY: 29 full- and 10 part-time   **AVERAGE CLASS SIZE:** 8

MISSION STATEMENT: The mission of The Kiski School is to prepare young men to succeed in college and in so doing, prepare them to succeed in life. Kiski defines success in two ways: the cultivation of academic excellence, and the development of a boy's character, integrity, self discipline and good manners. The traditional learning environment at Kiski: small classes, close student/faculty interaction, required athletics, formal meals, a dress code, and family dormitory living, creates an atmosphere where boys can make their mark based on their individual character, ability, and passion to try. The Kiski experience prepares young men to know themselves, and to lead happy and productive lives.

SPECIAL COURSES: Nineteen AP courses, honors sections in virtually every subject area. Kiski School is a laptop school; each boy carries a laptop computer to classes, and uses it for homework, classwork, and research. Computers are provided by the school. Kiski's math students rated 20th out of 600 Pennsylvania schools in math competitions in 2003. Kiski's National Forensics League teams are strong in debate, drama, and public speaking competitions.

ATHLETICS: Competitive athletic teams fielded in football, cross-country, golf, lacrosse, soccer, basketball, baseball, swimming, diving, tennis, track and field, and wrestling.

CLUBS: "Kiski Players" produces several plays each year in Kiski's 350-seat theatre. Numerous clubs include astronomy, art, chess, glee club, horticulture, recycling, science fiction, math, science, Spanish, varsity, woodworking, international, photography, political forum, literary forum, National Forensic League, and National Honor Society. Many students are involved in WKRC-FM, the school's radio station.

PUBLICATIONS: Publications include "Cougar Online", the school's internet newspaper, and the yearbook

COMMUNITY INVOLVEMENT: Community service projects include "Read to Kids" at Saltsburg Elementary, Adopt-a-Mile, blood drives, Special Olympics, and work at the local elderly center.

PLANT: The fine arts center, Rogers Hall, contains practice rooms for music, art studios, several classrooms, a 350-seat theatre, a woodworking shop, and journalism and photography labs. The S.W. Jacke Fieldhouse contains three gymnasiums, two weight rooms, a natatorium, and extensive locker facilities. The J.A. Pidgeon Library was named Pennsylvania's Best School Library in 2001, and houses over 22,000 volumes. The McAtee Health Center is staffed by five RN's, around the clock. Other facilities include eight academic and administrative buildings, nine dormitories (with faculty apartments attached), assorted athletic fields and stadiums, and 17 faculty homes.

ADMISSION: Application, transcripts, test scores (ISEE or SSAT required for freshman and sophomore applicants), campus visit, references, and $35 application fee. The common application is accepted. Kiski offers 5 open houses per year, and admissions representatives travel widely to meet prospective parents.

TUITION: $27,500

FINANCIAL AID: Yes. SSS application and copy of 1040 required; financial aid applicants must first complete the admissions process.

BOOKS: $300   **DRESS CODE:** Tie and jacket required for classes and weekday meals

SUMMER PROGRAMS: Two programs available for middle and high school boys. Five weeks, $2,500

THE LAB SCHOOL OF WASHINGTON   202-965-6600   FAX 202-965-5106

4759 Reservoir Road, N.W., Washington, DC 20007
Founded 1967
HEAD: Sally L. Smith
DIRECTOR OF ADMISSIONS: Susan F. Feeley
WEBSITE: www.labschool.org   **E-MAIL:** diana@labschool.org
GRADES: K–12 ungraded in lower school   **ENROLLMENT:** 310 Co-ed
FACULTY: 90 full-time   **AVERAGE CLASS SIZE:** 4:1 student:teacher ratio
MISSION STATEMENT: Program designed for intelligent students with learning disabilities; experiential "hands-on" curriculum based on the Arts.
SPECIAL COURSES: Program designed for primary, elementary, junior and senior high school students of average to superior intelligence with learning disabilities. Primary and elementary students spend half day in classrooms with highly individualized prescriptive programs taught by Master teachers; half day learning academic skills through art forms (woodwork, ceramics, music, dance, drama, film making) with outstanding artists trained in Learning Disabilities. History, geography, civics and academic readiness skills are taught through a unique method called Academic Clubs in the lower school. The junior/senior high school programs emphasize college preparatory courses, arts, electives, and sports. Spanish is offered in high school. Math includes algebra, geometry, trigonometry and calculus. Science: physical science, biology, chemistry, physics, environmental science. History, geography, U.S. government, remedial reading, set design, Shakespeare, sculpture (high school).
EXTENDED DAY: 3:30–5:30 p.m.
ATHLETICS: 2 years High School P.E. Varsity boys' and girls' basketball, varsity co-ed soccer, softball, track and field, swimming and diving
CLUBS: Drama club, Student Council
PUBLICATIONS: Yearbook, literary magazine
PLANT: Library 6,000 volumes. Modern 3-story classroom building, an historic mansion, carriage house, expanded speech and language rooms, occupational therapy annex, new Arts and Athletic Center. Media Center with extensive tapes and cassettes. Baltimore campus
ADMISSION: Registration fee $100. Educational, neurological, psychological tests. Interview. Child visits school for half day. Child must be of average to superior intelligence with specific learning disabilities (i.e., dyslexia, attention deficit) that impede academic success. Deadline is first week in February.
TUITION: $20,895
FINANCIAL AID: Tuition funded through D.C. and Maryland if approved by public school system.
OTHER FEES: Related services
DRESS CODE: No jeans/t-shirts: junior high and high school.
SUMMER PROGRAMS: 6-week summer session (K–12) of arts, recreation, remedial instruction and study skills, mid-June through July. Scholarships available

LAKE SHORE CHRISTIAN ACADEMY   410-437-3529

860 Swift Road, Pasadena, MD 21122
HEAD: Pastor McClure
GRADES: K4–grade 12   **ENROLLMENT:** 70 Co-ed

SPECIAL COURSES: A Beka program K–4, ACE program 5–12
TUITION: $2,900
DRESS CODE: Uniforms

LANDON SCHOOL   301-320-3200   FAX 301-320-1133
6101 Wilson Lane, Bethesda, MD 20817
Founded 1929
HEAD: Damon F. Bradley
WEBSITE: www.landon.net   **E-MAIL:** jeanne_hamrick@landon.net
GRADES: 3–grade 12   **ENROLLMENT:** 660 boys
FACULTY: 100 full-and 20 part-time   **AVERAGE CLASS SIZE:** 15
MISSION STATEMENT: Landon School prepares talented boys for productive lives as accomplished, responsible and caring men whose actions are guided by the principles of perseverance, teamwork, honor and fair play.
SPECIAL COURSES: French, Latin, Spanish, Chinese (all 5–12) Math through calculus, computer. Science: general science, biology, chemistry, physics. History: geography, ancient, modern world, U.S., modern Soviet, Contemporary World Issues, term courses. Art: history, design, appreciation and studio, pottery, ceramics, photography. Music: history and theory, harmony, choir, glee club, jazz band, string orchestra, concert band, drama AP: In most disciplines; cross registration with Holton-Arms School (nearby girls' school) for AP courses.
ATHLETICS: Football, cross-country, soccer, basketball, wrestling, hockey, swimming, riflery, lacrosse, baseball, track and field, tennis, golf
CLUBS: Music and drama, School Service and numerous special interest clubs
PUBLICATIONS: Yearbook, newspaper, literary magazine, www.landon.net website
COMMUNITY INVOLVEMENT: State and nationally recognized community service projects. Recommended by the Governor of Maryland as a model program for other schools.
PLANT: Library 25,000 volumes, 75-acre campus, 9 science labs, 8 art studios, 2 gyms, auditorium, 7 playing fields, 12 tennis courts, Performing Arts Center, all-weather track, rifle range, greenhouse, ropes course, 3 computer labs, 3 traveling computer labs computer lab, AV room, science labs, media center.
ADMISSION: Application and appointment for tour. Applicants to grades 5–6 and forms I–IV must take ISEE. Teacher recommendations, transcripts
TUITION: $20,000 grades 3–5; $21,800 grade 6–form VI
FINANCIAL AID: Available
TRANSPORTATION: Available   **DRESS CODE:** Yes
SUMMER PROGRAMS: Academic, sports, travel and specialty camps available. Call Summer Program Office at 301-320-1044 for information.
FUTURE PLANS: Completion of football stadium

THE LANGLEY SCHOOL   703-356-1920   FAX 703-790-9712
1411 Balls Hill Road, McLean, VA 22101
Founded 1942
HEAD: Doris Cottam
DIRECTOR OF ADMISSIONS: Holly Hartge
WEBSITE: www.langley.edu.net
GRADES: N–grade 8   **ENROLLMENT:** 475 Co-ed (236 boys/239 girls)
FACULTY: 69 full- and 14 part-time   **AVERAGE CLASS SIZE:** 15–22

MISSION STATEMENT: The Langley School is committed to the pursuit of excellence offering a challenging and enriched curriculum geared toward attracting students with promise and potential from diverse backgrounds throughout the greater Washington area who demonstrate the ability and readiness to participate and progress within Langley's curriculum. Emphasis is placed on educating the whole child in a comprehensive, well-rounded program that helps each child reach her/his fullest potential in a nurturing and stimulating environment where learning is enjoyed and sharing is commonplace. We want our students to leave Langley feeling good about themselves and on their way to becoming contributing and caring members of their adult community.

SPECIAL COURSES: French and Spanish, algebra, geometry, general science, earth science, physical and life science. Technology curriculum K–8, art, band, music, handbells, computer graphics, drama, life skills. Field trips throughout metro area, overnight trips for middle school

EXTENDED DAY: After school until 6:00 p.m.

ATHLETICS: Boys' and girls' varsity and junior varsity soccer, basketball, lacrosse. Member of Capitol Athletic Conference

CLUBS: Student Council   **PUBLICATIONS:** Yearbook, newspaper

COMMUNITY INVOLVEMENT: Community service at all grade levels

PLANT: Library 24,000 volumes, 4 computer labs, AV room, science labs, art studios, gyms, playing fields, 10.2 acres

ADMISSION: Apply September–January. Parent tour and interview. Child visit and assessment; transcripts and recommendations. Application fee $75

TUITION: $10,200–$18,500

FINANCIAL AID: Need-based financial aid available to Nursery–grade 8

BOOKS: Included   **OTHER FEES:** Transportation

TRANSPORTATION: Available. $1,000–$1,900   **DRESS CODE:** Yes

SUMMER PROGRAMS: Day camp, ages 3–12; 8 week summer day camp with extended day program. This supplements 6 week summer school of reading, math enrichment, foreign language, computers, drama and art enrichment

FUTURE PLANS: Fine arts center construction to begin in 2003- 2004

LANHAM CHRISTIAN SCHOOL   301-552-9102   FAX 301-552-2021
8400 Good Luck Road, Lanham, MD 20706
Grace Brethren 1977
HEAD: Gene B. Pinkard
WEBSITE: www.LanhamGBC.org   **E-MAIL:** LCS@lanhamgbc.org
GRADES: Kindergarten–grade 12   **ENROLLMENT:** 292 Co-ed (124 boys/168 girls)
FACULTY: 16 full- and 7 part-time   **AVERAGE CLASS SIZE:** 18
MISSION STATEMENT: Lanham Christian School seeks to instill a thoroughly Christian world view within all students, equipping them to succeed spiritually, academically, physically and socially.
SPECIAL COURSES: Prince Georges Community College concurrent enrollment classes available to qualified Juniors and Seniors on LCS campus.
EXTENDED DAY: 7:00 a.m.–5:30 p.m.
ATHLETICS: Interscholastic sports available at middle and high school levels
ADMISSION: Interview of student and parent required. Formal testing for Kindergarten applicants only. Others are admitted on the basis of school records and the interview. Agreement with the statement of faith and regular church

attendance at a Bible teaching church required.

TUITION: $4,895

BOOKS: Included   **LUNCH:** $3.50 per day

OTHER FEES: Discount for siblings. Monthly payments available, discount for prepayment. Discount for full time Christian workers. Application fee $50 per student, $100 maximum per family. Registration $175 per student, $350 maximum per family. Technology fee $80 per student grades 1–6

DRESS CODE: School uniform required

THE LEARNING ACADEMY   202-889-7441   FAX 202-889-7183
1634 16th Street, S.E., Washington, DC 20020

Founded 1996

HEAD: Kevin Hubbard

GRADES: Nursery–grade 3

ADMISSION: Visit, interview, application deadline August 31

TUITION: $5,228 one child, 10% tuition discount for 2nd child

THE LEARNING COMMUNITY INTERNATIONAL
410-730-0073   FAX 301-230-9021

9085 Flame Pool Way, Columbia, MD 21045

Non-denominational 1984

HEAD: Manfred Smith

DIRECTOR OF ADMISSIONS: Manfred Smith, general school

WEBSITE: www.tlcn.org or www.schoolfinders.net

E-MAIL: manfredsmith@comcast.net

GRADES: Nursery to postgraduate   **ENROLLMENT:** Varies as families enroll

FACULTY: 5 full- and 2 part-time   **AVERAGE CLASS SIZE:** 5-8:1 or 1:1

MISSION STATEMENT: TLC strives to offer an educational program that empowers each individual learner to reach his/her highest potential as a human being. To achieve this TLC supports: The realization and expression of the special interests and talents of each young person, the achievement of intellectual independence, respect for unique learning styles, timetables and learning approaches and educating children in accordance with the values and beliefs of the family. The goal of education at TLC is the gaining of knowledge, experience and skills necessary to create a meaningful life.

SPECIAL COURSES: Consultants are available for science, math, special needs, advanced learners, international students and students taking college courses. The Rockville Learning Facility is designed to work with students who are bored, at risk of failure in traditional school settings, have health issues, have left school and wish to return or need help with specific learning differences.

EXTENDED DAY: Available at Rockville location

CLUBS: Experiential learning, multiple field trips, internships, exchange programs, science and social studies fairs, invention conventions, poetry contests, art exhibits and fairs, SAT prep courses and college consultation available

PUBLICATIONS: Publications throughout the year

PLANT: Two locations–9085 Flame Pool Way in Columbia, Maryland and 6001 Montrose Road in Rockville, Maryland

ADMISSION: Open house in Columbia to apply to the independent learner homeschool program. Call 410-730-0073 for schedule. Individual appointments for

Rockville facility. Call 301-230-9010 for appointment. E-mail is schoolfind@aol.com.
Director of Admissions at Rockville Learning Facility: Judith Greenberg
TUITION: Varies by program
FINANCIAL AID: Some partial
SUMMER PROGRAMS: Full summer school K–12 in all subjects
FUTURE PLANS: More learning facility sites, homeschool college

THE LEARNING COMMUNITY OF NORTHERN VIRGINIA & CORTONA SCHOOL
703-464-0034 FAX 703-796-6690
Serves students in VA, MD, and DC
Founded 1992
HEAD: Sharon P. Strauchs, M.Ed.
DIRECTOR OF ADMISSIONS: Sharon P. Strauchs, M.Ed.
WEBSITE: www.tlc-nv.com **E-MAIL:** Info@tlc-nv.com
GRADES: grades 4–12, college 1st & 2nd year college courses
ENROLLMENT: 80–100 Co-ed (50 boys/50 girls)
FACULTY: 5 full- and 12 part-time **AVERAGE CLASS SIZE:** 4
SPECIAL COURSES: Toll-free: 877-851-2010 In Maryland: 301-215-7788
Our no-fail, positive, total-respect-for-the-student philosophy is critical to helping students achieve potential and realize dreams. Each student's customized course of study is designed to focus on their gifts, natural abilities, and goals. All school work is done on lap tops with organization and proven, revolutionary study systems taught in ALL classes. Our special focus is on science, technology, and the arts, but all students are welcome! Teachers hold a minimum of Master's degrees, but 1/3 hold Ph.D.'s in the subject taught, inspiring competence, confidence and self-esteem in their students. 100% college acceptance, many with scholarships. One-on-one courses available for acceleration or remediation, allowing students to make up for time lost, repeat courses to improve grades, or finish high school early. College courses available to our high school students, eliminating the AP test requirements. Bi-monthly trips to science and cultural venues inspire motivation and create mentoring opportunities to fulfill many Congressional Award requirements. LD and GT specialists on site with full testing services completed upon request. Rolling admission available.
ATHLETICS: Done as part of Congressional Award work
COMMUNITY INVOLVEMENT: Continual volunteer activities planned as part of the yearly calendar
ADMISSION: By interview and application. March deadline for September entry, but open admission throughout the year always considered. Toll-free number for application: 877-851-2010
TUITION: $2,600–$15,500 for 4–8, depending on number of courses. $16,500 average for 9–12, although 9 and 10 done in one year, creating the possibility of final year being a combination of high school and college for those requesting this
FINANCIAL AID: Partial for many students
BOOKS: $50–$500 **LUNCH:** Approximately $300
OTHER FEES: Field trips to NYC extra and optional
TRANSPORTATION: Transportation may be arranged. No cost
DRESS CODE: Yes
FUTURE PLANS: Satellite campuses (planned for fall 2004) throughout Washington area

LEARY SCHOOL OF PRINCE GEORGE'S COUNTY
301-839-5486   FAX 301-839-6392
7100 Oxon Hill Road, Oxon Hill, MD 20745
Founded 1964
HEAD: Dr. Ed Schultze
WEBSITE: www.learyschool.org   **E-MAIL:** learyschool@verizon.net
GRADES: 1–12 grades, ages 6–22
SPECIAL COURSES: See listing for Leary School of Virginia
ADMISSION: Most children are referred by their local public school system
TUITION: Placement in the school through a public agency pays the full tuition, related service costs, and transportation

LEARY SCHOOL OF VIRGINIA   703-941-8150   FAX 703-941-4237
6349 Lincolnia Road, Alexandria, VA 22312
Founded 1964
HEAD: Dr. Ed Schultze
WEBSITE: www.learyschool.org   **E-MAIL:** learyschool@verizon.net
GRADES: 1–12 grades, ages 6–22
SPECIAL COURSES: The Leary School is a private, day, co-educational, special education facility which serves students who have learning, emotional, and behavioral problems. Each child's identified learning styles, strengths, and weaknesses suggest the preferred methods of educational intervention. An individualized educational program is formulated for each child in consultation with public school personnel, parents, and, when appropriate, the child. Psychological services, counseling, and when needed, career development
ADMISSION: Most children are referred by their local public school system
TUITION: Placement in the school through a public agency pays the full tuition, related service costs, and transportation

LEESBURG CHRISTIAN SCHOOL   703-777-4220   FAX 703-771-1626
21336 Evergreen Mills Road, Leesburg, VA 20175
Non-denominational 1969
HEAD: Terry Overstreet
WEBSITE: www.leesburgchristianschool.org   **E-MAIL:** leesburgbeliever@aol.com
GRADES: Pre-K3–grade 12   **ENROLLMENT:** 150 Co-ed
FACULTY: 20 full- and 2 part-time   **AVERAGE CLASS SIZE:** 15
SPECIAL COURSES: French, computer literacy 1–12, general science, world history, remedial reading and math, art, music, chorus. Religious studies required. A Beka and Bob Jones programs. BJLINC satellite for chemistry, biology, geometry and Spanish
ATHLETICS: P.E. required. Interscholastic: soccer, baseball, softball, basketball, volleyball
TUITION: $3,300–$4,400
BOOKS: Extra.   **LUNCH:** Hot lunch program
TRANSPORTATION: Limited   **DRESS CODE:** Uniform required K5–12

LEONARD HALL JUNIOR NAVAL ACADEMY   301-475-8029   FAX 301-475-8518
P.O. Box 507, Leonardtown, MD 20650
Founded 1909

HEAD: Sam Brick
WEBSITE: www.lhjna.com   **E-MAIL:** lhjna@yahoo.com
GRADES: 6–12   **ENROLLMENT:** 110 Co-ed (95 boys/15 girls)
FACULTY: 11 full- and 1 part-time   **AVERAGE CLASS SIZE:** 15
SPECIAL COURSES: Leadership, advanced math, Spanish, Naval Science, military drill, marching units
ATHLETICS: Interscholastic lacrosse, basketball, soccer and volleyball
CLUBS: National Honor Society, National Junior Honor Society, Student Council, drama, Latin Club and military drill
PUBLICATIONS: Yearbook
PLANT: Library, science lab, computer lab, and drill hall
ADMISSION: Entrance test by appointment. Fee $50
TUITION: $4,523 middle school; $4,820 high school
FINANCIAL AID: Available
BOOKS: Included   **LUNCH:** Daily fees
TRANSPORTATION: Available only for students out of St. Mary's County
DRESS CODE: Uniforms
FUTURE PLANS: To focus on Maritime Academy Matriculation

LINDEN HALL SCHOOL FOR GIRLS   717-626-8512   FAX 717-627-1384
212 East Main Street, Lititz, PA 17543
Founded in 1746
HEAD: Thomas W. Needham
DIRECTOR OF ADMISSIONS: Madelyn P. Nix
WEBSITE: www.lindenhall.org   **E-MAIL:** admissions@lindenhall.org
GRADES: 6–12, Postgraduate   **ENROLLMENT:** 126 girls boarding from grade 6
FACULTY: 30 full- and 3 part-time   **AVERAGE CLASS SIZE:** 8–10
MISSION STATEMENT: Linden Hall School for Girls, founded by the Moravian Church in 1746, is the oldest girls' boarding school in the United States. For more than 250 years its mission has been the fulfillment of the school's motto: "Non Scholae Sed Vitae Discimus" or "We are learning not only for school but for life."
SPECIAL COURSES: College preparatory school; AP classes: calculus AB, calculus BC, English literature, European history, American history, Spanish, French, Latin; ESL; music, art, photography, vocal/instrumental, dance, equestrian studies
ATHLETICS: Tennis, volleyball, basketball, soccer, riding, softball, swimming, lacrosse
PUBLICATIONS: Newspaper, yearbook, literary magazine ("Echo"- the oldest continuing publication in the United States)
COMMUNITY INVOLVEMENT: Community service required for every girl each year
PLANT: 47 acres, new sports and fitness center with dance studio, new fine and performing arts building, indoor pool, indoor and outdoor riding rings, 22-stall stable, tennis courts, softball and soccer/lacrosse field, library, dorms, classroom and administration buildings, faculty-staff housing
ADMISSION: Rolling admission, application with fee, transcript, 2 recommendations, campus visit with interview. Alternate phone number is 800-258-5778.
TUITION: $29,770 7-day boarding; $28,030 5-day boarding; $13,100 day
FINANCIAL AID: Available

BOOKS: $700   OTHER FEES: $350
DRESS CODE: Yes
SUMMER PROGRAMS: Day camp, Summer Riding Camp

LINTON HALL SCHOOL   703-368-3157   FAX 703-368-3036
9535 Linton Hall Road, Bristow, VA 20136
Catholic 1922
HEAD: Robert F. Manning
WEBSITE: www.lintonhall.com
E-MAIL: lintonhall@aol.com
GRADES: Kindergarten–grade 8
ENROLLMENT: 186 Co-ed (84 boys/102 girls)
FACULTY: 15 full- and 4 part-time   AVERAGE CLASS SIZE: 22
MISSION STATEMENT: Linton Hall School is an independent Catholic school for children in Kindergarten through grade eight. The school is owned and operated by the Benedictine Sisters of Virginia. The development of the student is based on Christian beliefs and values: a reverence for God, self, and others. The guiding principle for achieving the fullest development of the student is the collaboration of the family, school personnel, and students. The mission of Linton Hall School is to provide educational experiences that allow students to master basic learning skills, to develop a sense of self-worth and integrity, and to learn to live effectively with others.
SPECIAL COURSES: Technology K–grade 8, algebra grade 8, Spanish I grade 8. Outdoor, Conservation, Environment, Wildlife (OCEW) K–grade 8
EXTENDED DAY: Call for information.
ATHLETICS: Boys' and girls' basketball and soccer, cheerleading
CLUBS: Leo Club, fife and drum corps, voice and handbell choirs
PLANT: 120-acre campus including full size gymnasium, soccer fields, swimming pool, baseball field, playgrounds
ADMISSION: Refer to Linton Hall School website at www.lintonhall.com.
TUITION: $6,020
FINANCIAL AID: Available.
DRESS CODE: Uniform required
SUMMER PROGRAMS: Summer Adventure (Technology)

LITTLE FLOCK CHRISTIAN SCHOOL   703-591-1216   FAX 703-591-3030
11911 Braddock Road, Fairfax, VA 22030
Founded 2003
HEAD: Adel Messeh
WEBSITE: www.littleflockschool.org
E-MAIL: admin@littleflockscool.org
GRADES: K3 and K4, grades to be added
ENROLLMENT: Co-ed
SPECIAL COURSES: Foreign language, P.E., music, computers
EXTENDED DAY: 7:30 a.m.–5:30 p.m.
PLANT: Brand new building, large indoor gymnasium, playground equipment
ADMISSION: Apply by March 1
TUITION: Call for information.
FUTURE PLANS: Add one or more grades each year until reaching grade 8

LITTLE FLOWER SCHOOL   301-320-3273   FAX 301-320-2867
5601 Massachusetts Avenue, Bethesda, MD 20816
Catholic
HEAD: Sister Rosemaron Rynn, IHM
WEBSITE: www.littleflowerschool.org   **E-MAIL:** lfbeth@erols.com
GRADES: Pre-K–grade 8   **ENROLLMENT:** 250 Co-ed
EXTENDED DAY: After care
TUITION: $4,600 one child in parish. Includes fees
DRESS CODE: Uniforms required K–8

LITTLE FLOWER SCHOOL   301-994-0404   FAX 301-994-2055
P.O. Box 257, Great Mills, MD 20634
Catholic
HEAD: Patty Gehring
WEBSITE: www.littleflowercatholic.org   **E-MAIL:** lfs@gmpexpress.net
GRADES: Pre-K–8   **ENROLLMENT:** Co-ed
TUITION: Call for information.
DRESS CODE: Uniforms
SUMMER PROGRAMS: Summer Camp

LONE OAK MONTESSORI SCHOOL   301-469-4888
10201 Democracy Boulevard, Potomac, MD 20854
HEAD: Patricia Swann
WEBSITE: www.loneoakmontessorischool.com
GRADES: Ungraded ages 2–12 years   **ENROLLMENT:** 158 Co-ed on two campuses
FACULTY: 18 full- and 5 part-time
SPECIAL COURSES: Montessori program. This campus includes children from ages 2–12.
EXTENDED DAY: 7:45–9:00 a.m. and 3:00–5:30 p.m.
TUITION: $2,500–$8,900
FINANCIAL AID: Limited

LONE OAK MONTESSORI SCHOOL   301-469-4888
10100 Old Georgetown Road, Bethesda, MD 20814
HEAD: Patricia Swann
WEBSITE: www.loneoakmontessorischool.com
GRADES: Ungraded ages 2–12 years
ENROLLMENT: 158 Co-ed on two campuses
FACULTY: 18 full- and 5 part-time
SPECIAL COURSES: Montessori program. This campus includes children from ages 3–6
EXTENDED DAY: 7:40–9:00 a.m. and 3:00–5:30 p.m.
TUITION: $2,500–$8,900
FINANCIAL AID: Limited
SUMMER PROGRAMS: In-house program available for ages 3–6

LOUDOUN COUNTRY DAY SCHOOL   703-777-3841   FAX 703-771-1346
237 Fairview Street, N.W., Leesburg, VA 20176
Founded 1953

HEAD: Dr. E. Randall Hollister
DIRECTOR OF ADMISSIONS: Pam Larimer
WEBSITE: www.lcds.org   **E-MAIL:** lcds@aol.com
GRADES: Pre-K–grade 8   **ENROLLMENT:** 264 Co-ed
FACULTY: 41 full- and 4 part-time   **AVERAGE CLASS SIZE:** 16
MISSION STATEMENT: Loudoun Country Day School, an accredited, independent, coeducational school, educates students in Pre-Kindergarten through eighth grade. We cultivate the intellectual, social, emotional, and physical growth of each child. We pride ourselves on our rigorous core curriculum, nurturing environment, and extensive programs in foreign languages, arts, computers, and athletics. LCDS inspires excellence and builds character, preparing each child for the challenges ahead.
SPECIAL COURSES: French and Spanish PK–8. Geometry, computer, hands-on science, civics, American history, art, music, remedial reading and math. Resource teacher for students who need remediation.
EXTENDED DAY: 7:00–8:30 a.m. and 3:20–6:00 p.m.; Pre-K 12:00–3:20 p.m.
ATHLETICS: Required all grades. Intramural and interscholastic. Soccer, field hockey, basketball, lacrosse, flag football, swimming, track
CLUBS: Drama, art, video clubs, Destination Imagination
PUBLICATIONS: School newspaper
COMMUNITY INVOLVEMENT: Community service projects
PLANT: Library 9,000 volumes, science lab, computer lab, playing fields, art studio, gym, auditorium
ADMISSION: Call for packet of general information. School tour. $60 application fee
TUITION: $7,300 Pre-K; $11,000 K–5; $11,400 6–8
FINANCIAL AID: Available.
TRANSPORTATION: Available. Approximately $2,500/year
DRESS CODE: Uniform required, starting at grade 1–8

LOVE OF LEARNING MONTESSORI SCHOOL
410-715-9600   FAX 410-715-9667
9151 Rumsey Road, Columbia, MD 21045
Founded 1983
HEAD: C. Awilda Torres
WEBSITE: www.lolms.com   **E-MAIL:** info@lolms.com
GRADES: Ungraded age 1–grade 6
SPECIAL COURSES: Spanish, gym programs
EXTENDED DAY: Before and after care
CLUBS: Many activities such as drama, yoga, crafts, gymnastics
ADMISSION: Call for Open House information.
TUITION: Call for information.
SUMMER PROGRAMS: Summer Camp

LOWELL SCHOOL   202-577-2000   FAX 202-577-2001
1640 Kalmia Road, N.W., Washington, DC 20012
Founded 1965
HEAD: Abigail B. Wiebenson
WEBSITE: www.lowellschool.org   **E-MAIL:** awiebenson@lowellschool.org
GRADES: Pre-K–grade 6   **ENROLLMENT:** 315 Co-ed

FACULTY: 40 full- and 12 part-time **AVERAGE CLASS SIZE:** 16–18
MISSION STATEMENT: Our philosophy emanates from three main principles—mutual respect, effective communication and an understanding of the developmental stages in physical, emotional and social and cognitive growth.
SPECIAL COURSES: Integrated curriculum- Spanish, creative movement, laptop program, music, chorus, drama, design technology, art
EXTENDED DAY: 3:15–6:00 p.m.
ATHLETICS: Aquatics, community playground.
CLUBS: Mini-courses- K–6
PLANT: Indoor pool, library, 3 art workshops, dining room, dance studio, technology lab, playgrounds, field, science lab, music room, gymnasium
ADMISSION: Tour the school; child visits/observation; some testing
TUITION: $10,150–$16,990
FINANCIAL AID: Available
OTHER FEES: Technology fee **DRESS CODE:** None
SUMMER PROGRAMS: Programs available for both pre-primary and primary. Programs include field trips, swimming, dance, Spanish, arts and crafts, etc.

—M

THE MADEIRA SCHOOL   703-556-8253   FAX 703-821-2845
8328 Georgetown Pike, McLean, VA 22102
Founded 1906
HEAD: Dr. Elisabeth Griffith
WEBSITE: www.madeira.org **E-MAIL:** admissions@madeira.org
GRADES: 9–12 **ENROLLMENT:** 308 girls, 160 boarding
FACULTY: 50 full- and 8 part-time
AVERAGE CLASS SIZE: 13 6:1 student/faculty
MISSION STATEMENT: A girls' school by design, where every aspect of academic, social and athletic life is directed toward educating young women. Exceptional training for college and beyond.
SPECIAL COURSES: AP offerings in all subject areas. Co-curriculum program Unique experiential learning program that uses D.C. as an extended classroom. Colleges attended by recent graduates include: University of Virginia, Harvard University, Yale University, University of Pennsylvania, and Wellesley College.
ATHLETICS: 13 varsity and junior varsity sports.
PLANT: 400 acres overlooking the Potomac River. Some of the finest athletic facilities in the region. Indoor pool, ropes course, indoor riding arena
ADMISSION: Selective admissions process. SSAT required
TUITION: $22,300 day; $29,520 boarding
FINANCIAL AID: Available
BOOKS: $400 **LUNCH:** Included   **DRESS CODE:** Neat and clean
SUMMER PROGRAMS: Camp Greenway; Girls First! leadership camp, Just Girls! sports camp, Riding Camp, Tennis Adventure

MANASSAS CHRISTIAN SCHOOL   703-393-6555   FAX 703-393-6655
9296 West Carondelet Drive, Manassas, VA 20111
WEBSITE: www.manassaschristianschool.org
GRADES: 1–8 **ENROLLMENT:** Co-ed
EXTENDED DAY: Before and after care

MANOR MONTESSORI SCHOOL   301-299-7400   FAX 301-299-7908
10500 Oaklyn Drive, Potomac, MD 20854
Founded 1962
HEAD: Katherine Damico
GRADES: Ungraded Pre-K–age 8   **ENROLLMENT:** 200 co-ed
FACULTY: 38   **AVERAGE CLASS SIZE:** 28
SPECIAL COURSES: Montessori Curriculum: Practical Life, Sensorial, math, languages, geography, science, Spanish and computer
EXTENDED DAY: 7:30–9:00 a.m. and 3:00–6:00 p.m.
ATHLETICS: Soccer
PLANT: Two locations: Potomac (ages 2 1/2–8) and Rockville (ages 2 1/2– 6)
ADMISSION: After application is received, an informal interview with Director is scheduled. $50 registration fee
TUITION: Call for school brochure
TRANSPORTATION: Available- see school brochure
SUMMER PROGRAMS: June–August with a Toddler program

MARET SCHOOL   202-939-8814   FAX 202-939-8884
3000 Cathedral Avenue, N.W., Washington, DC 20008
Founded 1911
HEAD: Marjo Talbott
WEBSITE: www.maret.org   **E-MAIL:** admissions@maret.org
GRADES: K–grade 12   **ENROLLMENT:** 600 Co-ed (293 boys/307 girls)
FACULTY: 87 full-time   **AVERAGE CLASS SIZE:** 12–15
SPECIAL COURSES: Latin 5–12, French and Spanish K–12. Math: geometry, advanced geometry, algebra I and II, Topics in Finite Math, functions, statistics, trigonometry, pre-calculus; Science: biology, chemistry, physics, environmental science, Chemistry in the Community, Anatomy and Physiology, Waves, Optics and Modern Physics, Geology and Geophysics. Computer: Computer Science and Programming in Java, Introduction to Digital Video, Advanced Computer Graphics. Humanities: Modern Peoples, U.S. history, Russian history, Civil Liberties, History and the Aesthetics of Film, Race, Gender and Religions, American literature, creative writing, Modern drama, Psychological Themes in Literature, African American Literature, Latino Literature and Culture, Comparative Literature. Art: Ceramics, woodworking, painting, mixed media, sculpture, computer graphics and video, photography. Music: Chorus, band, chamber choir, advanced music theory and composition. AP: Latin, French, Spanish, chemistry, physics AB and BC, calculus AB and BC, U.S. history. Faculty members work with juniors and seniors interested in developing an independent study course as a tutorial in a specific discipline or a senior option course. Intensive Study Week: one week program in February, opportunity for students/teachers to propose different topics, create new classes. Senior Project.
EXTENDED DAY: Until 6:00 p.m.
ATHLETICS: Required K–12. Intramural and interscholastic: football, soccer, volleyball, softball, baseball, weight training, aerobics, martial arts, wrestling, tennis, lacrosse, track and field, cross-country, modern dance, "Ultimate Frisbee", golf, Pilates and weight training
CLUBS: Engineering Team, "It's Academic", grades 9–12 musical, Amnesty International, peer facilitators, SADD, Model U.N.

PUBLICATIONS: Yearbook, literary and visual arts magazine, newspaper
COMMUNITY INVOLVEMENT: Community service required and service learning is incorporated into the curriculum school-wide
PLANT: 2 libraries (10,000 volumes), 6 science labs, field, 2 gyms, auditorium, 5 art studios, math lab, music room, 2 computer rooms with 40 computers, all housed in 6 buildings
ADMISSION: Tour/interview, recommendations and transcripts; SSAT and ISEE for grades 6–11. Some testing K–5
TUITION: $17,812–$21,140
FINANCIAL AID: Available
BOOKS: $250–$400   **DRESS CODE:** Neat and appropriate
SUMMER PROGRAMS: Credit, remedial and enrichment programs for grades 5–12 (full, half day). Theatre and sports camps. Summer study: Florida, France and Spain

MARTIN BARR ADVENTIST   301-261-0078   FAX 410-721-4910
2365 Bell Branch Road, Gambrills, MD 21054
Seventh-day Adventist
HEAD: Sandra J. Miller
GRADES: Kindergarten–grade 8   **ENROLLMENT:** 20 Co-ed (12 boys/8 girls)
AVERAGE CLASS SIZE: 2–3
TUITION: $3,400
OTHER FEES: Registration fee $200, activity fee $100
DRESS CODE: Yes

MARY OF NAZARETH CATHOLIC SCHOOL
301-869-0940   FAX 301-869-0942
14131 Seneca Road, Darnestown, MD 20874
Catholic
HEAD: Michael J. Friel
WEBSITE: www.maryofnaz.org   **E-MAIL:** marynaz@comcast.net
GRADES: Kindergarten–grade 8   **ENROLLMENT:** Co-ed
EXTENDED DAY: Before and after care
TUITION: $3,900
DRESS CODE: Uniforms

THE MARYLAND INTERNATIONAL DAY SCHOOL
301-567-9101   FAX 301-567-9103
6400 Livingston Road, Oxon Hill, MD 20745
Founded 2001
HEAD: Esther Donawa
DIRECTOR OF ADMISSIONS: Mayra Fernandez Martinez
WEBSITE: www.themidschool.org   **E-MAIL:** info@themidschool.org
GRADES: Pre-K–5   **ENROLLMENT:** 45 Co-ed
FACULTY: 5 full- and 1 part-time   **AVERAGE CLASS SIZE:** 15
MISSION STATEMENT: The mission of The Maryland International Day School is to encourage and enable students to become lifelong learners and responsible members of a diverse world community.
SPECIAL COURSES: Spanish immersion classes in Pre-Kindergarten through

3rd grade are conducted entirely in Spanish two and three days a week, based on the knowledge that young children respond well to immersion in a second language. Through both organized and spontaneous activities, children develop comprehension skills and then establish and expand their working vocabulary in Spanish. Instruction in grades 4–5 is bilingual. Reading, writing and associated language skills are taught through two languages of instruction, as are science, history, mathematics and geography. Classes such as sports, music, drama, art, and information technology are taught by specialists in both English and Spanish.
EXTENDED DAY: 7:30 a.m.–7:00 p.m.
ATHLETICS: Tae kwon do, year-round soccer team, tennis lessons
CLUBS: Piano and violin lessons, foreign language programs
ADMISSION: See website for an application and procedures:
www.themidschool.org
TUITION: $6,000
BOOKS: $350   **LUNCH:** Not provided
OTHER FEES: Each family must pay a $750 capital fund fee per year
DRESS CODE: Uniforms.
SUMMER PROGRAMS: Around the World Summer Camp

MASSANUTTEN MILITARY ACADEMY   540-459-2167   FAX 540-459-5421

614 S. Main Street, Woodstock, VA 22664
United Church of Christ 1899
HEAD: Roy F. "Rick" Zinser, Colonel (Ret.) USA
DIRECTOR OF ADMISSIONS: Frank Thomas
WEBSITE: www.militaryschool.com   **E-MAIL:** admissions@militaryschool.com
GRADES: 6- 12 and postgraduate
ENROLLMENT: 149 Co-ed(115 boys/34 girls) 142 board
FACULTY: 19 full- and 5 part-time   **AVERAGE CLASS SIZE:** 9:1
MISSION STATEMENT: Our mission is to provide every cadet with an academic, character, leadership, and physical education of excellence, which ensures their development and readiness for college, leadership, and citizenship. We achieve our mission through discipline, fostered with structure, and a firm, fair, consistent and supportive environment.
SPECIAL COURSES: Boarding begins in grade 6. JROTC Army Leadership Education and Training (school year and summer program), Postgraduate College Readiness Program, AP courses in social sciences and English, English as a second language, SAT/ACT preparation
ATHLETICS: 22 competitive athletic teams (cross-country, varsity, junior varsity and middle school football, golf, boys' soccer, girls' and boys' volleyball, varsity, junior varsity and girls' basketball, co-ed swim team, weightlifting and power-lifting, physical fitness training, wrestling, fencing, track and field, baseball, softball, varsity and middle school tennis, rifle marksmanship, lacrosse, Raiders and military drill team
CLUBS: National Honor Society, National Junior Honor Society, Boy Scouts, Explorers
PUBLICATIONS: Academy yearbook (The Adjutant)
PLANT: 43 acres in rural Woodstock, Virginia; three boys' dormitories, including the newly-renovated Lantz Hall; girls' dormitory is air-conditioned and has a security alarm system, an aerobic center, laundry and kitchen; classrooms are housed in Benchoff, Harrison, Lantz and Sperry halls; the library is located in

Harrison Hall; both the computer lab and library have internet-accessible computers available and wireless laptops are available in the girls' dormitory, cadet activity center, and for classroom use; the Hayes Activity Center contains several pool tables, foosball, ping pong table, two large screen plasma TV's with DVD, VCR and two gaming systems

ADMISSION: Call the Admissions Office at (877)466-6222 and speak with an Admissions Counselor or complete the online inquiry form at www.militaryschool.com. Campus visit, open houses, online virtual tour

TUITION: $18,945 tuition includes 7 day boarding, initial issue of uniforms, infirmary, laundry, haircuts, activities, athletics and technology fees

FINANCIAL AID: Please contact and Admissions Counselor to discuss financial aid.

BOOKS: $50–$300 **LUNCH:** Included

OTHER FEES: Optional fees include ESL, band, art, photography, or ceramics course fees, yearbook, Boy Scouts and allowance

TRANSPORTATION: Available. Cost TBD. **DRESS CODE:** Uniform

SUMMER PROGRAMS: Summer Cadet Program (take two repeat or one new course), Summer JROTC Leadership Education and Training Program (take the 180 hour LET course for a transferable elective credit recognized throughout the U.S.), Adventure Camp (for young men to enjoy a wilderness experience)

FUTURE PLANS: Postgraduate men's and women's basketball program

MATER AMORIS MONTESSORI SCHOOL   301-774-7468   FAX 301-774-5232
18501 Mink Hollow Road (P.O. Box 97), Ashton, MD 20861
Founded 1968
HEAD: Charlotte Kovach Shea
WEBSITE: www.materamoris.com
GRADES: Ungraded ages 2 1/2–12   **ENROLLMENT:** 139 Co-ed
FACULTY: 10 AMI trained teachers   **AVERAGE CLASS SIZE:** 22
SPECIAL COURSES: Art, music, general science, biology, history, dance, drama
EXTENDED DAY: 7:30 a.m.–6:00 p.m.
ATHLETICS: Softball, kickball, field hockey, basketball, soccer, volleyball
PLANT: Library, science lab, auditorium, playing fields, stables, 13-acre farm in Ashton, Maryland
ADMISSION: Parent visit and interview, child visits class
TUITION: Call for information.
FINANCIAL AID: Some available
TRANSPORTATION: Available between D.C. and Ashton

MATER DEI SCHOOL   301-365-2700   FAX 301-365-2710
9600 Seven Locks Road, Bethesda, MD 20817
Catholic 1960
HEAD: Edward N. Williams
GRADES: 1–8   **ENROLLMENT:** 225 Boys
FACULTY: 14 full- and 6 part-time   **AVERAGE CLASS SIZE:** 20
SPECIAL COURSES: Latin 8, art, music. Substantial reading requirement. Religious studies required, computer
ATHLETICS: Intramural & interscholastic 5–8; All sports offered
PUBLICATIONS: Newspaper, "The Blue Blazer"
PLANT: Library 6,000 volumes. Chapel, gym, art studio, swimming pool, playing fields

ADMISSION: Application, interview, test and recommendations
TUITION: $9,200
FINANCIAL AID: Available
BOOKS: $350
DRESS CODE: Uniform required
SUMMER PROGRAMS: Boys' sports camp, 8 weeks in summer

McDONOGH SCHOOL   410-363-0600   FAX 410-581-4777
8600 McDonogh Road, Owings Mills, MD 21117
Founded 1873
HEAD: W. Boulton-Dixon
WEBSITE: www.mcdonogh.org   **E-MAIL:** admissions@mcdonogh.org
GRADES: K–grade 12   **ENROLLMENT:** 1271 Co-ed day & boarding (at 9th)
SPECIAL COURSES: College preparatory
EXTENDED DAY: K–grade 4 after care
ATHLETICS: 26 interscholastic sports
CLUBS: Extensive offering of extracurricular clubs
TUITION: Call for information.
DRESS CODE: Yes
SUMMER PROGRAMS: Summer Camps

McLEAN SCHOOL OF MARYLAND   301-299-8277   FAX 301-299-1637
8224 Lochinver Lane, Potomac, MD 20854
Founded 1954
HEAD: Darlene B. Pierro
DIRECTOR OF ADMISSIONS: Catherine A. Biern
WEBSITE: www.mcleanschool.org   **E-MAIL:** admission@mcleanschool.org
GRADES: K–grade 12   **ENROLLMENT:** 400 Co-ed
FACULTY: 71 full- and 4 part-time   **AVERAGE CLASS SIZE:** 14–16
MISSION STATEMENT: McLean School of Maryland is an independent, coeducational day school for students in Kindergarten through grade 12. It is a unique place that challenges and encourages students to grow to be independent learners while recognizing and fostering their own particular learning style.
SPECIAL COURSES: English, literature, Spanish, Latin, history, science. For full curriculum see website
EXTENDED DAY: 8:30 a.m.–3:20 p.m.
ATHLETICS: Boys–soccer, basketball, lacrosse; girls–field hockey, basketball, volleyball, lacrosse: co-ed- track, cross-country
CLUBS: Drama club
PUBLICATIONS: Literary magazine, yearbook
PLANT: 85,000-square feet in a single building on 9.13 acres, 45 classrooms, 10,000-square foot gym; 2 playing fields, playground
ADMISSION: Application deadline mid-February, decision sent out mid-March. Open Houses in fall- see website for dates
TUITION: Average $18,975 plus $500 in fees.
FINANCIAL AID: Available
LUNCH: Extra $5.00/day
TRANSPORTATION: Available. About $2,500
SUMMER PROGRAMS: Available

MELVIN J. BERMAN HEBREW ACADEMY

HARRY A. EPSTEIN CAMPUS   301-962-9400   FAX 301-962-3991

13300 Arctic Avenue, Rockville, MD 20853

Jewish 1944

HEAD: Rabbi William Altshul

WEBSITE: www.mjbha.org   **E-MAIL:** MJBHAinfo@mjbha.org

GRADES: N (age 2)–grade 12   **ENROLLMENT:** 795 Co-ed

FACULTY: 117 full- and part-time   **AVERAGE CLASS SIZE:** 20

SPECIAL COURSES: Remedial reading, remedial math, art, music, religious studies required. Hebrew N–12, half day; academic studies half day. Comprehensive Judaic and general studies programs.

EXTENDED DAY: Until 5:30 p.m.

ATHLETICS: Soccer, track, volleyball, basketball, baseball and tennis

CLUBS: Ensemble band, jazz band, girls' choir, Hebrew Academy Dramatic Arts Society, Mock Trial, Model U.N., debate club, Hebrew Song and Art Club, tae kwon do, Hebrew Language, Stock Market Club, fencing, chess and science clubs

PUBLICATIONS: Award winning yearbook, student newspaper, literary magazine

COMMUNITY INVOLVEMENT: Programs emphasizing character and values development such as community service requirements

PLANT: 200,000-square foot facility on 20 acres including full size track, tennis courts, soccer fields, 4 science labs, 1,100 fixed-seat performance hall, David Lichy Kollel Library, gymnasium, weight room, auxiliary gym, computer labs, Parenting Center, Helene Berman Seidenfeld Visual Arts Center

ADMISSION: Interview required

TUITION: Call for information.

LUNCH: Daily, balanced hot meals   **OTHER FEES:** Scholarship fee

TRANSPORTATION: Available. Call school for information.

DRESS CODE: See website for details.

MERCERSBURG ACADEMY   717-328-6173   FAX 717-328-6319

300 East Seminary Street, Mercersburg, PA 17236

Founded 1893

HEAD: Douglas Hale

DIRECTOR OF ADMISSIONS: Christopher R. Tompkins

WEBSITE: www.mercersburg.edu

E-MAIL: admission@mercersburg.edu

GRADES: 9–12, post-graduate

ENROLLMENT: 430 (242 boys/ 188 girls) 363 board

FACULTY: 83 full- and 8 part-time   **AVERAGE CLASS SIZE:** 13

MISSION STATEMENT: Mercersburg Academy prepares young men and women from diverse backgrounds for college and for life in a global community. Students at Mercersburg pursue a rigorous and dynamic curriculum while learning to live together harmoniously in a supportive residential environment. Mercersburg's talented faculty instill in students the value of hard work and the importance of character and community as they teach students to think for themselves, to approach life thoughtfully and creatively, to thrive physically, to act morally, to value the spiritual dimension of human existence, and to serve others.

SPECIAL COURSES: 140 traditional courses, not including independent or directed studies. 19 Advanced Placement courses offered: English, art history,

U.S. and modern European history, government, language (French, German, Latin and Spanish), French literature, Spanish literature, calculus AB, calculus BC, computer science, statistics, biology, chemistry, environmental science and physics. Foreign languages offered: Chinese, French, German, Latin and Spanish. School Year Abroad (SYA) program in Rennes, France; Zaragoza, Spain; and Viterbo, Italy

ATHLETICS: Interscholastic: baseball, basketball, cross-country, diving, field hockey, football, golf, lacrosse, soccer, squash, swimming, tennis, track & field, volleyball, and wrestling

CLUBS: AASU, Academic Team, Amnesty International, Asian Club, bike club, Blue Review, 4 choral groups, concert and jazz band, Environmental Club, Fifteen, foreign language clubs, Gay Straight Alliance, Green Team, Greater Respect of Women (GROW), International Club, math team, Model U.N., Muslim Students' Association, Outdoor Adventure Club, photography club, Students Against Destructive Decisions (SADD), ski club, string ensemble, Stony Batter (dramatic club), student council, Trek Club, ultimate frisbee

PUBLICATIONS: Mercersburg News, Karux (yearbook)

COMMUNITY INVOLVEMENT: Community service

PLANT: The campus occupies 300 acres. Lenfest Hall, library: history department and classrooms, Boone Hall Theatre: music, stagecraft, and dance. Irvine Hall: art, music, foreign language, math, science facilities, and the Writing Center. Rutledge Hall: English department and classrooms. Astronomy building opened in 2002. 7 dormitory buildings. Edward E. Ford Hall: dining room, student center, post office and 2 school stores. Nolde Gymnasium: fitness center, swimming pool, 3 basketball courts, 8 squash courts, exercise rooms, wrestling center, and locker rooms. Other facilities include a 400-meter all-weather track, jumping pits, 8 playing fields, Smoyer Tennis Center and Frantz Pavilion, cross-country course, and a sand volleyball court.

ADMISSION: Students apply by completing the forms in our application packet (available from the Admission Office or online at www.mercersburg.edu). SSAT (for those entering grade 9 or grade 10), SSAT or PSAT (for those entering grade 11), SAT (for those entering the senior or postgraduate year). For admission to Mercersburg, all applicants must have sufficient English proficiency to pursue a regular course of study, as determined by the SSAT, TOEFL, or placement examinations. We require a personal interview, which must be on campus whenever possible, and a writing sample in addition to the application forms.

TUITION: $30,900 boarding; $23,000 day

FINANCIAL AID: 38% of the student body receives need-based aid.

BOOKS: $500 **TRANSPORTATION:** Yes. Cost varies

DRESS CODE: Monday evening meal: semi-formal dress

SUMMER PROGRAMS: Individual sport camps and enrichment programs in June, July, and August

FUTURE PLANS: New performing arts center, new squash center, and 50 meter Olympic pool

THE MERIT SCHOOL   703-670-9650   FAX 703-730-5171
14308 Spriggs Road, Woodbridge, VA 22193
E-MAIL: merit5@minnieland.net
GRADES: Kindergarten–3   **ENROLLMENT:** Co-ed
EXTENDED DAY: Before and after care   **TUITION:** Call for information.

MERRITT ACADEMY   703-273-8000   FAX 703-591-1431
9211 Arlington Boulevard, Fairfax, VA 22031
Founded 1963
HEAD: Toni Crouch
WEBSITE: www.merrittacademy.org   **E-MAIL:** admissions@merrittacademy.org
GRADES: Preschool–grade 8   **ENROLLMENT:** 380 Co-ed
FACULTY: 60 full- and 30 part-time   **AVERAGE CLASS SIZE:** 15–20
MISSION STATEMENT: "All children have talents." Rachel O. Merritt, Founder
For over 40 years, the mission of Rachel O. Merritt Academy has been to nourish and challenge the intellectual abilities, creative talents, and spiritual growth of children. We fulfill this mission by providing a safe, loving, and faith-centered educational environment, which is modeled on the family and time-honored tradition.
SPECIAL COURSES: Journalism, Spanish, accelerated curricula, French, Latin, music, computers, art, Award-winning Character Education Program, Intergenerational Programs, Handbell Choir, public speaking, theater arts, library, monthly field trips
EXTENDED DAY: 6:45 a.m.–6:15 p.m.
ATHLETICS: P.E., Intramural teams in soccer, bowling, basketball, softball (ABC League member). Karate, dance, gymnastics
CLUBS: Art, computer, Boy Scouts, Girl Scouts, cooking club, chess, Spanish, drama
PLANT: 7 1/2 acres, soccer/softball fields, sports court, in-ground pool, new gymnasium, 3 playgrounds, cafeteria
ADMISSION: Parent/child interview, entrance exam, transcript review. Enrollment is accepted year round, as space permits. Applications/Open House for new enrollments begins February of each year for coming Fall
TUITION: $11,230 Preschool (12 month program) full-time $8,900 elementary (K–5); $10,200 middle school (6–8) Extended care $2,250 annually (including snack) $12,810 toddler 24 months– nursery; $14,070 infant 6 weeks–24 months Books are included
FINANCIAL AID: Available
BOOKS: Included   **LUNCH:** Included in Preschool/optional lunch/milk K–8
TRANSPORTATION: Available within a 3–5 mile radius
DRESS CODE: Dress code is established K–8. Contact school for information.
SUMMER PROGRAMS: Day Camp (K–8) with weekly themes & field trips (Co-ed). Available in addition: swimming lessons, extended care (7:00 a.m.–6:00 p.m.), tutoring, AfterCamp activities program. $200 registration fee. Camp sessions $255 junior camp (K–5)/$275 senior camp (6–8)

METROPOLITAN DAY SCHOOL, INC.   202-234-3210   FAX 202-234-3214
1240 Randolph Street, NE, Washington, DC 20017-2628
Baptist 1998
HEAD: W.I. Woodard
DIRECTOR OF ADMISSIONS: Mark Woodson
WEBSITE: www.metropolitandayschool.org
E-MAIL: learn@metropolitandayschool.org
GRADES: Preschool 3.5, Pre-K–grade 6
ENROLLMENT: 99 Co-ed (53 boys/46 girls)
FACULTY: 14 full- and 2 part-time   **AVERAGE CLASS SIZE:** 17

MISSION STATEMENT: (Excerpted) Our mission is to develop the minds, bodies and spirits of children, creating in them a passion for lifelong learning, a commitment to caring for others, and habits of healthy living. We are committed to the pursuit of excellence, integrating learning and faith that our students may become the people God would have them to be.

SPECIAL COURSES: Africentric curriculum

EXTENDED DAY: 7:00–8:15 a.m. and 3:30–6:00 p.m.

ATHLETICS: Boys' and girls' basketball

CLUBS: Drill team, pom pom squad, African drumming, drama club, art club, Kuk Sol Won, book club

COMMUNITY INVOLVEMENT: Community ministry program

ADMISSION: Open houses, call for dates. Submit application with $50 fee

TUITION: $7,300

FINANCIAL AID: Available

BOOKS: Included   **LUNCH:** Available for a fee, but optional

OTHER FEES: After school care program $1,425

MILLER SCHOOL   434-823-4805   FAX 434-823-6617

1000 Samuel Miller Loop, Charlottesville, VA 22903

Founded 1878

HEAD: Lindsay R. Barnes

DIRECTOR OF ADMISSIONS: Jay Reeves

WEBSITE: www.millerschool.org   **E-MAIL:** jay@millerschool.org

GRADES: 6–12   **ENROLLMENT:** 160 Co-ed boarding begins in 6

FACULTY: 29 full-time   **AVERAGE CLASS SIZE:** 10–12

MISSION STATEMENT: "The Miller School of Albemarle is, first and foremost, an educational community, the primary purpose of which is to serve the best interests of its students by developing their minds, hands, and hearts and, in so doing, preparing them for successful entry into adult society."

SPECIAL COURSES: AP (English language & composition, European history, U.S. history, government & politics, French, Spanish, Calculus A/B & B/C, biology, environmental science, studio art); ESL; studio and performing arts

ATHLETICS: 17 athletic teams   **CLUBS:** Multiple clubs

PUBLICATIONS: Yearbook, newspaper, literary journal

COMMUNITY INVOLVEMENT: Community service

PLANT: The campus features 1,600 acres, a 12-acre lake, and a mix of buildings that include several on the Virginia Board of Historic Resources' list of Virginia Historic Landmarks

ADMISSION: Contact the Admission Office at 434-823-4805 or at www.millerschool.org for an application; interview required

TUITION: $9,885 day; $21,120 boarding

FINANCIAL AID: Available

DRESS CODE: Yes

MITCHELLVILLE CHILDREN'S HOUSE   301-249-9187   FAX 301-249-9742

12112 Central Avenue, Mitchellville, MD 20721

Founded 1992

HEAD: Gloria Panton-Harvey

WEBSITE: www.mmontesorisch.org   **E-MAIL:** ghrv129@aol.com

GRADES: Ungraded ages 2–10   **ENROLLMENT:** Co-ed
AVERAGE CLASS SIZE: 24
MISSION STATEMENT: The school's mission is the education of the whole person through the Montessori approach, addressing the intellectual, social, emotional, physical and spiritual needs of each child. Our goal is to foster independence, develop concentration, a sense of internal order and coordination; and to help the child to construct the adult personality she/he is in the process of becoming.
SPECIAL COURSES: Montessori program: Primary 3–6 and elementary 6–10. Music, Spanish
EXTENDED DAY: 6:30–8:30 a.m. and 3:00–6:00 p.m.
CLUBS: Dance, computer club
ADMISSION: Applications are accepted each year starting in February until slots are filled.
TUITION: $5,500
BOOKS: $180   **LUNCH:** Carried lunch
OTHER FEES: Trip fees $75   **DRESS CODE:** Uniform
SUMMER PROGRAMS: Enrichment program; Montessori Camp
FUTURE PLANS: Add a grade each year starting in September 2003, to the 6th grade

MONTESSORI ACADEMY AT BELMONT GREENE

703-729-7200   FAX 703-729-6957
20300 Bowfonds Street, Ashburn, VA 20147
Founded 2000
HEAD: Beth Theriot
DIRECTOR OF ADMISSIONS: Bart Theriot
WEBSITE: www.Montessori-BelmontGreene.com
E-MAIL: info@Montessori-BelmontGreene.com
GRADES: Ungraded ages 2–10   **ENROLLMENT:** 160 Co-ed
FACULTY: 23 full-time   **AVERAGE CLASS SIZE:** 24
MISSION STATEMENT: The Montessori Academy at Belmont Greene (MAB) is a diverse and engaging educational partnership of parents, teachers, children and community. We strive to nurture a child's love of learning and sense of personal and social responsibility using the child-centered Montessori philosophy and curriculum to develop the intellectual, spiritual, physical, artistic and academic excellence inherent in each child.
SPECIAL COURSES: Spanish, music, art, computers, dance
EXTENDED DAY: 7:30 a.m.–6:00 p.m.
CLUBS: Dance
ADMISSION: Contact Bart Theriot, Head of School Administration, for details.
TUITION: See website
LUNCH: Parents provide   **DRESS CODE:** Yes
SUMMER PROGRAMS: Montessori Camps offered throughout the summer
FUTURE PLANS: Expansion of facilities to include grades 4 through 6

MONTESSORI CHILDREN'S HOUSE OF LOUDOUN

703-421-1112   FAX 703-421-9356
880 West Church Road, Sterling, VA 20165
Founded 1997
HEAD: Claudine Norton, Bharti Shah, Meg Brown

DIRECTOR OF ADMISSIONS: Claudine Norton
WEBSITE: www.mchl.org   **E-MAIL:** mchl@erols.com
GRADES: Toddlers, preschool, K   **ENROLLMENT:** 180 Co-ed
FACULTY: 22 full- and 5 part-time   **AVERAGE CLASS SIZE:** 24–28
SPECIAL COURSES: Music, Spanish, Summer Camp, computers, yoga
EXTENDED DAY: 7:20 a.m.–6:00 p.m.
ADMISSION: Application with $25.00 application fee
TUITION: Varies
LUNCH: $2.50   **SUMMER PROGRAMS:** Camp
FUTURE PLANS: Adding two new classes in 2004

MONTESSORI INTERNATIONAL CHILDREN'S HOUSE   410-757-7789
1641 Winchester Road, Annapolis, MD 21401
Founded 1985
HEAD: Jean Burgess
E-MAIL: MICHPME@yahoo.com
GRADES: Ungraded ages 1 1/2–11   **ENROLLMENT:** 170 Co-ed
FACULTY: 7 full- and 7 part-time   **AVERAGE CLASS SIZE:** 20
SPECIAL COURSES: Montessori method. Spanish conversation taught. Music, art, creative dramatics, creative movement, cooking, P.E.
EXTENDED DAY: 7:30 a.m.–6:00 p.m.
PLANT: Library, modern facility designed specifically for Montessori primary and elementary programs in country setting
ADMISSION: Interview with parent and child, testing for elementary, $35 application fee
TUITION: $3,500–$6,700
LUNCH: Bring
SUMMER PROGRAMS: 6 week Montessori program for ages 18 months to 6

MONTESSORI SCHOOL OF ALEXANDRIA   703-960-3498   FAX 703-960-4667
6300 Florence Lane, Alexandria, VA 22310
Founded 1970
HEAD: Corrina Salahi
WEBSITE: www.montschoolalex.com
E-MAIL: montschoolalex@starpower.net
GRADES: Ungraded ages 3–13   **ENROLLMENT:** Co-ed
AVERAGE CLASS SIZE: 25
EXTENDED DAY: 7:30 a.m.–6:00 p.m.
TUITION: Call for information.

MONTESSORI SCHOOL OF HERNDON   703-437-8229   FAX 703-481-0249
840 Dranesville Road, Herndon, VA 22071
Founded 1984
HEAD: Nasim Kahn
WEBSITE: www.montessori-va.com   **E-MAIL:** director@montessori.com
GRADES: Ungraded ages 2 1/2–8   **ENROLLMENT:** Co-ed
SPECIAL COURSES: Montessori-based
CLUBS: Tap, ballet, karate, soccer
TUITION: Call for information.

MONTESSORI SCHOOL OF HOLMES RUN

703-573-4652   FAX 703-573-2807
3527 Gallows Road, Falls Church, VA 22042
Founded 1973
HEAD: Judith W. Clarke
WEBSITE: www.vamontessori.com
E-MAIL: mshr_fcch@hotmail.com
GRADES: Ungraded Pre-K–grade 6
ENROLLMENT: 150 Co-ed with FCCH
FACULTY: 12 full- and 10 part-time
AVERAGE CLASS SIZE: 20
MISSION STATEMENT: Parental involvement is actively encouraged. College preparatory, with emphasis on independence and self-motivation.
SPECIAL COURSES: French, music (Orff), guitar club. Classes are ungraded with 2 lower elementary classes for grade 1–3, and an upper elementary class for grades 4–6. Computers in all classes. Drama, P.E., and art at the elementary level. Pre-K and K classes held at Falls Church Children's House of Montessori.
EXTENDED DAY: Club program available before and after school 7:30–5:00
COMMUNITY INVOLVEMENT: Community service is done school-wide to benefit homeless families as well as UNICEF.
PLANT: Two campuses: one on Gallows Road, one on Annandale Road.
ADMISSION: Call for information and to schedule an observation, apply for enrollment and schedule a visit to the school by your child.
TUITION: $8,000 includes books
BOOKS: Included
OTHER FEES: Application fee $75. Activity fee, acceptance fee
TRANSPORTATION: Available. Call for details.
SUMMER PROGRAMS: Tenth month in June available to children enrolled at the elementary school

MONTESSORI SCHOOL OF MCLEAN   703-790-1049   FAX 703-790-1962

1711 Kirby Road, McLean, VA 22101
Founded 1973
HEAD: Joan Marie Parasine
GRADES: Ungraded ages 3–12   **ENROLLMENT:** 165 Co-ed
FACULTY: 14 full- and 20 part-time   **AVERAGE CLASS SIZE:** 25
MISSION STATEMENT: (Excerpted) The Montessori School of McLean strives to offer programs that challenge the child physically, mentally and emotionally so the child may reach their greatest potential. It is the goal of the organization to meet this challenge in a caring, compassionate and nurturing environment that fosters well being in the child, their family and the community.
SPECIAL COURSES: Ungraded classes, multi-age program. French or Spanish (elementary), computers all levels, art, dance and drama (elementary). Music and P.E. all levels.
TUITION: $7,900–$9,990
TRANSPORTATION: $2,000 round trip, $1,600 one way. 5 mile radius around school
DRESS CODE: Neat attire, no jeans in Preschool. Uniform required in elementary grades
SUMMER PROGRAMS: Available in June and July. Call for dates and information.

MONTESSORI SCHOOL OF NORTHERN VIRGINIA

577   FAX 703-256-9851

ic Lane, Annandale, VA 22003

_D. betsy Mitchell

WEBSITE: www.msnv.org   **E-MAIL:** info@msnv.org
GRADES: Ungraded, ages 2–9   **ENROLLMENT:** 135 Co-ed
FACULTY: 15 full- and 10 part-time   **AVERAGE CLASS SIZE:** 12–26
SPECIAL COURSES: Montessori curriculum, Spanish/French, Orff music program, art, P.E., cultural studies, Creative Dramatics. High level of parent involvement in many aspects of school life
EXTENDED DAY: All day program available, 7 a.m.–6 p.m.
CLUBS: Recorder, art
PLANT: Library; spacious bright classrooms that open to outside gardens, shady, park-like playground, amphitheater
ADMISSION: Parents visit and observe, interview. Application and $50 fee by January 15 for fall admission; mid-year admission from waiting list
TUITION: $2,824–$7,400 books included
FINANCIAL AID: Available
BOOKS: Included   **OTHER FEES:** Co-op fee $150
DRESS CODE: Comfortable clothing
SUMMER PROGRAMS: 8 weeks, ages 3–9. Wide range of activities, including Montessori, special interest studies, arts and crafts, outdoor play, food preparation, nature study

MONTESSORI SCHOOL OF OAKTON   703-715-0611

12113 Vale Road, Oakton, VA 22124
Founded 1981
HEAD: Carolyn Linke
GRADES: Ungraded 3–12 years   **ENROLLMENT:** Co-ed
SPECIAL COURSES: Spanish, music, art
TUITION: Call for information.

MONTROSE CHRISTIAN SCHOOL   301-770-5335   FAX 301-881-7345

5100 Randolph Road, Rockville, MD 20852
Founded 1977
HEAD: Tracy Mohr
DIRECTOR OF ADMISSIONS: Bonnie Liegey
WEBSITE: www.montrosechristian.org   **E-MAIL:** bliegy@montrosechristian.org
GRADES: Infant 6 weeks–grade 12   **ENROLLMENT:** 400 Co-ed
FACULTY: 45 full- and 6 part-time   **AVERAGE CLASS SIZE:** 18–20
MISSION STATEMENT: The mission of Montrose Christian School is to partner with parents to provide an outstanding education by inspiring wisdom, teaching discipline and nurturing faith.
SPECIAL COURSES: Child Development Center (6 weeks–4 years). Elementary (K–5) offers special enrichment courses including art, music, Spanish, P.E. and computers. Secondary (6–12) offers full Honors and AP courses in chemistry, British literature, calculus, biology, U.S. history and European history. Other courses offered include speech and debate, show choir, drama, Spanish, Latin,

home economics, apologetics, photography and more.

EXTENDED DAY: 7:00 a.m.–6:00 p.m.

ATHLETICS: Variety and junior varsity sports include basketball, soccer, volleyball, baseball, softball, and cheerleading. Elementary- Kids Sports program (ages 4–12)

CLUBS: National Honor Society, Student Government, drama productions, chorus, band, chess

COMMUNITY INVOLVEMENT: 20 hours of community service are required for all students in grades 9–12.

PLANT: Library and media center; child development center with 2 playgrounds, gym, auditorium, middle school and high school science labs, lower and upper school computer labs, 3 school playgrounds fully equipped and baseball batting cage

ADMISSION: Contact Bonnie Liegey at ext. 212 to schedule a tour. Elementary (K–5) Tuesdays 9:30 a.m., middle school (6–8) Wednesdays at 9:30 a.m. and high school tours Thursdays 9:30 a.m.

TUITION: $9,400 K–5; $9,900 6–12

FINANCIAL AID: Available. All families, returning and new must fill out a new form to SSS each school year to be reevaluated based on need. Funds are dispersed first come first served based on the individual family need.

BOOKS: Included   **LUNCH:** $3.50/day and a la carte menu available

OTHER FEES: Non-refundable application fee $250; $500 international (F–1) students. Student activity fees $100 (K–5) $295 (6–8) $325 (9,10) $395 (11) $425 (12). Re-enrollment $200 per student annually

TRANSPORTATION: Available   **DRESS CODE:** Uniforms required (K–12)

SUMMER PROGRAMS: Montrose Adventure Camp ages 5–12 contact Patti Schooler at 301-613-7930.

MOTHER CATHERINE SPALDING SCHOOL

301-884-3165   FAX 301-472-4469
38833 Chaptico Road, Helen, MD 20635
Catholic
HEAD: Robert Ligday
WEBSITE: www.mothercatherinespalding.com   **E-MAIL:** mcsadmin@erols.com
GRADES: Pre-K–grade 8   **ENROLLMENT:** Co-ed
EXTENDED DAY: Before and after care
TUITION: $2,636.25 one child in parish; $2,826.25 one child out of parish
DRESS CODE: Uniforms

MOTHER OF GOD SCHOOL   301-990-2088   FAX 301-947-0574

20501 Goshen Road, Gaithersburg, MD 20879
Catholic 1987
HEAD: Ann Jurkowski
DIRECTOR OF ADMISSIONS: Mary Sykes
WEBSITE: www.mogschool.com   **E-MAIL:** mogsadmn@erols.com
GRADES: Kindergarten–grade 8   **ENROLLMENT:** 241 Co-ed (99 boys/142 girls)
FACULTY: 11 full- and 9 part-time
AVERAGE CLASS SIZE: 28
MISSION STATEMENT: Mother of God School seeks to prepare students who, grounded in sound academics and strong faith go forth bearing Christ to the

world in their interpersonal and professional lives. With Mary as its model, the school accomplishes this in an atmosphere of love and respect: through academic excellence in the humanities, arts and sciences, and in living the Good News through worship and service.

SPECIAL COURSES: Algebra I, Spanish K–8

EXTENDED DAY: 7:00–8:30 a.m. and 3:25–6:00 p.m.

ATHLETICS: Soccer, CYO basketball

CLUBS: Student Council, Math Counts, chess club, Bible study, choir, band, Girl Scouts, Brownies and Daisies, Boy Scouts, School Safety Patrols

PLANT: Mother of God School is an independent Catholic school affiliated with the Archdiocese of Washington. Sponsored by Mother of God Community, an Archdiocesan-recognized association for the faithful, the school provides a faith-filled environment designed to promote the academic, spiritual and social development of its students. Mother of God School has a spacious campus, including an impressive full-court gymnasium and provides ample space for the Kindergarten through eighth grade program.

ADMISSION: Grade one applicants are screened individually. Other students are scheduled for entrance testing upon receipt of all application materials. $150 non-refundable application fee. Upon acceptance, $325 registration fee is submitted, applicable to student's tuition.

TUITION: $4,725 first child; $4,325 second child; $3,425 third child; $1,865 fourth child

FINANCIAL AID: Tuition assistance is available through the Archdiocese of Washington, and limited funds are available through the Mother of God School's Scholarship Program.

BOOKS: $300   **LUNCH:** Carry   **DRESS CODE:** Uniforms

MOUNT CALVARY CATHOLIC SCHOOL   301-735-5262   FAX 301-736-5044

6704 Marlboro Pike, Forestville, MD 20747

Catholic 1950

HEAD: Valerie M. Carroll

DIRECTOR OF ADMISSIONS: Maryanne Arena

WEBSITE: www.mtccs.org   **E-MAIL:** mtcalcs@erols.com

GRADES: Nursery–grade 8   **ENROLLMENT:** 280 Co-ed

FACULTY: 30 full- and 2 part-time   **AVERAGE CLASS SIZE:** 25

MISSION STATEMENT: (Excerpted) Our aim is to provide an environment that fosters spirituality and growth in faith, and education program that builds academic success, and leadership that promotes strong character and a love for service to others. At Mount Calvary Catholic School, the formation of our young people is carried out with care in ways that are based on the life and teachings of Jesus Christ.

SPECIAL COURSES: Inclusion program (for students with documented learning disabilities), enrichment program, Spanish (Pre-K–grade 8), math lab, state of the art computer lab, P.E., music, art, computer and library. Junior high grades (30 in homeroom classes, split 15/15 for all academic courses.)

EXTENDED DAY: 6:45 a.m.–6:00 p.m.

ATHLETICS: CYO athletic program (including, depending on level of interest: basketball, track and field, soccer, baseball, softball and cheerleading.) Intramural flag football

CLUBS: Drama club, instrumental music, liturgical dance team, National Junior Honor Society, Student Government Association, Afternoon Tea and Book Club, Frederick Douglass Oratorical Society, National Geographic Geography Bee, Reader's Digest Word Challenge

PUBLICATIONS: Yearbook

COMMUNITY INVOLVEMENT: Monthly Sandwich Day (Martha's Table), Ladies of Charity Food Pantry and many other community service opportunities. Junior high students (6,7,8 grades) are required to give 10 hours each year in community service.

PLANT: Mount Calvary is located on the campus with Mount Calvary Catholic Church, parish offices and Catholic Charities. The school is a three level building with classrooms, cafeteria and multipurpose room. In addition there is a large play area with a playground and athletic field.

ADMISSION: Please call registrar for detailed information.

TUITION: $3,800 participating Catholic families; $5,100 non-participating families

FINANCIAL AID: Available. Financial aid forms must be submitted no later than February 15th of the year you are interested in your child beginning school.

BOOKS: Included

LUNCH: Fees dependent on age of child

OTHER FEES: Junior High Fee for grades 6,7,8 $300 per child

DRESS CODE: Uniform

SUMMER PROGRAMS: Summer School is offered as well as an enrichment program. Extended care is an option during the summer as well.

FUTURE PLANS: Renovations to the physical plant

MOUNT PLEASANT BAPTIST CHURCH CHRISTIAN ACADEMY

703-793-1196
2516 Squirrel Hill Road, Herndon, VA 20171
Baptist 2000
HEAD: Margaret Aghayere
WEBSITE: www.mtpleasantbaptist.org
GRADES: K4–grade 3
SPECIAL COURSES: A Beka curriculum, computer, library
EXTENDED DAY: 6:30 a.m.–6:00 p.m.
CLUBS: Arts and crafts, STEP team
PLANT: Computer/library room
ADMISSION: Open enrollment
TUITION: Call for information.
FUTURE PLANS: Add grade levels until reaching grade 12

MUNGER ACADEMY   703-430-2781   FAX 703-430-5740

624 West Church Road, Sterling, VA 20164
HEAD: Paula Munger
WEBSITE: www.mungeracademy.com
GRADES: N (age 2)–grade 3
ENROLLMENT: 200 Co-ed
EXTENDED DAY: Before and after care for enrolled students only
TUITION: Call for information.
SUMMER PROGRAMS: Summer Camp

MUSLIM COMMUNITY SCHOOL   301-340-6713   FAX 301-340-7339

7917 Montrose Road, Potomac, MD 20854

Islamic, Non-Sectarian 1984

HEAD: Salim Mahdi

WEBSITE: www.muslimcommunityschool.com   **E-MAIL:** mcschool@erols.com

GRADES: Pre-K–grade 11   **ENROLLMENT:** 200 Co-ed   **AVERAGE CLASS SIZE:** 16

MISSION STATEMENT: MCS' educational philosophy is deeply rooted in the Holy Quran and is shaped around the prayer of the Holy Prophet Muhammad (S.A.W.):"My Lord! Grant me knowledge that is useful to humanity." Therefore, the Administration and Instructional Staff of MCS continuously work hard to develop an environment where students can acquire academic and life skills they will find constructive, positive, and useful as they march forward in life.

SPECIAL COURSES: Arabic and Religious Studies K–11. In addition to the 4 core subject areas, computer science and applications, P.E. and Leadership classes are also taught. General science to physics, general math to calculus, history: U.S., world, national, state and local government, civics and Islamic History are taught; language arts, literature and spelling, ESOL. Al classes except Arabic are taught in English.

ATHLETICS: Tae kwon do team   **CLUBS:** Drama club

PUBLICATIONS: Yearbook

PLANT: Computer lab, science lab and library media center

ADMISSION: Meet state age requirement for Pre-K, Kindergarten and 1st grade. Medical history and immunization records required for registration. The completion of MCS registration papers and tuition contract with letter of recommendation for students entering 6–11 grades. Interview with parents and student to understand school rules and expectations.

TUITION: $430 per month. Reduction in tuition cost for siblings

FINANCIAL AID: The amount of financial aid available depends on student enrollment and parent willingness and availability to volunteer time in school to help where needed.

BOOKS: Supplied   **LUNCH:** Catered, $2.00

OTHER FEES: Registration fee of $350 per child to cover book cost

TRANSPORTATION: $120 1st child and limited

DRESS CODE: Uniform required

FUTURE PLANS: Working on plans to add 12th grade

—N

NANNIE HELEN BURROUGHS SCHOOL, INC.

202-398-5266   FAX 202-398-5652

601 50th Street, N.E., Washington, DC 20019

Baptist 1909

HEAD: Shirley Hayes

WEBSITE: www.nhburroughs.org   **E-MAIL:** sagh66@hotmail.com

GRADES: N–grade 6   **ENROLLMENT:** 200 Co-ed

FACULTY: 11 full- and 8 part-time   **AVERAGE CLASS SIZE:** 20

SPECIAL COURSES: Spanish, music, science includes aerospace and computer science. Bible classes K–6. After school program in cultural arts. Emphasis on Leadership Training

EXTENDED DAY: 7:00 a.m.–6:00 p.m.   **TUITION:** $4,200 N and K; $4,000 1–6

GRADES: N (age 2 1/2)–grade 12   **ENROLLMENT:** 85 Co-ed
SPECIAL COURSES: French, Swahili, African Youth Organization and Dance, drill team, computer club
EXTENDED DAY: 7:00 a.m.–6:00 p.m.
TUITION: $4,250 (1–9); $4,500 (10–12); $4,500 pre-primary
DRESS CODE: Yes. Call for information
SUMMER PROGRAMS: Academic and recreational

NATIVITY CATHOLIC ACADEMY   202-722-0611   FAX 202-291-0219
6008 Georgia Avenue, N.W., Washington, DC 20011
Catholic 1908
HEAD: Dr. Thomas M. Simpson
DIRECTOR OF ADMISSIONS: Dr. Thomas M. Simpson
WEBSITE: www.centercityconsortium.org   **E-MAIL:** NCALearn2@aol.com
GRADES: Pre-K–grade 8   **ENROLLMENT:** 198 Co-ed
FACULTY: 10 full- and 4 part-time   **AVERAGE CLASS SIZE:** 17
MISSION STATEMENT: "Learning Christian Living and Hope" is Nativity Catholic Academy's motto. The Academy's elementary education (Pre-K through 8th) environment contributes to the growth of the whole person and prepares each for his/her unique role in this world. The pursuit of knowledge, Christian values, and the encouragement of Christian achievement calls for the cooperation of all. We will communicate openly and honestly with parents and encourage involvement in their child's learning process. Given in the Name of the Gospel, this collaboration is witness to Christ as the cornerstone of our Catholic community.
EXTENDED DAY: 7:00 a.m.–6:00 p.m.
ATHLETICS: Cheerleading, lacrosse, soccer, football, basketball
ADMISSION: (Excerpted) Registration for the new school year takes place in the month of March. Contact school for admission requirements and procedures. All families of enrolled students must agree to complete twenty hours of service during the course of the school year.
TUITION: $3,245
FINANCIAL AID: Available
DRESS CODE: Girls: heather plaid jumper/skirt, yellow blouse peter-pan collar/oxford, navy blue cardigan, navy blue slacks/shorts. Boys: navy blue slacks, light blue golf shirt/oxford, navy blue tie, navy blue v-neck/crew neck sweater.

NATIVITY CATHOLIC SCHOOL   703-455-2300   FAX 703-569-8109
6398 Nativity Lane, Burke, VA 22015
Catholic 1996
HEAD: Maria Kelly
DIRECTOR OF ADMISSIONS: Lillian Feltman
WEBSITE: www.nativityschool.org
E-MAIL: nativityschool@nativityschool.org
GRADES: Pre-K–grade 8   **ENROLLMENT:** 268 Co-ed (149 boys/119 girls)
FACULTY: 9 full- and 6 part-time   **AVERAGE CLASS SIZE:** 30
MISSION STATEMENT: The mission of Nativity Catholic School is to develop in the students a desire for learning in an atmosphere where every child is valued as a unique child of God. Our mission then is to encourage students to develop their full potential, spiritually, emotionally, and academically.

EXTENDED DAY: 7:00–8:00 a.m and 3:00–6:00 p.m.
ATHLETICS: Sports   **CLUBS:** Band, CYO
TUITION: $3,100–$3,960
BOOKS: $200   **OTHER FEES:** Registration $75–$100   **DRESS CODE:** Uniform

NAYLOR ROAD SCHOOL   202-584-5114   FAX 202-583-0687
2403 Naylor Road, S.E., Washington, DC 20020
Founded 1944
HEAD: Patricia A. Ward
DIRECTOR OF ADMISSIONS: Sherrie Ruggles, Principal
WEBSITE: www.naylorroadschool.com   **E-MAIL:** patnay@aol.com
GRADES: Pre-K 3–grade 8   **ENROLLMENT:** 300 Co-ed
FACULTY: 31 full- and 4 part-time   **AVERAGE CLASS SIZE:** 18
SPECIAL COURSES: Spanish, music, computers, general academic courses in math, reading, language, science, social studies and phonics
EXTENDED DAY: 6:30 a.m.–6:00 p.m.
CLUBS: United Nations Club, math club
PUBLICATIONS: Middle school newspaper
PLANT: Library 3,000 volumes, computer lab, language lab, science lab. Computers in each classroom
ADMISSION: Applications accepted in March. Testing grades 2–7
TUITION: $4,500–$5,500 Payment plans available
OTHER FEES: Registration fee, book fee   **DRESS CODE:** Uniform
SUMMER PROGRAMS: Available

NEW CITY MONTESSORI SCHOOL   301-559-8488
3120 Nicholson Street, Hyattsville, MD 20782-3108
Founded 1968
HEAD: Shirley Windsor
WEBSITE: www.newcitymontessori.com   **E-MAIL:** NCMS68@aol.com
GRADES: Ungraded ages 2 1/2–9   **ENROLLMENT:** 60 Co-ed
FACULTY: 6 full- and 4 part-time   **AVERAGE CLASS SIZE:** 20
SPECIAL COURSES: Montessori curriculum, ungraded
EXTENDED DAY: 7:30 a.m.–6:00 p.m.
PLANT: Spacious classrooms with floor-to-ceiling windows, large fenced and well-equipped playground with wooded areas on two sides. Convenient to two Metro stations
ADMISSION: Application form, fee, informal interview with parent and child. Observation by parent encouraged prior to interview
TUITION: $4,200–$5,900
LUNCH: Bring   **OTHER FEES:** Materials fee

NEW COVENANT CHRISTIAN ACADEMY
301-277-2596
FAX 301-277-9303
3805 Lawrence Street, Colmar Manor, MD 20722
HEAD: Dr. Cleola Spears
GRADES: N(age 2)–grade 8   **ENROLLMENT:** Co-ed
TUITION: Call for information.

DRESS CODE: Uniforms   **SUMMER PROGRAMS:** Summer Camp
FUTURE PLANS: Will add grade 9

NEW HOPE ACADEMY   301-459-7311   FAX 301-459-2813
7009 Varnum Street, Landover Hills, MD 20784
Non-denominational
HEAD: Joy Morrow
WEBSITE: www.newhopeacademy.org   **E-MAIL:** admin@newhopeacademy.org
GRADES: Pre-K3–grade 12   **ENROLLMENT:** 270 Co-ed
FACULTY: 29 full- and 9 part-time   **AVERAGE CLASS SIZE:** 16–20
MISSION STATEMENT: New Hope Academy is dedicated to academic excellence and character education. It supports parents to raise moral children, and promotes inter-cultural harmony. Founded on principles universal to people of all faiths, New Hope recognizes that belief in the Parenthood of God leads to the brotherhood of humanity.
SPECIAL COURSES: Character Education, Korean language, Spanish language, P.E., information technology, library, art, music. Optional after school dance program includes ballet and ethnic dance
EXTENDED DAY: 7:15–8:15 a.m. and 3:30–6:00 p.m.
ATHLETICS: Martial arts
CLUBS: Kindermusik, Boy Scouts, Girl Scouts, band, drill ream, Harvest Festival, Spring Fair, book fair, African-Caribbean Night, Asian-Mediterranean Night
PUBLICATIONS: Yearbook club
COMMUNITY INVOLVEMENT: Service for Peace Club
PLANT: 8-acre campus.
ADMISSION: Call for information packet. Orientation and tour, application and fee, release of records form, observation or testing, enrollment packet forms
TUITION: $6,000–$6,950
FINANCIAL AID: Limited. Second and third child discounts, co-op work opportunities and "finder's fee" for successful referrals
OTHER FEES: $500 deposit. Educational materials, books, technology, equipment, recreation and field trips: Preschool $200, K–8 $435, 9–12 $585
DRESS CODE: Modesty code, optional uniform
SUMMER PROGRAMS: Summer camp which includes field trips, swimming, sports, arts and crafts and snacks
FUTURE PLANS: Expanded science lab, improved library, new playground, new roof

NEW LIFE CHRISTIAN SCHOOL   301-663-8418   FAX 301-698-1583
5909 Jefferson Pike, Frederick, MD 21703
Foursquare Gospel 1988
HEAD: Rev. Paul H. Kemp
DIRECTOR OF ADMISSIONS: Donald Lewis
WEBSITE: www.newlifecs.org
GRADES: Kindergarten–grade 12   **ENROLLMENT:** 251 Co-ed (120 boys/131 girls)
FACULTY: 35 full- and 2 part-time   **AVERAGE CLASS SIZE:** 22
MISSION STATEMENT: New Life Christian School is an interdenominational Christian day school serving students in the Greater Frederick area, offering classes from Kindergarten through high school. NLCS provides a sound academic program presented from a distinctly Christian world-view. The school joins with parents

and home churches in developing young people well prepared to integrate their knowledge with their faith in their homes, churches, and workplace. New Life Christian School is committed to "Sowing Excellence and Christian Character" in all its students.

SPECIAL COURSES: AP English, AP calculus, computer lab, Spanish 1-4
ATHLETICS: Soccer, basketball, volleyball
CLUBS: Youth group, choir, Chapel and drama
PLANT: Rural setting off Jefferson Pike on over 20 acres. Air-conditioned gymnasium and separate computer lab
ADMISSION: See our website www.newlifecs.org
TUITION: $2,400 K half day; $3,900 elementary 1–5; $4,300 middle school 6–8; $4,500 high school 9–12 Reduction for siblings
FINANCIAL AID: Available only to returning students at this time.
BOOKS: Included **LUNCH:** Bring your own
OTHER FEES: Registration and activities fees.
DRESS CODE: Uniforms
SUMMER PROGRAMS: Basketball and volleyball camps
FUTURE PLANS: Expansion to 300–350 students maximum

THE NEW SCHOOL OF NORTHERN VIRGINIA

703-691-3040   FAX 703-691-3041
9431 Silver King Court, Fairfax, VA 22031
Founded 1989
HEAD: John Potter
DIRECTOR OF ADMISSIONS: Denise Jones grades 3-8; John Potter grades 9-12
WEBSITE: www.nsnva.pvt.k12.va.us
E-MAIL: val@nsnva.pvt.k12.va.us
GRADES: 3–12   **ENROLLMENT:** 125 Co-ed
FACULTY: 15 full- and 5 part-time   **AVERAGE CLASS SIZE:** 10–12
MISSION STATEMENT: Our central academic goal is to prepare students to enter college as self-motivated and accomplished writers, thinkers, collaborators and communicators.
SPECIAL COURSES: Essential schools philosophy: exhibitions, Socratic seminars, portfolios. AP English, U.S. government, studio art, U.S. history; plan to add more. ESL instruction available. Spanish, French, German, Latin. Drama, music 3–12. Fine arts include traditional media plus stone & wax sculpture, computer graphics, animation, digital photography. Computer programming, web design, powerpoint, internet in every room. Travel courses in history, science, foreign language. Student government, fairness committee, admissions committee, curriculum committee and more.
ATHLETICS: Soccer, basketball, ultimate frisbee, volleyball
CLUBS: Chess, art, electronics, Amnesty International, computer graphics, digital photography, sports, crafts, films
PUBLICATIONS: Yearbook, literary magazine, zines
COMMUNITY INVOLVEMENT: Community service requirement grades 7–11
PLANT: Two buildings, wooded site, sand volleyball court, basketball court, access to fields for softball, soccer, frisbee. Plans awaiting approval to build multimedia center, athletic space, library, additional classrooms.
ADMISSION: Rolling, but recommended before May 1. Interview, application,

recommendations, student visit. Fee $75. Tuition deposit $1,000 until May 1, increases after that date

TUITION: $13,500 3–6; $15,000 7–8; $16,600 9–12

FINANCIAL AID: Limited; returning students have priority. Must submit FAFSA form

OTHER FEES: Book and activity fee $200 3–6, $275 7–12. Annual registration fee $100; optional after school homework group: $650/semester

TRANSPORTATION: To and from Vienna Metro only: $350/semester

DRESS CODE: Liberal

SUMMER PROGRAMS: High school academic courses for credit; state of the art computer camps in 2-week intensive units

FUTURE PLANS: Building construction; interscholastic sports; SACS accreditation within two years

THE NEWPORT SCHOOL   301-942-4550   FAX 301-949-2654

10914 Georgia Avenue, Silver Spring, MD 20902
Founded 1930
HEAD: Ronald Stephens
DIRECTOR OF ADMISSIONS: Marilyn Grossblatt
WEBSITE: www.newportschool.org
GRADES: N–grade 12   **ENROLLMENT:** 105 Co-ed
FACULTY: 21 full- and 7 part-time   **AVERAGE CLASS SIZE:** 8

MISSION STATEMENT: The Newport School, committed to educating well-rounded, responsible young men and women, has a seventy-year track record of ensuring educational success. The Newport School's mission is to provide a nurturing environment where students benefit from individual attention within a diverse community of students, where strong value-based teaching fosters independent thinking. A Newport education combines a challenging curriculum and high academic standards using both traditional and innovative thinking.

SPECIAL COURSES: Spanish Pre-K–12, French 7–12, science, biology, chemistry, physics. History: world & American, political theory, government, economics. Arts: dance, music, theater & visual. AP psychology, biology, calculus, American history, English literature and composition

EXTENDED DAY: 7:00 a.m.–6:00 p.m.

ATHLETICS: After school sports program, karate

CLUBS: Chess club. Art programs & festival, lower and middle Fine and Performing Arts Night

PUBLICATIONS: Yearbook

PLANT: Senior and junior libraries, lower school/prep science lab, art room, computer room, all-purpose room

ADMISSION: Rolling admissions. Interview 6–12, Test, Pre-K, K; Application fee $50, visit

TUITION: $10,580–$16,960

FINANCIAL AID: Available

BOOKS: Included   **LUNCH:** Included

DRESS CODE: Uniform: 1–11, dress code grade 12

SUMMER PROGRAMS: Recreational: designed for 3 years and up–swimming lessons, science exploration

157

THE NORA SCHOOL   301-495-6672   FAX 301-495-7829
955 Sligo Avenue, Silver Spring, MD 20910
Founded 1964
HEAD: David E. Mullen
WEBSITE: www.nora-school.org   **E-MAIL:** elaine@nora-school.org
GRADES: 9–12   **ENROLLMENT:** 60 Co-ed (32 boys/28 girls)
FACULTY: 9 full- and 2 part-time   **AVERAGE CLASS SIZE:** 9
MISSION STATEMENT: Small classes and individual attention provide a supportive and challenging environment which fosters personal and intellectual growth and responsible independence.
SPECIAL COURSES: College preparatory curriculum plus the following: Civil Rights and Holocaust Studies; Rites of Passage and Women's Literature; Genre Studies in Science Fiction and Horror Literature; Remedial Writing; History of Religion; music theory, art, craft, photography, drama. Untimed SAT's for qualifying students
ATHLETICS: Interscholastic soccer, basketball and softball
CLUBS: Student Government. Peer mediation. International travel during Spring Break
PUBLICATIONS: Yearbook
PLANT: Formerly Washington Ethical High School. All new facility opened June 2000 in Silver Spring, Maryland. Convenient to Metrorail, Metrobus, and Montgomery County Ride-On. State of the art computer lab, science lab and art space
ADMISSION: Applicant and parent interview. Applicant visits for a half day. Contact Director of Admissions
TUITION: $16,150
FINANCIAL AID: Available
BOOKS: $250   **OTHER FEES:** Activities fee $250 **DRESS CODE:** Appropriate.
SUMMER PROGRAMS: Selected classes offered by individual teachers in summer

NORBEL SCHOOL   410-796-6700   FAX 410-796-7661
6135 Old Washington Road, Elkridge, MD 21075
WEBSITE: www.norbelschool.org
E-MAIL: fpugliese@norbelschool.org
GRADES: 1–11   **ENROLLMENT:** Co-ed
AVERAGE CLASS SIZE: 6:1 student/teacher ratio
MISSION STATEMENT: Norbel School's mission is to educate children of average to gifted intelligence who have language difficulties, learning disabilities, and/or attention deficit disorders. Norbel's environment is designed to nurture both the mind and the creative spirit of each child while providing a support for the development of emotional and social maturity.
SPECIAL COURSES: Norbel School is a national model of education for students with a wide variety of learning disabilities. By individualizing instruction, using multiple teaching methods, and integrating an affective curriculum, Norbel maximizes the academic success of each student. Through ongoing research, Norbel defines best practices for educating children. Norbel School serves children with average to gifted intelligence that also have language and/or learning differences. In this unique educational environment, children learn through a flexible, individualized academic program that is complemented with training in essential interpersonal skills.
ATHLETICS: Athletic programs
PLANT: 8.5 acre campus located in a residential area of Historic Elkridge,

Howard County, Maryland. Athletic field, basketball court, playground, several science labs, computer lab, art studio, performing arts center, three-story media center that boasts an integrated wireless computer network with access to numerous library databases

ADMISSION: Rolling admissions policy. Parent/student interviews and review of current assessments

TUITION: $17,650 lower/upper school; $19,000 high school

FINANCIAL AID: Available

TRANSPORTATION: Limited. Additional fee

FUTURE PLANS: Add 12th grade

NORTHERN VIRGINIA FRIENDS SCHOOL   703-281-6837   FAX 703-757-3898

2854 Hunter Mill Road (P.O. Box 411), Oakton, VA 22124

Quaker 2003

HEAD: Barbara Wille

DIRECTOR OF ADMISSIONS: Barbara Wille

WEBSITE: www.QuakerEd.com   **E-MAIL:** QuakerSchool@aol.com

GRADES: Pre-K–6   **ENROLLMENT:** 176 Co-ed maximum

AVERAGE CLASS SIZE: 16–18

MISSION STATEMENT: (Excerpted) The mission of Northern Virginia Friends School is to provide a loving, challenging academic environment that reflects the central Quaker belief that there is that of God in everyone. We strive to provide a school that fosters a life-long love of learning in all members of our community.

SPECIAL COURSES: Spanish beginning in Pre-Kindergarten. Conflict resolution is incorporated into the curriculum at all grade levels.

EXTENDED DAY: 6:30 a.m.–6:30 p.m.

PLANT: Opening in the fall of 2003, Northern Virginia Friends School's facilities are brand new. The building, completed by Unity Church of Fairfax in November, 2002, includes computer wiring in all classrooms to allow networking. With bright classrooms and inviting play spaces, NVFS opens only a few miles from Metro's Vienna station.

ADMISSION: Parents are encouraged to request admission material. Applications are accepted from November through January 15 (or as space allows thereafter.) Transcripts and/or referral forms are due by February 1.

TUITION: $9,500

FINANCIAL AID: Yes

BOOKS: $350

SUMMER PROGRAMS: Beginning in 2004, summer camp will run from late June to mid-August.

NORWOOD SCHOOL   301-365-2595   FAX 301-365-4277

8821 River Road, Bethesda, MD 20817

Founded 1952

HEAD: Richard T. Ewing, Jr.

WEBSITE: www.norwoodschool.org   **E-MAIL:** info@norwoodschool.org

GRADES: K–grade 8   **ENROLLMENT:** 506 Co-ed

FACULTY: 63 full- and 14 part-time   **AVERAGE CLASS SIZE:** 12

MISSION STATEMENT: The School's mission is to assure that each of its children grows intellectually, morally, physically and socially. The School provides outstanding instruction in fundamental skills and logical and analytical thinking, while encouraging independence of mind, intellectual curiosity, moral growth and creative self-expression.

SPECIAL COURSES: Educational technology at all grade levels; French and Spanish (grades 2–8); Latin (grades 7 and 8); art, music, drama, P.E. for all grades, instrumental or choral music classes (grade 5–8)

EXTENDED DAY: 2:30–5:50 p.m. Monday–Thursday; 12:30–5:50 p.m. Friday

ATHLETICS: Interscholastic sports

CLUBS: Debate club, computer club, rocket club, social club, yearbook committee, newspaper committee. Private music lessons available

PUBLICATIONS: Magazine, curriculum overview

COMMUNITY INVOLVEMENT: Each grade participates in an outreach project approved by the administration which parents help organize and implement. There are also 3 school-wide community service drives.

PLANT: 2 libraries, 5 science classrooms, 2 computer labs, 4 art classrooms, 3 gyms, 2 combined lacrosse/soccer/field hockey fields, 1 baseball field, 1 softball field, 1 playground, playing fields. Music/arts/drama building, fitness room, cafeteria.

ADMISSION: Applications taken September–mid-January for following year. Parent tour, personal interview with parents, each child visit to current grade, IQ test for grades K–5, SSAT or ISEE for grades 6–8. Notification by mid-March

TUITION: $17,130 K,1,2; $17,600 3,4; $17,790 5,6; $18,210 7,8

FINANCIAL AID: Available

LUNCH: Grades 5–8   **OTHER FEES:** K–4 $575; 5–6 $1,400; 7–8 $1,750

DRESS CODE: Serviceable school clothes

SUMMER PROGRAMS: Summer at Norwood Day Camp, ages 3–14; sports camp, ages 5–14; Adventure Camp, grades 4–8; study skills course, grades 5–8

NOTRE DAME ACADEMY   540-687-5581   FAX 540-687-3552

35321 Notre Dame Lane, Middleburg, VA 20117

Catholic 1965

HEAD: Sister Cecilia Liberatore, SND

DIRECTOR OF ADMISSIONS: Christopher A.L. Nittle

WEBSITE: www.notredameva.org   **E-MAIL:** cnittle@notredameva.org

GRADES: 9–12   **ENROLLMENT:** 285 Co-ed (50% boys/50% girls)

AVERAGE CLASS SIZE: 14

MISSION STATEMENT: An independent Catholic, coeducational, college preparatory school serving grades nine through twelve, Notre Dame Academy offers a challenging program complemented by competitive interscholastic sports teams, an outstanding arts program and a meaningful commitment to community service. All NDA graduates attend college, 85% of faculty hold advanced degrees, and the current faculty-to-student ratio is one to nine.

SPECIAL COURSES: French and Spanish. History: global studies, American history, government, Virginia history, sociology, economics. Science: Psychology, general science, chemistry, biology, and physics. Computer science, keyboarding. Religious studies required. Drama, art-drawing, design, studio ceramics, graphics. Music: choral, instrumental, orchestra, photography. AP: English, biology, calculus, American history, government. Senior career internship, independent study, dual enrollment- Shenandoah University

ATHLETICS: Required. Interscholastic. Volleyball, soccer, cross-country, basket-

ball, softball, baseball, tennis, field hockey, lacrosse
CLUBS: Campus Ministry, language club, Ambassadors, choral, drama
PUBLICATIONS: Newspaper, yearbook
COMMUNITY INVOLVEMENT: 26 hours of volunteer service required each year. Food and clothing assistance, Living Tree, Oxfam banquet, Senior Citizens Day. Students may volunteer to teach religion to children in local parish.
PLANT: Library 10,000 volumes, 190+-acre campus, science labs, auditorium, gym, playing fields, tennis courts, art studio, greenhouse.
ADMISSION: Competitive and selective. Interview required. $50 application fee. February 7th application deadline
TUITION: $13,500
FINANCIAL AID: Average grant is approximately 50% of the tuition obligation. Almost 50% of families receive some form of financial aid. Strictly need-based
BOOKS: Extra   **LUNCH:** Extra   **TRANSPORTATION:** Available
DRESS CODE: Yes   **SUMMER PROGRAMS:** Basketball camp; art camp

NYSMITH SCHOOL FOR THE GIFTED   703-435-7711   FAX 703-713-3336
13625 Eds Drive, Herndon, VA 20171
Founded 1983
HEAD: Carole Nysmith
WEBSITE: www.Nysmith.com   **E-MAIL:** KNysmith@Nysmith.com
GRADES: 3 years–grade 8   **ENROLLMENT:** 620 Co-ed (310 boys/310 girls)
FACULTY: 120 full- and part-time
AVERAGE CLASS SIZE: teacher/student ratio 1:9
MISSION STATEMENT: Nysmith offers a highly individualized, accelerated curriculum for students who have demonstrated high levels of curiosity, motivation and a desire to learn. Our program and educators are unique and offer students an exceptional environment for intellectual stimulation and emotional growth. Our goal is to assist children in achieving their full potential in an atmosphere that is loving and nurturing. We strive to make learning an ongoing adventure, piquing and maintaining the natural curiosity within each child.
SPECIAL COURSES: French. Math: algebra, geometry, algebra II- trigonometry; Science: biology, chemistry, physics, earth science, computer science (197 computers in use N–8). Art, music (including Orff program); Counseling (K–8). American history, ancient history
EXTENDED DAY: 6:30 a.m.–6:30 p.m.
ATHLETICS: P.E. required, sports, fencing, karate
CLUBS: Student Council, art, poetry, competitive math, geography, French
PUBLICATIONS: Yearbook, literary magazine, newsletters
PLANT: 55,000 square feet on 13.25 acres. Large sunlit classrooms in a new state of the art building. 3 computer labs and media center total over 300 computers used by every child daily
ADMISSION: Testing from K and older, visitation, teacher recommendation
TUITION: $11,420–$17,730
FINANCIAL AID: Available
LUNCH: Optional for K–8 **TRANSPORTATION:** Available
SUMMER PROGRAMS: Sports, art, cooking, karate, fencing, computers, drama, tennis and daily swimming

OAK CHAPEL SCHOOL   301-598-7249
14500 Layhill Road, Silver Spring, MD 20906
Methodist
HEAD: Maurice Hartlove
DIRECTOR OF ADMISSIONS: Maurice Hartlove
WEBSITE: www.oakchapelschool.com   **E-MAIL:** dloring@cpcug.org
GRADES: 2 years–grade 8   **ENROLLMENT:** 75 Co-ed
FACULTY: 7 full- and 3 part-time   **AVERAGE CLASS SIZE:** 13
MISSION STATEMENT: Our goal is to provide a safe, nurturing environment where your child will develop their natural curiosity and desire to learn. By presenting your child with the basic building blocks of learning, they will be equipped with everything necessary to begin their formal quest for learning. In addition to the child's cognitive development, Oak Chapel School is dedicated to giving each child a safe, fun experience with equal emphasis on their physical, social, emotional, and spiritual growth.
SPECIAL COURSES: Grades 1–8: English/language arts, mathematics, science and social studies, and Aesthetic Arts–Media Skills, P.E., music, art, religion, dramatic arts and computer skills. Time is taken to ensure that all students work at their own rate and ability level to complete objectives in each area of study.
EXTENDED DAY: 6:30 a.m.–6:00 p.m.
ATHLETICS: Martial arts class
CLUBS: Dramatic arts productions from preschool through grade 8. Children's Choir ages 5 and up. Private piano lessons available. Home economics, art, homework club, theatre, and Student Government
PUBLICATIONS: Yearbook
ADMISSION: Contact Mr. Hartlove.
TUITION: Changes yearly. Call for information.
LUNCH: Included in tuition   **OTHER FEES:** Change yearly
DRESS CODE: Uniforms
SUMMER PROGRAMS: Special summer excursions camp in addition to enriched summer program.

OAK HILL CHRISTIAN SCHOOL, HERNDON CAMPUS   703-796-6887
3063-C Centreville Road, Oak Hill, VA 20171
Founded 1997
HEAD: Robert Thoburn II
DIRECTOR OF ADMISSIONS: Robert Thoburn II
WEBSITE: www.oakhillcs.com   **E-MAIL:** RLThoburn@aol.com
GRADES: Pre-K, Kindergarten ages 3,4,5
ENROLLMENT: 120 Co-ed (60 boys/60 girls)
FACULTY: 10 full- and 5 part-time   **AVERAGE CLASS SIZE:** 12
MISSION STATEMENT: Our mission is to be of service to parents in instructing their children from a Christian perspective. We offer an exceptional academic program in a pleasant and orderly setting and use curriculum for classical Christian schools.
SPECIAL COURSES: Phonics and reading starting at age 3. We offer 3, 4, and 5 year old Kindergarten at our Oak Hill/Herndon and at our Reston campus. Children from both campuses continue in first grade and beyond at the Reston campus.

EXTENDED DAY: 7:30 a.m.–6:15 p.m.

PLANT: Classrooms and playground located at McLearen Square. Library for students, teachers and parents

ADMISSION: Parents may schedule a tour and student interview. Application with $150 application fee

TUITION: Call for information.

FINANCIAL AID: Available

BOOKS: Included   **LUNCH:** Bring own

TRANSPORTATION: Available   **DRESS CODE:** Uniform

SUMMER PROGRAMS: 8 weeks full day academic camp, arts. Sign up weekly

OAK HILL CHRISTIAN SCHOOL, RESTON CAMPUS   703-796-6887

11480 Sunset Hills Road, Reston, VA 20190

Founded 1997

HEAD: Robert Thoburn II

DIRECTOR OF ADMISSIONS: Robert Thoburn II

WEBSITE: www.oakhillcs.com   **E-MAIL:** RLThoburn@aol.com

GRADES: Pre-K3–grade 9   **ENROLLMENT:** 120 Co-ed (60 boys/60 girls)

FACULTY: 10 full- and 5 part-time   **AVERAGE CLASS SIZE:** 12

MISSION STATEMENT: Our mission is to be of service to parents in instructing their children from a Christian perspective. We offer an exceptional academic program and orderly setting and use curriculum for classical Christian schools.

SPECIAL COURSES: Reading starting at age 3, logic, Latin, an unusually good writing program, cathedral voice, piano lessons

EXTENDED DAY: 7:30 a.m.–6:15 p.m.

ATHLETICS: Soccer team, bicycling club   **CLUBS:** Latin club

PLANT: New private 7,500-square foot campus near Reston Town Center, overlooking peaceful golf course; large shaded play areas, library for student, teacher and parent use

ADMISSION: Parents may schedule a tour and student interview, application with $150 registration fee

TUITION: Call for information.

FINANCIAL AID: Available

BOOKS: Included   **LUNCH:** Bring own

TRANSPORTATION: Available   **DRESS CODE:** Uniform

SUMMER PROGRAMS: 8 weeks full day academic summer camp, arts. Sign up weekly

FUTURE PLANS: Add grades 10–12

OAKCREST SCHOOL   703-790-5450   FAX 703-790-5380

850 Balls Hill Road, McLean, VA 22101

Founded 1976

HEAD: Ellen M. Cavanagh

DIRECTOR OF ADMISSIONS: Amy Jolly

WEBSITE: www.oakcrest.org   **E-MAIL:** admissions@oakcrest.org

GRADES: 6–grade 12   **ENROLLMENT:** 205 girls

FACULTY: 29 full-time   **AVERAGE CLASS SIZE:** 12–18

MISSION STATEMENT: Oakcrest School is an independent college preparatory school for girls in grades 6 through 12 which focuses on academic excellence, character development, and active parent involvement.

SPECIAL COURSES: Strong college preparation–100% of graduates go on to attend college. Accelerated/AP courses available. Courses include: Art: studio art I & II, AP studio art, art history. Computers: keyboarding and introduction to computer applications, computer applications I & II; English: Introduction to Literature, Understanding Literature, Intro to Literary Genres and Expository Writing, Writer's Workshop & Communication Skills, Survey of American Literature (AP), Survey of British Literature (AP), Survey of World Literature (AP). Foreign language: Latin I, II & III, French I-IV (AP), Spanish I-IV (AP). History: Geography & World Cultures, Western Civilization I & II, American History I (AP), U.S. History II (AP), European History (AP), 20th Century and Modern World/Government & Law. Mathematics: pre-algebra, algebra I, algebra II & Trigonometry, geometry, pre-calculus, AP calculus. Music: vocal and instrumental, chorus, music appreciation. P.E. available for 6-10 grade. Science: general science, life science, integrated science, biology (AP), chemistry (AP), Science-Technology-Society, physics. Theology: Catholic Foundations, Christian Doctrine I & II, Introduction to Sacred Scripture, Ethics and Moral Theology, Social Ethics and the History of the Catholic Church, Introduction to Metaphysics and the History of Philosophy.

EXTENDED DAY: Students may be on campus until 4:30 every day

ATHLETICS: (PVAC): varsity soccer, cross-country, basketball, tennis, softball and track and field

CLUBS: Student Council, Ambassador Club, Service Club, National Honor Society, arts club, debate club, journalism club, Respect Life Club, Spring musical comedy production

PUBLICATIONS: Yearbook (Cresens)

PLANT: Library, science lab, art studio, gym, theatre, Chapel. Conveniently located in McLean, Virginia exit #44 off the Capital Beltway.

ADMISSION: Tour, interview, applicants must visit for a day, recommendations and transcript. SSAT testing. $50 application fee. Deadlines: mid-December for 9th grade applicants; 1st week in February for middle school applicants; rolling admissions for Transfers or as space is available

TUITION: $10,617 grades 9–12; $9,425 grades 7–8; $8,700 grade 6 Books and uniforms are additional

FINANCIAL AID: Available

DRESS CODE: Uniform required

OAKLAND SCHOOL   434-293-9059   FAX 434-296-8930
Boyd Tavern, Keswick, VA 22947
Founded 1950
HEAD: Carol Smieciuch
WEBSITE: www.oaklandschool.net   **E-MAIL:** csoakland@earthlink.net
GRADES: Ungraded though 9th   **ENROLLMENT:** 60 Co-ed (40 boys/20 girls)
FACULTY: 18 full-time   **AVERAGE CLASS SIZE:** 4–5
MISSION STATEMENT: To encourage and help students with learning problems to achieve their potential, so that they will develop a love of learning as well as respect for themselves and others.
SPECIAL COURSES: Emphasis on basic skills in reading, math, English/written language and study skills. We provide individualized instruction in reading with

a 1:1 session with a private reading teacher for every student, each day. Oakland also employs four part-time clinical child psychologists and a part time speech/language pathologist, with services on an as-needed basis. Our residential staff receives year round training and are separate from the teachers. They act as dorm parents, work with the children on social and emotional goals and plan all of the sports and recreational activities.

ATHLETICS: Horseback riding, interscholastic soccer and basketball, intermural team sports, tennis, hiking, biking

CLUBS: Outdoor activities, arts and crafts, cooking club, music club

PUBLICATIONS: Yearbook, student newspaper, literary magazine.

COMMUNITY INVOLVEMENT: Community service

PLANT: 450 acres, 5 dorms, dining hall, gym and recreation center, 16-stall stable and riding ring, 2 tennis courts, swimming pool, hiking trails, pre-Revolutionary "Main House", 5 classroom buildings and summer camp complex.

ADMISSION: Telephone interview; send application form and records, personal interview. Admission ongoing

TUITION: $31,950 boarding; $17,500 day

DRESS CODE: Guidelines

SUMMER PROGRAMS: Yes

OAKMONT SCHOOL   301-947-3761   FAX 301-947-3764
17051 Oakmont Avenue, Gaithersburg, MD 20850
Founded 1997
HEAD: Denise Flora
DIRECTOR OF ADMISSIONS: Denise Flora or Susan Rail
WEBSITE: www.oakmontschool.com
E-MAIL: dflora@oakmontschool.net
GRADES: 6–12   **ENROLLMENT:** 45 Co-ed
FACULTY: 14 full-time   **AVERAGE CLASS SIZE:** 9

MISSION STATEMENT: (Excerpt) At Oakmont School we identify and build upon our students' strengths to help each one achieve success in an academic environment. We believe that by addressing students' emotional and learning needs, his or her success in school will follow.

SPECIAL COURSES: The Oakmont School will provide a therapeutic and academic program for grades 6–12 which may culminate in a diploma from their home school. Courses offered include: English 6–12, Social Studies– U.S. history, government, world history, and World Studies (grades 6–8).Science–science 6, life science, earth science, Matter & Energy, biology and chemistry. Mathematics-math 6, 7, & 8, pre-algebra, algebra I, geometry, algebra II, and Consumer Math. P.E. & health 6–12, art 6–12, Spanish. Technology Education- Introduction to Computers, Advanced Computer Applications

ATHLETICS: Volleyball, basketball, badminton, softball

CLUBS: Drama, chess   **PUBLICATIONS:** Yearbook

COMMUNITY INVOLVEMENT: Curriculum includes emphasis on community service completed outside the school day.

PLANT: Located in a beautiful wooded area in Gaithersburg, Maryland. The school has four large classrooms, media center, gymnasium with locker rooms, art room and a cafeteria.

ADMISSION: Parent/student tour and interview. Some testing and paperwork required prior to interview. Most referrals received by Local Education Agency (LEA)

TUITION: Call for information.
BOOKS: Provided   **LUNCH:** Student provides
OTHER FEES: Approximately $50
TRANSPORTATION: Provided by Local Education Agency (LEA)
DRESS CODE: No uniforms.
SUMMER PROGRAMS: Mandatory summer program in July

OAKWOOD SCHOOL   703-941-5788   FAX 703-941-4186

7210 Braddock Road, Annandale, VA 22003
Founded 1971
HEAD: Robert McIntyre
DIRECTOR OF ADMISSIONS: Muriel Jedlicka
WEBSITE: www.oakwoodschool.com
E-MAIL: jwoodruff@oakwoodschool.com
GRADES: 1–8   **ENROLLMENT:** 113 Co-ed (85 boys/28 girls)
FACULTY: 35 full- and 7 part-time   **AVERAGE CLASS SIZE:** 10
MISSION STATEMENT: It is the mission of Oakwood School to provide the highest quality educational opportunities for learning disabled students of average to gifted potential. To accomplish the goal of preparing young people for their future, the school's professional staff combines proven educational strategies of the past with effective, innovative methods and technologies of the present, in a nurturing environment that builds good character.
SPECIAL COURSES: General science, biology, earth science. History: U.S. and world, geography, reading/language arts, math, music appreciation, perception art, P.E.(regular and adaptive), speech/language therapy, occupational therapy. All subjects taught remedially for the bright learning disabled child as needed.
ATHLETICS: Required. Volleyball, football, softball, soccer, hockey, gymnastics, weights, trampoline. All taught as part of the P.E. program for all students.
PLANT: Library 5,000 volumes; Large bright classrooms, science and math labs, computer lab, reading lab, speech/language therapy clinic, P.E. room, weight room, athletic field, custom-designed playground.
ADMISSION: Interview with parents or referring professional. Parents complete confidential history. Transcripts of other evaluations and school records. Oakwood "short form" educational evaluation. Conference with parents at which placement recommendation is made. Students   are LD, Gifted LD, have Speech/Language Disfunctions- mild to moderate range of disabilities. Oakwood is not appropriate for MR, ED or those who are seriously physically handicapped.
TUITION: $21,100
FINANCIAL AID: Small student aid fund available based on need
DRESS CODE: Appropriate, modest and clean

OASIS SCHOOL   703-437-1444

11480 Sunset Hills Road, Reston, VA 20190
Founded 2002
HEAD: Janelle Blanchard
WEBSITE: www.OasisSchool.ws
GRADES: 3–8   **ENROLLMENT:** 10 girls

FACULTY: 7 part-time   AVERAGE CLASS SIZE: 4

MISSION STATEMENT: Oasis School offers the benefits of a single-gender learning environment for girls during the years when there are extensive developmental differences between genders. It guides girls through gender-based developmental stages in an environment designed to foster self-esteem and independence. Students learn processes that allow them to become creative and independent thinkers as well as mastering necessary concepts, data, and skills. A longer school day is designed to complete most work at school rather than relying on extensive homework. Oasis actively recruits multicultural staff and student body.

SPECIAL COURSES: Strong academic program in language arts, history, mathematics (including algebra), and science. Foreign languages (Spanish, French, Latin). Additional classes in culture/geography, art, drama, music, research and computer skills, P.E. Varied teaching approaches allow for accommodation of some learning differences. Small environment well-suited to assisting students not working to academic potential.

EXTENDED DAY: 4:00–6:00 p.m.

CLUBS: After-school instrumental music   PUBLICATIONS: School newspaper

COMMUNITY INVOLVEMENT: Community service projects included in curriculum

PLANT: Secluded building in heart of Reston overlooks green space with outdoor play area. Computer lab, library over 2,000 volumes.

ADMISSION: Parent tour and interview. Student visit. Applications due March 1; later rolling admissions

TUITION: $12,500

FINANCIAL AID: Limited partial tuition reduction based on need.

OTHER FEES: All costs included in tuition

DRESS CODE: Appropriate attire, but no uniforms

SUMMER PROGRAMS: Weekly art camps, private tutoring

FUTURE PLANS: New school, gradually growing to class sizes of 12–15

ODENTON CHRISTIAN SCHOOL   410-674-5625   FAX 301-912-2334

8410 Piney Orchard Parkway, Odenton, MD 21113

Baptist 1976

HEAD: Dr. T.E. Pike

WEBSITE: www.ocs1.org   E-MAIL: tpike@ocs1.org

GRADES: K3–grade 12   ENROLLMENT: 350 Co-ed

FACULTY: 30 full- and 5 part-time   AVERAGE CLASS SIZE: 23

MISSION STATEMENT: To assist parents in rearing their children in the nurture and admonition of the Lord by providing an education that is Bible-based, Christ-centered, Holy Spirit-controlled and student oriented.

SPECIAL COURSES: Math through calculus, foreign language

EXTENDED DAY: 6:00 a.m.–6:00 p.m.

ATHLETICS: Soccer, basketball   CLUBS: Music

PUBLICATIONS: Yearbook

ADMISSION: Open enrollment K3–grade 5; grades 6–12 require interviews

TUITION: $3,000

BOOKS: $270

OTHER FEES: $200 activities

DRESS CODE: Uniform required

OLD MILL CHRISTIAN ACADEMY   410-987-4744   FAX 410-987-4784
649 Old Mill Boulevard, Millersville, MD 21108
Christian 1974
HEAD: Dr. Ron Carter
WEBSITE: www.thecalvarytemplechurch.com
GRADES: Pre-K–grade 12   **ENROLLMENT:** 150 Co-ed
FACULTY: 14 full- and 3 part-time   **AVERAGE CLASS SIZE:** 15–20
SPECIAL COURSES: Spanish 9–12, computer lab, computer basics and basic programming, general science, biology, chemistry, U.S. and world history, Constitutional History, geography, remedial reading and math. Religious studies required. Typing, home economics, auto mechanics, music, chorus. P.E. required.
TUITION: Call for information.
BOOKS: Extra   **LUNCH:** Bring   **DRESS CODE:** Uniform required
FUTURE PLANS: Offer extended day 6:00 a.m.–6:00 p.m.

OLDFIELDS SCHOOL   410-472-4800   FAX 410-472-6839
1500 Glencoe Road, Glencoe, MD 21152
Founded 1867
HEAD: George S. Swope
DIRECTOR OF ADMISSIONS: Kimberly Loughlin
WEBSITE: www.OldfieldsSchool.org
E-MAIL: admissions@oldfieldsschool.org
GRADES: 8–12 boarding and day
ENROLLMENT: 185 girls (80% boarding/20% day)
FACULTY: 47 full- and 2 part-time
AVERAGE CLASS SIZE: 8   student/faculty ratio 4:1
MISSION STATEMENT: Oldfields School is committed to the intellectual and moral development of young women. In a culture of kindness and mutual respect, we encourage each student to make the most of her academic and personal potential. We seek to guide each student to grow in character, confidence, and knowledge by encouraging her to embrace the values of personal honesty, intellectual curiosity, and social responsibility.
SPECIAL COURSES: All core courses are available on both the A and B tracks. This unique, dual track college preparatory program allows a student's academic schedule to be individualized according to the student's strengths and weaknesses. Technology is integrated into the curriculum, as 100% of teachers and students use laptops. Public areas on campus, including all classrooms, are wired for Internet access. Elective and AP courses are available in addition to regular course offerings. In 2002-2003, AP courses in American history, biology, calculus AB, English language, English literature, world history, French, Spanish and studio art were offered. The following elective courses were also available: creative writing, theater, dance technique, photography, ceramics, astronomy, marine biology, equine veterinary science, contemporary American and World history, international politics, World War II/Holocaust, web page design. May program, a two-week experiential learning program provides students with the opportunity to travel abroad, to take part in other off-campus experiences, or to choose from the on-campus courses offered in a wide array of academic disciplines.
ATHLETICS: Required for all students. Field hockey, volleyball, tennis, soccer, basketball, lacrosse, badminton, softball, horseback riding, dance, aerobics

CLUBS: Model U.N., Art Club, Global Awareness Club, Black Awareness Club, Student Council, Dubious Dozen (a capella group), Images (a capella group), Tour Guides, FOCUS

PUBLICATIONS: "Crosswalks" (newspaper),"Rarebit" (yearbook), "Tidbit" (literary magazine)

COMMUNITY INVOLVEMENT: Weekend activities include the opportunity to work at local soup kitchens and homeless shelters. Students also participate in Race for the Cure, Walk for the Homeless and other awareness-raising events.

PLANT: Caesar Rodney Hall, the main academic building, houses most classrooms and a fine arts wing. A 24,000-square foot addition to this building, opened in the fall of 2000, containing a new library and five state of the art science labs, along with four new classrooms, tutorial space and a new technology center. McCulloch Commons houses the dining hall, bookstore, student bank and post office, and lounges. Athletic facilities include a gym, workout rooms, 4 playing fields, 5 tennis courts, an indoor riding arena, 2 outdoor riding rings, stables, and dance studio. The David Niven Theatre, 3 darkrooms, music rooms, and additional classrooms are contained in Old House, along with the health center and administrative offices. 7 dormitories.

ADMISSION: All students must submit an application, essay and fee, transcript, 2 teacher recommendations, standardized testing (SSAT, ISEE or WISC). An interview is also required. Regular admission deadline is February 1 with a notification date of March 10. Rolling admission continues on a space available basis after March 10.

TUITION: $31,200 boarding; $20,000 day

FINANCIAL AID: Available. Deadline for receipt of paperwork is February 15.

BOOKS: $400

OTHER FEES: Students must have a laptop computer, which may be purchased through the school. Families who qualify for financial assistance may inquire about leasing a laptop. Weekend activities, riding lessons, music lessons, and other school-related expenses are billed individually.

DRESS CODE: No jeans, sweatshirts, athletic gear or commercial t-shirts may be worn during the school day. Clothing must be clean and in good repair.

FUTURE PLANS: Oldfields is embarking on a strategic plan in conjunction with the school's most successful Capital Campaign to date. As part of this plan, the school will increase the financial aid budget, update campus facilities, grow the endowment, and improve faculty benefits.

OLNEY ADVENTIST PREPARATORY SCHOOL

301-570-2500   FAX 301-570-0400

4100 Olney-Laytonsville Road, Olney, MD 20832

Seventh-day Adventist 1997

HEAD: Kimberlie J. Hogan

DIRECTOR OF ADMISSIONS: Linda Dooley

WEBSITE: www.olneyprep.org   **E-MAIL:** olneyprep@olneyprep.org

GRADES: Kindergarten–grade 8

ENROLLMENT: 115 Co-ed (60 boys/55 girls)

FACULTY: 10 full- and 10 part-time   **AVERAGE CLASS SIZE:** 16–20

MISSION STATEMENT: To go above and beyond to treat students as individuals spiritually, emotionally, and academically.

SPECIAL COURSES: Spanish (K–8), etiquette (K–8)
EXTENDED DAY: M–Th 3:30–6:00 p.m. F 2:00–4:30 p.m.
CLUBS: Orchestra K–8, handbells choir 6–8, strings K-8, flute, chimes 1–5
PLANT: 5 scenic acres, 3 buildings, playground, field
ADMISSION: Call for application and tour, schedule visitation and interview
TUITION: $4,400 Seventh-day Adventists; $5,700 non-Seventh-day Adventists
BOOKS: $350   **LUNCH:** Bag lunch
OTHER FEES: $50 application, $200 graduation   **DRESS CODE:** Uniform
SUMMER PROGRAMS: Varies
FUTURE PLANS: Grow K–8 to 240 students. Build new facility within 10 miles

ONENESS-FAMILY SCHOOL   301-652-7751   FAX 301-718-6214
6701 Wisconsin Avenue, Chevy Chase, MD 20815
Founded 1988
HEAD: Andrew Kutt
WEBSITE: www.onenessfamily.org
GRADES: 3 years–grade 8   **ENROLLMENT:** 100 Co-ed
FACULTY: 13 full- and 10 part-time
AVERAGE CLASS SIZE: 13:1 student:faculty ratio
MISSION STATEMENT: Oneness-Family School is an international peace academy dedicated to non-violence and multi-cultural understanding and unity.
SPECIAL COURSES: Spanish, French, yoga, P.E., art and music
EXTENDED DAY: 7:30 a.m.–6 p.m.
CLUBS: Woodworking, drama club, chess club and a variety of others
PLANT: St. John's Episcopal Church
ADMISSION: Tour/ open house attendance, application with $100 fee, child visit, parent/teacher meeting, two confidential evaluation forms, transcripts
TUITION: $9,750–$12,250
FINANCIAL AID: Available
DRESS CODE: Casual, no violent images

OUR LADY OF GOOD COUNSEL HIGH SCHOOL
301-942-1155   FAX 301-942-4967
11601 Georgia Avenue, Wheaton, MD 20902
Catholic 1958
HEAD: Arthur Raimo
DIRECTOR OF ADMISSIONS: Thomas Campbell
WEBSITE: www.olgchs.org   **E-MAIL:** tcampbell@gchs.com
GRADES: 9–12   **ENROLLMENT:** 1050 Co-ed
AVERAGE CLASS SIZE: 22
MISSION STATEMENT: As a Xaverian Brothers sponsored school Our Lady of Good Counsel is dedicated to academic excellence, fostering Christian faith, and encouraging leadership and community service.
SPECIAL COURSES: International Baccalaureate, Advanced Placement, honors, college prep and Ryken (for students with mild learning disabilities)
ATHLETICS: Over 50 teams, intramurals, compete in Washington Catholic Athletic Conference
CLUBS: Over 25 traditional and non-traditional clubs and activities including 8 musical ensembles (some for academic credit), Student Government, speech and

debate, International Students Association and Key Club
COMMUNITY INVOLVEMENT: Camp Good Counsel, 100 hour service requirement
PLANT: Media center, 3 computer labs, 3 science labs, 2 music rooms, 2 art studios, college resource room, 2 gyms, weight room, lighted playing field, Chapel. Relocating to 50+-acre campus in Olney in 2005
ADMISSION: 9th grade applications due in January. 10th and 11th grade applications considered on rolling basis beginning in April. For details contact admissions office at extension 105.
TUITION: $9,975
FINANCIAL AID: Available
BOOKS: Extra   **LUNCH:** Cafeteria
OTHER FEES: $50 technology fee
TRANSPORTATION: Available. Cost varies
DRESS CODE: Yes
SUMMER PROGRAMS: Basketball (boys/girls), football (boys), technology classes
FUTURE PLANS: New Olney campus 2005

OUR LADY OF GOOD COUNSEL SCHOOL   703-938-3600
8601 Wolftrap Road, Vienna, VA 22182
Catholic
HEAD: Austin Poole
WEBSITE: www.olgcschool.homestead.com
GRADES: Kindergarten–grade 8   **ENROLLMENT:** Co-ed
TUITION: Call for information.
DRESS CODE: Uniforms

OUR LADY OF LOURDES SCHOOL   301-654-5376   FAX 301-654-2568
7500 Pearl Street, Bethesda, MD 20814
Catholic 1941
HEAD: Ed Lindekugel
WEBSITE: www.bethesda-lourdes.org   **E-MAIL:** bethesdaolol@yahoo.com
GRADES: Pre-K, K, grades 1–8   **ENROLLMENT:** 218 Co-ed (103 boys/115 girls)
FACULTY: 10 full- and 9 part-time   **AVERAGE CLASS SIZE:** 22
MISSION STATEMENT: Our Lady of Lourdes School is a community of faith comprised of parents, students and teachers. It strives to guide each child in growing and maturing in knowledge and in the Catholic faith as expressed in the Gospel of Jesus Christ. Our Lady of Lourdes School exists so that the moral, intellectual, social and physical potential of each student may be developed according to his/her age and ability. In doing this, it shares a responsibility with the family and the Catholic Church.
SPECIAL COURSES: Spanish classes twice a week for grades 3–8
EXTENDED DAY: Dismissal until 6:00 p.m.
ATHLETICS: Soccer, baseball, softball, track, basketball
PUBLICATIONS: Yearbook
PLANT: Building, library, science lab, art studio, music room, gymnasium, playing field, playground
ADMISSION: $500 registration fee, kindergarten testing

TUITION: $4,575
FINANCIAL AID: Available
DRESS CODE: Uniform required
SUMMER PROGRAMS: Summer day camp and away camp "A Long Summer Camp"

OUR LADY OF MERCY SCHOOL   301-365-4477   FAX 301-365-3423
9222 Kentsdale Drive, Potomac, MD 20854
Catholic
HEAD: Joan Hosmer
E-MAIL: mercyhos@aol.com
GRADES: Kindergarten–grade 8   **ENROLLMENT:** Co-ed
EXTENDED DAY: After care
TUITION: $5,750
DRESS CODE: Uniforms
SUMMER PROGRAMS: Summer Camp and academics

OUR LADY OF PERPETUAL HELP   202-678-0211   FAX 202-610-1519
1604 Morris Road, S.E., Washington, DC 20020
Catholic
HEAD: Charlene Hursey
E-MAIL: ladymorr@erols.com
GRADES: 5–8   **ENROLLMENT:** Co-ed   **PLANT:** Grades Pre-K–4 at V Street campus
TUITION: $3,100
DRESS CODE: Uniforms
SUMMER PROGRAMS: Summer Camp

OUR LADY OF PERPETUAL HELP   202-889-1662   FAX 202-610-1519
1409 V Street, S.E., Washington, DC 20020
Catholic
HEAD: Charlene Hursey
E-MAIL: ladyvst@erols.com
GRADES: Pre-K–grade 4   **ENROLLMENT:** Co-ed
EXTENDED DAY: Before and after care
PLANT: Grades 5–8 located at Morris Road campus
TUITION: $3,100 one child in parish
DRESS CODE: Uniforms
SUMMER PROGRAMS: Summer Camp

OUR LADY OF SORROWS SCHOOL   301-891-2555   FAX 301-891-1523
1010 Larch Avenue, Takoma Park, MD 20912
Catholic
HEAD: Gail Riffin
WEBSITE: www.oloschurchtp.com   **E-MAIL:** gruffin248@aol.com
GRADES: Pre-K–grade 8   **ENROLLMENT:** Co-ed
SPECIAL COURSES: Academic/performing arts school
EXTENDED DAY: Before and after care
TUITION: $3,800 one child in parish
DRESS CODE: Uniforms   **SUMMER PROGRAMS:** Summer school and camp

OUR LADY OF VICTORY SCHOOL   202-337-1421   FAX 202-338-4759

4755 Whitehaven Parkway, N.W., Washington, DC 20007

Catholic 1954

HEAD: Susan Milloy

WEBSITE: www.olvdc.com   **E-MAIL:** olvsdc@erols.com

GRADES: Nursery–grade 8   **ENROLLMENT:** 165 Co-ed

FACULTY: 10 full- and 8 part-time   **AVERAGE CLASS SIZE:** 17

MISSION STATEMENT: To provide quality Catholic education in a secure, caring community. In cooperation with the families of our school and parish, we help students experience self-worth and develop their full potential while pursuing academic excellence.

SPECIAL COURSES: Spanish, computer, art, study skills, library skills, algebra, general science. Resource teacher on staff

EXTENDED DAY: 7:30 a.m.–6:00 p.m.

ATHLETICS: P.E., after school soccer, softball, basketball

CLUBS: Band, choir, geography club, chess club, after school book club

PUBLICATIONS: Newspaper

PLANT: Library, computer room, auditorium

ADMISSION: Tour, visiting day, testing

TUITION: $4,900 in parish; $5,800 out of parish

BOOKS: $250   **DRESS CODE:** Uniform required

OUR LADY STAR OF THE SEA SCHOOL   410-326-3171   FAX 410-326-9478

90 Alexander Lane, Solomons, MD 20688

Catholic

HEAD: Sister Rosella Summe, CDP

E-MAIL: olssprincipal@comcast.net

GRADES: Kindergarten–grade 8   **ENROLLMENT:** Co-ed

EXTENDED DAY: 3:00–6:00 p.m.

TUITION: $2,850 one child in parish

DRESS CODE: Uniforms

OUR SAVIOR LUTHERAN SCHOOL   703-892-4846   FAX 703-892-4847

825 South Taylor Street, Arlington, VA 22204

Lutheran 1952

HEAD: Barbara Huehn

WEBSITE: www.OSVA.org   **E-MAIL:** osloffice@juno.com

GRADES: K–grade 8   **ENROLLMENT:** 180 Co-ed

FACULTY: 8 full- and 5 part-time

AVERAGE CLASS SIZE: 20

MISSION STATEMENT: It is the mission of Our Savior Lutheran School to provide quality education centered in Christ and to reach out to all people with the Gospel.

SPECIAL COURSES: Self-contained classrooms, religious training, phonics, outdoor camping for 6th grade, band, keyboard

EXTENDED DAY: 7:00 a.m.–6 p.m.

CLUBS: Chess club

PLANT: 9 classrooms, computer lab, library 2,400 volumes, gym, church and fellowship hall

ADMISSION: Interview, testing, $170 registration fee

TUITION: $3,600 1 child; $5,840 2 children; $7,360 3 children
FINANCIAL AID: Available
TRANSPORTATION: Only bus transportation available for BAFB students
DRESS CODE: Uniform dress

OUR SAVIOR'S SCHOOL   301-420-5076   FAX 301-420-4153
3111 Forestville Road, Forestville, MD 20747
Nondenominational
HEAD: Douglas Sorenson
GRADES: K4–7   **ENROLLMENT:** 125 Co-ed (55 boys/70 girls)
FACULTY: 12 full- and 7 part-time   **AVERAGE CLASS SIZE:** 18
MISSION STATEMENT: Quality education built on Christian values.
EXTENDED DAY: 6:45 a.m.–6:00 p.m.
ADMISSION: Admission is closed when class is filled.
TUITION: $3572 for one year, paid over 9 months $397
BOOKS: $175 a year   **LUNCH:** $3.00 a day
OTHER FEES: Registration fee $100   **DRESS CODE:** Uniforms
SUMMER PROGRAMS: Available for Our Savior's School students
FUTURE PLANS: Add eighth grade

—P

PAINT BRANCH MONTESSORI SCHOOL   301-937-2244   FAX 301-937-2266
3215 Powder Mill Road, Adelphi, MD 20783
Founded 1975
HEAD: Manjit K. Singh
DIRECTOR OF ADMISSIONS: Sandra Thomas
WEBSITE: www.pbmontessori.com   **E-MAIL:** pbms@erols.com
GRADES: Ungraded ages 2–12   **ENROLLMENT:** 100 Co-ed
FACULTY: 10 full- and 4 part-time   **AVERAGE CLASS SIZE:** 16
MISSION STATEMENT: To aid children in their own natural development which includes physical, emotional, and cognitive skills necessary for functioning in society.
SPECIAL COURSES: Full day program for those 3 and up. Art, music, P.E., Spanish
EXTENDED DAY: 7:30 a.m.–6:00 p.m.
PLANT: Located on five acres of land with two streams running through property. Each room has one wall of windows looking out to trees and bird feeders.
ADMISSION: School visit. For elementary program 6 years and older by November 30
TUITION: $4,254 half day; $6,688 full day; $6,882 lower elementary; $7,026 upper elementary

PALADIN ACADEMY   703-397-0555   FAX 703-397-0565
3753 Centerview Drive, Chantilly, VA 20151
HEAD: Penny Lindblom
WEBSITE: www.paladinacademy.org
GRADES: Kindergarten–grade 8   **ENROLLMENT:** 35 Co-ed
FACULTY: 7 full- and 2 part-time   **AVERAGE CLASS SIZE:** 8
MISSION STATEMENT: To provide a unique and nurturing environment for

students with mild to moderate learning challenges through a multi-sensory, individualized educational program that builds a foundation for lifelong success.

SPECIAL COURSES: All Paladin programs incorporate multi-sensory strategies that are used to teach, remediate and facilitate the student's individual learning. These strategies address learning challenges in eight specific areas: visual/auditory processing, encoding/decoding, writing, reading, mathematics, study skills, behavior modification/management, and social skills. Auxiliary Programs: Prescriptive clinics address specific academic issues.

ATHLETICS: All Paladin students participate in the P.E. program.

ADMISSION: Interview with parents. Parents complete confidential history. Transcripts or other evaluation and school records. Current Educational Psychological testing. Student interview/visit. Paladin testing

TUITION: $16,035

FINANCIAL AID: Available

LUNCH: Hot lunch   **OTHER FEES:** $900

DRESS CODE: Uniform

SUMMER PROGRAMS: Summer academic camp (6 week summer program)

PALADIN ACADEMY   703-404-0202   FAX 703-421-7874
46100 Woodshire Drive, Sterling, VA 20166
WEBSITE: www.paladinacademy.org
GRADES: Kindergarten–grade 8   **ENROLLMENT:** 35 Co-ed
FACULTY: 7 full- and 2 part-time   **AVERAGE CLASS SIZE:** 8
MISSION STATEMENT: To provide a unique and nurturing environment for students with mild to moderate learning challenges through a multi-sensory, individualized educational program that builds a foundation for lifelong success.
SPECIAL COURSES: All Paladin programs incorporate multi-sensory strategies that are used to teach, remediate and facilitate the student's individual learning. These strategies address learning challenges in eight specific areas: visual/auditory processing, encoding/decoding, writing, reading, mathematics, study skills, behavior modification/management, and social skills. Auxiliary Programs: Prescriptive clinics address specific academic issues.
ATHLETICS: All Paladin students participate in the P.E. program.
ADMISSION: Interview with parents. Parents complete confidential history. Transcripts or other evaluation and school records. Current Educational Psychological testing. Student interview/visit. Paladin testing
TUITION: $16,035
FINANCIAL AID: Available
LUNCH: Hot lunch   **OTHER FEES:** $900   **DRESS CODE:** Uniform
SUMMER PROGRAMS: Summer academic camp (6 week summer program)

PALADIN ACADEMY   703-759-3000   FAX 703-759-5526
9525 Leesburg Pike, Vienna, VA 22182
WEBSITE: www.paladinacademy.org
GRADES: Kindergarten–grade 8   **ENROLLMENT:** 35 Co-ed
FACULTY: 7 full- and 2 part-time   **AVERAGE CLASS SIZE:** 8
MISSION STATEMENT: To provide a unique and nurturing environment for students with mild to moderate learning challenges through a multi-sensory, individualized educational program that builds a foundation for lifelong success.

SPECIAL COURSES: All Paladin programs incorporate multi-sensory strategies that are used to teach, remediate and facilitate the student's individual learning. These strategies address learning challenges in eight specific areas: visual/auditory processing, encoding/decoding, writing, reading, mathematics, study skills, behavior modification/management, and social skills. Auxiliary programs: Prescriptive clinics address specific academic issues.

ATHLETICS: All Paladin students participate in the P.E. program.

ADMISSION: Interview with parents. Parents complete confidential history. Transcripts or other evaluation and school records. Current Educational Psychological testing. Student interview/visit. Paladin testing

TUITION: $16,035

FINANCIAL AID: Available

LUNCH: Hot lunch   **OTHER FEES:** $900   **DRESS CODE:** Uniform

SUMMER PROGRAMS: Summer academic camp (6 week summer program)

PARKMONT SCHOOL   202-726-0740   FAX 202-726-0748
4842 16th Street, N.W., Washington, DC 20011
Founded 1972
HEAD: Ron McLain
DIRECTOR OF ADMISSIONS: Gina Duffin
WEBSITE: www.parkmont.org   **E-MAIL:** gduffin@parkmont.org
GRADES: 6–12   **ENROLLMENT:** 65 Co-ed
FACULTY: 9 full- and 5 part-time   **AVERAGE CLASS SIZE:** 7–12

MISSION STATEMENT: How do we help adolescents develop the confidence and skills they need to move ahead energetically with their lives? At Parkmont we create a community where they ally themselves with creative adults whose driving concern is their success and well-being. We provide them with substantial experience in the world beyond school that invites them to see more clearly the possibilities ahead. And we challenge them with an academic program that fuses adolescent interests with traditional disciplines and respects the variety of their talents and motivations. They get ready to chart their own course; we make sure they're prepared for the journey.

SPECIAL COURSES: Innovative small school dedicated to fostering individual growth and enthusiasm for learning. Unique academic structure of short, intensive courses and challenging, high interest curriculum. We are committed to experiential learning and make considerable use of the city and its resources. Individual attention and close adult-student relationships provide support when needed, build a strong sense of community and enable our students to thrive. Internships in the areas of Community Service and other areas of interest.

ATHLETICS: Soccer program, tennis, volleyball, softball, canoeing and camping, dance. Participate in the WSSA athletic league

PLANT: Science lab, art room, all-purpose room, ceramics studio, photo lab, computer lab

ADMISSION: Parent interview with Director followed by a full day student visit. $50 application fee. Rolling admission

TUITION: $18,200

FINANCIAL AID: Available

BOOKS: Included   **LUNCH:** Not included   **OTHER FEES:** Included in tuition

SUMMER PROGRAMS: Math and English (high school)

PATUXENT MONTESSORI SCHOOL   301-464-4506   FAX 301-464-8792

14210 Old Stage Road, Bowie, MD 20720
Founded 1992
HEAD: Suzanne Damadio
WEBSITE: www.patuxent-montessori.org
GRADES: Ungraded nursery–age 12
ENROLLMENT: 70 Co-ed (34 boys/36 girls)
FACULTY: 4 full- and 5 part-time   **AVERAGE CLASS SIZE:** 24
SPECIAL COURSES: AMI Montessori Method; P.E.; art, music, outdoor education, challenging educational program
EXTENDED DAY: 7:30 a.m.–5:30 p.m.
PLANT: New 8,200-square foot building on 6 wooded acres, 4 classrooms, child care room, library, kitchen, large outdoor play area
ADMISSION: Interview with parent/child conducted all year
TUITION: $5,200–$6,400
FUTURE PLANS: Multi-purpose building; outdoor gardens and nature paths

PAUL VI CATHOLIC HIGH SCHOOL   703-352-0925   FAX 703-383-3974

10675 Lee Highway, Fairfax, VA 22030
Catholic 1983
HEAD: Philip V. Robey
DIRECTOR OF ADMISSIONS: Eileen B. Hanley
WEBSITE: www.paulvi.net   **E-MAIL:** gopvi@paulvi.net
GRADES: 9–12   **ENROLLMENT:** 1150 Co-ed(575 boys/575 girls)
FACULTY: 85 full- and 5 part-time   **AVERAGE CLASS SIZE:** 22
MISSION STATEMENT: The mission of Paul VI High School is to provide an excellent Catholic education to young men and women in the Washington Metropolitan area. The school is devoted to graduating responsible, moral young adults so that they will continue to "grow in grace and wisdom." Paul VI is a College Preparatory School.
SPECIAL COURSES: Courses are available on four levels: Advanced Placement, Honors, College Prep, and General. Advanced Placement courses are available in all subject areas. Wide variety of electives in fine arts, social studies, technology, English and Family and Consumer Science. Learning Centers available. No ESL.
ATHLETICS: 43 athletic teams compete in the WCAC- Washington Catholic Athletic Conference
CLUBS: 42 clubs including honor societies, service clubs and special interest clubs
PUBLICATIONS: Three publications
COMMUNITY INVOLVEMENT: Service required all four years. Student body is extremely active within the school and community.
PLANT: State of the art facility in historic setting. Multimillion dollar new student activity center; newly renovated library, auditorium, computer labs and classrooms
ADMISSION: 9th grade–Admission test required. Deadline 2/1 of 8th grade. Transcripts and recommendation required. Transfer students- rolling admission on space available basis. Transcripts and recommendation required.
TUITION: $7,035 Catholic; $9,135 Non-Catholic
FINANCIAL AID: Available
BOOKS: $400–$500   **LUNCH:** Full cafeteria service. Cost varied.

OTHER FEES: $350   TRANSPORTATION: Available. $1,100–$1,200 yearly.
DRESS CODE: Uniform
SUMMER PROGRAMS: Study skills, sports and theater camps. Intro to English and math, computer classes
FUTURE PLANS: Renovations

PHELPS SCHOOL   610-644-1754   FAX 610-644-6679
583 Sugartown Road (P.O. Box 476), Malvern, PA 19355
Founded 1946
HEAD: Norman T. Phelps, Jr.
WEBSITE: www.phelpsschool.org   E-MAIL: admis@phelpsschool.org
GRADES: 7–12, PG   ENROLLMENT: 165 boys, boarding and day
FACULTY: 30 full- and 2 part-time   AVERAGE CLASS SIZE: 7
SPECIAL COURSES: Students represent 27 states and 13 countries. Academic Support Program for Learning Differences. Remedial and Developmental Programs. Strong program for underachievers and ADD. ESL individualized programs. Photography
ATHLETICS: Interscholastic soccer, cross-country, basketball, baseball, lacrosse, riding, golf, tennis, ropes course, climbing wall, fitness center
PLANT: Located 22 miles west of Philadelphia. 70-acre campus. Library, Academic Support Center, darkroom, gym, fitness center, auditorium, all-weather tennis courts, indoor and outdoor equestrian facilities, 9 dormitories, woodshop, dining hall addition, visual arts studio.
ADMISSION: Application fee, interview, recommendations, transcript and current educational testing
TUITION: $25,000
FINANCIAL AID: Some available
BOOKS: $300   OTHER FEES: $1,000–$1,500
DRESS CODE: Shirt and tie (jacket Monday)
SUMMER PROGRAMS: 5 week remedial classes in reading, English, math, computers and study skills. Credit is possible. Trips, activities and athletics

PINECREST SCHOOL   703-354-3446   FAX 703-354-0502
7209 Quiet Cove, Annandale, VA 22003
Founded 1977
HEAD: Pamela Kenney
WEBSITE: www.pinecrestschool.org   E-MAIL: pinecrst@patriot.net
GRADES: N3–grade 5   ENROLLMENT: 120 Co-ed
FACULTY: 8 full- and 5 part-time   AVERAGE CLASS SIZE: 12–15
MISSION STATEMENT: (Excerpted) Pinecrest School is committed to providing a positive social and emotional environment for student development. The school provides an atmosphere that bolsters self-confidence and equips its students with the cognitive skills necessary to undertake and succeed in rigorous academic pursuits throughout their lives. It strives to reinforce basic values such as honesty, integrity, respect for others, and an appreciation for diversity.
SPECIAL COURSES: French, music, P.E., computer
EXTENDED DAY: 3:00–5:00 p.m.
PUBLICATIONS: Student-produced newspaper
ADMISSION: $50 application fee, transcript, recommendation, classroom visit,

rolling admissions, $150 registration fee
TUITION: $3,600–$8,250
FINANCIAL AID: Available
BOOKS: $175–$200   **LUNCH:** Lunch not offered/ Preschool snack provided.
OTHER FEES: Preschool materials fee $80
TRANSPORTATION: Available. $1,700–$2,000 both ways/$1,400–$1,600 one way
DRESS CODE: None
SUMMER PROGRAMS: Enrichment and remedial tutoring
FUTURE PLANS: New upper school building opening November 2003.

POTOMAC HEIGHTS CHRISTIAN ACADEMY
301-753-9350   FAX 301-743-5400
37-A Glymont Road, Indian Head, MD 20640
Christian 1975
HEAD: Greg Judy
WEBSITE: www.phbc.com   **E-MAIL:** greg@phbc.com
GRADES: K5–grade 8   **ENROLLMENT:** 150 Co-ed
SPECIAL COURSES: A Beka curriculum. Art, music, P.E., Spanish, computer. Umbrella school for homeschoolers
EXTENDED DAY: 6:30 a.m.–6:00 p.m.
CLUBS: Christmas musical, spring musical. Chapel once a week
PLANT: Computer lab, Chapel, playground
ADMISSION: Application. Grades 1–8 entrance test for placement
TUITION: $3,600
LUNCH: Bring
TRANSPORTATION: Available through Charles County public school buses
DRESS CODE: Uniforms

THE POTOMAC SCHOOL   703-356-4101
1301 Potomac School Road (P.O. Box 430), McLean, VA 22101
Founded 1904
HEAD: Geoffrey Jones
DIRECTOR OF ADMISSIONS: Charlotte Nelson
WEBSITE: www.potomacschool.org
GRADES: K–grade 12   **ENROLLMENT:** 875 Co-ed
FACULTY: 140 full- and part-time
SPECIAL COURSES: Spanish, French, Latin and Japanese. Math through advanced calculus, statistics, computer programming. Science: biology, chemistry, physics, and electives. History: Global Studies, American, government, and electives. AP courses: American history, government, Spanish, French, Latin, biology, chemistry, physics, statistics, calculus, computer science, art history, and music theory. Ethics course, health education, month-long Senior Project.
EXTENDED DAY: 3:10–6:00 p.m.
ATHLETICS: Required. Interscholastic. Football, cross-country, squash, soccer, baseball, lacrosse, track and field, basketball, field hockey, wrestling, softball, swimming
CLUBS: Chorus, madrigals, band, jazz band, string ensemble, drama productions, video, dance club, Student Government, Model Congress, Model U.N., debate, chess, environmental, Black Student Union, and Gay Straight Alliance

PUBLICATIONS: Two newspapers, yearbook, literary magazine
COMMUNITY INVOLVEMENT: Community Service Program, K–12
PLANT: 83-acre campus, 3 libraries (more than 35,000 volumes), 11 science labs, 6 computer labs, 5 art studios, nature trails, playing fields, 2 gyms, fitness center, outdoor swimming pool, tennis courts, squash courts, wresting facility, and Performing Arts Center
ADMISSION: Applications by January 15. Fee $60. Testing in January and February; decisions in March. Visits by parents requested. School seeks broad ethnic, geographic and socio-economic diversity within its community.
TUITION: $17,550–$20,190
FINANCIAL AID: Available
BOOKS: Extra   **LUNCH:** $790 (9–12)
TRANSPORTATION: Available. $695–$1,250
DRESS CODE: Dress code K–3; 9–12. Uniform 4–8

POWHATAN SCHOOL   540-837-1009   FAX 540-837-2558
49 Powhatan Lane, Boyce, VA 22620
Founded 1948
HEAD: John G. Lathrop
DIRECTOR OF ADMISSIONS: Clare M. Hamman
WEBSITE: www.powhatan.pvt.k12.va.us **E-MAIL:** hammancm@powhatans.org
GRADES: K–grade 8   **ENROLLMENT:** 245 Co-ed
FACULTY: 30 full- and 5 part-time   **AVERAGE CLASS SIZE:** 15
MISSION STATEMENT: Powhatan School offers a strong foundation in the traditional academic disciplines in a supportive environment. The school provides educational experiences that promote academic skills, problem solving, and analytical thinking. We strive to build cooperation through teamwork, to encourage trust and respect for self and others, and to instill a lifelong love for learning and excellence.
SPECIAL COURSES: Spanish K–4, 6–8; French 5, 6–8; algebra, geometry, computer, general science, biology, history: U.S., ancient, reading resource, art, music
ATHLETICS: Athletics required. Soccer, field hockey, lacrosse, basketball, track, dance, skiing, climbing wall
PUBLICATIONS: Yearbook, newspaper
COMMUNITY INVOLVEMENT: Required 7 and 8. Local nursing home, local food bank donation drive, family adoption at holiday times, foster child
PLANT: Library, science lab, auditorium, gym, art studio, playing fields, music and dance facility, 20-acre campus, nature trails
ADMISSION: $50 application fee; testing in January, February and April; classroom visits encouraged
TUITION: $10,550 full day K; $10,950–$11,650   1–8
FINANCIAL AID: Available   **OTHER FEES:** $450–$550 teaching materials
TRANSPORTATION: Available. $450–$985
DRESS CODE: Dress code K–3; uniform required 4–8
SUMMER PROGRAMS: Summer camps: Sports Camp, Adventure Camp, general camp
FUTURE PLANS: Expansion underway to two classes per grade with no more than 15 students in a teaching class. Opening of new arts and science building in the fall of 2003

PREPARATORY SCHOOL OF THE DISTRICT OF COLUMBIA
202-723-0079   FAX 202-723-0204
6017 Chillum Place, N.E., Washington, DC 20011
Founded 1984
HEAD: Betty North
E-MAIL: preparatoryschoolofdc@yahoo.com
GRADES: Nursery–grade 6
ENROLLMENT: Co-ed
SPECIAL COURSES: Foreign language, accelerated reading classes, music, P.E.
EXTENDED DAY: Before and after care
CLUBS: Ski program, band, martial arts program
PLANT: Gym, computer lab, media center
ADMISSION: Open enrollment
TUITION: $8,000
SUMMER PROGRAMS: Summer Camp

THE PRIMARY DAY SCHOOL   301-365-4355   FAX 301-469-8611
7300 River Road, Bethesda, MD 20817
Founded 1944
HEAD: Louise K. Plumb
DIRECTOR OF ADMISSIONS: Ivy C. Velte
WEBSITE: www.theprimarydayschool.org
GRADES: Pre-Kindergarten–grade 2
ENROLLMENT: 160 Co-ed
FACULTY: 19 full- and 4 part-time
AVERAGE CLASS SIZE: teacher/student ratio 1:9
MISSION STATEMENT: The Primary Day School is a diverse, coeducational, independent school for children in Pre-Kindergarten through Second Grade. The school's warm and supportive atmosphere encourages the intellectual, moral, physical and emotional development of students and fosters a lifelong love of learning.
SPECIAL COURSES: The traditional curriculum emphasizes fundamental skills, sound work habits and an appreciation of the arts. The school was founded as a demonstration school for the Phonovisual Method, a multi-sensory phonetic system which provides the foundation for language arts instruction. Students participate in weekly assemblies designed to develop poise and public speaking, and performance skills.
ATHLETICS: P.E., after school ice-skating, soccer, tennis and tae-kwon-do, coordinated by parents off-site
PLANT: 7,000+ volume library: math, computer and science labs: art and music studios; auditorium, well-equipped playground, playing fields and Sport Court
ADMISSION: Applications accepted Sept. 1–Jan. 15 for the next academic year. Child activity visit, classroom visit and teacher recommendation are required.
TUITION: $9,000–$12,500 includes books
FINANCIAL AID: Available
BOOKS: Included
LUNCH: Students bring
DRESS CODE: Comfortable school clothes
FUTURE PLANS: Expand the science and educational technology program

PRIMARY MONTESSORI DAY SCHOOL   301-309-9532

14138 Travilah Road, Rockville, MD 20850
WEBSITE: www.primarymontessori.com
E-MAIL: info@primarymontessori.com
GRADES: Age 3–grade 2   **ENROLLMENT:** Co-ed
SPECIAL COURSES: Spanish, computers, tae kwon do. 11-month program from September–end of July
EXTENDED DAY: Until 6:00 p.m.
TUITION: Call for information.

PRINCE WILLIAM ACADEMY/ EARLY YEARS ACADEMY

703-590-3659   FAX 703-590-3755
13817 Spriggs Road, Manassas, VA 20112
Founded 1987
HEAD: Dr. Samia Harris
WEBSITE: www.Princewilliamacademy.com
E-MAIL: drsamiaharris@comcast.net
GRADES: Preschool–grade 6   **ENROLLMENT:** 160 Co-ed (80 boys/80 girls)
FACULTY: 15 full- and 3 part-time   **AVERAGE CLASS SIZE:** 15
MISSION STATEMENT: The mission of Prince William Academy is to provide a safe, healthful and stimulating educational environment within which to prepare your child for the future.
SPECIAL COURSES: High academic standards, phonics-based language arts curriculum. Combination McMillan and Math Their Way, Spanish and French as a second language, P.E., computers, science, social studies, music
EXTENDED DAY: 6:00 a.m.–6:30 p.m.
ATHLETICS: Sports, gym, ice skating   **CLUBS:** Chorus, chess
PLANT: 5.5-acre campus includes 3 buildings, sports field, basketball court, 3 large playgrounds
ADMISSION: Interview and evaluation, registration
TUITION: $4,500
FINANCIAL AID: Limited availability
BOOKS: $120   **LUNCH:** Not provided
TRANSPORTATION: Field trips and library only
DRESS CODE: Blue and white
SUMMER PROGRAMS: Accredited by the American Camping Association
FUTURE PLANS: To expand to 7th and 8th grades

PROGRESSIVE CHRISTIAN ACADEMY   301-449-3160   FAX 301-449-0382

5408 Brinkley Road, Camp Springs, MD 20748
HEAD: Yolanda Davis
WEBSITE: www.progressivechristianacademy.org
GRADES: K3–grade 9   **ENROLLMENT:** Co-ed
EXTENDED DAY: Before and after care
TUITION: Call for information.

PROVIDENCE CHRISTIAN SCHOOL   301-549-3725   FAX 301-549-3591

4515 Sandy Spring Road, Burtonsville, MD 20866
WEBSITE: www.go2pcs.org

GRADES: Kindergarten–grade 6
SPECIAL COURSES: Latin grades 3–6. Art, music and P.E. offered to home-schoolers.
TUITION: Call for information.

QUEEN ANNE SCHOOL   301-249-5000   FAX 301-249-3838
14111 Oak Grove Road, Upper Marlboro, MD 20774
Episcopal 1964
HEAD: J. Temple Blackwood
DIRECTOR OF ADMISSIONS: Brenda B. Walker
WEBSITE: www.queenanne.org
GRADES: 6–12   **ENROLLMENT:** 272 Co-ed (133 boys/139 girls)
FACULTY: 43 full- and 5 part-time   **AVERAGE CLASS SIZE:** 17
MISSION STATEMENT: Queen Anne School is a private, Episcopal-affiliated, coeducational day school for students in grades 6–12. Based on a rigorous academic curriculum, a Queen Anne education develops intellectual, moral, physical, social, and spiritual growth in each student. A dedicated staff emphasizes the development of individual responsibility, integrity, compassion, and respect. Students assume leadership and discover and delight in the
diversity of their community and wider world.
SPECIAL COURSES: AP classes offered in all areas of study. Virtual classes available.
EXTENDED DAY: 8:00 a.m.–3:30 p.m.
ATHLETICS: Competitive sports such as: soccer, cross-country, basketball, tennis, baseball, softball, lacrosse, track and field. Swim and golf are offered as club sports.
CLUBS: Drama program, photography, ceramics as part of a full art department. Music and band
PLANT: Approximately 50 acres in rural Upper Marlboro, Maryland. There are 8 different academic buildings set on a college style campus.
ADMISSION: Recommendations are required from English, math and Principal or Guidance. Independent School Entrance Exam is used, writing sample, transcripts from current school and interview
TUITION: $13,200–$14,700
FINANCIAL AID: Offered on a need basis
BOOKS: $250   **LUNCH:** Offered at a separate cost
TRANSPORTATION: Available. $1,300 approximate depending on location from school
DRESS CODE: Golf shirts and dress slacks
SUMMER PROGRAMS: Fun and enrichment
FUTURE PLANS: A second field house and theatre

QUEEN OF APOSTLES CATHOLIC SCHOOL   703-354-0714   FAX 703-354-1820
4409 Sano Street, Alexandria, VA 22312
Catholic 1965
HEAD: Mary L. West
WEBSITE: www.queenofapostles.org   **E-MAIL:** qofak8@verizon.net
GRADES: Kindergarten–grade 8   **ENROLLMENT:** 270 Co-ed
FACULTY: 15 full- and 2 part-time   **AVERAGE CLASS SIZE:** 17 K–2, 30 3–8

MISSION STATEMENT: (Excerpted) In partnership with parents, we focus on the spiritual, moral, academic, physical, aesthetic, and social development of each student. To this aim, we employ a variety of teaching strategies and provide a curriculum and environment that will foster spiritual growth, promote academic excellence and give all students a chance to develop to their highest potential.

SPECIAL COURSES: Algebra offered to qualifying 8th grade students. Title I program to qualifying students. Art, music, P.E. and computer

EXTENDED DAY: begins at 7:00 a.m./ dismissal–6:00 p.m.

CLUBS: Choir (grades 4–8), band (grades 4–8), Spanish, Spirit Club, Quiz Bowl, safety patrols, student council, spelling and geography bees, student ushers (grade 8)

PUBLICATIONS: Yearbook, art and literary magazine

COMMUNITY INVOLVEMENT: Student Volunteer Corps

PLANT: Single level; air-conditioned; handicapped access. New gym, new computer lab

ADMISSION: Registration begins last week in January–rolling admissions policy. Application packet available. $85 application fee

TUITION: Varies as to category

FINANCIAL AID: Available

LUNCH: Hot lunch 2 times per week.　**DRESS CODE:** Uniform

SUMMER PROGRAMS: Thematic weekly programs

—R

RANDOLPH-MACON ACADEMY　　800-272-1172　FAX 540-636-5419

200 Academy Drive, Front Royal, VA 22630

Methodist 1892

HEAD: Major General Henry M. Hobgood USAF Ret.

DIRECTOR OF ADMISSIONS: Celeste Brooks, Associate Director

WEBSITE: www.rma.edu　**E-MAIL:** admissions@rma.edu

GRADES: grade 6–postgraduate

ENROLLMENT: 438 Co-ed (337 board)

FACULTY: 45 full-time　**AVERAGE CLASS SIZE:** 12–15

MISSION STATEMENT: Randolph-Macon Academy is dedicated to educating young people to succeed in top colleges, universities and in life. The Academy provides an advanced curriculum, a superior faculty and staff, and a disciplined structure in a religious and secure environment. Students learn to live together harmoniously in a supportive and diverse community by developing moral character, citizenship and a passion for excellence and lifelong learning.

SPECIAL COURSES: AP (10 courses) ESL (3 levels) and TOEFL prep, Honors Program. Postgraduate: up to 62 hours of college credit through Shenandoah University. Flight training program (ground school, solo, pilot's license, instrument rating)

EXTENDED DAY: 5:30–9:00 p.m.

ATHLETICS: 21 varsity-level sports, JV sports program, middle school sports program, complete intramural program

CLUBS: Award-winning band, chorus; co-curricular program including drama, debate, literary club, etc. Various clubs and organizations such as computer club, language clubs, Kitty Hawk Air Society, Interact Club and ham radio club. Numerous weekend activities

PUBLICATIONS: Yearbook, literary magazine, newspaper

PLANT: Located near the entrance of the Skyline Drive and the Shenandoah River, R-MA sits on 135 acres overlooking historic Front Royal, Virginia. The Campus consists of 10 major buildings for students including 2 gyms, swimming pool, full athletic facilities, and 3 computer labs.

ADMISSION: Contact Admissions Office for application package (application, transcript release form and two recommendations). Come to R-MA for an interview and tour.

TUITION: $16,480 RB&T

FINANCIAL AID: Available

DRESS CODE: 6–8 casual uniform; 9–PG Air Force JROTC uniform

SUMMER PROGRAMS: Academic 9–12, enrichment 6–8, flight training, full ESL and TOEFL prep

FUTURE PLANS: $18 million expansion program underway. Will add 6 major buildings.

RENAISSANCE CHRISTIAN ACADEMY   301-568-8171   FAX 301-516-7742

2101 Shadyside Avenue, Suitland, MD 20746

Christian

HEAD: Lisa Weathers

GRADES: N3–grade 8   **ENROLLMENT:** Co-ed

SPECIAL COURSES: A Beka curriculum, Spanish, computers, music

EXTENDED DAY: 6:30 a.m.–6:00 p.m.

TUITION: Call for information.

DRESS CODE: Uniforms

RESTON MONTESSORI SCHOOL   703-481-2922   FAX 703-435-9308

1928 Isaac Newton Square West, Reston, VA 20190

Founded 1986

HEAD: Kathleen Lanfear

WEBSITE: www.restonmontessorischool.com   **E-MAIL:** RMSKM@aol.com

GRADES: Ungraded, age 2–12   **ENROLLMENT:** 180 Co-ed

FACULTY: 28 full- time   **AVERAGE CLASS SIZE:** 24

MISSION STATEMENT: The school's mission is the education of the whole person using the Montessori method, which addresses the intellectual, social, emotional, and physical needs of each child.

SPECIAL COURSES: French program. Computers in class for grades 1–6. Kindermusik and Orff music program

EXTENDED DAY: 7:00 a.m.–6:30 p.m.

ATHLETICS: Soccer, gymnastics

CLUBS: Kinderdance, chess

PLANT: Library, multi-purpose room, playground, open field, spacious classroom building

ADMISSION: Call for brochure and appointment. Visit, parent and child interview

TUITION: $6,550–$10,800

LUNCH: Bring

DRESS CODE: Uniform Kindergarten and elementary

SUMMER PROGRAMS: Sports, crafts, swimming, creative writing, math and science, computers

RIVENDELL SCHOOL   703-532-1200   FAX 703-532-3003
5700 Lee Highway, Arlington, VA 22207
Founded 1989
HEAD: Bentley Craft and Byron List
DIRECTOR OF ADMISSIONS: Lyle Peterson
GRADES: Kindergarten–grade 8   **ENROLLMENT:** 148 Co-ed
FACULTY: 13 full-time   **AVERAGE CLASS SIZE:** 16
MISSION STATEMENT: Helping Children explore God's world and discover their place in it.
SPECIAL COURSES: Small LD program
COMMUNITY INVOLVEMENT: All 8th graders complete service projects in the community.
PLANT: Library 7,000 volumes, computer room, music room, Chapel, auditorium, playground
ADMISSION: Applications received 9/1–1/31. Decisions made by 3/15 for following school year
TUITION: $4,925 K; $6,250 1–8
FINANCIAL AID: Available
DRESS CODE: Uniforms

THE RIVER SCHOOL   202-337-3554   FAX 202-337-3534
4880 MacArthur Boulevard, N.W., Washington, DC 20007
Founded 2000
HEAD: Nancy K. Mellon
DIRECTOR OF ADMISSIONS: Rachel Goldstein
WEBSITE: www.riverschool.net   **E-MAIL:** tarmstrong@riverschool.net
GRADES: Preschool (18 months)–grade 3
ENROLLMENT: 200 Co-ed (108 boys/92 girls)
FACULTY: 28 full- and 5 part-time   **AVERAGE CLASS SIZE:** 10
MISSION STATEMENT: To provide successful educational experiences for children by combining a child centered, experience based approach to learning with master's level professionals in child development and language. In addition, to promote clinical research and training in language development and literacy.
SPECIAL COURSES: 1 Master level educator and 1 Speech and Language Pathologist per classroom with additional graduate students. Offer art, music, creative movement/dance, science and library
EXTENDED DAY: 3:00–5:00 p.m.   **CLUBS:** Active Parent's Association.
PLANT: Spacious, open building, science laboratory, art studio, library, 2 playgrounds and gymnasium
ADMISSION: Parent tour/student visit. Application deadline January 30
TUITION: $6,500–$15,000
FINANCIAL AID: Available
SUMMER PROGRAMS: The River School has an 11-month school year.

RIVERDALE BAPTIST SCHOOL   301-249-7000   FAX 301-249-3425
1133 Largo Road, Upper Marlboro, MD 20774
Baptist 1971
HEAD: Terry Zink
WEBSITE: www.rbschool.org   **E-MAIL:** lcolmus@rbschool.org

GRADES: Preschool 3 year old–grade 12   **ENROLLMENT:** 1,000 Co-ed
FACULTY: 75   **AVERAGE CLASS SIZE:** 25
MISSION STATEMENT: Riverdale Baptist School exists for the purpose of providing the opportunity for our students to develop a personal relationship with the Lord Jesus Christ and to receive a Christ-centered biblically-based education.
SPECIAL COURSES: Spanish, algebra, geometry, trigonometry, calculus, math analysis, accounting, college keyboard, basic computing, Cobol/Pascal, general science, physical science, anatomy, environmental science, biology, chemistry, physics, psychology, geography, U.S. history, world history, modern history, European history, American government, creative writing, journalism, art, mechanical drawing, choir, band (5–12), speech, drama, driver's ed.
EXTENDED DAY: 7:00 a.m.–6:00 p.m.
ATHLETICS: Not required. Football, wrestling, soccer, basketball, tennis, baseball, track, volleyball, softball, cheerleading
CLUBS: National Honor Society, Student Council
PUBLICATIONS: Yearbook
PLANT: Library 15,000 volumes, computer lab, science lab, gym, auditorium, playing fields
ADMISSION: Achievement test scores, transcript, personal evaluation form, interview
TUITION: Call for information.
FINANCIAL AID: By application
TRANSPORTATION: Available
DRESS CODE: Uniform required

ROCK CREEK INTERNATIONAL SCHOOL   202-965-8700   FAX 202-965-8973
1550 Foxhall Road, N.W., Washington, DC 20007
Founded 1988
HEAD: J. Daniel Hollinger, Ph.D.
DIRECTOR OF ADMISSIONS: Alejandra Maudet
WEBSITE: www.rcis.org   **E-MAIL:** admission@rcis.org
GRADES: Pre-K–grade 8   **ENROLLMENT:** 200 Co-ed (95 boys/105 girls)
FACULTY: 30 full- and 6 part-time   **AVERAGE CLASS SIZE:** 12
MISSION STATEMENT: RCIS offers a unique bilingual (English and Spanish, French or Arabic), co-ed education for Pre-Kindergarten through grade eight, in a caring environment and an international community.
SPECIAL COURSES: International Baccalaureate Organization (IBO) Accredited School. Bilingual dual immersion programs in Spanish/English, French/English and Arabic/English. ESL, SSL, FSL and ASL offered.
EXTENDED DAY: 3:30–6:00 p.m.
ATHLETICS: Basketball, soccer, tennis
CLUBS: Enrichment programs: art, ballet, chess, computer technology, cooking, cricket, digital movie-making, drama, graphic design, Japanese language and karate, music, and web page design. Annual 5th grade Costa Rica trip
PUBLICATIONS: Yearbook
PLANT: Lower school Pre-Kindergarten–grade 4 at 1550 Foxhall Road, N.W. Washington, D.C. 20007. Middle school grades 5–8 at 1621 New Hampshire Avenue, N.W. Washington, D.C. 20009. Separate art and technology rooms on

each campus. Separate libraries on each campus; volumes in English, Spanish, French and Arabic.

ADMISSION: Application deadline February 20. Child visit, assessment, transcript and recommendation are required. We invite the prospective student to visit the school. For Pre-Kindergarten and Kindergarten the visit will last for approximately ninety minutes, with half the time spent in the classroom playing with other children and half in our Admission Office for a developmental in-house test. Students applying for grades 1–8 are invited for a full day, during which they will be given a placement test to determine their academic level.

TUITION: $16,975

FINANCIAL AID: Available

OTHER FEES: Parents Association fee $50

TRANSPORTATION: Available. Cost varies

SUMMER PROGRAMS: Summer Language Immersion Programs in English, Spanish, French or Arabic

FUTURE PLANS: To add upper school

ROOTS ACTIVITY LEARNING CENTER   202-882-5155   FAX 202-882-5157
6222 North Capitol Street, N.W., Washington, DC 20011
Founded 1977
HEAD: Faheem A.-Khabeer
WEBSITE: www.rootsalc.org   **E-MAIL:** Faheem@rootsalc.org
GRADES: 6 weeks–grade 8   **ENROLLMENT:** 150 Co-ed
FACULTY: 15 full-time   **AVERAGE CLASS SIZE:** 16
MISSION STATEMENT: Our philosophy is that exposure is the key to intelligence.
SPECIAL COURSES: Spanish, French and Kiswahili. Full academic curriculum. Computer. Specialize in African-American History and Culture
EXTENDED DAY: 7:00 a.m.–6 p.m. Before care $181 After care $223
ADMISSION: First come first served on the first week day in May
TUITION: Infant $873/month(lunch included); age 3–4 $711/month (lunch and books included); age 5 $651/month (lunch and books included); grades 1–8 $467/month (Extended care not included for grades 1–8) Extended day included. Books included.
BOOKS: Included
LUNCH: Not included
SUMMER PROGRAMS: Summer programs June–August

RUXTON COUNTRY SCHOOL   410-356-9603   FAX 410-356-9690
11202 Garrison Forest Road, Owings Mills, MD 21117
Founded 1913
HEAD: Dennis Grubbs
DIRECTOR OF ADMISSIONS: Roberta Garfield
WEBSITE: www.ruxtoncountryschool.org
GRADES: Kindergarten–grade 8
ENROLLMENT: Co-ed 225
EXTENDED DAY: Before and after care
TUITION: Call for information.

SACRED HEART ACADEMY   540-662-7177   FAX   540-722-2894

110 Keating Drive, Winchester, VA 22601
Catholic
HEAD: Bonnie McGann
GRADES: Pre-K–grade 8   **ENROLLMENT:** Co-ed
EXTENDED DAY: After care
TUITION: Call for information.
DRESS CODE: Uniforms

SACRED HEART SCHOOL   202-265-4828   FAX   202-265-0595

1625 Park Road, N.W., Washington, DC 20010
Catholic 1907
HEAD: Juana Tancig-Brown
DIRECTOR OF ADMISSIONS: Juana Tancig-Brown
WEBSITE: www.centercityconsortium.org
E-MAIL: brownj@centercityconsortium.org
GRADES: Pre-K–grade 8   **ENROLLMENT:** 225 Co-ed
FACULTY: 18 full- and 4 part-time   **AVERAGE CLASS SIZE:** 20
MISSION STATEMENT: Sacred Heart School is dedicated to providing an education that values academic excellence, service to others, and spiritual values rooted in the Catholic faith. We strive to nurture and engage students in the learning process. We work with students to help them realize their potential, to be critical and independent thinkers, and able to create opportunities for themselves and others in their community.
SPECIAL COURSES: Bilingual academic program using the 50/50 immersion model. Language arts, math, and all specials classes taught in English and Spanish. Language arts, science and social studies instruction in Spanish. English as a Second language (ESOL) and Spanish as a Second Language (SSL). Instruction is focused on Learning for Understanding, helping students use multiple entry points of knowledge. Studio arts includes pottery and print making. Our music program includes theory, music history, and choral arts. Language arts, science, math, social studies, and religion form the core curriculum supplemented by the arts and P.E. programs.
ATHLETICS: Girls' and boys' basketball, lacrosse, soccer, aerobics, yoga, badminton, volleyball
CLUBS: Art club, dance club, drama club, science club, Brain Twisters Club, hiking club, and Social Justice Club
PUBLICATIONS: Yearbook
COMMUNITY INVOLVEMENT: All middle school students are required to complete community service hours.
PLANT: Originally opened as an all girls academy, the school was relocated to the present facility in 1939, the year we began our co-ed elementary program. The classrooms are housed on four floors with recent renovations adding an art room with a pottery annex, computer lab, library, gym, and science lab. The school is networked, with access to the internet available in the computer lab and most classes.
ADMISSION: Prospective students submit an application along with a copy of the last report card, most recent standardized test, and a teacher/principal

lation. Admissions test , interview with the school principal. School ...eduled for parents and new students by appointment. New students ...ed to spend a morning in the school.

.200

...AL AID: Financial aid is available from the Archdiocese of Washington ...nd from the Center City Consortium. Families are asked to complete a financial aid form for each.

BOOKS: Included   **LUNCH:** Additional

OTHER FEES: Activity fee of $200. Each family is asked to complete 10 hours of service to the school each year.

DRESS CODE: Uniform

SUMMER PROGRAMS: Spanish immersion camp and academic summer school

FUTURE PLANS: Each year a new grade will transition into the bilingual program, continuing until completion of the program to the eighth grade.

ST. AGNES CATHOLIC SCHOOL   703-527-5423   FAX 703-525-4689

2024 North Randolph Street, Arlington, VA 22207
Catholic
HEAD: Vivian Uthe
WEBSITE: www.saintagnes.org
GRADES: Pre-K–grade 8   **ENROLLMENT:** 350 Co-ed
SPECIAL COURSES: Computer, art, music, P.E., Spanish and library
EXTENDED DAY: Before and after care
ATHLETICS: CYO sports
CLUBS: Junior Great Books, band, Scouts   **PUBLICATIONS:** Yearbook, newspaper
PLANT: State of the art computer and science lab
TUITION: Call for information.
DRESS CODE: Uniforms

ST. ALBANS SCHOOL   202-537-6435   FAX 202-537-5613

Wisconsin & Massachusetts Avenues, N.W., Washington, DC 20016
Episcopal 1909   Al Gore went here
HEAD: Vance Wilson
WEBSITE: www.sta.cathedral.org   **E-MAIL:** sta_admission@cathedral.org
GRADES: 4–12   **ENROLLMENT:** 563 boys (28 boarding)
FACULTY: 68 full- and 12 part-time   **AVERAGE CLASS SIZE:** 15
SPECIAL COURSES: Latin, French, Spanish: all 8–12; Japanese, 9–12. Math through calculus. Science: biology, chemistry, physics, earth science. History: ancient Rome, ancient Greece, omnibus-American and European history, history and culture of Islam. Fine arts: painting and drawing, graphics, 3-dimensional art, studio. Music: survey of Western music, music theory, instrumental-orchestra. Computer. Religious studies required: The Bible, Question of God. Drama, filmmaking. AP: English, languages, math, computer, history, science. Coordinate classes with National Cathedral School for Girls; Boys in both the Boys Choir and the Men's Choir at the Cathedral often attend classes at St. Albans. Student exchange program with Russia and Japan.
EXTENDED DAY: Grades 4–8 only, 3:30–6 p.m.
ATHLETICS: Required. Intramural and interscholastic (13 varsity sports); basketball, soccer, swimming, wrestling, track, lacrosse, weight training, football,

baseball, tennis, cross-country, golf, rock climbing, kayaking, crew, ice hockey
CLUBS: Glee, Madrigals, orchestra, press, drama, service, government, art, band
PUBLICATIONS: Newspaper, yearbook, literary magazine
COMMUNITY INVOLVEMENT: 60 hours of Social Service prior to senior year are required for graduation.
PLANT: Library 24,000 volumes. (A computer system now links the libraries of St. Albans with those at National Cathedral School for Girls.) 3 science labs, 3 art studios, 2 gyms, auditorium, playing fields, swimming pool, 8 tennis courts, computers, music room.
ADMISSION: ISEE or SSAT October–January. Interview, transcript, teacher recommendations. Fee $75. Lower school has its own testing in January for grades 4 and 5.
TUITION: $21,837 day (includes lunch); $30,889 boarding
FINANCIAL AID: Full and partial scholarships available.
BOOKS: Extra   **DRESS CODE:** Coat and tie
SUMMER PROGRAMS: Academic programs. Summer Camp: tennis, soccer, basketball, baseball, sports clinics. Early June Program; late afternoon program 3:00–6 :00 p.m., ages 6–12.

ST. AMBROSE SCHOOL   301-773-0223   FAX 301-773-9647
6310 Jason Street, Cheverly, MD 20785
Catholic
HEAD: Vincent Spadoni
GRADES: Pre-K–grade 8
EXTENDED DAY: Before and after care
TUITION: $3,562 one child in parish
DRESS CODE: Uniforms
FUTURE PLANS: To add a Summer Camp

ST. AMBROSE SCHOOL   703-698-7171   FAX 703-698-7170
3827 Woodburn Road, Annandale, VA 22003
Catholic
HEAD: Virginia Connell
WEBSITE: www.stambroseschool.org
GRADES: Kindergarten–grade 8
ENROLLMENT: Co-ed
EXTENDED DAY: Before and after care begins at 7:00 a.m., ends at 6:00 p.m.
TUITION: Call for information.
DRESS CODE: Uniforms

ST. ANDREW APOSTLE SCHOOL   301-649-3555   FAX 301-649-2352
11602 Kemp Mill Road, Silver Spring, MD 20902
Catholic
HEAD: Catherine Medlock
WEBSITE: www.standrewapostle.org
E-MAIL: standrew20902@yahoo.com
GRADES: Pre-K–grade 8   **ENROLLMENT:** Co-ed
EXTENDED DAY: After care
TUITION: $4,845 one child in parish 1–8
DRESS CODE: Uniforms

ST. ANDREW THE APOSTLE SCHOOL   703-817-1774   FAX 703-817-1721
6720-B Union Mill Road, Clifton, VA 20124
Catholic
HEAD: Phyllis Hammang
E-MAIL: office@standrewtheapostleschool.org
GRADES: Pre-K–grade 8   **ENROLLMENT:** Co-ed
TUITION: Call for information.
DRESS CODE: Uniforms

ST. ANDREW'S EPISCOPAL SCHOOL   301-983-5200   FAX 301-983-4620
8804 Postoak Road, Potomac, MD 20854
Episcopal 1978
HEAD: Robert Kosasky
DIRECTOR OF ADMISSIONS: Julie Jameson
WEBSITE: www.saes.org   **E-MAIL:** admission@saes.org
GRADES: 6–12 grade   **ENROLLMENT:** 450 Co-ed approx 50% boys/50% girls
FACULTY: 62 full- and 12 part-time   **AVERAGE CLASS SIZE:** 15
MISSION STATEMENT: St. Andrew's mission is to provide a comprehensive coeducational college preparatory program for students in grades six through twelve in a cooperative environment that embodies the faith and perspective of the Episcopal church. The school values the educational advantages of a diverse student body composed of a wide spectrum of racial, religious, socioeconomic, and cultural backgrounds.
SPECIAL COURSES: Latin, French, and Spanish, 7–12; AP French, AP Spanish. Math 6–12, including geometry, algebra I–III, algebra II/trigonometry, pre-calculus, statistics and finance, AP calculus. English 6–12, including accelerated English, AP English, journalism, creative writing. History 6–12, including Modern European History, U.S. History to 1877, America in the World, Asian Studies, Globalization, Modern Middle East, History of Violence, Race and Culture, AP history, and Advanced History Consortium courses ranging from AP economics to Media Studies to The Civil Rights Movement in America. Science 6–12, including Applied Science and Technology, biology, AP biology, chemistry, Fundamentals of Organic and Biochemistry II, earth science, conceptual physics, physics I–II, and accelerated physics. Religion (one trimester/high school year), including Church History and Society, World Religions, The Bible, Theology, Ethics and Philosophy of Religion. Art (2 trimesters/high school year), including dance, acting, improvisation, public speaking, play production, band, guitar, keyboard, musical theater, Music in History, chorus, orchestra, jazz band, computer graphics, drawing, painting, studio art, animation, ceramics, photography, video and AP art. Human Development and Family Life and P.E. (see athletics below).
EXTENDED DAY: 3:30–6:00 p.m.
ATHLETICS: Aikido, baseball, basketball, cross-country, dance, equestrian team, fitness, golf, soccer, softball, track, tennis, volleyball, and wrestling
CLUBS: Band, jazz band, orchestra, string ensemble, instrumental lessons, chorus, dance, play productions, musical productions, stage crew, Student Government, Amnesty International, badminton club, chess club, diversity club, electronics club, environmental club, fashion club, HART (service) club, I-2-I (women's issues), Latin club, Leadership Weekend, Model U.N., Student Vestry, swing dance, TGIF club, and tour guides

PUBLICATIONS: Literary magazines, newspaper, yearbook

COMMUNITY INVOLVEMENT: Community service required each year, with a variety of possible organizations or trips to fulfill requirement.

PLANT: St. Andrew's is situated on a beautiful 19.2-acre campus with state of the art classrooms, science and technology laboratories, 13,000-volume library, theater/assembly hall, sports fields, four tennis courts, photography and computer labs, art studios, and dance studio.

ADMISSION: Submit an application form with $50 fee; call for an appointment and personal interview, submit transcript and teacher recommendations from English and math teachers, and take the SSAT examination. February 1 deadline for all forms and exams for potential admission the following fall

TUITION: $21,895 grades 9–12; $20,580 grades 6–8

FINANCIAL AID: Available

BOOKS: $400–$700   **LUNCH:** Included

OTHER FEES: Graduation fee of $200, optional parent association fee of $50; optional tuition refund insurance plan of approximately $375

TRANSPORTATION: Available. $1,200 round trip, $750 one way. No charge for the St. Andrew's shuttle service for those families who qualify for financial aid

DRESS CODE: Neat shirts with collars, nice pants, skirts, or dresses. No blue jeans

SUMMER PROGRAMS: Summer Day Camp for ages 4–18, variety of classes and sports. 9:00 to 3:30, before and after care

ST. ANDREW'S UNITED METHODIST DAY SCHOOL   410-266-0952

4 Wallace Manor Road, Edgewater, MD 21037
Methodist 1985
HEAD: Kristine Angelis
WEBSITE: www.standrewsum.com   **E-MAIL:** k2sandsch@aol.com
GRADES: N–grade 8   **ENROLLMENT:** 398 Co-ed
SPECIAL COURSES: Spanish, computer, art, music, religion, P.E.
EXTENDED DAY: 7:00 a.m.–6:30 p.m.
TUITION: $2,845–$6,489
FINANCIAL AID: Available
DRESS CODE: Uniforms

ST. ANN ELEMENTARY SCHOOL   703-525-7599

980 North Frederick Street, Arlington, VA 22205
Catholic
HEAD: Sally Berra
WEBSITE: www.stann.org   **E-MAIL:** stann@stann.org
GRADES: Kindergarten–grade 8   **ENROLLMENT:** Co-ed
EXTENDED DAY: Before and after care
TUITION: Call for information.
DRESS CODE: Uniforms

ST. ANN'S ACADEMY   202-363-4460   FAX 202-362-6560

4404 Wisconsin Avenue, N.W., Washington, DC 20016
Catholic
HEAD: Barbara A. Kelly
E-MAIL: stannofc@erols.com

GRADES: Pre-K–grade 8   ENROLLMENT: Co-ed
EXTENDED DAY: Before and after care
TUITION: $5,400 one child
DRESS CODE: Uniforms K–8
SUMMER PROGRAMS: Summer school

ST. ANNE'S DAY SCHOOL   410-263-8650   FAX 410-280-8720
3112 Arundel on the Bay Road, Annapolis, MD 21403
Episcopal 1960(PK)/1992
HEAD: Fran Lukens
DIRECTOR OF ADMISSIONS: Caroline Aras
WEBSITE: www.saintannes.org   E-MAIL: caras@saintannes.org
GRADES: 3's program–grade 8   ENROLLMENT: 388 Co-ed (176 boys/212 girls)
FACULTY: 30 full- and 7 part-time   AVERAGE CLASS SIZE: 16–20
MISSION STATEMENT: (Excerpted) St. Anne's Day School is an independent, co-educational, Episcopal school for motivated and capable students from pre-school through eighth grade. St. Anne's students learn in an innovative, experiential and student-centered program that prepares graduates for success in demanding, college-preparatory programs.
SPECIAL COURSES: French, Spanish, art, music, computer, Language Arts Plus
EXTENDED DAY: 7:15 a.m.–6:00 p.m.
ATHLETICS: P.E., Intramural and interscholastic. Field hockey, soccer, basketball, lacrosse, cross-country, tennis
CLUBS: Instrumental music, chorus, drama
PUBLICATIONS: Weekly "Monday Memo" parent newsletter, "Star" quarterly news magazine
COMMUNITY INVOLVEMENT: Community service required. Class projects
PLANT: 10-acre campus, 45,600 square footage. Traditional classroom setting. Library, computer technology center, 3 playgrounds, sports fields, auditorium/gym, music center, art center, foreign language lab, seminar room.
ADMISSION: Parents may apply for new student admission between October 1 and February 15 for the following academic year. Applications submitted after February 15 will be considered by the Admissions Committee on a rolling basis.
TUITION: $5,145–$11,975
FINANCIAL AID: Available
LUNCH: Brown bag/pizza Fridays/taco Fridays
OTHER FEES: $50 application $75 screening fee
DRESS CODE: Uniform required (K–8)
SUMMER PROGRAMS: The Summer Camp at St. Anne's
FUTURE PLANS: Possible third floor

ST. ANNE'S-BELFIELD SCHOOL   434-296-5106   FAX 434-979-1486
2132 Ivy Road, Charlottesville, VA 22903
Founded 1910
HEAD: Reverend George E. Conway
DIRECTOR OF ADMISSIONS: Jean Craig
WEBSITE: www.stab.org   E-MAIL: admission@stab.org
GRADES: Pre-K–grade 12   ENROLLMENT: 835 Co-ed/ 37 boarding begins in 9
FACULTY: 95 full-and 6 part-time   AVERAGE CLASS SIZE: 15

MISSION STATEMENT: (Excerpted) We at St. Anne's-Belfield believe that the transmission of knowledge, the encouragement of curiosity, the development of rational thought, and the cultivation of responsible, honorable behavior are the great ends of education. In asking students to master a specific body of knowledge, we seek not to impart knowledge alone, but to instill the lifelong habit of learning.

SPECIAL COURSES: ESL program, 11 AP courses, a number of honors/accelerated courses 7–12

EXTENDED DAY: 7:30 a.m.–5:30 p.m.

ATHLETICS: Interscholastic sports: hockey, volleyball, cross-country, basketball, lacrosse, wrestling, soccer, football, baseball, softball, tennis, golf, squash. Competitive athletics grades 7–12

CLUBS: Honor Council, SADD, Amnesty International, drama, Pop Quiz, Art Forum. Fine and performing arts

PUBLICATIONS: Newspaper, literary magazine, yearbook

COMMUNITY INVOLVEMENT: Community service requirement

PLANT: 40+ acres adjacent to The University of Virginia- 2 libraries, 3 gyms, 2 auditoriums, 8 science labs, 2 computer labs, 5 playing fields, 6 courts, Fine Arts Building with wheels and kiln, photography darkroom.

ADMISSION: Rolling admissions. Interview and class visit. SSAT required for 7-12. Send application, transcript and recommendations.

TUITION: $6,990- $14,600 day; $12,577- $21,716 boarding

FINANCIAL AID: Available

BOOKS: $200   **LUNCH:** $3.00- $4.00 per lunch

DRESS CODE: Collared shirts–no t-shirts or jeans

SUMMER PROGRAMS: 8-week camp, sports camps, remedial/enrichment classes. Summer programs for Pre-K–grade 8

FUTURE PLANS: Expansion of boarding facilities and fine arts center

ST. ANSELM'S ABBEY SCHOOL   202-269-2350   FAX 202-269-2373

4501 South Dakota Avenue, N.E., Washington, DC 20017
Catholic 1942
HEAD: Rev. Peter Weigand, OSB, M.T.S.
DIRECTOR OF ADMISSIONS: Patrick I. Parsons
WEBSITE: www.saintanselms.org   **E-MAIL:** mainoffice@saintanselms.org
GRADES: 6–12   **ENROLLMENT:** 260 boys
FACULTY: 45 full-time   **AVERAGE CLASS SIZE:** 15
MISSION STATEMENT: The School strives to provide a "liberal education with maximum intellectual challenge" within a community of learning that reflects "the Rule of St. Benedict: peace and fraternity, respect for the value of work, self-discipline, and the development of personal talents for the service of others."
SPECIAL COURSES: Latin 7–12, French and Spanish 8–12, Greek 11–12. Math includes calculus and computer. General science, biology, chemistry, physics. History: U.S., Western Civilization, world history, Native American history, economics. Religious studies required. Art, music. AP: English literature, composition, American literature, Latin, French literature and conversation, physics, chemistry, biology, U.S. history, European history, comparative governments, U.S. politics and government and calculus
ATHLETICS: All students in grades 6–10 are required to participate weekly in

intramural sports: basketball, softball, soccer, volleyball, stickball. Optional co-ed recreational program offered grades 9–12. Interscholastic: soccer, basketball, baseball, tennis, cross-country, wrestling, track and field

CLUBS: Forensics, Priory Players, Latin Bowl, Cultural Student Organization, Math Counts, "It's Academic," theater, film, science

PUBLICATIONS: Yearbook, newspaper, literary magazine

COMMUNITY INVOLVEMENT: 2 1/2 hours a week of community service to various off-campus agencies in the metro area required for all students in grades 11–12

PLANT: Library 12,500 volumes, 3 science labs, art studio, auditorium, greenhouse, 2 playing fields, 4 tennis courts, Chapel, new athletic complex, Brian K. Devine Performing Arts Center. 35 acres of land

ADMISSION: Rolling admission. Apply November-March. Entrance test required. $35 application fee

TUITION: $14,800–$15,100

FINANCIAL AID: Need-based

OTHER FEES: Additional fees $650–$900

TRANSPORTATION: School accessible by Red and Green Metro lines

DRESS CODE: Jacket and tie

SUMMER PROGRAMS: Academic: Remedial courses in math, languages. Enrichment courses in science, math, English, study skills. Sports Camp, Outdoor Adventure Camp

ST. ANTHONY CATHOLIC SCHOOL   202-526-4657   FAX 202-832-5567
12th & Lawrence Streets, N.E., Washington, DC 20017
Catholic
HEAD: William Eager
E-MAIL: santhonydc@juno.com
GRADES: Pre-K–grade 8   **ENROLLMENT:** Co-ed
EXTENDED DAY: Before and after care
TUITION: $3,535 one child in parish
DRESS CODE: Uniforms

ST. AUGUSTINE SCHOOL   202-667-2608   FAX 202-667-2610
1421 V Street, N.W., Washington, DC 20009
Catholic
HEAD: Donna Edwards
GRADES: Pre-K–grade 8   **ENROLLMENT:** Co-ed
EXTENDED DAY: Before and after care
TUITION: $3,255 one child in parish

ST. BARTHOLOMEW SCHOOL   301-229-5586   FAX 301-229-8654
6900 River Road, Bethesda, MD 20817
Catholic
HEAD: Kathleen Miller
WEBSITE: www.stbartholomew.org   **E-MAIL:** kathleen@stbartholomew.org
GRADES: Kindergarten–8   **ENROLLMENT:** Co-ed
EXTENDED DAY: Before and after care
TUITION: $4,740 one child
DRESS CODE: Uniforms

ST. BENEDICT THE MOOR SCHOOL   202-397-3897   FAX 202-388-7874
320 21st Street, N.E., Washington, DC 20002
Catholic
HEAD: Rose Thomas
DIRECTOR OF ADMISSIONS: Rose Thomas
E-MAIL: st_benedict_the_moor@hotmail.com
GRADES: Pre-K–grade 8   **ENROLLMENT:** 235 Co-ed
FACULTY: 17 full- and 3 part-time   **AVERAGE CLASS SIZE:** 25
EXTENDED DAY: 7:00–8:00 a.m. and 3:00–6:00 p.m.
TUITION: $3,255 one child in parish
FINANCIAL AID: Available through the Archdiocese of Washington
DRESS CODE: Uniform

ST. BERNADETTE SCHOOL   301-593-5611   FAX 301-593-9042
80 University Boulevard East, Silver Spring, MD 20901
Catholic
HEAD: Janet Cantwell
WEBSITE: www.st-bernadetteelem.com
GRADES: Kindergarten–grade 8   **ENROLLMENT:** Co-ed
EXTENDED DAY: Before and after care
TUITION: $4,450 one child in parish
DRESS CODE: Uniforms
SUMMER PROGRAMS: Summer school

ST. BERNADETTE SCHOOL   703-451-8696
7602 Old Keene Mill Road, Springfield, VA 22152
Catholic
HEAD: Sister Maureen Vellon
GRADES: Kindergarten–grade 8   **ENROLLMENT:** Co-ed
TUITION: Call for information.
DRESS CODE: Uniforms

ST. BERNARD OF CLAIRVAUX SCHOOL   301-864-3801   FAX 301-864-2912
5811 Riverdale Road, Riverdale Park, MD 20737
Catholic 1952
HEAD: Philip E. Buckley
WEBSITE: www.stbsriverdale.org   **E-MAIL:** Buckley@stbsriverdale.org
GRADES: Kindergarten–grade 8   **ENROLLMENT:** 210 Co-ed (100 boys/110 girls)
FACULTY: 15 full- and 3 part-time   **AVERAGE CLASS SIZE:** 27
EXTENDED DAY: After care 3:00–6:00 p.m. Before care please call 301-864-2798
ATHLETICS: Sponsored by Church affiliated organization
CLUBS: Student Council, drama club, choir, Book and Garden Club
PUBLICATIONS: Yearbook, school newsletter
ADMISSION: Rolling admissions- contact Principal or admissions committee.
TUITION: $3,545 in parish
FINANCIAL AID: Available
BOOKS: Included   **OTHER FEES:** Application $50, registration $190
DRESS CODE: Uniform
SUMMER PROGRAMS: Call for information.

ST. CAMILLUS CATHOLIC SCHOOL   301-434-2344   FAX 301-434-7726

1500 St. Camillus Drive, Silver Spring, MD 20903
Catholic 1954
HEAD: Dr. John Black
WEBSITE: www.rc.net\washington\st_camillus   **E-MAIL:** camillad@erols.com
GRADES: Kindergarten–grade 8   **ENROLLMENT:** 270 Co-ed
FACULTY: 14 full- and 10 part-time   **AVERAGE CLASS SIZE:** 27
MISSION STATEMENT: St. Camillus offers a Catholic education, consistent with the educational mission of the church, to students of all ethnic groups. The mission of St. Camillus Catholic School is to offer experiences in an environment which will enable students to proclaim and celebrate the Good News of Jesus Christ, to build a community of Faith and to reach out in service to others for the sake of peace and justice.
SPECIAL COURSES: Recognized by the U.S. Department of Education in 1997 as a "National School of Excellence." Algebra, religion, English/language arts, math, science, art, music, social studies, P.E., Spanish, ESL program
EXTENDED DAY: 7:00–8:15 a.m. and 3:00–6:00 p.m.
ATHLETICS: Sports
CLUBS: Spanish, science, French, drama, dance, computer, band
PLANT: Brick building, computer lab, library, gym, all-purpose room
ADMISSION: All new students will be accepted on probation after consideration of previous academic records, screening and placement test and an interview.
TUITION: $3,600
FINANCIAL AID: Available
DRESS CODE: Uniform required
FUTURE PLANS: New playground equipment and air conditioning

ST. CATHERINE LABOURE   301-946-1717   FAX 301-946-9572

11811 Claridge Road, Wheaton, MD 20902
Catholic 1953
HEAD: Sister Mary Gilbart, DC
DIRECTOR OF ADMISSIONS: Julie Fox
WEBSITE: www.stcatherine.com   **E-MAIL:** sclscl@stcatherine.com
GRADES: Pre-K–grade 8   **ENROLLMENT:** 463 Co-ed (220 boys/243 girls)
FACULTY: 35 full- and 3 part-time   **AVERAGE CLASS SIZE:** 25
MISSION STATEMENT: At SCL we incorporate strong religious values, academic challenges, and a sense of personal and community responsibility in all aspects of life. We attempt to create an environment that allows each student to be successful and fosters an appreciation of diversity.
SPECIAL COURSES: ESOL available, Teacher Learning Center in 5th grade, inclusive practices
EXTENDED DAY: Call for information.
ATHLETICS: CYO athletics
CLUBS: Chess club, band, chorus, reading clubs, math club
PUBLICATIONS: Yearbook
ADMISSION: Application, screening, references, etc.
TUITION: $3,000 Parish
FINANCIAL AID: Available through the Archdiocese of Washington and SCL Parish

BOOKS: $150   LUNCH: Weekly cost
DRESS CODE: Uniform
SUMMER PROGRAMS: Summer Camp

ST. CHARLES CATHOLIC SCHOOL   703-527-0608

3299 North Fairfax Drive, Arlington, VA 22201
Catholic 1922
HEAD: Sister Benedict Kesock, OSB
DIRECTOR OF ADMISSIONS: Sister Benedict Kesock, OSB
WEBSITE: www.stcharles.k12.va.us   E-MAIL: office@stcharles.k12.va.us
GRADES: Kindergarten–grade 8   ENROLLMENT: 240 Co-ed
FACULTY: 15 full- and 5 part-time   AVERAGE CLASS SIZE: 24
MISSION STATEMENT: Keeping in mind that we are born into three societies-
the home, the community and the church- St. Charles Catholic School is dedicat-
ed to assisting parents in fulfilling their God-given duty of educating their chil-
dren spiritually, intellectually, ethically, socially and physically. This mission has
never been more important, with so many assaults on our security and trust and
on the values and standards we hold so dear. When a child is entrusted to our
care, we attempt to build on their faith experience and to enhance what the child
has already learned from their parents, their first teachers.
SPECIAL COURSES: Algebra grades 7 and 8
EXTENDED DAY: 7:00–8:00 a.m. and 3:00–6:00 p.m.
ATHLETICS: Basketball (girls grades 6,7,8; boys grades 5,6,7,8)
CLUBS: Safety Patrols, Scouts
PLANT: Library, cafeteria, playground, new gymnasium fall 2003, computer in
each classroom. The school is a short walk from either the Clarendon or Virginia
Square Metro stops on the Orange Line. It is 5 minutes from the Pentagon and I-
95 and 2 minutes from I-66 Glebe Road exit.
TUITION: $3,289–$5,389 per child, depending upon parish affiliation. Family
discounts given
FINANCIAL AID: Available
BOOKS: $150
LUNCH: Hot lunch available for purchase each day
OTHER FEES: $75 registration $50 each technology and playground
TRANSPORTATION: Bus available from Bolling Air Force Base for residents of
Base. Van transportation after school only provided by Ft. Myer for Ft. Myer
dependents
DRESS CODE: Uniforms
FUTURE PLANS: New gymnasium and Community Center open in fall 2003.
Preschool in fall 2004.

ST. COLETTA SCHOOL   703-683-3686

207 South Peyton Street, Alexandria, VA 22314
Catholic
HEAD: Sharon Raimo
WEBSITE: www.stcoletta.org
GRADES: Ungraded ages 4–22   ENROLLMENT: Co-ed
SPECIAL COURSES: For developmentally disabled children
FUTURE PLANS: Will open new building in Washington. D.C. in 2005

ST. COLUMBA SCHOOL   301-567-6212   FAX 301-567-6907
7800 Livingston Road, Oxon Hill, MD 20745
Catholic
HEAD: Donna Potenza
WEBSITE: www.rc.net/washington/stcolumba   **E-MAIL:** stcolmd@aol.com
GRADES: Kindergarten–grade 8   **ENROLLMENT:** Co-ed
EXTENDED DAY: Before and after care
TUITION: $2,953 one child in parish (non-Kindergarten)
DRESS CODE: Uniforms

ST. ELIZABETH CATHOLIC SCHOOL   301-881-1824   FAX 301-881-6035
917 Montrose Road, Rockville, MD 20852
Catholic
HEAD: Cheryl Murzyn
WEBSITE: www.stelizabethschoolmd.org   **E-MAIL:** office@stelizabethschool.org
GRADES: Kindergarten–grade 8   **ENROLLMENT:** Co-ed
TUITION: $4,900 one child in parish
DRESS CODE: Uniforms
SUMMER PROGRAMS: Summer Camp

ST. FRANCIS DE SALES SCHOOL   202-529-5394   FAX 202-529-1620
2019 Rhode Island Avenue, N.E., Washington, DC 20018
Catholic
HEAD: Matt Johnson
E-MAIL: johnsonm@centercityconsortium.org
GRADES: Pre-K–grade 8   **ENROLLMENT:** Co-ed
EXTENDED DAY: Before and after care Pre-K–8
TUITION: $3,100 one child in parish
DRESS CODE: Uniforms grades 1–8

ST. FRANCIS EPISCOPAL DAY SCHOOL   301-365-2642   FAX 301-299-0412
10033 River Road, Potomac, MD 20854
Episcopal 1988
HEAD: Walter T. McCoy
DIRECTOR OF ADMISSIONS: Joanne T. Zinsmeister
WEBSITE: www.sfeds.org   **E-MAIL:** last name(no space)1st initial@sfeds.org
GRADES: Preschool–grade 5   **ENROLLMENT:** 252 Co-ed(124 boys/128 girls)
FACULTY: 29 full- and 5 part-time
AVERAGE CLASS SIZE: 7:1 student/teacher ratio
MISSION STATEMENT: St. Francis Episcopal Day School is a parish school whose primary purpose is to provide an excellent educational program for preschool and elementary students. The school cultivates intellectual curiosity while engaging heart and spirit. St. Francis Episcopal Day School educates the whole child in the context of the Christian story encouraging students to live healthy and productive lives.
SPECIAL COURSES: All grade levels: Christian Studies, music, science lab, library, P.E., cultural arts enrichment program, community outreach, Chapel. K–5: Spanish, technology, art 3–5: Music involves, recorder, chorus, and music class. Nurturing, self-esteem building environment with a challenging curriculum

EXTENDED DAY: 3:15–4:45 p.m.

CLUBS: Curriculum-related field trips. After school programs include: chess, tae kwon do, tone chimes, art, gymnastics, cooking, drama, scouts, tennis and soccer

PLANT: Multi-purpose room, library with over 9,000 books, creative playgrounds, soccer field, hard court/basketball. Art, computer lab, music room, science lab and tutoring areas

ADMISSION: Application fee $50.00 with applications accepted throughout the year. Children applying to preschool participate in play-group evaluations. Elementary grades spend a day at school with assessment testing in reading, writing, and math. Transcripts and teacher recommendations required for all grades. Parents tour school, and interview with Director of Admissions.

TUITION: $3,874–$12,409

FINANCIAL AID: Yes

BOOKS: Included   **LUNCH:** Bring

OTHER FEES: Technology, activity, Parents Association dues. Tuition Refund Plan is optional.

DRESS CODE: Uniforms for grades K–5

SUMMER PROGRAMS: Summer Journeys for ages 3–11: a creative, social, academic and athletic program

FUTURE PLANS: 2003–2004: second section of 3rd grade with second sections planned for future 4th and 5th grades.

ST. FRANCIS OF ASSISI SCHOOL   703-221-3868   FAX 703-221-0700
18825 Fuller Heights Road, Triangle, VA 22172
Catholic
HEAD: Dr. Tricia Barber
WEBSITE: www.stfas.org
GRADES: Pre-K–grade 8   **ENROLLMENT:** Co-ed
EXTENDED DAY: 6:30 a.m.–6:30 p.m.
TUITION: Call for information.
DRESS CODE: Uniforms

ST. FRANCIS XAVIER SCHOOL   202-581-2010   FAX 202-581-1142
2700 O Street, S.E., Washington, DC 20020
Catholic
HEAD: Harold Thomas
GRADES: Pre-K to grade 8   **ENROLLMENT:** 222 Co-ed
SPECIAL COURSES: Computer, technology, music, art, P.E.
EXTENDED DAY: 6:30 a.m.–6:00 p.m.
TUITION: Call for information.
DRESS CODE: Uniforms

ST. GABRIEL SCHOOL   202-726-9212   FAX 202-726-3378
510 Webster Street, N.W., Washington, DC 20011
Catholic
HEAD: Monica Arce
GRADES: Kindergarten–grade 8   **ENROLLMENT:** Co-ed
EXTENDED DAY: After care
TUITION: Call for information.

ST. HUGH'S SCHOOL   301-474-4071   FAX 301-474-3950
145 Crescent Road, Greenbelt, MD 20770
Catholic
HEAD: Mary Elizabeth Whelan
GRADES: Kindergarten–grade 8   **ENROLLMENT:** Co-ed
EXTENDED DAY: Before and after care
TUITION: Call for information.

ST. IGNATIUS SCHOOL   301-567-4090   FAX 301-567-0156
2317 Brinkley Road, Ft. Washington, MD 20744
Catholic
HEAD: Linda Bourne
WEBSITE: www.saintignatiusschool.org
GRADES: Pre-K–grade 8   **ENROLLMENT:** Co-ed
EXTENDED DAY: Before and after care
TUITION: $4,000 one child
DRESS CODE: Uniforms

SAINT JAMES SCHOOL   301-733-9330   FAX 301-739-1310
St. James, MD 21781
Episcopal 1842
HEAD: Rev. D. Stuart Dunnan, Ph.D.
WEBSITE: www.stjames.edu   **E-MAIL:** admissions@stjames.edu
GRADES: 8–12   **ENROLLMENT:** 228 Co-ed Boarding 164
FACULTY: 30 full-time   **AVERAGE CLASS SIZE:** 12
MISSION STATEMENT: To prepare young men and women for academic success in college and to challenge and inspire them to be leaders for good in the world. We seek to do this within a small and familial residential community which values the moral and spiritual development of our students.
SPECIAL COURSES: Languages: Latin, Spanish, French. Math: math II, algebra I, algebra II, geometry, pre-calculus, calculus, AP calculus AB/SC. Science: Introduction to Physical Science, biology, chemistry, physics, environmental. History: ancient history, modern European history, Developing Nations, U.S. history, political economy, Biblical theology, Old and New Testament studies. Fine Arts: art, studio art, studio art II, music, music history, music theory. AP: calculus, biology, chemistry, U.S. history, European history, French, Spanish, Latin, English.
ATHLETICS: Required. Interscholastic. Member of the MAC (Mid-Atlantic Conference). Football, basketball, soccer, tennis, cross-country, wrestling, baseball, field hockey, lacrosse, golf, volleyball, softball, dance, strength and conditioning, martial arts. Indoor soccer
CLUBS: Acolytes, art, Cum Laude Society, disciplinary committee, Honor Council, Lay Readers, Maroon Key (tour guides), Mummers Society (drama), Latin club, photography, Student Activities Committee, choir
PUBLICATIONS: Yearbook, newspaper, literary magazine
COMMUNITY INVOLVEMENT: Big Brother/Big Sister
PLANT: Library 20,000 volumes, 4 science labs, art studio, large field house, new fitness center, 7 playing fields, 12 tennis courts, pottery studio, Chapel, 5 dormitories, student center, 3 computer labs, Fine Arts Center.
ADMISSION: SSAT grades 8–12, or PSAT/SAT for grades 11–12. Transcript,

math and English teacher recommendations, interview
TUITION: $25,000 Boarding; $16,700 Day
FINANCIAL AID: Available
BOOKS: $350–$500
DRESS CODE: Boys: coat and tie; Girls: skirt/dress/slacks and a blazer
SUMMER PROGRAMS: Sports Camp

ST. JAMES SCHOOL   703-533-1182   FAX 703-532-8316
830 West Broad Street, Falls Church, VA 22046
Catholic
HEAD: Sister Teresa Ballisty, IHM
WEBSITE: www.saintjamesschool.org
GRADES: Kindergarten–grade 8   **ENROLLMENT:** Co-ed
EXTENDED DAY: Before and after care
TUITION: Call for information.
DRESS CODE: Uniforms
SUMMER PROGRAMS: Summer Camp

ST. JANE DE CHANTAL SCHOOL   301-530-1221   FAX 301-530-1688
9525 Old Georgetown Road, Bethesda, MD 20814
Catholic
HEAD: Elizabeth Hamilton
GRADES: Kindergarten–grade 8   **ENROLLMENT:** Co-ed
EXTENDED DAY: Before and after care
TUITION: $3,950 one child Catholic
DRESS CODE: Uniforms
SUMMER PROGRAMS: Special programs

ST. JEROME'S SCHOOL   301-277-4568   FAX 301-779-2428
5207 42nd Place, Hyattsville, MD 20781
Catholic
HEAD: Dr. Joyce Volpini, SND
DIRECTOR OF ADMISSIONS: Ethel Jenkyns
WEBSITE: www.stjeromes.org   **E-MAIL:** office@stjeromes.org
GRADES: Infants, Pre-K–grade 8   **ENROLLMENT:** Co-ed
SPECIAL COURSES: St. Jerome Child Center accepts infants– Pre-K.
EXTENDED DAY: 7:00–8:00 a.m. and 2:40–6:00 p.m. and Summer Program
TUITION: $3,325
BOOKS: $185
DRESS CODE: Uniforms
SUMMER PROGRAMS: St. Jerome Summer Program 8 weeks

ST. JOHN NEUMANN SCHOOL   703-492-1272
13900 Church Hill Drive, Woodbridge, VA 22194
Catholic
WEBSITE: www.stjohnneumannschool.org
GRADES: 7–12   **ENROLLMENT:** Co-ed
TUITION: Call for information.
DRESS CODE: Uniforms

ST. JOHN REGIONAL CATHOLIC SCHOOL   301-662-6722   FAX 301-695-7024
114 East 2nd Street, Frederick, MD 21701
Catholic
HEAD: Joyce Connelly
WEBSITE: www.sjrcs.org
GRADES: Kindergarten–grade 8
EXTENDED DAY: 2:30–6:00 p.m.
TUITION: Call for information.
DRESS CODE: Uniforms

ST. JOHN SCHOOL   703-356-7554   FAX 703-448-3811
6422 Linway Terrace, McLean, VA 22101
Catholic
HEAD: Christine Wells
WEBSITE: www.stjohncatholicmclean.org
GRADES: Pre-K–grade 8   **ENROLLMENT:** Co-ed
EXTENDED DAY: After care until 6:00 p.m.
TUITION: Call for information.
DRESS CODE: Uniforms

ST. JOHN THE BAPTIST CATHOLIC SCHOOL
301-622-3076   FAX 301-622-2453
12319 New Hampshire Avenue, Silver Spring, MD 20904
Catholic
HEAD: Marianne Moore
E-MAIL: sjbssprincipal@yahoo.com
GRADES: Kindergarten–grade 8   **ENROLLMENT:** Co-ed
EXTENDED DAY: After care 3:00–6:00 p.m.
TUITION: $4,400 one child in parish
DRESS CODE: Uniforms

ST. JOHN THE EVANGELIST SCHOOL   410-647-2283   FAX 410-431-5438
669 Ritchie Highway, Severna Park, MD 21146
Catholic
WEBSITE: www.stjohnsp.org
GRADES: K3–grade 8   **ENROLLMENT:** 600 Co-ed
EXTENDED DAY: 7:00–8:00 a.m. and 3:00–6:00 p.m.
TUITION: Call for information.
DRESS CODE: Uniforms

ST. JOHN THE EVANGELIST SCHOOL   301-868-2010   FAX 301-856-8941
8912 Old Branch Avenue, Clinton, MD 20735
Catholic
HEAD: Sister Jean Louise Bachetti, IHM
WEBSITE: www.saintjohnsschool.org
E-MAIL: stjohn.clinton@verizon.net
GRADES: Kindergarten–grade 8   **EXTENDED DAY:** Call for information.
TUITION: $3,465 one child in parish
DRESS CODE: Uniforms

ST. JOHN THE EVANGELIST SCHOOL   301-681-7656   FAX 301-681-0745
10201 Woodland Drive, Silver Spring, MD 20902
Catholic
HEAD: Sister Kathleen Lannak, IHM
WEBSITE: www.sjte.org   **E-MAIL:** srkathleen@sjte.org
GRADES: Pre-K–grade 8   **ENROLLMENT:** Co-ed
EXTENDED DAY: Before and after care
TUITION: $3,450 one child in parish
DRESS CODE: Uniforms

ST. JOHN THE EVANGELIST SCHOOL   540-347-2458   FAX 540-349-8007
111 King Street, Warrenton, VA 20186
Catholic
HEAD: Elizabeth Roach
GRADES: Preschool–grade 8   **ENROLLMENT:** Co-ed
EXTENDED DAY: Before and after care
TUITION: Call for information.
DRESS CODE: Uniforms

ST. JOHN'S COLLEGE HIGH SCHOOL   202-363-2316   FAX 202-686-5162
2607 Military Road, N.W., Washington, DC 20015
Catholic 1851
HEAD: Brother Thomas Gerrow, FSC
DIRECTOR OF ADMISSIONS: Edward A. Miele
WEBSITE: www.stjohns-chs.org
E-MAIL: admissions@stjohns-chs.org
GRADES: 9–12   **ENROLLMENT:** 985 Co-ed
FACULTY: 68 full- and 4 part-time   **AVERAGE CLASS SIZE:** 23
SPECIAL COURSES: College preparatory with AP and honors courses in all areas. Scholars Program for advanced students. Benilde Program for Learning Differences. Optional JROTC Program.
ATHLETICS: Sports in all major areas. Athletic program participates in the Washington Catholic League.
CLUBS: Include Student Government, theater and band
PUBLICATIONS: Yearbook, newspaper
COMMUNITY INVOLVEMENT: Hours of community service required
PLANT: 29-acre campus, library 13,000 volumes, 5 science labs, 2 computer labs, Chapel, auditorium, 2 gyms, football/baseball stadium, soccer/lacrosse field, softball field, 4 tennis courts, rifle range, new athletic complex.
ADMISSION: Archdiocese admissions tests, transcript, recommendations, $35 application fee
TUITION: $9,470; $11,370 Benilde Program
FINANCIAL AID: Available.
BOOKS: $400
TRANSPORTATION: Available. Bus service as well as shuttle from Metro
DRESS CODE: Uniform.
SUMMER PROGRAMS: Advanced and enrichment courses. All Benilde students attend summer school. Numerous sports camps
FUTURE PLANS: Renovate Chapel; install artificial grass on soccer/lacrosse field

ST. JOHN'S EPISCOPAL SCHOOL   301-774-6804   FAX 301-774-2375

3427 Olney-Laytonsville Road, Olney, MD 20832
Episcopal 1961
HEAD: John Zurn
DIRECTOR OF ADMISSIONS: Wes Wehunt
WEBSITE: www.stjes.com   **E-MAIL:** wes.wehunt@stjes.com
GRADES: Kindergarten–grade 8
ENROLLMENT: 320 Co-ed (160 boys/160 girls)
FACULTY: 45 full- and 10 part-time   **AVERAGE CLASS SIZE:** 18 maximum
MISSION STATEMENT: To provide: a structured and challenging academic program; an everyday focus on Christian values and moral character: a community centered approach to learning.
SPECIAL COURSES: Leadership, technology, Spanish, French, art, religion, research, library, Latin, environmental ed, robotics, international travel, drama, band, chorus
EXTENDED DAY: 7:00 a.m.–6:00 p.m.
ATHLETICS: Soccer, basketball, field hockey, lacrosse, cross-country, swimming
PLANT: Library, science lab, technology lab, art studio, playing fields, gymnasium, stage, Chapel
ADMISSION: There are three Open House dates during the school year. Tours are available upon receipt of application. Please contact our Admission Office with any inquiries: (301) 774-6804.
TUITION: $9,692
FINANCIAL AID: Available
BOOKS: $400   **LUNCH:** Bring   **DRESS CODE:** Uniform required
SUMMER PROGRAMS: Day camp, athletic camps, museum tours, art camp, writing and math enrichment programs

ST. JOHN'S LITERARY INSTITUTION AT PROSPECT HALL

301-662-4210   FAX 301-662-5166
889 Butterfly Lane, Frederick, MD 21703
Catholic 1829
HEAD: Richard E. Fairley
WEBSITE: www.stjph.org   **E-MAIL:** sjphadmissions@yahoo.com
GRADES: 9–12   **ENROLLMENT:** 325 Co-ed
FACULTY: 40   **AVERAGE CLASS SIZE:** 17
SPECIAL COURSES: AP level courses. French, Spanish, Latin. Math through calculus. Science: includes physics. Philosophy. Religion required. Art, music, computer science. Honors courses 9–12 with children placed according to testing
ATHLETICS: Soccer, volleyball, basketball, baseball, softball, golf, tennis, cross-country, football, cheerleading, track
CLUBS: Ski, science, National Honor Societies, Student Council, drama, mock trial, SADD
PUBLICATIONS: Yearbook, student-alumni newsletter
COMMUNITY INVOLVEMENT: Nursing home, soup kitchen in Washington monthly. Each grade involved in ongoing projects
PLANT: Main building nominated to National Historic Trust. Library, computer lab, Chapel, gym, playing fields, science labs, 5 portable classrooms. Art/publications cottage

ADMISSION: Placement testing, transcript, recommendations, interview
TUITION: $8,250
FINANCIAL AID: Available.
BOOKS: Extra   LUNCH: Cafeteria optional
TRANSPORTATION: Available to Montgomery County
DRESS CODE: Uniform required
SUMMER PROGRAMS: SJPH basketball camp. Baseball, football, soccer, computer camps.

ST. JOHN'S PARISH DAY SCHOOL   410-465-7644   FAX 410-465-7748
9130 Frederick Road, Ellicott City, MD 21042
Episcopal 1965
HEAD: Anna Puma
WEBSITE: www.stjohnspds.com
E-MAIL: annapuma@aol.com
GRADES: Pre-K–2   ENROLLMENT: 300 Co-ed
FACULTY: 10 full- and 10 part-time   AVERAGE CLASS SIZE: 15
MISSION STATEMENT: (Excerpted) The mission of St. John's Parish Day School is to provide education in a spiritual environment for the children of the parish and the community it serves.
SPECIAL COURSES: Art, music, science lab, P.E., Spanish, technology
EXTENDED DAY: 8:00 a.m.–until start of school and 3:15–6:00 p.m.
PLANT: Renovated preschool building and brand new lower school with auditorium, multi-purpose room, art workshop, science lab
ADMISSION: In person registration for preschool. Call for admissions materials for elementary grades. Complete application and submit
TUITION: Call for information.
FINANCIAL AID: Available
DRESS CODE: Yes
SUMMER PROGRAMS: In future plans
FUTURE PLANS: Expansion through 5th grade to be completed in 2006

ST. JOHN'S SCHOOL   301-373-2142   FAX 301-373-4500
P.O. Box 69, St. John's Road, Hollywood, MD 20636
Catholic
HEAD: Patricia T. Suit
E-MAIL: stjohnshollywood@erols.com
GRADES: Kindergarten–grade 8   ENROLLMENT: Co-ed
TUITION: $3,100 one child in parish
DRESS CODE: Uniforms

ST. JOSEPH SCHOOL   703-437-3014   FAX 703-437-0765
750 Peachtree Street, Herndon, VA 20170
Catholic
HEAD: Joan Cargill
WEBSITE: www.sjcherndon.org
GRADES: Kindergarten–grade 8   ENROLLMENT: Co-ed
TUITION: Call for information.
DRESS CODE: Uniforms

ST. JOSEPH'S SCHOOL   301-937-7154   FAX 301-937-1467
11011 Montgomery Road, Beltsville, MD 20705
Catholic 1962
HEAD: Mr. Wroblewski
WEBSITE: www.stjosephbeltsville.org
E-MAIL: office@stjosephbeltsville.org
GRADES: Pre-K–grade 8   **ENROLLMENT:** 215 Co-ed
FACULTY: 13 full- and 3 part-time
AVERAGE CLASS SIZE: 21
MISSION STATEMENT: The goal of the pastor, principal, faculty, and staff is to develop and extend in cooperation with the families, the foundations of education which are study, work, and play. The school provides each child with the opportunity to grow in all areas of his or her life- spiritual, intellectual, emotional, social and physical- as an individual and as a member of the community.
SPECIAL COURSES: Pre-algebra in 7th grade, algebra in 8th grade. Technology lab and program. Sacramental preparation
EXTENDED DAY: 6:45 a.m. until school starts, then from dismissal until 6:00 p.m.
CLUBS: Student Government, active CYO, altar servers, instrumental music program, after and before care program
COMMUNITY INVOLVEMENT: Adopt-a-Road
PLANT: Newly-renovated stage for theater productions, new Church built within the last 3 years
ADMISSION: For information call 301-937-7154.
TUITION: $3,879
FINANCIAL AID: Archdiocese of Washington may offer assistance.
BOOKS: $130
OTHER FEES: Technology $50, milk $20, Home & School $25, application fee $250
DRESS CODE: Uniform

ST. JUDE CATHOLIC SCHOOL   301-946-7888   FAX 301-929-8927
4820 Walbridge Street, Rockville, MD 20853
Catholic
HEAD: Mary Ellen Jordan
WEBSITE: www.users.erols.com/sjkids
E-MAIL: stjude1@erols.com
GRADES: Pre-K–grade 8   **ENROLLMENT:** Co-ed
EXTENDED DAY: Before and after care
TUITION: $3,900 one child
DRESS CODE: Uniforms

ST. LEO THE GREAT CATHOLIC SCHOOL   703-273-1211   FAX 703-273-6913
3704 Old Lee Highway, Fairfax, VA 22030
Catholic
HEAD: Diane Drews
WEBSITE: www.saintleothegreatschool.org
GRADES: Pre-K–grade 8   **ENROLLMENT:** Co-ed
EXTENDED DAY: Before and after care
TUITION: Call for information.
DRESS CODE: Uniforms

ST. LOUIS CATHOLIC SCHOOL   703-768-7732
2901 Popkins Lane, Alexandria, VA 22306
Catholic
HEAD: Noreen Gilmour
WEBSITE: www.stlouisschool.org
GRADES: Kindergarten–grade 8   **ENROLLMENT:** Co-ed
EXTENDED DAY: Before and after care
TUITION: Call for information.
DRESS CODE: Uniforms

ST. LUKE SCHOOL   703-356-1508   FAX 703-356-1141
7005 Georgetown Pike, McLean, VA 22101
Catholic 1962
HEAD: David J. DiPippa
WEBSITE: www.stlukeschool.com   **E-MAIL:** (1st initial/last name)@stlukeschool.com
GRADES: Kindergarten–grade 8   **ENROLLMENT:** 250 Co-ed (130 boys/120 girls)
FACULTY: 15 full- and 10 part-time   **AVERAGE CLASS SIZE:** 27
MISSION STATEMENT: (Excerpted) Following strong instructional and organizational practices based on the current Diocesan Curriculum Guidelines, the administration, faculty and staff of Saint Luke's School encourage and challenge each student to fulfill his or her potential. The school is divided into self-contained classrooms for grades K–5 and has a middle school format for grades 6–8. Classes are well organized by teachers current in the disciplines who maximize the student's engagement in learning pursuits and who tailor their teaching techniques to the individual learning needs of each student.
SPECIAL COURSES: French. Accelerated reader is offered. Students participate in Johns Hopkins math testing.
EXTENDED DAY: 3:00–6:00 p.m.
ATHLETICS: Sports are through Catholic Youth Organization
CLUBS: Math club, chess club, hand bells, choristers, safety patrol, art club
PUBLICATIONS: Yearbook, bi-annual student newspaper
PLANT: One-level school separate from the Church. Grades K–5 are in self-contained classrooms. Middle school has separate hallway and classrooms for science, math, social studies/Religion and English/reading. Library, music room, art room, computer room, French room, Enrichment Center and school store. The gym is separate and includes the cafeteria and auditorium.
ADMISSION: Sibling applications are due from September–December prior to the year of entering. All other applications for Kindergarten are due on the first Monday in January after we return from the Christmas holidays. Applications for grades 1–8 are accepted through the year.
TUITION: Varies according to number of children, in-parish/out-of-parish and Catholic/non-Catholic status. $3,490–$19,700
FINANCIAL AID: A limited amount of financial aid is available to eligible families who are registered, in-boundary, participating St. Luke parishioners. Please check with school office for details.
BOOKS: $150   **LUNCH:** Lunchroom fee $60 per family
OTHER FEES: Application $100, Re-registration $200, computer $175, milk $30, PTO dues $50 Kindergarten fee $150, closing exercises $125 8th only
FUTURE PLANS: Plant maintenance

ST. MARGARET OF SCOTLAND SCHOOL   301-336-3113   FAX 301-350-1322
410 Addison Road South, Seat Pleasant, MD 20743
Catholic
HEAD: Mrs. Hines
E-MAIL: stmadmin@erols.com
GRADES: Pre-Kindergarten–grade 8   **ENROLLMENT:** Co-ed
EXTENDED DAY: Before and after care
TUITION: $2,850 one child in parish
DRESS CODE: Uniforms

ST. MARGARET'S SCHOOL   804-443-3357   FAX 804-443-6781
P.O. Box 158 444 Water Lane, Tappahanock, VA 22560
Episcopal 1921
HEAD: Margaret R. Broad
DIRECTOR OF ADMISSIONS: Kimberly McDowell
WEBSITE: www.sms.org   **E-MAIL:** admit@sms.org
GRADES: 8–12   **ENROLLMENT:** 158 girls(114 boarding begins 8 gr)
FACULTY: 34 full- and 1 part-time   **AVERAGE CLASS SIZE:** 10–12
MISSION STATEMENT: (Excerpted) "As we grow in age, may we grow in grace." St. Margaret's School's motto reflects our commitment to the growth of young women in every area of their lives; growth in intellectual ability, spiritual maturity, social responsibility, and physical well-being. We offer a diverse curriculum, challenging to each individual.
SPECIAL COURSES: River Program that uses the Rappahannock as a living laboratory for science classes, including marine biology and environmental science. Exchanges with sister schools in Australia and New Zealand. Two-week winter "Minimester" term for experimental learning in non-traditional subjects and educational travel (in 03-04: France/Spain, Florida coast by houseboat, sailing in the Bahamas, repairing homes in rural South Carolina). Senior internships in fields of career interest. Advanced Placement and honors courses, as well as math and writing labs for students who need additional structure/support.
ATHLETICS: SMS competes in the League of Independent Schools in basketball, crew, cross-country, field hockey, lacrosse, soccer, softball, swimming, tennis and volleyball. After school activities include aerobics, fitness center, golf and horseback riding.
CLUBS: A complete weekend activity program offers outdoor activities and cultural events, as well as mixers at other schools and shopping excursions. Musical performance groups, student government. In recent years, girls have started a gospel choir and a poetry club.
COMMUNITY INVOLVEMENT: Annual requirement. Girls may also participate in student service organization.
PLANT: Riverfront campus blending historic and modern facilities, located in beautiful rural area about 2 hours south of D.C. Community/Technology Center (1999) housing dining room, science classrooms, labs and computer room; library; art and music studios; gym, field, new tennis courts and outdoor pool; two air-conditioned dormitories (one renovated 2002) with adjoining faculty apartments; neighborhood campus homes. Fully networked campus with internet and e-mail access from all rooms.
ADMISSION: About half of our boarding students come from the D.C. metro

area. Admission is rolling but applicants are encouraged to apply by February 1. SSAT and personal interview required

TUITION: $29,800 boarding; $11,800 day

FINANCIAL AID: Available. Need-based; provided to approximately 30% of the student body

OTHER FEES: $1,500 deposit for books, supplies and activities. Piano lessons are available for an additional fee.

TRANSPORTATION: Available. Cost for day students $1000

DRESS CODE: Flexible uniform (we call it a "wardrobe")

FUTURE PLANS: Completing final two years of five-year strategic plan. Implementing campus master plan that calls for construction of additional small dormitories.

ST. MARIA GORETTI HIGH SCHOOL   301-739-4266   FAX 301-739-4261
1535 Oak Hill Avenue, Hagerstown, MD 21742-2980
Catholic
WEBSITE: www.goretti.org
GRADES: 9–12   **ENROLLMENT:** Co-ed
TUITION: Call for information.

ST. MARK THE EVANGELIST   301-422-7440   FAX 301-422-7710
7501 Adelphi Road, Hyattsville, MD 20783
Catholic 1957
HEAD: Karen Murphy
DIRECTOR OF ADMISSIONS: Karen Murphy
WEBSITE: www.stmarkhyattsville.org
E-MAIL: principal@stmarkhyattsville.org
GRADES: Preschool–grade 8   **ENROLLMENT:** 500 Co-ed
FACULTY: 45 full-time
EXTENDED DAY: Until 6:00 p.m.
TUITION: Call for information.

ST. MARTIN'S LUTHERAN SCHOOL   410-269-1955   FAX 410-280-2024
1120 Spa Road, Annapolis, MD 21403
Lutheran 1965
HEAD: Margaret Wolfe
DIRECTOR OF ADMISSIONS: Joyce MacCrory
WEBSITE: www.stmartinsls.org
GRADES: Pre-Kindergarten–grade 8   **ENROLLMENT:** 235 Co-ed
FACULTY: 15 full- and 6 part-time   **AVERAGE CLASS SIZE:** 24
MISSION STATEMENT: St. Martin's Lutheran School, in partnership with families, will assist in carrying out the God-given privilege and responsibility of raising children by providing Christian instruction, academic education and extra curricular activities with the goal of equipping children for God pleasing and productive lives.
SPECIAL COURSES: Music, art, computer, P.E., Spanish, religion. Resource teacher for gifted and talented
EXTENDED DAY: 7:00 a.m.–6:00 p.m.
ATHLETICS: Co-ed soccer, field hockey, boys' and girls' basketball, boys' and girls' lacrosse

CLUBS: Chess, sign language, student government, drama, stock market, science, tutoring

PUBLICATIONS: Yearbook **COMMUNITY INVOLVEMENT:** Active PTO

PLANT: Gymnasium, science lab, computer lab, library

ADMISSION: Applications due January 31. Students tested: teacher recommendations; class visit; transcripts required

TUITION: $4,210 Pre-K; $5,858 K–5; $7,220 6–8

FINANCIAL AID: Limited

BOOKS: Provided **LUNCH:** Hot lunch available

ST. MARTIN'S SCHOOL   301-840-1748   FAX 301-840-1733

115 South Frederick Avenue, Gaithersburg, MD 20877

Catholic

HEAD: Donald E. Jackson

WEBSITE: www.erols.com/sanmarti

GRADES: Kindergarten–grade 8 **ENROLLMENT:** Co-ed

EXTENDED DAY: Before and after care

TUITION: $3,200 one child in parish

DRESS CODE: Uniforms

SUMMER PROGRAMS: Academics

ST. MARTIN'S-IN-THE-FIELD DAY SCHOOL   410-647-7055   FAX 410-647-7411

375-A Benfield Road, Severna Park, MD 21146

Episcopal 1957

HEAD: Sharon Holsclaw

WEBSITE: www.stmartinsdayschool.org

GRADES: N3–grade 5 **ENROLLMENT:** Co-ed

AVERAGE CLASS SIZE: Limited to 18–20

SPECIAL COURSES: Integrated humanities curriculum: social studies, literature, fine arts, Sacred Studies. Inquiry-based science

TUITION: Call for information.

FUTURE PLANS: Expanding one grade per year until reaching grade 8

ST. MARY OF THE ASSUMPTION SCHOOL

301-627-4170   FAX 301-627-6383

4610 Largo Road, Upper Marlboro, MD 20772

Catholic

HEAD: Patricia Petruzzelli

WEBSITE: www.stmarysum.com   **E-MAIL:** stmaryum@erols.com

GRADES: Kindergarten–grade 8 **ENROLLMENT:** 300 Co-ed

EXTENDED DAY: Before and after care.

TUITION: $3,500 one child in parish

DRESS CODE: Uniforms

ST. MARY OF THE MILLS SCHOOL   301-498-1433   FAX 301-498-1170

106 St. Mary's Place, Laurel, MD 20707

Catholic

HEAD: Darcy Ann Tomko

WEBSITE: www.stmarys.laurel.md.us   **E-MAIL:** principal@stmarys.laurel.md.us

GRADES: Kindergarten–grade 8   **ENROLLMENT:** Co-ed
EXTENDED DAY: 7:00–8:00 a.m. and 3:00–6:00 p.m.
TUITION: $3,910.58 one child in parish
DRESS CODE: Uniforms
SUMMER PROGRAMS: Summer Experience

ST. MARY STAR OF THE SEA SCHOOL   301-283-6151   FAX 301-283-4368
6485 Indian Head Highway, Indian Head, MD 20640-9727
Catholic
HEAD: Howard Dent
WEBSITE: www.stmarystar.com   **E-MAIL:** dgrimes@stmarystar.com
GRADES: Kindergarten–grade 8   **ENROLLMENT:** Co-ed
EXTENDED DAY: 6:30–8:50 a.m. and 3:00–6:00 p.m.
TUITION: $3,000 one child in parish
DRESS CODE: Uniforms

ST. MARY'S CATHOLIC SCHOOL   301-577-0031   FAX 301-577-5485
7207 Annapolis Road, Landover Hills, MD 20784
Catholic
HEAD: Susan J. Varrone
WEBSITE: www.stmaryslandoverhills.org   **E-MAIL:** marylh@erols.com
GRADES: Preschool–grade 8   **ENROLLMENT:** 300 Co-ed
EXTENDED DAY: 7:20–8:20 a.m. and 3:00– 6:00 p.m.
TUITION: $3,065 one child Catholic; $3,985 one child non-Catholic
DRESS CODE: Uniforms

ST. MARY'S ELEMENTARY SCHOOL   410-263-2869   FAX 410-269-6513
111 Duke of Gloucester Street, Annapolis, MD 21401
Catholic
WEBSITE: www.stmarysannapolis.org
GRADES: Kindergarten–grade 8   **ENROLLMENT:** Co-ed
TUITION: Call for information.

ST. MARY'S HIGH SCHOOL   410-263-3294   FAX 410-269-7843
Duke of Gloucester Street, Annapolis, MD 21401
Catholic 1946
HEAD: Dr. Charles L. Ritter
WEBSITE: www.stmarysannapolis.org   **E-MAIL:** ecotton@stmarysannapolis.org
GRADES: 9–12   **ENROLLMENT:** 574 Co-ed
FACULTY: 45   **AVERAGE CLASS SIZE:** 20
SPECIAL COURSES: Four period day, intensive schedule. Honors courses in all grade levels in English, social studies, math, science, and foreign language. Religious studies. AP: English, calculus, chemistry, biology, U.S. history, European history, American government, French. 92% of the faculty have Masters Degrees or beyond.
ATHLETICS: Football, field hockey, soccer, volleyball, cross-country, basketball, wrestling, ice hockey, swimming, lacrosse, baseball, softball, tennis, golf
CLUBS: National Honor Society, Fellowship of Christian Athletes, Amnesty International, Junior Civitan, drama, environmental and many others

PUBLICATIONS: Yearbook, newspaper, literary magazine

COMMUNITY INVOLVEMENT: Service hours required for graduation. Volunteer projects at all levels

ADMISSION: Application fee, tours and interview available, acceptance based on academic records grades 6-8, standardized testing, recommendations. Students must be on grade level.

TUITION: Call for information.

FINANCIAL AID: Academic and financial need-based

DRESS CODE: Uniform required

ST. MARY'S RYKEN HIGH SCHOOL   301-475-2814   FAX 301-475-7972

22600 Camp Calvert Road, Leonardtown, MD 20650
Catholic 1981
HEAD: Fr. Paul Tipton
DIRECTOR OF ADMISSIONS: Dawn Simpson
WEBSITE: www.smrhs.org
GRADES: 9–12   **ENROLLMENT:** 650 Co-ed (313 boys/337 girls)
FACULTY: 46 full- and 2 part-time   **AVERAGE CLASS SIZE:** 22
MISSION STATEMENT: St. Mary's Ryken is an independent Catholic college preparatory high school, operated under the Xaverian Brothers' sponsorship, committed to academic excellence and to individualized student growth in faith, moral probity, physical health, social demeanor, and responsible citizenship.

SPECIAL COURSES: Honors Courses: Literature and composition, American literature and composition, World Literature, French I–IV; Spanish I–IV; Latin II–IV, World History, U.S. history, American government, algebra I, geometry, algebra II, trigonometry and pre-calculus, calculus, probability and statistics, biology, chemistry, and physics. AP courses: Art history, English literature and composition, U.S. history, world history, government and politics, biology, chemistry, physics, calculus I, calculus II, Spanish, French, computer science, art and music theory. St. Mary's Ryken offers the Ryken Program. This program is designed for those students who have documented difficulty in learning. The focus of this program is to help students develop coping strategies and skills to deal with their individual learning style. While in this program, students continue to take college preparatory classes.

ATHLETICS: Member of the Washington Catholic Athletic Conference (WCAC), one of the oldest, most competitive athletic conferences in the country. Nearly 65 percent of our students compete on at least one of our varsity or junior varsity teams. Baseball, basketball, cheerleading, cross-country, field hockey, golf, ice hockey, lacrosse, soccer, softball, tennis, track and field, volleyball, and wrestling teams provide a wide variety of opportunities for our students to participate in sports all year long.

CLUBS: Ambassadors Club, art club, Campus Ministry Club, drama club, foreign language club, Future Business Leaders of America, Key Club, Mock Trial, National Honor Society, photography club, Science, Ecology and Technology Club, Student Activity Council (SAC), SADD, Shakespearean Drama Club, speech and debate, and Students Helping Other People (SHOP)

PUBLICATIONS: Literary magazine, newspaper, and yearbook

COMMUNITY INVOLVEMENT: 50 hours of community service required for graduation.

PLANT: St. Mary's Ryken provides students the opportunity to learn in a college-like setting. Our 105-acre campus, which overlooks the Breton Bay, includes four academic buildings, plus a full service cafeteria. These buildings feature the Chapel of Charity, a 300-seat auditorium/theater, state of the art computer and science labs, media center, college resource center, art studio, darkroom, and a full size gymnasium.

ADMISSION: To be considered for admission to St. Mary's Ryken, students must submit an application for admission, along with academic records and teacher recommendations. Students must also take an admissions/placement test and attend an interview.

TUITION: $6,400

FINANCIAL AID: Merit-based and need-based tuition assistance. Need-based tuition assistance is also available through the Archdiocese of Washington.

BOOKS: $300

LUNCH: Purchased

OTHER FEES: Activity fee $100, retreat fee $35, sports fee $25 per sport

TRANSPORTATION: Free within St. Mary's County; a fee is charged to students in surrounding counties (approx. $120 per month)

DRESS CODE: Specific uniform wardrobe required

ST. MARY'S SCHOOL   301-762-4179   FAX 301-762-9550
600 Veirs Mill Road, Rockville, MD 20852
Catholic
HEAD: Beverly Consilvio
E-MAIL: maryrcka@erols.com
GRADES: Pre-K–grade 8   **ENROLLMENT:** Co-ed
EXTENDED DAY: After care
TUITION: $3,427 one child in parish

ST. MARY'S SCHOOL   301-932-6883   FAX 301-274-0626
13735 Notre Dame Place, Bryantown, MD 20617
Catholic
HEAD: Jeanette Coleman
WEBSITE: www.bryantown.org
E-MAIL: office@bryantown.org
GRADES: Kindergarten–grade 8   **ENROLLMENT:** Co-ed
EXTENDED DAY: Before and after care
TUITION: $2,742 one child in parish
DRESS CODE: Uniforms

ST. MARY'S SCHOOL   703-549-1646   FAX 703-549-0840
400 Green Street, Alexandria, VA 22314
Catholic
HEAD: Kathy Dolan
WEBSITE: www.stmarys-alexva.org
GRADES: Pre-K–grade 8   **ENROLLMENT:** Co-ed
EXTENDED DAY: After care
TUITION: Call for information.
DRESS CODE: Uniforms

ST. MARY'S SCHOOL OF PISCATAWAY   301-292-2522   FAX 301-292-2534
13407 Piscataway Road, Clinton, MD 20735
Catholic
HEAD: Patrick Hanus
WEBSITE: www.stmaryspiscataway.org
E-MAIL: school@stmaryspiscataway.org
GRADES: Kindergarten–grade 8   **ENROLLMENT:** Co-ed
EXTENDED DAY: Before and after care
TUITION: $3,200 one child in parish
DRESS CODE: Uniforms

ST. MATTHIAS APOSTLE SCHOOL   301-577-9412   FAX 301-577-2060
9473 Annapolis Road, Lanham, MD 20706
Catholic
HEAD: Mary Frey
WEBSITE: www.stmatthias.org   **E-MAIL:** schooloffice@stmatthias.org
GRADES: Pre-K–grade 8   **ENROLLMENT:** Co-ed
EXTENDED DAY: Before and after care
TUITION: Call for information.
DRESS CODE: Uniforms

ST. MICHAEL CATHOLIC SCHOOL   703-256-1222
7401 St. Michael's Lane, Annandale, VA 22003
Catholic
HEAD: Sister Dorothy Mayer, IHM
GRADES: Kindergarten–grade 8   **ENROLLMENT:** Co-ed
TUITION: Call for information.
DRESS CODE: Uniforms

ST. MICHAEL SCHOOL   301-585-6873   FAX 301-587-1142
824 Wayne Avenue, Silver Spring, MD 20910
Catholic
HEAD: Sister Mary Raymond Logue, SSND
WEBSITE: www.st-michaelschool.org   **E-MAIL:** tech824@erols.com
GRADES: Kindergarten–grade 8   **ENROLLMENT:** 239 Co-ed
EXTENDED DAY: 3:00–6:00 p.m.
TUITION: $2,850 one child in parish
DRESS CODE: Uniforms

ST. MICHAEL'S SCHOOL   301-872-5454   FAX 301-872-4047
16560 Three Notch Road, Route 235 South, Ridge, MD 20680
Catholic
HEAD: Regina Housel
WEBSITE: www.saint-michaels-school.org
E-MAIL: administration.stmichaels@verizon.net
GRADES: Kindergarten–grade 8   **ENROLLMENT:** Co-ed
TUITION: Call for information.
DRESS CODE: Uniforms
SUMMER PROGRAMS: Summer Camp

ST. PATRICK CATHOLIC SCHOOL   540-786-2277

9151 Ely's Ford Road, Fredericksburg, VA 22407
Catholic
HEAD: George Elliott
WEBSITE: www.saintpatrickschool.com
GRADES: Preschool–grade 8   **ENROLLMENT:** Co-ed
EXTENDED DAY: Before and after care
TUITION: Call for information
DRESS CODE: Uniforms

ST. PATRICK'S EPISCOPAL DAY SCHOOL   202-342-2805   FAX 202-342-7001

4700 Whitehaven Parkway, N.W., Washington, DC 20007-1586
Episcopal 1956
HEAD: Peter A. Barrett
DIRECTOR OF ADMISSIONS: Jennifer S. Donish
WEBSITE: www.stpatsdc.org
E-MAIL: admission@stpatsdc.org
GRADES: N age 3–grade 8   **ENROLLMENT:** 470 Co-ed
FACULTY: 44 full- and 17 part-time
AVERAGE CLASS SIZE: 1:8 teacher/student ratio
MISSION STATEMENT: (Excerpted) St. Patrick's Episcopal Day School educates children in Nursery through grade 8. The active, growing, changing individuals within this diverse learning community–students, teachers, parents–recognize the infinite value of every participant as a child of God. We strive to create an atmosphere of trust and cooperation in which to nourish each child's growth toward personal integrity and a lifetime of service.
SPECIAL COURSES: Computer, video production, science, art, music, religion, library skills, choir, handbell choir, recorder consort, French, Spanish, cooking, crafts
EXTENDED DAY: Until 6:00 p.m. (contract students only)
ATHLETICS: P.E. required. Varied after-school sports programs, including gymnastics, karate
PUBLICATIONS: Yearbook
COMMUNITY INVOLVEMENT: Grate Patrol, Martha's Table
PLANT: Library 15,000 volumes with CD-ROM computerized card catalog; Technology Center (computer/video production), amphitheater, 2 science labs, 2 art studios, 2 music/rehearsal rooms, gym/auditorium, 2 acre playing field, 4 playgrounds.
ADMISSION: Deadline is January 30th, application fee is $65. Parent interview, student visit, testing K–8, transcript, teacher recommendations
TUITION: $9,760 N half day; $12,940 N (5 mornings/2 afternoons)l $15,270 N (5 mornings/4 afternoons); $17,800 K–3; $18,700 4–8
FINANCIAL AID: Available
BOOKS: Included
LUNCH: Bring.
OTHER FEES: Activity fee $110 N/PK, $250 K–3, $800 4–8
DRESS CODE: Conservative
SUMMER PROGRAMS: Day Camp ages 3–12. Swimming, sports, arts, drama and Early Bird Academic

ST. PAUL'S LUTHERAN SCHOOL   410-766-5790   FAX 410-766-8758
308 Oak Manor Drive, Glen Burnie, MD 21061
Lutheran
HEAD: Ruth Colross
WEBSITE: www.stpaulsgb.org
GRADES: K3–grade 8
EXTENDED DAY: 7:00 a.m.–6:00 p.m.
TUITION: Call for information.

ST. PETER'S INTERPARISH SCHOOL   202-544-1618   FAX 202-547-5101
422 Third Street, S.E., Washington, DC 20003
Catholic 1868
HEAD: Pamela J. Klobulowski
WEBSITE: www.stpetersinterparish.org
E-MAIL: info@stpetersinterparish.org
GRADES: Pre-K4–grade 8   **ENROLLMENT:** 230 Co-ed
AVERAGE CLASS SIZE: 25
MISSION STATEMENT: St. Peter's is a family of learners serving the Capitol Hill parishes and community. We provide students with an education that is founded on love of God and service to others, characterized by Catholic values and academic excellence, and dedicated to addressing each child's unique talents.
SPECIAL COURSES: Art, music, P.E., computer, Spanish, French
EXTENDED DAY: 7:30 a.m.–6:00 p.m.
ADMISSION: Begins in February; runs until class full; wait list
TUITION: $4,546 in parish $5,397 out of parish, non-Catholic
BOOKS: $150   **LUNCH:** Bring own
OTHER FEES: Application fee $75, Pre-K/K fee $500, facilities fee $175, technology fee $100
DRESS CODE: Uniform

ST. PETER'S SCHOOL   301-843-1955   FAX 301-843-6371
3310 St. Peter's Drive, Waldorf, MD 20601
Catholic
HEAD: Judith DeLucco
E-MAIL: stpeters@erols.com
GRADES: Kindergarten–grade 8   **ENROLLMENT:** Co-ed
EXTENDED DAY: Before and after care
TUITION: $2,585 one child in parish

ST. PETER'S SCHOOL   301-774-9112   FAX 301-924-6698
2900 Sandy Spring Road, Olney, MD 20832
Catholic
HEAD: Carol A. Mikoni
E-MAIL: peterol@reols.com
GRADES: Kindergarten–grade 8
ENROLLMENT: Co-ed
EXTENDED DAY: Before and after care
TUITION: $3,870 one child in parish
DRESS CODE: Uniforms

ST. PHILIP THE APOSTLE SCHOOL   301-423-4740   FAX 301-423-4716
5414 Henderson Way, Camp Springs, MD 20746
Catholic
HEAD: Linda Cullinan
WEBSITE: www.erols.com/st.phils   **E-MAIL:** phisch@erols.com
GRADES: Pre-K–grade 8   **ENROLLMENT:** Co-ed
EXTENDED DAY: 6:45–7:45 a.m. and 3:00–6:00 p.m.
TUITION: $3,465 one child in parish
DRESS CODE: Uniforms

ST. PIUS X REGIONAL SCHOOL   301-262-0203   FAX 301-805-8875
14710 Annapolis Road, Bowie, MD 20715
Catholic
HEAD: Robert S. Love
WEBSITE: www.stpiusbowie.org   **E-MAIL:** thungate@stpiusbowie.org
GRADES: Kindergarten–8   **ENROLLMENT:** Co-ed
EXTENDED DAY: Before and after care
TUITION: 3,620 one child in parish
DRESS CODE: Uniforms

ST. RITA ELEMENTARY SCHOOL   703-548-1888   FAX 703-519-9389
3801 Russell Road, Alexandria, VA 22305
Catholic
HEAD: Mary Pat Schlickenmaier
WEBSITE: www.saintrita-school.org
GRADES: Kindergarten–grade 8   **ENROLLMENT:** Co-ed
EXTENDED DAY: Before and after care
TUITION: Call for information.
DRESS CODE: Uniforms

ST. STEPHEN'S & ST. AGNES SCHOOL   703-212-2706
4401 West Braddock Road, Alexandria, VA 22304
GRADES: 6–8   **SPECIAL COURSES:** See following listings.

ST. STEPHEN'S & ST. AGNES SCHOOL   703-212-2705   FAX 703-838-0032
400 Fontaine Street, Alexandria, VA 22302
GRADES: Jr Kindergarten age 5–grade 5
SPECIAL COURSES: See following listing.

ST. STEPHEN'S & ST. AGNES SCHOOL   703-212-2706
1000 St. Stephen's Road, Alexandria, VA 22304
Episcopal 1924/1944 merged 1991
HEAD: Joan G. Ogilvy Holden
DIRECTOR OF ADMISSIONS: Tim Doyle
WEBSITE: www.sssas.org
GRADES: grades 9–12 this campus
ENROLLMENT: 1,153 Co-ed (581 boys/572 girls)
FACULTY: 145 full-and 17 part-time   **AVERAGE CLASS SIZE:** 13–16
MISSION STATEMENT: St. Stephen's and St. Agnes School is a college prepara-

tory Episcopal Church School in the Diocese of Virginia that educates boys and girls from junior kindergarten through twelfth grade. To help our students succeed in a complex and changing world, we seek to inspire a passion for learning, an enthusiasm for athletic and artistic endeavor, a striving for excellence, a celebration of diversity and a commitment to service. Our mission is to pursue goodness as well as knowledge and to honor the unique value of each of our members as a child of God in a caring community.

SPECIAL COURSES: Single gender math and science classes grades 6–8. Math: algebra I–III, geometry, trigonometry, calculus, finite math, computer science (Jr.K–12). Science: general science (Jr.K–7), Principles of Science (grade 8), biology, environmental science, chemistry, physics, field studies, forensics, bioethics. History: 9–12 Ages of Humanity-Interdisciplinary, Multi-cultural History course (3 years required), Medieval History (grade 6), Twentieth Century World History (grade 7). Languages: Latin 6–12, French and Spanish 4–12. Music: chorus, band, orchestra, chamber music, jazz band; drama, playwriting, directing. Religious studies required. Studio art. AP: English, calculus AB, BC, statistics, studio art, sculpture, art history, computer science, Latin, Spanish, French, history, biology, environmental science, chemistry, physics, U.S. government, modern European, American.

EXTENDED DAY: 7:00 a.m.–6:00 p.m.

ATHLETICS: Required to grade 11. Intramural and interscholastic. Basketball, football, baseball, tennis, field hockey, soccer, lacrosse, track and field, wrestling, volleyball, cross-country, swimming, golf, ice hockey

CLUBS: Lower school: Enrichment- private art, gymnastics, science, computer and Scouting. Middle school: Generated by students Upper school: Language, debate, Model O.A.S. and U.N., library, service, Unity and NCBI (Multicultural Organization)

PUBLICATIONS: Yearbook, newspapers, literary magazines

COMMUNITY INVOLVEMENT: Service projects at all grade levels. Required service project, 40 hours for upper school students

PLANT: Schools are divided into 3 campuses: 400 Fontaine Street, Alexandria Junior Kindergarten–grade 5 4401 W. Braddock Road, Alexandria   grades 6–8 1000 St. Stephen's Road, Alexandria   grades 9–12 Libraries, language labs, computer labs, media centers, science labs, art studios, gym, playing fields, tennis courts, large multi-purpose room, performing arts rooms, weight room, dining facilities. New Chapel/Performing Arts building on upper campus

ADMISSION: Grades Jr.K–1: Parent tour and interview, Child Play Day Activity. Testing: age less than 6 years, Wechsler Preschool and Primary Scale of Intelligence (WPPSI-III); age over 6 years, Wechsler Intelligence Scale for Children (WISC-III), transcripts, 1 teacher recommendation (2 for 1st grade), application and $60 fee Grades 2–5: Parent and child tour and interview, Child Group Achievement Testing and WISC-III, transcripts, 2 teacher recommendations, application and $60 fee. Grades 6–12: Tour and interview, campus visit. Testing: ISEE or SSAT, transcripts, essay, 2 teacher recommendations, application and $60 fee. Students generally fall into above average to superior range of ability.

TUITION: $12,780 Jr.K; $17,470 K–5; $18,530 6–8; $19,600 9–12

FINANCIAL AID: Available, based on need

LUNCH: $580–$730   **OTHER FEES:** $325–$920   Extended day $850–$2,800

TRANSPORTATION: $790–$1,300 round trip

DRESS CODE: Appropriate attire expected at all times- specific rules for lower (uniform), middle and upper schools
SUMMER PROGRAMS: Enrichment courses for all grades. Classes daily early June–early August. Also SAT Prep Course. For rising seniors: internships in area business, and Oxford Study Program in England. Summer Camp: Day Camp early June–early August, Co-ed, ages 3–11: Sports, computer, swimming, arts and crafts, music/drama, field trips. All Sports Camps: boys' and girl's lacrosse, soccer, basketball, softball, tennis, football, field hockey, weight training

ST. THERESA SCHOOL   703-729-3577   FAX 703-729-8068
21370 St. Theresa Lane, Ashburn, VA 20147
Catholic
HEAD: Jacqueline MacKenzie   **GRADES:** Kindergarten–grade 8
ENROLLMENT: Co-ed
TUITION: Call for information.
DRESS CODE: Uniforms

ST. THOMAS MORE CATHEDRAL SCHOOL   703-528-1547   FAX 703-528-5048
105 North Thomas Street, Arlington, VA 22203
Catholic
HEAD: Kathy Swinehart
WEBSITE: www.stmschool.org
GRADES: Kindergarten–grade 8   **ENROLLMENT:** Co-ed
EXTENDED DAY: Before and after care
TUITION: Call for information.
DRESS CODE: Uniforms

ST. THOMAS MORE CATHOLIC SCHOOL   202-561-1189   FAX 202-562-2336
4265 Fourth Street, S.E., Washington, DC 20032
Catholic 1957
HEAD: Wilford X. Graham
DIRECTOR OF ADMISSIONS: Carolyn Berry
WEBSITE: www.centercityconsortium.org
E-MAIL: grahamw@centercityconsortium.org
GRADES: Pre-K–grade 8   **ENROLLMENT:** 178 Co-ed (98 boys/80 girls)
FACULTY: 16 full-time   **AVERAGE CLASS SIZE:** 22
MISSION STATEMENT: To create a spirit of love, understanding, and inquiry that nurtures each child in pursuing an agenda of spiritual development, positive self-awareness, and academic excellence.
SPECIAL COURSES: Music, art, P.E.
EXTENDED DAY: 6:30–7:50 a.m. and 3:00– 6:00 p.m.
ATHLETICS: CYO sports, lacrosse, intramural basketball, cheerleading
CLUBS: Student Government, safety patrols, Knights of St. Peter Claver, Altar Servers
COMMUNITY INVOLVEMENT: Community Action- S.O.M.E.
PLANT: Single story building
ADMISSION: Complete an application packet which is obtainable from the school's office. Bring completed application form to school. All new applicants will meet with the principal and students in grades 1–7 will take a placement test.
TUITION: $3,100 one child in parish

FINANCIAL AID: Limited financial aid is available to qualifying families. An application for financial aid is included in the application packet.
OTHER FEES: Service credit $150- all parents/family members are obligated to complete 150 hours of service to the school or pay $150 for each hour not served. Fundraiser $200- each family must participate in our annual fundraising program. Parents who are unable to do fundraising pay $200.
DRESS CODE: School uniform and appropriate hairstyle
FUTURE PLANS: We hope to begin building our multipurpose gym.

ST. TIMOTHY SCHOOL   703-378-6932   FAX 703-378-1273
13809 Poplar Tree Road, Chantilly, VA 20151
Catholic
HEAD: Marilyn Valatka
GRADES: Kindergarten–grade 8   **ENROLLMENT:** Co-ed
EXTENDED DAY: After care for enrolled students
TUITION: Call for information.
DRESS CODE: Uniforms

ST. TIMOTHY'S SCHOOL   410-486-7400   FAX 410-486-1167
8400 Greenspring Avenue, Stevenson, MD 21153
Episcopal, 1882
HEAD: Randy Stevens
DIRECTOR OF ADMISSIONS: Patrick Finn
WEBSITE: www.sttims-school.org   **E-MAIL:** admis@sttims-school.org
GRADES: 9–12 and post-graduate   **ENROLLMENT:** 95 girls (50 boarding)
FACULTY: 31 full- and 6 part-time   **AVERAGE CLASS SIZE:** 9
MISSION STATEMENT: St. Timothy's School enrolls girls with intelligence, energy and character and builds in them the capability, confidence and integrity to compete and contribute effectively and ethically throughout their lives.
SPECIAL COURSES: French I–IV, Latin I–IV, Spanish I-IV. Science: physical science, biology, chemistry, physics. History: world history I and II, American history. Religious studies (required one year), introduction to law. Studio art, photography, piano, dance, drama. AP courses: English, French, Latin, Spanish, biology, chemistry, U.S. history, art history, studio art. Special programs such as English as a foreign language (EFL). Senior Independent Project. Cross-Curricular Connections. Academic Resource Center.
ATHLETICS: Required. Intermural and interscholastic. Field hockey, tennis, volleyball, basketball, soccer, ice hockey, lacrosse, softball, dance, riding
CLUBS: Choir, dramatics, madrigals, handbell choir, a capella, social activities, current events, EAC
PUBLICATIONS: Yearbook, literary magazine
COMMUNITY INVOLVEMENT: Community service (required), tutoring, Special Games Day
PLANT: State of the art athletic complex (opening fall 2003–basketball courts, fitness center, training room, locker rooms). Library 20,000 volumes. Academic resource center, 3 science labs, art studio, 350-seat theater, stables and indoor riding arenas, playing fields, swimming pool, 6 tennis courts, dance studio, music practice rooms with pianos, Chapel, dormitories, infirmary, faculty homes, darkroom.

ADMISSION: $40 fee. Transcript, interview, SSAT/ISEE; English, math and advisor recommendations, applicant essay, parent evaluation. Application deadline February 10
TUITION: $30,725 boarding/5-day boarding; $17,750 day
FINANCIAL AID: Available
BOOKS: $500
DRESS CODE: Uniform required

ST. VINCENT PALLOTTI HIGH SCHOOL   301-725-3228   FAX 301-776-4343

113 St. Mary's Place, Laurel, MD 20707
Catholic 1921
HEAD: Stephen J. Edmonds
DIRECTOR OF ADMISSIONS: Jane Burdette
WEBSITE: www.pallottihs.org   **E-MAIL:** admissions@pallottihs.org
GRADES: 9–12   **ENROLLMENT:** 460 Co-ed
FACULTY: 37 full- and 3 part-time   **AVERAGE CLASS SIZE:** 20
MISSION STATEMENT: (Excerpted) Inspired by the gospel message of Jesus Christ and faithful to our founder St. Vincent Pallotti, the Missionary Sisters of the Catholic Apostolate sponsor the work of Catholic education at St. Vincent Pallotti High School. Mindful of the mandate of our founder to proclaim and revive faith and to deepen the love of God among all people, we will strive to create an atmosphere in our schools in which the Lord's call to know, to love, and to serve Him will inspire students, faculty, and staff to contribute their best to the growth and development of their God-given talents and abilities.
SPECIAL COURSES: College preparatory, including 12 Advanced Placement courses (math, English, history, science, and foreign language). Academic honors courses. Learning Center that focuses on students who have mild learning disabilities. Band, drama, chorus, photography, web design, sculpture and yearbook.
ATHLETICS: 17 varsity and junior varsity sports for males and females including football, volleyball, soccer, basketball, wrestling, softball, baseball, lacrosse and cross-country
CLUBS: Over 20 different extra-curricular activities and clubs including: Mock Trial, foreign language club, ski club, multicultural club, National Honor Society and Student Government Association
PUBLICATIONS: Yearbook, literary magazine, school newspaper
COMMUNITY INVOLVEMENT: Christian Service Class
PLANT: Library, audio-visual center. Brand new athletic complex and gymnasium, 3 computer labs, 3 science labs, resource center, college counseling center, Guidance Center and athletic playing fields
ADMISSION: $50 application fee. Required forms differ depending on whether student is coming from a Washington Archdiocese school or a non-Archdiocesan school. Please contact the Office of Admissions for further details.
TUITION: Tuition is set yearly and includes books.
FINANCIAL AID: Financial aid applications are due in early January. Please call the Business Office for the official date.
BOOKS: Included   **LUNCH:** $4.00- $6.00
DRESS CODE: School uniform   **SUMMER PROGRAMS:** Summer School
FUTURE PLANS: The school just completed an 8 million dollar athletic complex. The school is currently completing a 3 million dollar Chapel addition.

ST. WILLIAM OF YORK CATHOLIC SCHOOL   540-659-5207
3130 Jefferson Davis Highway, Stafford, VA 22554
Catholic
HEAD: Claire Dougherty
GRADES: Preschool–grade 8   **ENROLLMENT:** Co-ed
EXTENDED DAY: Before and after care
TUITION: Call for information.
DRESS CODE: Uniforms

SAN MIGUEL MIDDLE SCHOOL   202-232-1193
1525 Newton Street, N.W., Washington, DC 20010
Catholic 2002
HEAD: Brother Francis Eells
GRADES: 6–8   **ENROLLMENT:** Boys
ATHLETICS: Soccer, basketball
ADMISSION: Apply before May 1
TUITION: Call for information.
LUNCH: National lunch program
SUMMER PROGRAMS: July academic extension

SANDY SPRING FRIENDS SCHOOL   301-774-7455   FAX 301-924-1115
16923 Norwood Road, Sandy Spring, MD 20860
Quaker 1961
HEAD: Dr. Kenneth W. Smith
WEBSITE: www.ssfs.org   **E-MAIL:** admissions@ssfs.org
GRADES: Pre-Kindergarten–grade 12
ENROLLMENT: 510 Co-ed; 40 boarding (9–12 only)
FACULTY: 66 full- and 2 part-time   **AVERAGE CLASS SIZE:** 15
MISSION STATEMENT: Sandy Spring Friends School provides a welcoming and nurturing learning community with Friends testimonies and meeting for worship central to its life and vitality. A challenging academic curriculum, enriched arts program, inclusive athletics, and service opportunities promote intellectual excellence and strength of character. Recognizing the unique worth of each person, the School strives to develop individual talents and foster caring and effective citizens of the world.
SPECIAL COURSES: Spanish (K–12), French (6–12), ESL (9–12). English: African Literature, American Literature, British Literature, Early European Literature and Modern European Literature. History: Cultural Geography, Western Civilization, Italia, British History, Native American History. Math through calculus. Science: biology, chemistry, physics, astronomy, and environmental science. Arts: performing arts, music, modern dance, drama, stagecraft and handbells. Visual arts: painting, ceramics, printshop, video production and photography. AP: French, Spanish, British Literature, U.S. history, calculus, statistics, chemistry, environmental science, physics and music theory. Intersession: one to two week experiential learning programs: community service with Head Start or Habitat for Humanity, outdoor exploration, hiking in Maine, sailing in the British Virgin Islands, international travel to Italy, Finland, Dominican Republic, and France to name a few.
EXTENDED DAY: 7:30–8:00 a.m. and 3:30–6:00 p.m.

ATHLETICS: Required. Intramural and interscholastic: soccer, lacrosse, basketball, cross-country, volleyball, baseball, tennis, athletic conditioning, team games, softball, track and field and golf

CLUBS: Amnesty International, Multicultural Club, Torch (Student Government), ski club, French club, Spanish club, Culinary Club and more

PUBLICATIONS: Literary magazine, yearbook, newspaper

COMMUNITY INVOLVEMENT: Required on and off campus.

PLANT: Library 18,000 volumes; lower school, middle school, upper school, Science Center with observatory and greenhouse. Art studios, photography lab, theater, woodshop, dormitory with classrooms, dining hall, print shop, gym, 4 soccer/lacrosse fields, baseball field, tennis courts. All on a 140-acre property

ADMISSION: Applications due January 15 for first consideration. Interview, transcript, references, testing required at every grade level: Pre-K and K WPPSI-III; grades 1–5 WISC-IV; grades 6–10 SSAT

TUITION: $12,800–$13,775 lower; $14,750–$16,280 middle; $17,850–$18,380 upper; $25,100–$25,630 5 day boarding; $30,150–$30,680 7 day boarding; Deposit: $1,100

FINANCIAL AID: Available

BOOKS: $500 **LUNCH:** Included

OTHER FEES: Intersession Program: ranges from $100 to $2,000 depending on program. Most are $200–$500. ESL Program $1,600

TRANSPORTATION: Available $1,535 round trip/ $835 one way

DRESS CODE: Simple, neat and clean

SUMMER PROGRAMS: Summer Friends Day Camps- many offerings in sports, arts, Junior/Senior Camps, special interest: rocketry, robotics, etc.

FUTURE PLANS: New middle school, performing arts center and athletic facility

SENECA ACADEMY/CIRCLE SCHOOL   301-869-3728   FAX 301-869-3348

15601 Germantown Road, Darnestown, MD 20874

Founded 1983

HEAD: Joy B. Thurmond, M.Ed.

WEBSITE: www.senecaacademy.org

GRADES: Nursery–grade 6   **ENROLLMENT:** 310 Co-ed

FACULTY: 13 full- and 24 part-time   **AVERAGE CLASS SIZE:** 12–16

MISSION STATEMENT: Seneca Academy is a non-profit, independent day school dedicated to educating children in a safe and nurturing environment. Small classes assure that students will acquire a core of knowledge necessary for cultural literacy and success at higher levels of education.

SPECIAL COURSES: Foreign language K–6, art, music, P.E.

EXTENDED DAY: 8:00 a.m.–5:00 p.m.

PLANT: New building with 7.0-acre campus

ADMISSION: Elementary: application fee $50, school visit, teacher evaluation. Nursery: application fee $55

TUITION: $6,600 elementary   Nursery varies according to program 2,3,4,5 sessions per week.

FINANCIAL AID: Available.

OTHER FEES: Activity fee $175   **DRESS CODE:** Uniforms required at kindergarten

SUMMER PROGRAMS: Camp for ages 4–8 years old

FUTURE PLANS: Will add a grade a year until reaching grade 8

SETON JUNIOR AND SENIOR HIGH SCHOOL   703-368-3220
9314 Maple Street, Manassas, VA 22110
Catholic
HEAD: Anne Carroll
WEBSITE: www.seton-school.org
GRADES: 7–12   **ENROLLMENT:** Co-ed
TUITION: Call for information.
DRESS CODE: Uniforms

SEVERN SCHOOL   410-647-7700   FAX 410-544-9451
203 Water Street, Severna Park, MD 21146
Founded 1914
HEAD: William J. Creeden
DIRECTOR OF ADMISSIONS: Molly Moore Green
WEBSITE: www.severnschool.com
GRADES: 6–12   **ENROLLMENT:** 574 Co-ed (296 boys/278 girls)
FACULTY: 70 full- and 10 part-time   **AVERAGE CLASS SIZE:** 14
MISSION STATEMENT: Severn challenges its students to pursue excellence. In their pursuit, students are expected to develop and demonstrate scholarship, leadership, citizenship, sportsmanship, service to others, and respect for tradition and diversity. By balancing academics, activities, and athletics within its curriculum, Severn helps students learn both inside and outside the classroom.
SPECIAL COURSES: Severn School believes in educating the whole person in a student-centered school community. In addition to foreign languages, mathematics, science, English, history, fine arts, and performing arts, Severn offers advanced placement and honors classes, and a mentor program. Severn is among the nation's leaders in the implementation of instructional technology- not only in our numerous computer labs but in every classroom.
ATHLETICS: 30 athletic teams, including varsity, junior varsity and middle school; 4 athletic fields
CLUBS: Over 20 clubs
PLANT: 19-acre campus in the heart of Severna Park just north of Annapolis includes four athletic fields, four academic buildings, and Memorial Gymnasium
ADMISSION: Testing, transcripts, interviews, recommendations
TUITION: $16,000
FINANCIAL AID: Available.
DRESS CODE: Uniform. Boys shirt and tie; girls skirts or pants
SUMMER PROGRAMS: Summer school, day camp, sports camp
FUTURE PLANS: New athletic facility

SHERIDAN SCHOOL   202-362-7900   FAX 202-244-9696
4400 36th Street, N.W., Washington, DC 20008
Founded 1927
HEAD: C. Randall Plummer
DIRECTOR OF ADMISSIONS: Julie Calloway Lewis
WEBSITE: www.sheridanschool.org   **E-MAIL:** admission@sheridanschool.org
GRADES: K–grade 8   **ENROLLMENT:** 215 Co-ed
FACULTY: 30 full- and 4 part-time
AVERAGE CLASS SIZE: 23 with 2 teachers

MISSION STATEMENT: (Excerpted) Sheridan School's mission is t͜ confident, responsible and kind children who are well prepared to me lenges and demands of a complex and changing world. We believe͜ accomplished by faculty, staff and parents working together as a ͜c emphasizing high academic standards in a small, diverse, nurturing, and lea͜͞ centered environment. The School's two campuses, located in Northwest Washington, D.C. and the Shenandoah Valley of the Blue Ridge Mountains, provide a unique opportunity for its students and their families to combine academic and experiential learning.

SPECIAL COURSES: Strong academic program with emphasis on nurturing and challenging students. Central Subject (the study of language arts and history/social studies) topics include: Native Americans, American history, ancient civilizations, world cultures, Political Structures Around the World, and Human and Civil Rights and Responsibilities. Integrated approach to Everyday Math, general science, art, music and computers. French and Spanish K–8. Performing and fine arts program 3–8. Instrumental program K–8. Spring musical 6–8. Unique Mountain Campus in Luray, Virginia provides outdoor and environmental education including rock-climbing, caving and whitewater rafting.

EXTENDED DAY: 7:45–8:15 a.m. and 2:30–6:00 p.m.

ATHLETICS: Intramural basketball. Interscholastic: soccer, basketball, softball, track and field

CLUBS: Chess club   **PUBLICATIONS:** Yearbook

COMMUNITY INVOLVEMENT: All classes participate in at least one community service project per year as well as several school wide projects benefitting local and national organizations.

PLANT: Library 9,000 volumes, 2 science labs, art studio, gymnasium, playground, multi-purpose room, computer lab, foreign language pavilion. 130-acre Mountain Campus in Luray, Virginia

ADMISSION: Application given on school tour, parent interview, student visit, teacher recommendations, school grade reports, tests for K–8. $60 fee. Notification Mid-March

TUITION: $17,631–$19,577 includes lunch and books

FINANCIAL AID: Available

BOOKS: Included   **LUNCH:** Included

OTHER FEES: Parents Association   **DRESS CODE:** No

SUMMER PROGRAMS: Ages 3–16: Creative Arts and Summer Adventure on city campus. Ages 9–18: Shenandoah Summer at Mountain Campus

FUTURE PLANS: Building and grounds renovation

SIDWELL FRIENDS SCHOOL   202-537-8100   FAX 202-537-2401
3825 Wisconsin Avenue, N.W., Washington, DC 20016
Society of Friends 1883
HEAD: Bruce B. Stewart
WEBSITE: www.sidwell.edu
GRADES: Pre-K–grade 12   **ENROLLMENT:** 1,100 Co-ed (550 boys/550 girls)
FACULTY: 106 full-and 24 part-time   **AVERAGE CLASS SIZE:** 14–18
MISSION STATEMENT: "Sidwell Friends School, at heart, is about the life of the mind, integrity of character and authenticity of soul." —Bruce Stewart, Head of School
SPECIAL COURSES: Spanish (PK–12), Latin, French, Chinese (all 7–12), 1 year

dy in art required, 2 years of science. Environmental science, philosophy, physical science, scientific writing, physics, 21st century science. Math through calculus. History: global, ancient, medieval, modern European, English, American, American and Chinese studies program. Drama, technical theater, sculpture, music. School year abroad opportunities. Independent studies, seminars in consortium with other area schools: ancient Greek, German, Japanese, linear algebra, multivariable calculus. AP: Physics, biology, chemistry, math, languages, computer science

EXTENDED DAY: Close of school–6:00 p.m.

ATHLETICS: Interscholastic, recreational and instructional athletics. Boys compete in Mid-Atlantic Conference (MAC); girls in Independent School League (ISL). P.E. required. Baseball, softball, basketball, cross-country, field hockey, golf, indoor soccer, lacrosse, gymnastics, soccer, tennis, squash, track and field, volleyball, crew, swimming, diving, wrestling and weight lifting

CLUBS: More than 40 clubs

COMMUNITY INVOLVEMENT: Extensive community service

PLANT: Two campuses: lower school (Pre-K–4) in Bethesda, Maryland; middle and upper schools (5–12) on Wisconsin Avenue in Northwest Washington, D.C. Library 35,000 volumes, language lab, science labs, computer labs, auditorium, gym, playing fields, 6-lane track, tennis courts, arts center, Quaker Meeting Room.

ADMISSION: Applications accepted September 2–January 5 for next academic year. $50 application fee

TUITION: $19,975–$20,975

FINANCIAL AID: Available

BOOKS: $350–$600 **LUNCH:** Included

OTHER FEES: Minimal

TRANSPORTATION: Available $975–$1,495 lower school only

DRESS CODE: Neatness, simplicity

SUMMER PROGRAMS: Contact Summer Programs Office: 202-537-8133

SLIGO ADVENTIST SCHOOL   301-434-1417   FAX 301-434-4680
8300 Carroll Avenue, Takoma Park, MD 20912
Seventh-day Adventist 1940
HEAD: Ruth I. Satelmajer
DIRECTOR OF ADMISSIONS: Tammie Conway
E-MAIL: Tammie6905c@aol.com
GRADES: Preschool 2 1/2–4 1/2; K–8 **ENROLLMENT:** 350 Co-ed (165 boys/185 girls)
FACULTY: 22 full- and 5 part-time
AVERAGE CLASS SIZE: K–25; 1–2 25; 3–4 25; 6–8 30
SPECIAL COURSES: Remedial reading, art, music and computers
EXTENDED DAY: 7:00–8:30 a.m. and 3:30–6:00 p.m.
ATHLETICS: Boys' and girls' basketball   **CLUBS:** Sligo Strings
PUBLICATIONS: Yearbook
COMMUNITY INVOLVEMENT: Jump-a-Thon, Walk-a-Thon for Ad Com Serv
PLANT: Large, easy-access facility; art room, music, strings and band rooms; primary rooms have own restrooms and separate exits; gym track, playgrounds, computer labs.
ADMISSION: Testing for all new students, letter of recommendation from former school officials

TUITION: Call for information.
BOOKS: $155   LUNCH: $4.00   OTHER FEES: $280 Technology
TRANSPORTATION: Available on a limited basis   DRESS CODE: Yes

SOUTHERN MARYLAND CHRISTIAN ACADEMY
301-870-2550   FAX 301-934-2855
P.O. Box 1668, White Plains, MD 20695
HEAD: Colleen Gaines
GRADES: K3–grade 12   ENROLLMENT: 430 Co-ed
SPECIAL COURSES: Regular academic program, plus honors math and SAT
prep course, Spanish, French, computers, typing, music, band, art and drama
EXTENDED DAY: 6:00 a.m.–6:00 p.m.
TUITION: Call for information. Reduced rate for siblings
OTHER FEES: Registration fee

SPENCERVILLE ADVENTIST ACADEMY   301-421-9101   FAX 301-421-0007
15930 Good Hope Road, Silver Spring, MD 20905
Seventh-day Adventist 1943
HEAD: Jacqueline Messenger
GRADES: Kindergarten–grade 12   ENROLLMENT: 315 Co-ed
FACULTY: 23 full- and 3 part-time   AVERAGE CLASS SIZE: 25
MISSION STATEMENT: To provide Seventh-day Adventist education which is
committed to prepare, nurture, and inspire students for a Christ-centered life now
and forever.
SPECIAL COURSES: Keyboarding, computer application, virtual education:
Microsoft classes, computer building. Auto mechanics, life skills, work study,
English I and II, The American Experience, Honors American Literature, The
British Tradition, The World of Shakespeare, Spanish, drawing, concert band, bell
choir, choir, private music education, P.E., Life Guarding, Health Education,
world history, U.S. history, American Government, economics, political theory,
The Modern World, The Campaign Trail, Study Tours–New England and
England and Scotland, philosophy, psychology, algebra, geometry, pre-calculus,
Introduction to World Religions, Basic SDA Beliefs and the Rise of the Christian
Church, biology, chemistry, anatomy and physiology.
EXTENDED DAY: 3:15–6:00 p.m.
ATHLETICS: Basketball- "The Hornets", volleyball, cheerleading program
CLUBS: Student Council
COMMUNITY INVOLVEMENT: All students take part in a variety of age-
appropriate missionary activities such as nursing home visitation, neighborhood
projects, card ministry, chapel activities, and ministry to the homeless.
PLANT: Three-story brick structure
ADMISSION: Application with $35 fee, character and academic recommenda-
tions for transfer students, plus transcripts and related forms. Current SAA stu-
dents must apply each year before registration.
TUITION: $3,080–$8,420 Different rates apply depending on half or full day and
constituent/non-constituent and non-SDA status
OTHER FEES: Registration fees, music fees, sports fees, milk fee, testing fee, book fee
DRESS CODE: Uniform required
FUTURE PLANS: To build a new school

SPRINGFIELD ACADEMY   703-256-3773
5236 Backlick Road, Springfield, VA 22151
Founded 1958
HEAD: Jack Merritt
WEBSITE: www.springfieldacademy.com
GRADES: Age 6 weeks–grade 4   **ENROLLMENT:** 180 Co-ed
FACULTY: 12 full- and 5 part-time   **AVERAGE CLASS SIZE:** 15 (K–2)
SPECIAL COURSES: Remedial reading and math. Ballet, art, music
EXTENDED DAY: 6:30 a.m.–6:30 p.m.
TUITION: $225 per week infants and toddlers; $180/191 per week N2; $170 per week grade N3 and up. Includes extended day and lunch
DRESS CODE: Moderate

STAR OF BETHLEHEM CHRISTIAN ACADEMY
703-221-4111   FAX 703-221-2823
19068 Bethlehem Church Road, Triangle, VA 22172
Baptist 1985
HEAD: Rev. Frederick S. Jones
DIRECTOR OF ADMISSIONS: Rev. Henry P. During
WEBSITE: www.starbethlehem.org   **E-MAIL:** sbca@mail.com
GRADES: 3 year olds–grade 6   **ENROLLMENT:** 67 Co-ed(38 boys/29 girls)
FACULTY: 15 full- and 5 part-time   **AVERAGE CLASS SIZE:** 10
MISSION STATEMENT: (Excerpted) SBCA's primary objective is to equip students with the best academic education by providing comprehensive instruction in core subjects. We are dedicated to teach divine principles of trust, loyalty, obedience, helpfulness, courtesy, kindness, cleanliness and a host of other lifelong Godly attributes.
EXTENDED DAY: 6:00–8:30 a.m. and 3:30–6:30 p.m.
ADMISSION: Interview with parents. Child must be 3 years old by December 31 of the same school year.
TUITION: $400 per month.
BOOKS: $80–$225   **LUNCH:** $55   **DRESS CODE:** Yes
SUMMER PROGRAMS: Summer Camp

STONE RIDGE SCHOOL OF THE SACRED HEART
301-657-4322   FAX 301-657-4393
9101 Rockville Pike, Bethesda, MD 20814
Catholic 1923
HEAD: Anne Dyer, RSCJ
DIRECTOR OF ADMISSIONS: Michelle McPherson
WEBSITE: www.stoneridge.org   **E-MAIL:** admissions@stoneridge.org
GRADES: Jr. K–grade 12   **ENROLLMENT:** 792 girls (boys welcome in JrK.-K)
FACULTY: 66 full- and 22 part-time   **AVERAGE CLASS SIZE:** 16
MISSION STATEMENT: Stone Ridge exists to offer a religious education which enables young women to develop a personal faith and prepares them to take their places as informed and active members of the Church and society. Consequently, the school aims at providing programs which expose students to the needs of the world, awaken their sense of personal responsibility as Christians, and equip them with the necessary skills for effective action.

SPECIAL COURSES: Stone Ridge offers a challenging college preparatory curriculum with a strong technology focus. Instruction in computer skills begins in the lower school and the school's laptop program begins in the 8th grade and is woven into every aspect of the upper school. AP classes are offered in history, biology, chemistry, English, art, French, Spanish, math, and computer science. Independent study, consortium classes, internships, and Network Exchange programs help broaden the academic offerings. Foreign language begins in middle school and Latin is required.

EXTENDED DAY: 3:00–6:00 p.m.

ATHLETICS: Basketball, cross-country, diving, field hockey, lacrosse, soccer, softball, swimming, tennis, track and volleyball

CLUBS: 20 in number, encompassing a wide variety of interests

PUBLICATIONS: Yearbook, literary magazine, newspaper

COMMUNITY INVOLVEMENT: Social Action Program for upper school students, taking them into the community every Wednesday afternoon

PLANT: 35 acres with Chapel, 3 libraries, 2 language labs, 5 science labs, 3 art studios, auditorium, 3 gyms, 3 playing fields, 4 tennis courts, 3 computer labs, photography labs, playgrounds, competition size swimming pool

ADMISSION: Application deadline January 15. Application fee of $50 and all files must be complete by February 2. Financial aid materials due by December 31. Testing (varies by grade level) and visit day required. Families encouraged to visit the campus and Admissions Office during Open House.

TUITION: $8,880–$16,650

FINANCIAL AID: Stone Ridge works hard to provide assistance to families who demonstrate financial need.

OTHER FEES: Book and uniform expenses: $220–$500

DRESS CODE: Uniform required

SUMMER PROGRAMS: Summer CampUS from mid-June through July, offering a variety of activities

STUART HALL   540-885-0356   FAX 540-886-2275
235 Frederick Street, Staunton, VA 24401
Episcopal 1844
HEAD: Rev. J. Kevin Fox
DIRECTOR OF ADMISSIONS: Stephanie C. Shafer
WEBSITE: www.stuart-hall.org   **E-MAIL:** admissions@stuart-hall.org
GRADES: 5-12 Co-ed day/8–12 girls board
ENROLLMENT: 146(34 boys/112 girls/53 board)
FACULTY: 24 full- and 3 part-time   **AVERAGE CLASS SIZE:** 10
MISSION STATEMENT: (Excerpted) Stuart Hall is one of Virginia's historic independent schools, affiliated since 1843 with the Episcopal Church. It is a college preparatory boarding and day school, serving young women and men in its upper school (grades 9–12) and both girls and boys in middle school (grades 6–8). Stuart Hall seeks to educate the whole child- mind, body, heart, and spirit- in a special context: a supportive, family-like, Christian environment which nurtures self-esteem and honor, leadership and industry, compassion and commitment to service.
SPECIAL COURSES: AP/ Honors. French, Spanish 9–12. Math: includes pre-algebra through AP calculus, computer processing. Science: General science, biology, chemistry, physics, environmental science. History: non-western world cultures,

world history, U.S. government I and II. Philosophy and religion, involves ethics and volunteer work. Art: all media including stained glass and ceramics. Music: appreciation, voice, piano. Drama. LRC- Learning Resource Center and ESL.

ATHLETICS: P.E. required. Intramural: volleyball, tennis, swimming. Interscholastic: Member Blue Ridge Conference: volleyball, soccer, basketball, tennis, softball. Cross-country. Skiing. Dance: ballet, tap, modern

CLUBS: FOCUS, SGA, Ambassadors, ecology

PUBLICATIONS: Yearbook, literary magazine, newspaper

COMMUNITY INVOLVEMENT: Senior community project; tutoring at local elementary school; hospitals, Special Olympics

PLANT: 8 acres, tennis courts, field hockey/soccer fields, new gymnasium, fitness center, science labs, art facilities, library 14,000 volumes, indoor pool, darkroom, science center

TUITION: $25,700

FINANCIAL AID: Available

OTHER FEES: Approximately $1000 for books, supplies, weekly allowance, activities

DRESS CODE: Coordinated dress look with specific colors

THE SUMMIT SCHOOL   410-798-0005   FAX 410-798-0008
664 East Central Avenue, Edgewater, MD 21037
Founded 1989
HEAD: Dr. Jane R. Snider
DIRECTOR OF ADMISSIONS: Kathleen Heefner
WEBSITE: www.thesummitschool.org
E-MAIL: kathy.heefner@thesummitschool.org
GRADES: 1–8   **ENROLLMENT:** 107 Co-ed (73 boys/34 girls)
FACULTY: 34 full-time   **AVERAGE CLASS SIZE:** 9–12
MISSION STATEMENT: The Summit School is a place for children who need to be educated to their full potential in light of their unique learning styles and academic needs. Literacy is our goal.
SPECIAL COURSES: Algebra, computer technology and keyboarding, speech and oral language, science fair, outdoor education
CLUBS: Social activities, Alumni activities, camping, chess club
PUBLICATIONS: Yearbook
COMMUNITY INVOLVEMENT: 8th grade community service project. Summit Outreach program provides testing and tutoring services.
PLANT: Library, new Student Activities Center with gymnasium and art and music rooms, soccer fields, basketball court, reading rooms, computer labs, outdoor amphitheatre, kitchen for student cooking activities
ADMISSION: Application fee $50, tours by appointment, WISC and Achievement Testing with application, speech and language evaluations helpful; summer testing required for newly enrolled students
TUITION: $21,800
FINANCIAL AID: Available
LUNCH: Available   **OTHER FEES:** Activity fee $100
DRESS CODE: Uniform required
SUMMER PROGRAMS: Available
FUTURE PLANS: Student sculpture garden

SUNSET HILLS MONTESSORI   703-481-8484   FAX 703-318-8274
11180 Ridge Heights Road, Reston, VA 20191
Founded 1994
HEAD: Eileen Dowds Minarik
WEBSITE: www.sunsethillsmontessori.com
E-MAIL: office@sunsethillsmontessori.com
GRADES: Ungraded toddler–grade 6   **ENROLLMENT:** 200 Co-ed
FACULTY: 30 full- and 6 part-time
AVERAGE CLASS SIZE: 25 student/teacher ratio 12:1
MISSION STATEMENT: The heart of the school is the warm, caring, qualified staff who are dedicated to the nurturing and education of children and to the philosophy of Dr. Maria Montessori.
SPECIAL COURSES: Music, Spanish, P.E., art appreciation. Montessori curriculum
EXTENDED DAY: 7:00 a.m.–6:30 p.m.
CLUBS: Roots and Shoots, chess club, Simple Machines, yoga, foreign languages, music
PLANT: 12,000-square foot former church building on 2 1/2 acres of land. 12,000 square foot addition to be built for 2004–2005 school year.
ADMISSION: Phone the school for information, schedule tour and observation. Submit application. Rolling admissions
TUITION: $4,500–$8,900
LUNCH: Milk only   **OTHER FEES:** $95–$200 activity fee
SUMMER PROGRAMS: Summer Camp

SYDENSTRICKER SCHOOL   703-451-4141   FAX 703-451-1493
7001 Sydenstricker Road, Springfield, VA 22152-2742
Founded 1965
HEAD: Ronnie Martinez
DIRECTOR OF ADMISSIONS: Ronnie Martinez
E-MAIL: Sydenschool@aol.com
GRADES: Ungraded age 3–grade 1   **ENROLLMENT:** 100 Co-ed
FACULTY: 9 full- and 2 part-time
AVERAGE CLASS SIZE: 15
MISSION STATEMENT: Program is designed to provide stimulating atmosphere, in which a child is relaxed, develops enthusiasm for learning and gains self-confidence, enabling him to make a smooth transition into other school systems.
SPECIAL COURSES: Half day and full day Kindergarten offered. Developmental reading, study skills, computer, science, music, art, Spanish
EXTENDED DAY: 7:00 a.m.–6:00 p.m.
CLUBS: Piano offered
PLANT: Library 2,000 volumes, 5 acres with woodland playground
ADMISSION: Apply starting in February until full- then waiting lists
TUITION: Call for information. Depends on age and hours in school
BOOKS: Fee
LUNCH: Provided by parents
OTHER FEES: Activity fee- call for information.
DRESS CODE: Appropriate
SUMMER PROGRAMS: Call for information.
FUTURE PLANS: Renovation in future

TABERNACLE BAPTIST ACADEMY   703-368-8610   FAX 703-365-0170

8275 Barrett Drive, Manassas, VA 20109
HEAD: Mike Brown
GRADES: Preschool–grade 12   **EXTENDED DAY:** Before and after care
TUITION: Call for information.
DRESS CODE: Uniforms

TAKOMA ACADEMY   301-434-4700   FAX 301-434-4814

8120 Carroll Avenue, Takoma Park, MD 20912
Seventh-day Adventist 1904
HEAD: Dr. L. Kromann
DIRECTOR OF ADMISSIONS: Joan H. Wilson
WEBSITE: www.ta.edu   **E-MAIL:** contact@ta.edu
GRADES: 9–12   **ENROLLMENT:** 392 Co-ed (193 boys/199 girls)
FACULTY: 30 full-time   **AVERAGE CLASS SIZE:** 20
MISSION STATEMENT: Takoma Academy's mission is redemptive: to guide students in developing a meaningful relationship with God, their church, their community, their family, and themselves. It is essential that students discover their true potential. When they realize that Christ died for them personally, they can recognize their individual worth. The school is an agent in this process of discovery.
SPECIAL COURSES: French I–II, Spanish I–II. Math honors courses in algebra, geometry, trigonometry, calculus. Science honors courses in biology I and II, chemistry, physics. Computer applications. AP American government, AP English literature. Full music and art programs. English honor classes. TV production. Economics/philosophy, multicultural history
ATHLETICS: Intramural sports in most areas. Interscholastic: soccer, basketball, cross-country, track
CLUBS: National Honor Society, ski club, biology club, pottery
PUBLICATIONS: Yearbook
COMMUNITY INVOLVEMENT: Community Service Day, mission trips to foreign countries
PLANT: Library 17,000 volumes, science lab, art room, auditorium, gym, tennis courts, auto mechanics department, playing fields, 400-meter track, weight lifting room
ADMISSION: Application fee $25, placement tests in math and English, interview, transcript, recommendations
TUITION: $5,950–$7,500 includes books
FINANCIAL AID: Available
BOOKS: Included   **LUNCH:** $3–$5   **OTHER FEES:** Locker, car permit
TRANSPORTATION: Public bus service from Takoma Park Metro station
DRESS CODE: Uniform required
FUTURE PLANS: Major physical plant improvements

TEMPLE BAPTIST SCHOOL   703-437-7422   FAX 703-437-7430

1545 Dranesville Road, Herndon, VA 20170
Baptist
HEAD: Sam Dalton
GRADES: N3–grade 12   **ENROLLMENT:** 200 Co-ed
TUITION: Call for information.

THORNTON FRIENDS SCHOOL (MIDDLE SCHOOL MD)
301-622-9033   FAX 301-622-4786
11612 New Hampshire Avenue, Silver Spring, MD 20904
Quaker 1973
HEAD: Michael DeHart
WEBSITE: www.thorntonfriends.org   **E-MAIL:** info@thorntonfriends.org
GRADES: 6–8 grades   **ENROLLMENT:** 36 Co-ed
FACULTY: 6 full- and 1 part-time   **AVERAGE CLASS SIZE:** 9
MISSION STATEMENT: (Excerpted) Founded in 1973, Thornton has always been a haven for bright and creative students seeking a more fulfilling school life. Our average class size is nine students, and the student/teacher ratio is about 6:1. Foremost among the Quaker values that inform our school are honesty; compassion; trust; openness; curiosity of mind; generosity of spirit; health of body, mind and spirit; and enthusiasm for the future.
SPECIAL COURSES: Emphasis on hands-on, experiential learning. Students travel off campus an average of 2–3 times per week. Curriculum is designed to prepare students for a college prep program which focuses on building solid skills in math, reading, writing, social studies, Spanish, science and the arts. Portfolio assessment at all grade levels. Chesapeake Bay environmental class
EXTENDED DAY: 3:30–5:00 p.m. enrichment
ATHLETICS: Interscholastic soccer and basketball
CLUBS: Drama
PUBLICATIONS: Yearbook, literary magazines
COMMUNITY INVOLVEMENT: Weekly community service
PLANT: Use of library, gym, pool, bowling, skating and nearby pond and streams
ADMISSION: Call for brochure. Transcript and recommendations. Interview with parents and student. Student visits classes. Rolling admission. We are looking for students who are curious, alert, lively, interesting, persuasive, and kind.
TUITION: $15,095
FINANCIAL AID: Available
OTHER FEES: $450 includes books.
TRANSPORTATION: Available on public bus line
DRESS CODE: Students may not advertise drugs, alcohol, smoking, violence or sex.

THORNTON FRIENDS SCHOOL (UPPER SCHOOL MD)
301-384-0320   FAX 301-236-9481
13925 New Hampshire Avenue, Silver Spring, MD 20904
Quaker 1973
HEAD: Michael DeHart
WEBSITE: www.thorntonfriends.org   **E-MAIL:** info@thorntonfriends.org
GRADES: 9–12 grades   **ENROLLMENT:** 54 Co-ed
FACULTY: 9 full- and 1 part-time   **AVERAGE CLASS SIZE:** 9
MISSION STATEMENT: See mission statement under Middle School Maryland listing.
SPECIAL COURSES: College preparatory. Communication skills emphasized (writing, listening, reading, speaking, thinking); development of strong inner self taught and learned; Socratic teaching method
ATHLETICS: Interscholastic: soccer, basketball, softball
CLUBS: Drama, chess

PUBLICATIONS: Yearbook, literary magazine, newspaper
COMMUNITY INVOLVEMENT: Forty hours per year graduation requirement
PLANT: Library, science labs, auditorium, tennis courts, playing field. Use of nearby gym, pool, bowling and skating
ADMISSION: Call for brochure. Transcript and recommendations. Interview with parents and student. Student visits classes. Rolling admission. We are looking for students who are curious, alert, lively, interesting, persuasive, and kind.
TUITION: $15,895
FINANCIAL AID: Available
BOOKS: $400
OTHER FEES: Included with books
TRANSPORTATION: Available on public bus line
DRESS CODE: Students may not advertise drugs, alcohol, smoking, violence or sex

THORNTON FRIENDS SCHOOL (UPPER SCHOOL VA)
703-461-8880   FAX 703-461-3697
3830 Seminary Road, Alexandria, VA 22304
Quaker 1973
HEAD: Michael DeHart
WEBSITE: www.thorntonfriends.org   **E-MAIL:** info@thorntonfriends.org
GRADES: 9–12 grade   **ENROLLMENT:** 40 Co-ed
FACULTY: 8 full-time   **AVERAGE CLASS SIZE:** 9
MISSION STATEMENT: See mission statement for Middle School Maryland listing.
SPECIAL COURSES: College preparatory. Communication skills emphasized (writing, listening, reading, speaking, thinking); development of strong inner self taught and learned; Socratic teaching method
ATHLETICS: Interscholastic: soccer, basketball, softball
CLUBS: Chess
PUBLICATIONS: Yearbook. literary magazine, newspaper
COMMUNITY INVOLVEMENT: Forty hours per year graduation requirement.
PLANT: Library, science labs, auditorium. Use of playing field, basketball court and nearby bowling
ADMISSION: Call for brochure. Transcript and recommendations. Interview with parents and student. Student visits classes. Rolling admission. We are looking for students who are curious, alert, lively, interesting persuasive and kind.
TUITION: $15,995
FINANCIAL AID: Available
BOOKS: $400   **OTHER FEES:** Included with books
TRANSPORTATION: Available on public bus line
DRESS CODE: Students may not advertise drugs, alcohol, smoking, violence or sex

THE TIDEWATER SCHOOL   410-257-0533
120 Cox Road, Huntingtown, MD 20639
Founded 1986
HEAD: Nancy Libertini
WEBSITE: www.thetidewaterschool.org
E-MAIL: tidewaterschool@chesapeake.net
GRADES: Pre-Kindergarten–grade 5   **ENROLLMENT:** Co-ed
TUITION: Call for information.

TORAH SCHOOL OF GREATER WASHINGTON
301-962-8003   FAX 301-962-9755
12721 Goodhill Road, Silver Spring, MD 20906
Jewish 1994
HEAD: Rabbi Yitzchak Charner
DIRECTOR OF ADMISSIONS: Rabbi Yitzchak Charner
GRADES: Kindergarten–grade 6
ENROLLMENT: 200 Co-ed (110 boys/90 girls)
AVERAGE CLASS SIZE: 16
EXTENDED DAY: Until 5:15 p.m.
TUITION: Call for information.

TOWN AND COUNTRY SCHOOL OF VIENNA
703-759-3000   FAX 703-759-5526
9525 Leesburg Pike, Vienna, VA 22182
Founded 1971
HEAD: Barbara Logan
DIRECTOR OF ADMISSIONS: Jocelyn Hayward
WEBSITE: www.tcvienna.com   **E-MAIL:** info@tcvienna.com
GRADES: Preschool (age 3)–grade 6
ENROLLMENT: 160 Co-ed (80 boys/80 girls)
FACULTY: 17 full- and 7 part-time
AVERAGE CLASS SIZE: 15
MISSION STATEMENT: To create a unique environment built on sound research, qualified instruction, and local communities of learning that foster academic excellence, instill a love of active learning, and provide experiences that enable all students to acquire a foundation of skills for lifelong achievement.
SPECIAL COURSES: Art, library, computer lab, music, Spanish, fitness, band, academic clinics. Enhanced student achievement through effective technology integration, state of the art networking and web connectivity; community based learning
EXTENDED DAY: 7:00 a.m.–6:00 p.m.
ATHLETICS: Gymnastics, soccer, karate, flag football
CLUBS: Woodwind instruments, piano, chorus, vocal, computers, art, academic clinics. Spring and Winter Break Camps
PLANT: Tree-lined, rustic campus on 6 acres: swimming pool, fields, playgrounds, library, computer lab, art studio, basketball court. Large, sunny, child-centered classrooms. Networked campus
ADMISSION: Applications accepted October–February for following year (later if space permits). Parent tour, child visit, testing, transcripts, recommendations
TUITION: $9,900 full day Preschool–6; $6,950 half day PS–PK
BOOKS: $190   **LUNCH:** Included
OTHER FEES: Activity fee $160, computer lab fee $45
TRANSPORTATION: Available $300–$375
DRESS CODE: Yes
SUMMER PROGRAMS: Camp for ages 3–12. Swimming instruction, arts and crafts, field trips, special themes and specialty camps. Extended care. Spring and Winter Break Camps
FUTURE PLANS: Currently assessing expansion options

IFE CHRISTIAN ACADEMY   410-761-6102
th Crain Highway, Suite 102, Glen Burnie, MD 21061
et Giles
lca@worldnet.att.net
GRADES: Kindergarten–grade 12   **ENROLLMENT:** Co-ed
EXTENDED DAY: After care
TUITION: Call for information.
DRESS CODE: Uniforms

TRINITY CHRISTIAN SCHOOL   703-273-8787   FAX 703-352-8522
11204 Braddock Road, Fairfax, VA 22030
Interdenominational 1987
HEAD: Todd J. Williams, Ph.D.
DIRECTOR OF ADMISSIONS: Mary Underwood
WEBSITE: www.tcsfairfax.org   **E-MAIL:** info@tcsfairfax.org
GRADES: 1–grade 12   **ENROLLMENT:** 413 Co-ed (195 boys/218 girls)
FACULTY: 30 full- and 5 part-time   **AVERAGE CLASS SIZE:** 25
MISSION STATEMENT: (Excerpted) Trinity Christian School of Fairfax exists to educate students to the glory of God by pursuing excellence for mind and heart.
SPECIAL COURSES: Spanish and French (grades 8–12), AP courses
ATHLETICS: Soccer, basketball, volleyball, lacrosse and cheerleading
PUBLICATIONS: Yearbook
COMMUNITY INVOLVEMENT: Christian Service Program
PLANT: Trinity will occupy a brand new campus at 11204 Braddock Road in Fairfax beginning September 2003.
ADMISSION: Admission is based upon assessment testing, previous school records, recommendations, a graded writing sample and an interview. Admissions office: 703-352-8520
TUITION: $5,500 1–5; $5,750 6–8; $6,750 9–12
FINANCIAL AID: Available
BOOKS: Included   **LUNCH:** Bring your own. Special lunches by PTO
OTHER FEES: Miscellaneous, athletics and field trips
DRESS CODE: Uniforms required
FUTURE PLANS: Additional buildings planned on Braddock Road campus: gymnasium, additional classroom building and Chapel/library. Add Kindergarten

TRINITY SCHOOL   410-744-1524   FAX 410-744-3617
4985 Ilchester Road, Ellicott City, MD 21043
Independent Catholic 1941
WEBSITE: www.trinitynews.org   **E-MAIL:** mainoffice@trinitynews.org
GRADES: Kindergarten–grade 8   **ENROLLMENT:** 390 Co-ed
EXTENDED DAY: Before and after care
TUITION: Call for information.

TRINITY SCHOOL AT MEADOW VIEW   703-876-1920   FAX 703-641-9220
2849 Meadow View Road, Falls Church, VA 22042
Ecumenical 1998
HEAD: Andrew J. Zwerneman
DIRECTOR OF ADMISSIONS: Andrew J. Zwerneman

WEBSITE: www.trinityschools.org
GRADES: 7–12 **ENROLLMENT:** 110 Co-ed (53 boys/57 girls)
FACULTY: 14 full- and 8 part-time **AVERAGE CLASS SIZE:** 12
MISSION STATEMENT: Trinity School at Meadow View offers a classical Christian education and is characterized by three educational essentials: ordered basic knowledge, basic skills or tools of learning and the habitual vision of greatness.
SPECIAL COURSES: Trinity School at Meadow View is the third in a line of the nationally-acclaimed Trinity Schools, first established in 1981. Core curriculum includes: 6 years of mathematics, including 2 years of calculus; 6 years of science including physics, chemistry and biology; 6 years of literature, writing, and history, including 4 years of Socratic seminars where the students are reading and discussing original works from authors including Homer, Plato, Augustine, Dante, Shakespeare, Cervantes, Rousseau, Locke, the Founding Fathers, Dostoyevsky, and T.S. Eliot; foreign language (4 years Latin, 2 years modern language); 5 years of theology, including 4 of Biblical studies; 4 years of music and art, and 2 years of drama.
ATHLETICS: For boys: soccer, basketball, and lacrosse. For girls: volleyball, basketball, and soccer
CLUBS: Chess club, choir, Trinity Life Committee (generating and directing school social events and charitable outreach efforts), Trinity School Union (sponsoring student participation in political and oratorical events)
PUBLICATIONS: Yearbook, fine arts journal
PLANT: 4 main buildings on 3 acres off Lee Highway, west of Falls Church city
ADMISSION: Contact school office. Application, aptitude test and interview required
TUITION: $10,450
FINANCIAL AID: Applications available upon request
BOOKS: $375
OTHER FEES: Approximately $50–$75 per extracurricular group
DRESS CODE: Uniform
SUMMER PROGRAMS: Trinity Classic Summer for rising 5th and 6th graders
FUTURE PLANS: 5th building to be developed in near future

TRUTH CHRISTIAN ACADEMY   301-733-0712   FAX 301-733-3924
41 Bryan Circle, Hagerstown, MD 21740
Church of God (Universal)
HEAD: Jackie Marquiss
GRADES: Kindergarten–grade 12   **ENROLLMENT:** 100 Co-ed
TUITION: Call for information.
DRESS CODE: Yes

VIENNA ADVENTIST ACADEMY   703-938-6200   FAX 703-938-3934
340 Courthouse Road, S.W., Vienna, VA 22180
Seventh-day Adventist 1920
HEAD: Elaine Pugh
WEBSITE: www.viennaadventistacademy.org   **E-MAIL:** eipugh@msn.com
GRADES: Kindergarten–grade 12   **ENROLLMENT:** 64 Co-ed
SPECIAL COURSES: Spanish, English handbells, choir

TUITION: $5,200–$5,300   Rate varies for members and non-members of the Adventist Church. Reductions for siblings
OTHER FEES: Registration/insurance/activity fee per year $275 K–8 $300 9–12
DRESS CODE: Dress code

VILLAGE MONTESSORI SCHOOL   301-977-5766
20301 Fulks Farm Road, Gaithersburg, MD 20886
HEAD: Laura Kerwin
GRADES: Ungraded age 2–grade 2   **ENROLLMENT:** Co-ed
TUITION: Call for information.

—W

WAKEFIELD SCHOOL   540-253-5393   FAX 540-253-5422
4439 Old Tavern Road, The Plains, VA 20198
Founded 1972
HEAD: Peter A. Quinn
DIRECTOR OF ADMISSIONS: Vicky Ann Lewis
WEBSITE: www.wakefieldschool.org
E-MAIL: vjannlewis@wakefieldschool.org
GRADES: Pre-K–grade 12   **ENROLLMENT:** 435 Co-ed
FACULTY: 59 full- time, 15 staff
AVERAGE CLASS SIZE: 15
SPECIAL COURSES: Part of UNESCO Association Schools Program. Latin, French, Spanish, German. Math through calculus, computer. Science: general science, forensic science, earth systems, environmental science, psychology, biology, chemistry and physics. History: British, U.S., world civilizations, political science, Eastern Studies, geopolitics, civics. Studio art, art history, Introduction to Theatre, photography, music theory and literature, instruments. AP: French, Spanish, Latin, English composition and literature, U.S. government and politics, U.S. history, European history, calculus AB and BC, statistics biology, physics, chemistry, music theory, art. Trips to foreign countries, JCL convention, sightseeing and theater opportunities. Student Strengths Program: Resiliency and Leadership. Kindergarten is full day. Everyday Math and Saxon Phonics.
ATHLETICS: Required to grade 10. Volleyball, soccer, basketball, cross-country, lacrosse, skiing, tennis, golf, fencing, mountain biking
CLUBS: Harvard Model Congress, Model U.N., environmental, Junior Classical League (highly competitive in Certamens), drama, math, poetry, investment, art, foreign language, service, history, Pop Quiz Team, Amnesty International, Young Republicans, World Culture Club, debate, Radio Theatre Society, Ultimate Frisbee, A Capella, Campus Conservation Club, Classic Movies Society, spirit club, Odyssey of the Mind.
PUBLICATIONS: Newspaper, award-winning literary and art magazines, yearbook
COMMUNITY INVOLVEMENT: Scout troops, Adopt a Highway Program, Abused Women's Shelter, Habitat for Humanity, food for needy and eldercare organizations
PLANT: 50-acre campus with 26 classrooms, library 8,000 volumes, 3 science labs, 2 computer labs, new art and music building, gym, 3 playing fields, playground, tennis courts, student activities building, renovated Manor House for administration/admissions/counseling.

ADMISSION: SSAT, Wakefield Placement Test, transcripts, recommen	ᴸ interview
TUITION: $9,100–$12,200
FINANCIAL AID: Available
BOOKS: $100–$800   **LUNCH:** Extra
TRANSPORTATION: Available. Fee depends on location
DRESS CODE: Uniform required
SUMMER PROGRAMS: Basketball camp Co-ed for ages 6–18. Volleyball and soccer camps. Specialty camps. Full range of educational and enrichment programs from Pre-K to Prep School

WASHINGTON CHRISTIAN ACADEMY   301-649-1070   FAX 301-649-9863

1820 Franwall Avenue, Silver Spring, MD 20902
Christian 1960
HEAD: Larry Danner
DIRECTOR OF ADMISSIONS: Karen Frank
WEBSITE: www.wca1.org   **E-MAIL:** webmaster@wca1.org
GRADES: Kindergarten–grade 12   **ENROLLMENT:** 365 Co-ed
FACULTY: 35 full- and 15 part-time   **AVERAGE CLASS SIZE:** 18
MISSION STATEMENT: "The mission of Washington Christian Academy is to educate covenant children from a Reformed, Christian perspective, developing students' God-given abilities so that they may occupy their places worthily in society, church, and state."
SPECIAL COURSES: AP: British literature, American history, chemistry, physics, biology, calculus
EXTENDED DAY: 7:00 a.m.–6:00 p.m.
ATHLETICS: Soccer, basketball, volleyball, softball, baseball, tennis, track and field
CLUBS: Student council, Model U.N., International Club, art, music
PUBLICATIONS: Yearbook, newspaper
COMMUNITY INVOLVEMENT: Various service projects
PLANT: Suburban location surrounded by fields; adjacent to park land. Library, auditorium, science lab, computer lab, outdoor basketball court
ADMISSION: Rolling admission. Download application materials from website or call for packet to be mailed.
TUITION: $7,155–$8,828
FINANCIAL AID: Available
BOOKS: Provided   **LUNCH:** Tuesday, Thursday, Friday
OTHER FEES: Application and registration
DRESS CODE: Yes, but no uniforms

WASHINGTON EPISCOPAL SCHOOL   301-652-7878   FAX 301-652-7255

5600 Little Falls Parkway, Bethesda, MD 20816
Episcopal 1986
HEAD: Stuart Work
DIRECTOR OF ADMISSIONS: Kathleen Herman
WEBSITE: www.w-e-s.org   **E-MAIL:** info@w-e-s.org
GRADES: N(age 3)–grade 8   **ENROLLMENT:** 320 Co-ed (165 boys/155 girls)
FACULTY: 34 full- and 18 part-time   **AVERAGE CLASS SIZE:** 16
MISSION STATEMENT: (Excerpted) Within an educational institution that sup-

orts the principles of the Episcopal Church while maintaining independent academic integrity, we propose to offer the best education possible- predicated on the tenets of traditional theory but continually modified in the light of recent research- to a heterogeneous student body.

SPECIAL COURSES: French, Spanish, Latin, computer, music, art, religion, P.E., movement, science

EXTENDED DAY: 3:30–6:00 p.m.   **ATHLETICS:** Tae kwon do, sports

CLUBS: Computer club, art club, chorus, science club, Christmas Crafts

PUBLICATIONS: Yearbook

PLANT: 6-acre campus, athletic field, gym, theater, art rooms, music rooms. Newly renovated building and playground, new library

ADMISSION: Applications accepted September–February (later if space is available.) Testing generally scheduled November–January. Transcript and Independent School Recommendation form. School visit by applicant required

TUITION: $9,300 N; $18,015 K–8

FINANCIAL AID: Available. School and Student Services

BOOKS: $350 grades 7–8   **DRESS CODE:** Uniform

SUMMER PROGRAMS: Academic program, recreational, sports, overnights

WASHINGTON HEBREW CONGREGATION
RABBI JOSEPH WEINBERG EARLY CHILDHOOD CENTER
AND WASHINGTON HEBREW CONGREGATION PRIMARY SCHOOL

301-279-7505   FAX 301-354-3200

11810 Falls Road, Potomac, MD 20854

Jewish, 1980

HEAD: Phyllis Shankman

E-MAIL: pshankman@whctemple.org

GRADES: Toddlers–grade 2   **ENROLLMENT:** 315 Co-ed

FACULTY: 7 full- and 49 part-time   **AVERAGE CLASS SIZE:** 17

MISSION STATEMENT: We recognize that every child is a unique individual, and that we must strive to assist our children in discovering themselves as well as the world around them. It is incumbent upon us to create a warm, positive environment for their learning.

SPECIAL COURSES: Specialists in the following areas: Hebrew, computer, music, creative movement, science, art

EXTENDED DAY: 11:45 a.m.–2:00 p.m. enrichment; 2:00–3:00 p.m. aftercare

ATHLETICS: After school soccer, ballet, tae kwon do   **CLUBS:** Science, arts and crafts

ADMISSION: Priority to Temple members; screenings for Kindergarten, 1st and 2nd grade

TUITION: $312–$10,040

FINANCIAL AID: Available for Temple members

OTHER FEES: Activity fees   **TRANSPORTATION:** Available- cost varies

SUMMER PROGRAMS: Six week camp program

WASHINGTON HEBREW CONGREGATION
EDLAVITCH-TYSER EARLY CHILDHOOD CENTER   202-895-6334

3935 Macomb Street, N.W., Washington, DC 20016

Jewish

HEAD: Carol Cohen

E-MAIL: ccohen@whctemple.org

GRADES: Toddlers through 4 year olds   ENROLLMENT: 120 Co-ed
FACULTY: 2 full- and 19 part-time   AVERAGE CLASS SIZE: 15
SPECIAL COURSES: The Washington Hebrew Congregation Edla'
Early Childhood Center is affiliated with the Washington Hebrew Co
Primary School.
EXTENDED DAY: 12:00–2:15 p.m.
TUITION: $313–$7,675
FINANCIAL AID: Available for Temple members only
SUMMER PROGRAMS: Six week camp program

WASHINGTON INTERNATIONAL SCHOOL
202-243-1800   FAX 202-243-1807
3100 Macomb Street, N.W., Washington, DC 20008
Founded 1966
HEAD: Richard P. Hall
WEBSITE: www.wis.edu   E-MAIL: admissions@wis.edu
GRADES: Pre-K–grade 12   ENROLLMENT: 825 Co-ed
FACULTY: 84 full- and 23 part-time   AVERAGE CLASS SIZE: 15
SPECIAL COURSES: French/Spanish immersion in Pre-K/K. Bilingual instruc-
tion in English/French, English/Spanish grades 1–8; English/Dutch grades 1–5.
International Baccalaureate Diploma Program in grades 11 and 12.
EXTENDED DAY: 7:30 a.m.–6:00 p.m.
ATHLETICS: Soccer, basketball, volleyball, tennis, track, cross-country, golf, soft-
ball, baseball
CLUBS: Drama, Student Government, debate   PUBLICATIONS: Newspaper
PLANT: 2 campuses, 8 acres, new Primary School campus opened in May 1998.
Middle and upper school arts and athletics center
ADMISSION: Apply by January 15; complete file by February 15. Selective, com-
petitive admissions
TUITION: $14,630–$20,070
FINANCIAL AID: Available
BOOKS: $300 (6–12)   LUNCH: $700 estimated
OTHER FEES: Capital levy $1000   TRANSPORTATION: Between campuses
DRESS CODE: "Clean and reasonably tidy."
SUMMER PROGRAMS: Recreational language camps: ages 3–12. Some aca-
demic options and travel opportunities up to age 14

WASHINGTON ISLAMIC ACADEMY   703-313-6977   FAX 703-313-6273
6666 Commerce Street, Springfield, VA 22150
Founded 2000
HEAD: Dr. Saleh M. Nusairat
WEBSITE: www.washingtonislamicacademy.org
E-MAIL: principal@washingtonislamicacademy.org
GRADES: Kindergarten–grade 6   ENROLLMENT: Co-ed
SPECIAL COURSES: Language arts, math, science and social studies. Quran,
Islamic Studies, Arabic language, Islamic History
TUITION: $300 per month
TRANSPORTATION: Available
FUTURE PLANS: Add one grade annually until reaching grade 12

WASHINGTON NEW CHURCH SCHOOL   301-464-5602   FAX 301-805-8835

1910 Chantilly Lane, Mitchellville, MD 20721
Swedenborgian 1970
HEAD: Rev. James P. Cooper
DIRECTOR OF ADMISSIONS: Rev. James P. Cooper
WEBSITE: www.washnewchurch.org   **E-MAIL:** secretary@washnewchurch.org
GRADES: Kindergarten–grade 10   **ENROLLMENT:** 47 Co-ed (26 boys/21 girls)
FACULTY: 8 full- and 5 part-time   **AVERAGE CLASS SIZE:** 5
MISSION STATEMENT: The Washington New Church School is a small, private school located in a quiet residential area of Mitchellville in Prince George's County. The Washington New Church School was established as the parish school of the Washington Society of the General Church of the New Jerusalem in 1970. Its primary purpose is to educate the children of church members. The school accepts applications from Christian families in the community who are affirmative to the principles on which the school was founded and continues to operate.
PLANT: The complex serves a variety of uses: the Washington Society of the General Church of the New Jerusalem operates the school. The main room is the Nave where worship services are held every Sunday at 11:00 a.m. There are four large modern classrooms and a library in the 1993 addition. There is a multipurpose room that is jointly used by the Church and School for assemblies, plays, church suppers and the like. The remaining rooms in the original part of the complex are used for additional classrooms, Sunday School rooms, and offices. There are large, safe play areas and a sports field.
ADMISSION: Application for September admission must be made by the previous April 30 in order to provide the school with enough time for the necessary meetings, records to be transferred, and testing. It is also important so that the correct supplies and text books can be ordered and received by the start of school. For the same reasons we do not accept midyear transfers except from other schools in the New Church system. The application procedure is simple, and begins by contacting the school office to schedule a meeting with the Principal for an introduction to the school and the facilities.
TUITION: $3,200
OTHER FEES: $300 surcharge for students in grades 7–10
DRESS CODE: Yes

WASHINGTON WALDORF SCHOOL   301-229-6107   FAX 301-229-9379

4800 Sangamore Road, Bethesda, MD 20816
Founded 1969
HEAD: Faculty directed
DIRECTOR OF ADMISSIONS: Edward J. Buckley
WEBSITE: www.washingtonwaldorf.org
E-MAIL: info@washingtonwaldorf.org
GRADES: Pre-K–grade 12   **ENROLLMENT:** 312 Co-ed (150 boys/162 girls)
FACULTY: 33 full- and 15 part-time
AVERAGE CLASS SIZE: 20 Preschool; 26 grade school; 20 high school
MISSION STATEMENT: (Excerpted) The Washington Waldorf School strives to seek, cultivate, and apply spiritual knowledge and insight to meet the needs of each child. We are committed to providing an education of head, heart, and hand,

such that each child's unique individuality is freed to seek its echoing spirit in the wider world. We are dedicated to inspiring these qualities in our students: a clear-thinking mind, a warm, compassionate heart, an appreciation of artistic life and form, a purposeful, creative, productive will, a sense of trust in and joy for the evolving human story, a sense of unity with all life.

SPECIAL COURSES: An international educational movement with over 800 Waldorf schools world-wide. Waldorf schools (Rudolph Steiner Education) offer a developmental and integrative approach balancing the academic, artistic, and practical to educate the whole child. Two foreign languages (German and Spanish) in grades 1–12. History includes ancient, medieval, renaissance, American, modern, social studies and geography. Art and crafts are an integral part of the curriculum (grades 1–12) and include painting, drawing, sculpture, woodwork, handwork and blacksmithing. Music, drama, and eurythmy (expressive movement to speech and music) are offered throughout. Recorder and strings. Middle and high school orchestra and chorus. High school math includes algebra 1 and 2, geometry, and calculus. Four years of high school science: biology, chemistry, physics, and earth science. High school Foreign Exchange Program

EXTENDED DAY: 3:00–6:00 p.m. for grades 1–6

ATHLETICS: Interscholastic sports program: member of Potomac Valley Athletic Conference (baseball, basketball, cross-country, soccer and softball)

CLUBS: High School Student Council, debate team, stage tech crew

PUBLICATIONS: Yearbook, literary magazine

COMMUNITY INVOLVEMENT: Class service projects

PLANT: The school's property encompasses 6 acres. Library (15,000 volumes), computer lab, 2 science labs, 2 art studios, music room, auditorium, woodworking shop, sewing and crafts room, weavery, eurythmy room, tennis courts, and playing fields.

ADMISSION: $40 application fee, admissions application, photo of applicant, transcripts, assessment of math and language skills, and teacher recommendations. Applications are accepted on a rolling basis. Preschool: parent and child interview with pre-school teachers; child has a class visit for 1–2 days. Grade school: parents and child interview with appropriate class teacher; child has class visit for 1 week. High school: parent and student interview with High School Faculty Admissions Committee; student has a class visit for 3 days

TUITION: $3,120–$13,450 preschool; $13,450 grade school; $14,100 high school

FINANCIAL AID: There is tuition assistance available based on demonstrated financial need.

LUNCH: Bring   **OTHER FEES:** Annual registration fee ranges from $160–$400

DRESS CODE: Clean, neat and practical

SUMMER PROGRAMS: Baseball, basketball, soccer, and Children's Garden programs for 4, 5, and 6 year-olds

FUTURE PLANS: Build a permanent home for the school

WASHINGTON-McLAUGHLIN CHRISTIAN SCHOOL   301-270-2760

6501 Poplar Avenue, Takoma Park, MD 20912
Interdenominational 1983
HEAD: Dr. Pauline Washington/ Sujjan John
E-MAIL: wmadcc@aol.com
GRADES: N–grade 6   **ENROLLMENT:** 200 Co-ed

FACULTY: 15 full-time **AVERAGE CLASS SIZE:** N 20; K–6 27
SPECIAL COURSES: Art, music, computer grade 2–6. Religious studies required
EXTENDED DAY: 7:00 a.m.–6 p.m.
TUITION: Call for information.
BOOKS: Extra **DRESS CODE:** Uniform required

WAY OF FAITH CHRISTIAN ACADEMY   703-573-7221   FAX 703-573-7248

8800 Arlington Boulevard, Fairfax, VA 22031
Assembly of God 1975
HEAD: Reverend Ellen K. Blackwell
E-MAIL: wayoffaith@juno.com
GRADES: Kindergarten 5–grade 12 **ENROLLMENT:** 200 Co-ed
AVERAGE CLASS SIZE: 15–20
MISSION STATEMENT: This school's primary purpose continues to be the provision of spiritual training and development of Christian character coupled with academic excellence.
SPECIAL COURSES: Spanish 9–12, computer, word processing and spreadsheet, art, P.E., Bible Study, character development training, accounting. Science: earth science, biology, chemistry and physics. History: U.S., World Cultures, government, geography and economics. Music: appreciation, vocal and instrumental. A Beka curriculum. Art, advanced language studies. Music and bank. Character First Education
EXTENDED DAY: 7:00 a.m.–6:00 p.m.
COMMUNITY INVOLVEMENT: Community outreach
PLANT: 30,000-square foot modern facility plus second building campus
ADMISSION: Application, admission testing where appropriate
TUITION: $3,800 includes registration, books and materials
BOOKS: Included **LUNCH:** Milk **DRESS CODE:** Yes
SUMMER PROGRAMS: Day Camp for Youth

WEST NOTTINGHAM ACADEMY   410-658-5556   FAX 410-658-9264

1079 Firetower Road, Colora, MD 21917
Founded 1744
HEAD: Dr. D. John Watson
DIRECTOR OF ADMISSIONS: Heidi K.L. Sprinkle
WEBSITE: www.wna.org **E-MAIL:** admissions@wna.org
GRADES: 6– PG (6–8 day only) **ENROLLMENT:** 200 Co-ed Boarding begins in 9
FACULTY: 45 full-time **AVERAGE CLASS SIZE:** 8
MISSION STATEMENT: West Nottingham Academy, founded in 1744, is a college preparatory school dedicated to the intellectual, spiritual, and social growth of each student. The Academy equips students to become successful in all aspects of life through individual attention within a diverse community and a safe environment.
SPECIAL COURSES: Advanced Placement and honors courses are offered in most subjects. Parallel curriculum offered through our Chesapeake Learning Center for students with diagnosed learning differences. English as a Second Language Program is also available.
ATHLETICS: Boys: football, soccer, cross-country, basketball, wrestling, baseball, tennis, track and field, lacrosse. Girls: field hockey, cross-country, volleyball,

basketball, cheerleading, softball, track and field, tennis, soccer
CLUBS: Student Government, National Honor Society, PDO, FCA, chorus, Ensemble, OM, computer club, swim club, powerlifting, drama, horseback riding
PUBLICATIONS: Yearbook
PLANT: 120-acre rural campus, 4 dorms, brand new Patricia A. Bathon Science Wing
ADMISSION: Rolling admission, first round of acceptance is March 10, Common Boarding School Application is accepted
TUITION: Varies by program. $14,385 traditional day; $27,960 traditional boarding $20,420 CLC day; $33,995 CLC boarding $33,995 ESL boarding; $8,370 middle school
FINANCIAL AID: Available
LUNCH: Included in tuition
DRESS CODE: Girls: nice pants, skirt or dress with dress shirt. Boys: khakis or slacks, dress shirt, tie

WESTMINSTER SCHOOL   703-256-3620   FAX 703-256-9621
3819 Gallows Road, Annandale, VA 22003
Founded 1962
HEAD: Ellis H. Glover
DIRECTOR OF ADMISSIONS: Nancy G. Schuler
WEBSITE: www.westminsterschool.com
E-MAIL: admissions@westminsterschool.com
GRADES: K–grade 8   **ENROLLMENT:** 305 Co-ed (147 boys/158 girls)
FACULTY: 28 full-time   **AVERAGE CLASS SIZE:** 15–18
MISSION STATEMENT: (Excerpted) Westminster School is dedicated to providing a superior elementary and middle-school education whose fundamental goals for each child are a disciplined and well-informed mind, strength of character, dedication to learning, generosity of spirit, and joy in the possibilities of life. The Westminster program is founded on a traditional curriculum, rigorous academic standards, and an atmosphere that promotes respect, integrity, kindness, and a sense of excellence.
SPECIAL COURSES: Structured, accelerated curriculum in all subjects/grades. Great Books K–8, integrated history and classical studies 3–8, French K–8, Latin 7–8, performing arts K–8, art and music K–8, study skills, after school academic help, subject-related field trips
EXTENDED DAY: 3:00–5:30 p.m.
ATHLETICS: Daily P.E., K–8. Interscholastic competition, grade 5–8. Basketball, soccer, softball, track
CLUBS: Builders Club (Junior Kiwanis Club), chess club, dance K–8
PUBLICATIONS: Literary magazine, yearbook
PLANT: 23 classrooms, library 15,000 volumes, gymnasium, auditorium, computer lab, science lab, art studio, music studio, athletic fields, playground
ADMISSION: Recommended application period: October–January. Placement testing, grades K–7; classroom visit, grades 1–7; transcripts and teacher recommendation; parent/child interview and tour of school. Application fee $100
TUITION: $10,824 K up to $13,360 8
FINANCIAL AID: Available
TRANSPORTATION: Door-to-door bus service available $1032–$1,800
DRESS CODE: Uniform required

SUMMER PROGRAMS: Academic review for new and returning students, grades 1–7; enrichment courses. Basketball Camp, Soccer Camp, Summer Fun Camp

FUTURE PLANS: Establishment of Band Program 2004. Long range: establish and construct Preschool

THE WINCHESTER SCHOOL   301-598-2266
3223 Bel Pre Road, Silver Spring, MD 20906
Founded 1970
HEAD: Mary L. Rhim
GRADES: Pre-K 3 and 4–Kindergarten   **ENROLLMENT:** 75 Co-ed
FACULTY: 6 full- and 3 part-time   **AVERAGE CLASS SIZE:** 8–10
SPECIAL COURSES: Art, music, cooking, baking
EXTENDED DAY: 7:30–9:00 a.m. and 3:00–6:00 p.m.
ADMISSION: Parent visit, interview, $25 application fee. No testing. Open to all children who are not severely handicapped, emotionally disturbed, or retarded
TUITION: $550 per month half day; $750 per month full day. Reduction for less than 5 days.
LUNCH: Bring
SUMMER PROGRAMS: Organized play program with art, music, stories, water play, field trips
FUTURE PLANS: Will expand the school to grades 1–6, adding one grade a year. An additional campus will be opened on Georgia Avenue in Olney, Maryland 4 miles from the Silver Spring Campus. First grade will be added September 2004. Please call Mary Rhim, Director at 301-299-5668 for information.

WONDERS OF WISDOM ACADEMY & DAYCARE   703-670-2500
13420 Minnieville Road, Woodbridge, VA 22192
GRADES: Nursery–grade 1   **ENROLLMENT:** Co-ed
EXTENDED DAY: Before and after care
TUITION: Call for information.

WOODBERRY FOREST SCHOOL   540-672-3900   FAX 540-672-0928
Woodberry Forest, VA 22989
Founded 1889
HEAD: Dr. Dennis Campbell
DIRECTOR OF ADMISSIONS: Joseph Coleman
WEBSITE: www.woodberry.org
GRADES: 9–12   **ENROLLMENT:** Boys, all boarding
TUITION: $28,400
FINANCIAL AID: Available

THE WOODS ACADEMY   301-365-3080   FAX 301-469-6439
6801 Greentree Road, Bethesda, MD 20817
Catholic 1975
HEAD: Mary C. Worch
DIRECTOR OF ADMISSIONS: Barbara Snyder
WEBSITE: www.woodsacademy.org   **E-MAIL:** admissions@woodsacademy.org
GRADES: Montessori ages 3–5; traditional 1–8

ENROLLMENT: 300 Co-ed (147 boys/153 girls)
FACULTY: 24 full- and 6 part-time   **AVERAGE CLASS SIZE:** 15–20
MISSION STATEMENT: A challenging and supportive educational program that encourages all students to reach their full intellectual, spiritual, emotional, social and physical potential.
SPECIAL COURSES: Daily French and Spanish, Chicago math, algebra, inquiry-based science, laboratory science, internet assisted learning, public speaking, fine art, music (guitar 6–8), religion, expanded upper school, small class size
EXTENDED DAY: 7:15–8 a.m. and 3:10–6:00 p.m.
ATHLETICS: Competitive sports: soccer, basketball, softball, cross-country
CLUBS: Chess, video, computer   **PUBLICATIONS:** Yearbook
COMMUNITY INVOLVEMENT: Community service is on-going
PLANT: State of the art student activity center, regulation size gym, stage for theatrical and musical performances, art studio, music studio, ten new classrooms, beautiful Chapel. All located on 6-acre, park-like campus.
ADMISSION: Applications should be received by February 15, (later if space available). School visit by applicant, recommendations, transcript, testing
TUITION: $7,975–$12,165   No additional fees.
FINANCIAL AID: Available
BOOKS: No fee   **LUNCH:** No fee   **DRESS CODE:** Uniform

WORD OF LIFE CHRISTIAN ACADEMY   703-354-4222   FAX 703-750-1306
5225 Backlick Road, Springfield, VA 22151
HEAD: Michael Burroughs
WEBSITE: www.wolca.org
GRADES: Pre-K–grade 12   **ENROLLMENT:** 360 Co-ed
SPECIAL COURSES: All academic courses. Spanish, computer, typing, Introduction to Business, home economics, Family Living, art, religious studies
EXTENDED DAY: 6:30 a.m.–6:00 p.m.
TUITION: Call for information.
SUMMER PROGRAMS: Recreational programs available

WORLD VIEW CHRISTIAN CENTER   301-372-0053
12700 Southeast Crain Highway, Brandywine, MD 20613
Non-denominational 1995
HEAD: Harold Tolbert
DIRECTOR OF ADMISSIONS: Angela Tolbert
GRADES: 6 weeks–grade 6   **ENROLLMENT:** Co-ed
AVERAGE CLASS SIZE: Elementary 1:15
SPECIAL COURSES: Foreign language: Spanish, French, Japanese, Chinese. Bible instruction, language development, homework assistance, auxiliary programs, music program
EXTENDED DAY: Before and after care
ATHLETICS: Gymnastics, tae kwon do
CLUBS: Reading/poetry club, math club, Student Government
PLANT: Computer lab
ADMISSION: Register by third week of March for upcoming school year
TUITION: Call for information.
LUNCH: Hot lunch

TRANSPORTATION: Available   DRESS CODE: Uniforms
SUMMER PROGRAMS: Summer Camp
FUTURE PLANS: Expanding physical plant to include adult school, church sanctuary and gymnasium. Add grades until reaching grade 12.

WYOMING SEMINARY   570-270-2100   FAX 570-270-2199

201 N. Sprague Avenue, Kingston, PA 18704
Methodist 1844
HEAD: H. Jeremy Packard
DIRECTOR OF ADMISSIONS: Randy Granger
WEBSITE: www.wyomingseminary.org
E-MAIL: pmitchell@wyomingseminary.org
GRADES: 9–postgraduate upper school
ENROLLMENT: 467 Co-ed(250 boys/217 girls)167 board
FACULTY: 44 full- and 32 part-time   AVERAGE CLASS SIZE: 15
MISSION STATEMENT: Wyoming Seminary, with a strong liberal arts tradition, prepares its students to succeed in college and to develop into caring, responsible adults of strong moral character, who will lead and serve their communities.
SPECIAL COURSES: Boarding begins grade 9. AP classes offered in all disciplines
ATHLETICS: 19 varsity sports
CLUBS: Superior performing arts program, varied student clubs
PUBLICATIONS: Yearbook and award-winning newspaper.
COMMUNITY INVOLVEMENT: Very active community service group.
PLANT: 15-acre suburban campus, 2 classroom buildings, three dorms, two gyms, 2 performing arts venues, several athletic fields
ADMISSION: Rolling admissions; contact 1-570-270-2160 or admissions@wyomingseminary.org.
TUITION: $31,000 boarding; $15,900 day
FINANCIAL AID: Available
LUNCH: $525   OTHER FEES: Technology: $325 boarding/$175 day students
DRESS CODE: No jeans
SUMMER PROGRAMS: Academic, music and ESL programs

YESHIVA OF GREATER WASHINGTON   301-649-7077   FAX 301-649-7053

1216 Arcola Avenue, Silver Spring, MD 20902
Jewish Orthodox 1963
HEAD: Rabbi Yitzchok Merkin
WEBSITE: www.yeshiva.edu   E-MAIL: registrar@yeshiva.edu
GRADES: 7–12   ENROLLMENT: 240 No Co-ed classes
FACULTY: 57   AVERAGE CLASS SIZE: 14
SPECIAL COURSES: Math through calculus; honors biology, chemistry, physics, English, Hebrew; AP English, biology, chemistry, physics, calculus, European history, American government, U.S. history, computer science, psychology; computer skills, Hebrew, family living; Required religious studies include Talmud, Prophets.
ATHLETICS: P.E. required, basketball teams at boys' and girls' schools. Other teams as interest determines
CLUBS: Drama, choir, dance

PUBLICATIONS: Yearbooks, literary magazine

COMMUNITY INVOLVEMENT: Hebrew Home for the Aged, local hospitals, other local community service activities

PLANT: Girls' campus and business office is located at 12721 Goodhill Road, Silver Spring, Maryland 20906. Effective August 2004 it will be located at 2010 Linden Lane, Silver Spring, 20910. Phone number is 301-962-5111, fax number is 301-962-8372. Boys' campus: newly renovated Judaic library and study hall, over 10,000 volumes, secular library, science lab, playing field. Girls' campus: library with over 5000 volumes, gym, science lab, playing field.

ADMISSION: Students admitted on basis of previous academic records and interviews. Ability to succeed in dual secular/Judaic curriculum

TUITION: Call for information.

FINANCIAL AID: Need-based, call for information.

TRANSPORTATION: Available from Baltimore at additional cost

DRESS CODE: Yes, call for information.

THE YOUNG SCHOOL   410-381-6191   FAX 410-381-9699
7175 Riverwood Drive, Columbia, MD 21046

DIRECTORS: Josh and JoAnn Young

WEBSITE: www.youngschool.com

GRADES: Kindergarten–grade 8   **ENROLLMENT:** 224 Co-ed

MISSION STATEMENT: The vision of The Young School is to foster personal excellence by providing a dynamic learning environment where each child discovers and develops his or her unique gifts and abilities.

SPECIAL COURSES: Traditional areas of study enriched with daily P.E. and Spanish. Art, music, technology, public library visits, project work, opportunities for cross-grade experiences.

EXTENDED DAY: Before and after care

ATHLETICS: Martial arts, gymnastics, sports clinics

CLUBS: Cub Scouts, Girl Scouts, dance, music

PLANT: Beautifully landscaped 9 acre campus featuring working wetlands for environmental studies, state of the art playground, sports fields, networked computer workstations, media center, two-story cafetorium offers a gym, cafeteria and auditorium stage, school store operated by students grades 3–5.

TUITION: Call for information.

SUMMER PROGRAMS: Academic enrichment, fine arts, sports clinics and traditional camp

EDUCATIONAL SPECIALISTS

Index to Educational Specialists

ABCs FOR LIFE SUCCESS, LLC   301-439-7697   FAX 301-408-3831
10801 Lockwood Drive, Suite 165, Silver Spring, MD 20901
E-MAIL: Abc4success@msn.com
DIRECTOR: Michelle R. Davis, M.Ed.
SERVICES:
"Academic and behavioral consultants committed to extraordinary service to families and educators."

Assist parents in understanding and navigating special education process to secure school placement and services for students with special needs. Conduct educational assessments, referrals for evaluation and services in every area. Life, school planning for students ages 3 to 21 with ADHD, learning disabilities, emotional disabilities, gifted potential, other health impairments and low-incidence disabilities. Advocacy, consulting by highly educated and trained professionals with extensive educational experience. Tutoring, social skills groups, and coaching available. Conduct teacher training and workshops.

JILL ADAMAN, Ph.D.   301-770-8682
6225 Executive Boulevard, Rockville, MD 20852
SERVICES:
Licensed Psychologist

Psycho-educational and social-emotional assessments; independent school admissions testings; psychotherapy with children, adolescents, and adults; psycho-educational groups. Specializing in learning disabilities, attention deficit hyperactivity disorder, stress management, and women's issues. Competence-based approach to therapy. VISA and MasterCard accepted.

BIOGRAPHY:
Ph.D. in Clinical Psychology, University of Miami, 1994. M.S.S. in Clinical Social Work, Bryn Mawr College, 1987. Extensive clinical experience with clients of diverse age, ethnicity, and socioeconomic status in a variety of inpatient and out-patient settings. Experience as a teacher and tutor of students with learning disabilities. Member of the American Psychological Association and Fellow of the Maryland Psychological Association.

JEAN H. BALDWIN, M.A.   202-363-0513   FAX 202-364-2667
4921 Tilden Street, N.W., Washington, DC 20016
E-MAIL: Baldwinconsult@aol.com
SERVICES:
Educational Consultant

An Independent School advising and referral service. Services are focused solely on preschool through high school age students. Regarded as a highly personalized process, the purpose is to gain a clear understanding of the uniqueness of each student cognitively, socially, emotionally, academically, and personally and then to determine the schools which would most benefit the student. In order to refer appropriately, a firm commitment is made to assess a broad range of programs through continual visits to day schools in the Washington, D.C. area and boarding schools throughout the United States. Clients include families with very young children preparing to enter school, families transferring to the Washington, D.C. area, older students desiring to explore day or boarding school options, students referred by their current school due to an unsuitable placement, families exploring independent schools for the first time, and students seeking testing for admission or educational purposes.

BIOGRAPHY:

Jean H. Baldwin, M.A. has worked in the Independent School admission field since 1988. An associate with Georgia K. Irvin for 4 years and Director of Lower School Admission at St. Stephen's and St. Agnes School for 7 years, she holds a Master's Degree in Psychological Services with an emphasis on educational testing and assessment. She is a member of the IECA (Independent Educational Consultants Association), WISER (Washington Independent Services for Educational Resources), ERB (Educational Records Bureau), SSATB (Secondary School Admission Test Board), and TASC (The Association of School Counselors.)

BEVERLY CELOTTA, Ph.D.   301-330-8803
LICENSED PSYCHOLOGIST
CHILD AND FAMILY PRACTICE
13517 Haddonfield Lane, Gaithersburg, MD 20878
E-MAIL: celotta@comcast.net
SERVICES:
My mission is to help children, teens and young adults become more competent and confident in all areas of their lives and to support parents and families as they help their children grow. I work with a wide range of psychological concerns affecting youngsters and their families. Services include individual therapy, parent consultations, family and marital therapy, psychological evaluation and case management.

BIOGRAPHY:

I am a licensed psychologist and Fellow of the Maryland Psychological Association with over thirty years of professional experience. My degrees are from Queens College (BA), Brooklyn College (MS and Advanced Certificate) and the University of Colorado (Ph.D.). I was a Graduate Faculty Member at the University of Maryland and a Faculty Associate at Johns Hopkins University. In addition to my private practice, I serve as a consultant to the Treatment and Learning Centers. I have given hundreds of workshops at the national, state and local levels and have written for many professional journals. I have also testified as an expert witness on youth suicide prevention for a U.S. House of Representatives subcommittee.

CENTER FOR APPLIED MOTIVATION, INC.   301-838-5584   FAX 301-838-8525
107 West Edmonston Drive, Rockville, MD 20852
WEBSITE: www.appliedmotivation.com
DIRECTOR: Peter A. Spevak, Ph.D.
SERVICES:
Established in 1984, the Center for Applied Motivation specializes in motivating underachievers. We are a private organization whose success in treating under-achievers is based on a developmental approach which addresses the problems of underachievement psychologically. Significant improvement in both attitude and performance can be achieved as a result of this approach. In addition to our Applied Motivation program for underachievers, we offer psychological assessment, and consultation and workshops to community, school, and parent groups.

As a public service, our newsletter, Issues in Development, Education, Achievement and Success (IDEAS) is available without charge.

Offices are conveniently located in Rockville, MD and Annandale, VA.

CHESAPEAKE PSYCHOLOGICAL SERVICES OF MARYLAND   301-562-8448
8607 Cedar Street, Silver Spring, MD 20910
WEBSITE: www.ChesapeakePsychological.com
E-MAIL: kathleen.nadeau@chesapeakepsychological.com
DIRECTOR: Kathleen Nadeau, Ph.D. Clinical Director
SERVICES:
Testing and assessment of attention and learning problems
School consultations
Parent Guidance
Counseling/Family therapy

CPS is a private clinic that specializes in the diagnosis and treatment of learning and attention problems. Dr. Nadeau is a nationally recognized authority on ADD and ADHD, and the author of numerous books on the topic. She works closely with her staff to provide top quality diagnostic and educational testing as well as follow-up counseling, parent guidance, and family therapy.

Dr. Nadeau has a particular interest and expertise in working with girls who experience problems with attention, learning, organization, memory, study skills, and processing speed issues. These issues for girls are frequently overlooked or misunderstood, even in the private school setting. Dr. Nadeau and her staff offer school and teacher consultations, as requested, following our extensive and detailed evaluations.

Chesapeake also works with high school juniors in preparing for a successful college experience as well as with college students with ADHD and LD issues.

(See ad at back of book.)

EDUCATIONAL ASSESSMENT ASSOCIATES   202-363-9805
5125 MacArthur Blvd, N.W., Suite 16, Washington, DC 20016
WEBSITE: www.EAADC.ORG
SERVICES:
Educational Assessment Associates was founded by the assessment staff of the former George Washington University Reading Center. The team of educational specialists and psychologists offers a full range of diagnostic testing and consulting services for children, adolescents and adults. EAA is an alternative site for the administration of the Secondary School Admissions Test (SSAT). Admission assessments for independent school applications are also available.

Our diagnostic assessments are individually designed to identify and provide a thorough understanding of the client's learning patterns, significant strengths, and areas which need further development. The assessment process is interactive: that is, the client's observations of his or her learning styles, problem-solving approaches and reactions to the assessments are integral parts of the evaluation.

F&A ASSOCIATES   301-925-8386
1300 Mercantile Lane, Suite 100-L, Largo, MD 20774
WEBSITE: www.flyntcollegefunds.com
E-MAIL: a312flynt@cs.com
DIRECTOR: Aubrey Flynt
SERVICES:
Independent Education Counselor

Mr. Flynt and his firm, F&A Associates College Funding and Preparation provides college preparation, funding, selection, counseling and career development to families (locally and out of state) with middle and high school students or adults who want to attend college. We also provide assistance to families by setting up a consultation with the family and the college bound student to determine the goals and objectives of the student and which colleges are of interest. F&A assists the family in preparing a student profile on the student and represents the family at twelve to fourteen major college/career fairs and reports back to the family who (colleges, universities or corporations) is interested in their child. F&A provides this assistance from middle school through the college years by providing information (videos, newspaper articles, internet) about special summer programs, funding (scholarships, grants and financial aid), internships, and co-ops, and will also help in negotiating with the college representative.

BIOGRAPHY:
Mr. Flynt earned a B.A. in political science (minoring in sociology), and a M.A. in public administration from the American University in Washington, D.C. He has over eight years of experience in working with families of college bound students. Some of his students attend or have graduated from University of Virginia, Duke, Hampton, Northern Virginia Community College, Howard, University of Maryland, Hawaii, Florida, Pittsburgh, Florida A&M, Georgia Tech, Duquesne, Morehouse, Fordham, Trinity, Bowie, Penn State and many other colleges and universities.
"Preparing Families of Today for Future Generations"

DENISE C.K. FORT, PH.D.   202-244-8686
5410 Connecticut Avenue, N.W., Suite 105, Washington, DC 20015
SERVICES:
Clinical Psychologist and Adult and Child Analyst

Evaluate and treat children, adolescents and adults. Individual psychotherapy. Parent counseling. School consultation. Couples therapy. Special interest in working with young children including the anxious child, the withdrawn or inhibited child and the gifted child with emotional difficulties.

BIOGRAPHY:
Ph.D. in Clinical Psychology, Catholic University; M.A. and M.S.N., Catholic University; B.S.N. Georgetown University. Postdoctoral Fellowship and Psychology Staff, Sheppard Pratt Hospital, 1983 to 1985. Medical Staff, Chestnut Lodge Hospital, 1985 to 2000. Graduate of the Washington Psychoanalytic Institute in both adult and child psychoanalysis. Faculty, Washington Psychoanalytic Institute. Faculty and Steering Committee of the Modern Perspectives on Psychotherapy Training Program, Washington Psychoanalytic Foundation. Faculty and Steering Committee of the Child and Adolescent Psychotherapy Training Program, Washington School of Psychiatry. Teach Human Development and Child Therapy. Private practice since 1984.

SHERYL GILBERT, M.S.   301-656-1753   FAX 301-656-1753
5402 Surrey Street, Chevy Chase, MD 20815
E-MAIL: sgtutor@aol.com
SERVICES:
Mathematics diagnostic testing and tutoring from elementary school through geometry. Reading comprehension and process writing. Organizational skills, test taking skills and strategies to improve overall memory. French tutoring at all levels. Experienced in general remediation, in working with children with learning disabilities, in coaching for the SSAT, PSAT and SAT, and in providing enrichment for the highly gifted.

BIOGRAPHY:
Primary and secondary education in France (bilingual). B.A., Brandeis University; M.S. in Biology, University of Pennsylvania. M.A. in Special Ed., American University (The Lab School of Washington). Associated with The Math Center since 1986, with Bill Stixrud and Associates since 1996 and with School Support Services since 1998. Member, National Council of Teachers of Mathematics and Independent Schools Mathematical Association of Washington.

ELLEN ARONIS HEARD INC.   301-946-1998   FAX 301-946-5024
9909 Connecticut Avenue, Kensington, MD 20895
WEBSITE: www.alternatives4teens.com
E-MAIL: ejaheard@alternatives4teens.com
DIRECTOR: Ellen Aronis Heard
SERVICES: Educational Consultant

Ellen Aronis Heard specializes in therapeutic residential school placements for youth who have slipped through the cracks in traditional school settings due to emotional or behavioral problems. Having had a struggling student of her own, Ellen lends a uniquely insightful perspective to families.

Drawing from hundreds of programs that she has personally visited both throughout the United States and abroad, Ellen is able to be the eyes and ears for her clients. From guiding parents through the entire placement process to supporting her students by visiting them at their schools once placed, Ellen shows a strong personal commitment to families. Her mantra has become: There is no shame in having a child who doesn't fit the mold; the shame is when nothing is done about it.

Ellen Aronis Heard is a member of the Independent Educational Consultants Association.

(See ad at front of book.)

RUTH C. HEITIN, PH.D.   703-519-7181   FAX 703-519-4737
100 West Howell Avenue, Alexandria, VA 22301
WEBSITE: www.educationalconsultingva.com

Educational Consulting Services of Northern Virginia

Dr. Heitin has more than 25 years experience as a teacher and/or administrator in educational settings ranging from the preschool to the university level. Her hands-on approach includes holding certification as a regular and special education teacher in elementary and middle schools and as an elementary Principal in Virginia. Dr. Heitin is also proficient in sign language. (PSE)

Dr. Heitin is an enthusiastic and powerful advocate for the educational rights of all children. Her practice includes psycho-educational assessment, support for identification of Attention Deficit Disorder, diagnosis of learning disabilities, support for the Gifted/Learning Disabled student, advocacy, and assistance in the special education process.

INDEPENDENT SCHOOL OPTIONS   703-671-8316   FAX 703-997-8438
1015 North Quaker Lane, Alexandria, VA 22302
WEBSITE: www.independentschooloptions.org
E-MAIL: lacahill@independentschooloptions.org
DIRECTOR: Leigh Ann Cahill
SERVICES:
Educational Consultant: and School placement for Pre-K through high school

Choosing a school for your son or daughter can be an overwhelming experience. During this time of exploration, you not only learn about the many different educational options in the area but you also learn a great deal about your child and your family. Leigh Ann will help guide you through this process by developing a comfortable and positive relationship with your child and family while sorting through the different education options available.

BIOGRAPHY:
Leigh Ann Cahill holds an undergraduate degree from The College of William and Mary and a Masters in Education from George Mason University. Her teaching experience for the past ten years has focused on middle and high school children in both public and private schools. The skills Leigh Ann has acquired for smaller children come from her work at The Garden Day Care Center in Washington, D.C., as a Counselor Intern Director and by raising her own child, Alex. "Leigh Ann's skills as a teacher, mentor, and innovator are paralleled by her cooperative and caring personal attributes. She likes children and interacts very well with them. She likes adults and knows how to work professionally with them."

GEORGIA K. IRVIN & ASSOCIATES, INC.   301-951-0131   FAX 301-951-1024
4701 Willard Avenue, Suite 227, Chevy Chase, MD 20815
WEBSITE: www.gkirvin.com
E-MAIL: georgia@gkirvin.com
DIRECTOR: Georgia K. Irvin, IECA, CEP
ASSOCIATES: Pamela Tedeschi, M.S.Ed., IECA, and Tiffany Hearn
SERVICES:
We work exclusively with children 18 years old and younger who are entering independent and public schools in greater Washington, as well as families interested in boarding schools and therapeutic programs throughout the United States and selected schools abroad. We believe that in order to identify schools in which a student will flourish, we must understand the child's strengths, interests and learning style; therefore, in addition to meeting with parents, we spend time getting to know the child. We address the unique characteristics that must be considered when selecting an appropriate school or program. We use our experience and expertise to help maximize the child's potential. Our goal is to find appropriate solutions for children and adolescents who are gifted and talented in a range of areas, those with learning disabilities (LD), attention disorders (ADD and ADHD), behavior disorders (BD), and other special needs. We are known for our personal involvement and commitment to each child and family, ability to identify the strengths and needs of children, and dedication to making every effort to place students in environments where they are successful and happy. We also provide information sessions for schools, parent groups, and business associations.

BIOGRAPHY:
Georgia K. Irvin served as Director of Admission and Financial Aid at the Sidwell Friends School for 15 years. She served on the faculty of the National Association of Independent Schools' workshops for admissions officers and held membership on the board of the School and Student Service for Financial Aid (SSS). She also served on committees of the Secondary School Admission Test Board (SSATB), was a Trustee of the Black Student Fund, and served as board member of a local

independent school. She is the recipient of SSATB's prestigious William B. Brentnall Award for exemplary contributions to the field of Independent School Admission.

In 2002, after more than three decades of experience, she wrote *Georgia Irvin's Guide to Schools: Metropolitan Washington, Independent and Public/Pre-K–12,* in which she shares her knowledge of schools, admission procedures and other areas of interest to parents. She is available to discuss this book with groups of parents.

Pam Tedeschi, M.S.Ed., an associate since 1999, has taught in public and independent schools, including the McLean School of Maryland. She has experience in educational evaluation and diagnosis and founded a resource class for LD and BD students in New York. She was also the director of a Montgomery County pre-school. Other experience includes mentoring science teachers, teaching gifted children, and developing educational materials.

(See ad at back of book.)

AUDREY V. KISSEL, PH.D.   202-365-5259
5101 River Road, Suite 106, Bethesda, MD 20816
SERVICES:
Licensed Clinical Psychologist

Individual private practitioner offering a variety of diagnostic and treatment services including admissions testing for Independent Schools and psychotherapy with children, adolescents, and adults.

BIOGRAPHY:
Dr. Kissel earned a Ph.D. in Clinical Psychology from American University in 2000 and a bachelor's degree from Cornell University in 1992. Postdoctoral training at Children's National Medical Center and State University of New York (SUNY) Medical Center's Department of Child and Adolescent Psychiatry.

MAUREEN E. LYON, Ph.D., ABPP   703-836-3217   FAX 703-548-9863
803 Franklin Street, Alexandria, VA 22314
E-MAIL: mlyon@cnmc.org
SERVICES:
Clinical Psychologist
Board Certified in Health Psychology
American Board of Professional Psychology

Psychological and Psychoeducational Testing and Individual Psychotherapy

Dr. Lyon provides diagnostic testing to assess for ADHD, Learning Disabilities, Gifted and Talented, and differential diagnosis for individuals aged 7–65 at her office in Old Town. In her private practice Dr. Lyon provides Individual

Psychotherapy for ages 12–65, specializing in health psychology (wellness, chronic illness, eating disorders). She also treats adolescents and adults with depression, anxiety and relationship problems. Dr. Lyon provides coaching for adolescents and adults who underachieve or have ADHD with a practical, problem-solving focus.

BIOGRAPHY:
Dr. Lyon earned a Ph.D. in psychology from The American University. She has fifteen years of experience as a clinical psychologist, including being on the research faculty of George Washington University Medical Center and Children's National Medical Center. Dr. Lyon is the author of numerous articles and lectures nationally. Dr. Lyon began her professional life as a junior high school teacher.

CATHLEEN J. MCGRATH, MD, FAAP   301-294-0931
1738 Elton Road, Suite 127, Silver Spring, MD 20903
2568A Riva Road, Suite 103, Annapolis, MD 21401   410-224-7667
E-MAIL: cjmcgrath@starpower.net
SERVICES:
Board Certified in Behavioral and Developmental Pediatrics
Board certified in General Pediatrics

Behavioral/Developmental Pediatric assessment and treatment.
(I also provide General Pediatric care in the Annapolis office.)

Dr. McGrath works closely with pediatricians, psychologists and educational specialists to evaluate and treat children from birth through high school who are experiencing a variety of developmental delays, behavioral problems and learning differences. She uses a variety of approaches, including medication when appropriate, to help children achieve their potential. She also provides guidance for parents on behavior modification techniques, relaxation strategies and stress reduction for children, and helps parents explore complementary approaches to managing these problems as well.

BIOGRAPHY:
Dr. McGrath received a medical degree from the Medical College of Ohio and did her Pediatric residency training and a Behavioral/Developmental Pediatric fellowship at the University of Maryland System in Baltimore. She has been a practicing pediatrician for 10 years, and has specialized in behavioral/developmental assessments for the past 3 years. She is currently on faculty in the Department of Pediatrics at the University of Maryland Medical Systems, is a consulting Developmental Pediatrician at Shady Grove Adventist Hospital and the Hospital for Sick Children in the District of Columbia, and sees patients in offices in Annapolis and Silver Spring.

MINDWORKS TUTORING AND EDUCATIONAL SERVICES
703-242-7951   FAX 703-242-2585
Vienna, VA 22180
WEBSITE: www.mindworkstutoringservices.com
E-MAIL: mindworksedu@earthlink.net
DIRECTOR: Grace McMullin, B.S.Ed., M.S.HR.
SERVICES:
Serving the Northern Virginia Area

Certified Education and Reading Specialist

Mindworks Services offers private tutoring for students ages 4–adult. Learning sessions are given in your home or location of choice to assure an optimal learning environment. About 90% of Mindworks educators have obtained master's or doctoral degrees with multiple years in teaching. We work closely with teachers, specialists and parents to assure the highest success possible for your child. Initial evaluations and consultations are available upon request. For complete subject and specialty area details please visit our website or call to request an information packet.

(See ad at back of book.)

LINDA SMOLING MOORE, Ph.D.   301-654-4320
5601 River Road, Suite C-19, Bethesda, MD 20816
SERVICES:
Clinical Psychologist

Dr. Moore works with children, adolescents and their families. Her services include consultation to schools and parents regarding a child's special education needs and appropriate academic placement, assessment, and Individual and Family Therapy. Special areas of interest include the Gifted LD student and struggling teens.

CHRISTINE OLLO, Ph.D.   301-257-6679
5411 West Cedar Lane, Suite 209-A, Bethesda, MD 20814
E-MAIL: clollo@aol.com
SERVICES:
Comprehensive assessment of attention, learning, memory, or other cognitive processing issues that affect success in children and adolescents. Independent school entrance evaluation, including intelligence and achievement (psychoeducational). Services include recommendations for remediation, consultation to parents and schools, and referral to appropriate providers and support services.

BIOGRAPHY:
Dr. Ollo is a licensed psychologist specializing in neuropsychological assessment. She was a Teaching Hospital Psychologist at University Hospital in Stony Brook, New York, where she obtained her degree, and a Fellow in clinical research at the

National Institute of Mental Health and National Institute of Drug Abuse. She was a Senior Neuropsychologist at the NeuroBehavioral Center of Green Spring/Magellan and NeuroBehavioral Associates in Columbia, Maryland. She brings twenty years of experience to her private practice in Bethesda, Maryland. Affiliations include Maryland Psychological Association, International Neuropsychological Society, and the National Academy of Neuropsychology.

PENNIMAN AND O'BRIEN   202-364-4263   FAX 202-966-4814
3522 Davenport Street, N.W., Washington, DC 20008
WEBSITE: www.mathteachingtoday.com
E-MAIL: paul@mathteachingtoday.com
SERVICES:
Mathematics Tutoring and Diagnosis

Paul Penniman and Erin O'Brien provide mathematics tutoring and diagnosis for ages 10–infinity at their offices on Davenport Street. Erin specializes in algebra and geometry, while Paul also does statistics and calculus.

BIOGRAPHY:
Mr. Penniman earned an B.A. in mathematical sciences and psychology from Johns Hopkins University. He has twenty years of experience as a mathematics instructor, including five years as head of the math department at the Edmund Burke School. Ms. O'Brien has a B.A. in mathematics from St. Mary's College of Maryland. She also has twenty years of experience as a mathematics instructor, including stints at The Madeira School and Maret School.

PETERSEN ACADEMIC GROUP   703-391-1280   FAX 703-391-0727
Linda S. Petersen, Ed. D.
11870 Sunrise Valley Drive, Suite 201, Reston, VA 20191
WEBSITE: www.PetersenAG.com
E-MAIL: PetersenAG@aol.com
DIRECTOR: Linda S. Petersen, Ed.D.
SERVICES:
The Petersen Academic Group was established in 1993 as an educational consulting service for students, parents, and educational institutions, both public and private, nationwide as well as internationally. Our services include: educational placement and diagnostic testing, study skill and learning style assessments, administration of and consultation for the SSAT test, individualized content area tutorials, and assistance with the admissions process for private school and college placement.

BIOGRAPHY:
Dr. Linda S. Petersen has a B.Ed. in Elementary Education, a M.Ed. in Reading, and an Ed.D. in Human Development. She has classroom experience in preschool to graduate school, and management experience with a large educational corporation. Dr. Petersen is a consultant for the NAESP and NASSP.

The Petersen Academic Group consultants and instructors are certified, credentialed teachers, content area specialists, or psychologists.

THE SCHOOL COUNSELING GROUP, INC.   202-333-3530   FAX 202-333-3212
4725 MacArthur Boulevard, N.W., Washington, DC 20007
WEBSITE: www.schoolcounseling.com
E-MAIL: guidance@schoolcounseling.com
DIRECTOR: Peter A. Sturtevant, Jr., M.A., IECA
Associates: Ethna Hopper, M.A., IECA, CEP
                   Jenifer Rideout, IECA
                   Clare Anderson, M.Ed.
                   Andrew Walpole, M.Ed., IECA
                   Sharon McCombe, M.Ed.
                   Janet Brennan

SERVICES:
The School Counseling Group is now under the leadership of Peter A. Sturtevant, Jr. Founded in 1979 by Ethna Hopper, we provide compassionate, professional counsel to families seeking better ways to address the unique educational and emotional needs of their children.

Our goal is to identify and evaluate schools, programs, and other resources continually, and to provide our families with current, thoughtful and effective choices. We see ourselves as educators and consultants, partners with our clients in the challenging and rewarding process that accompanies a successful search.

• Day school consultation–public and private, traditional and special needs, relocation
• Boarding school consultation–regional, national, and international, traditional and special needs
• College guidance–traditional and special needs, transitional, year-off
• Crisis intervention and placement for struggling teens
• Referrals to local professionals for testing, tutoring, counseling and school advocacy

(See ad at back of book.)

SCHOOL FINDERS, LLC   301-230-9010   FAX 301-230-9021
6001 Montrose Road, Suite 1001, Rockville, MD 20852
WEBSITE: www.schoolfinders.net
E-MAIL: schoolfind@aol.com
DIRECTOR: Judith E. Greenberg, Ph.D.

SERVICES:
School Finders is designed to meet the needs of families with children from pre-kindergarten through college age. We specialize in working with students who are bored, frustrated, at risk of failure and students who have learning differ-

ences. Families planning to stay with the public school system may find use of our advocacy for children to be of help. School Finders also helps find the right private school and college selection. We help families with applications, essays and interviews. We have an after school tutor center, summer school program and homeschool learning facility. Services also include: working with homeschoolers, expert testimony, scholarship searches, and references for ed./psych. testing and therapists. Judith Greenberg is the author of 37 books for children and teens and the host of an educational solutions radio program.

SCHOOL SUPPORT SERVICES, LLC   301-656-5200   FAX 202-337-1670
4701 Sangamore Road Suite 135-S, Bethesda, MD 20816
E-MAIL: schoolsupportLLC@aol.com
SERVICES:
Provides an array of educational services and clinical services to individual families and schools. A cadre of learning specialists, clinical and educational psychologists deliver services, with an emphasis on case management, diagnostic assessment and academic coaching. Diagnostic, coaching, and therapeutic services are provided based on a coordinated needs assessment with case management from intake to follow-up. Dr. Edelstein and Ms. Channick write a monthly column "School Support", in the Washington Parent newspaper. The School Support Group also presents workshops on issues that pertain to academic skill development, conflict resolution and diagnostic assessment.

BIOGRAPHY:
Terry Edelstein, Ph.D. is Clinical Director of School Support Services and is a Nationally Certified School Psychologist. She has a doctorate in Educational Psychology from the University of Pittsburgh and a B.S. in Special Education from the University of Michigan. Dr. Edelstein is specialized in psycho-educational assessment, school consultation and family intervention and has been in private practice for 25 years. She is a member of the National Association of School Psychologists, a Psychology Associate with McLaughlin Associates, and past president and current board member of WISER.

Kathy Channick, M.S., is Educational Director of School Support Services and certified in Elementary and Special Education for Learning Disabilities. She is a Reading Specialist and earned a master's degree from Johns Hopkins University and a B.A. from the University of Maryland. Ms. Channick is an experienced tutor, academic coach and college placement specialist. She has been a provider of services at the Barrie School for over 20 years. Ms. Channick has membership in the Council for Exceptional Children and WISER.

RUTH SPODAK & ASSOCIATES   301-770-7507   FAX 301-770-3576
6155 Executive Boulevard, Rockville, MD 20852
DIRECTOR: Ruth B. Spodak, Ph.D.
SERVICES:
A multidisciplinary team of professionals offering comprehensive psychological and educational evaluations to diagnose learning disabilities, Attention Deficit

Disorder, and related emotional issues. Clients receive a full written report and consultation providing academic modifications, therapeutic intervention and/or recommendations for school placement. We also include referral to highly trained specialists and academic therapists for additional support as needed.

Counseling is available for individuals and families to help in understanding and addressing learning disabilities within the school and family. Particular specialization with Gifted/Learning Disabled individuals. Serving preschool children through adults.

WILLIAM STIXRUD, Ph.D., AND ASSOCIATES   301-565-0534
8720 Georgia Avenue, Suite 300, Silver Spring, MD 20910
WEBSITE: www.Stixrud.com
SERVICES:
Neuropsychology Practice

Our group is comprised of neuropsychologists and clinical psychologists who specialize in the assessment of students with learning difficulties, problems with attention and organization, and/or challenges in the social/emotional area. Using a brain-based model for our comprehensive evaluations allows us to provide a clear profile of a student's cognitive, academic, and emotional strengths and weaknesses. This profile is then used to guide recommendations related to appropriate classroom instruction, as well as any interventions that may be needed to support the student's academic performance (including tutoring, speech/language or occupational therapy, psychotherapy or social skills training). For older students, the results from testing are also used to help guide decisions related to college selection, choosing an appropriate college major, and determining career direction. For information please contact Starr Stixrud at extension 225.

Tutoring Service

Our tutoring service provides specialized support for students with educational difficulties related to learning disabilities, attention deficit disorder, and/or organizational weaknesses. Our tutors make every effort to focus on their students' strengths while remediating their areas of academic weakness. All tutors are college educated and have received training from Dr. Stixrud. For tutoring information please contact Edward Strozier at extension 279.

STRATHMORE TUTORING LLC   301-758-1464
4921 Strathmore Avenue, Kensington, MD 20895
WEBSITE: www.strathmoretutoring.com
E-MAIL: strathmoretutor@yahoo.com
DIRECTOR: Shirley A. Miller, M.S., President
SERVICES:
Math and Science Tutoring

Strathmore Tutoring LLC provides professional, individual, in-home instruction in math and science. Our contracting tutors are mathematicians and scientists who work with students in all areas of math, chemistry, physics, and biology, including SAT I (math) and SAT II (math and sciences). We serve middle, high school, college, and graduate students in Montgomery County, Maryland, and vicinity.

Strathmore Tutors are content area experts. They represent an effective resource for the motivated student who struggles with the concepts, methods, or application of mathematic or scientific principles. Our tutors do not have any specialized training in education, however, and are not a recommended resource for poorly motivated students or those with significant special needs.

HISTORY:
Strathmore Tutoring LLC has been in business since 1999, with the sole mission of becoming the premier source of individual math and science coaching in the region. Since our inception, we have served over 200 students.

TIPS ON TRIPS AND CAMPS   301-670-1706   FAX 202-337-0681
P.O. Box 15068, Chevy Chase, MD 20825
WEBSITE: www.tipsontripsandcamps.com
E-MAIL: carey@tipsontripsandcamps.com
SERVICES:
Consultant: Carey Rivers

Since 1971, we have provided parents with the information needed to choose a summer program that is right for their child. Our service is a central source for over 400 carefully selected summer experiences including traditional and specialty sleep away camps, wilderness expeditions, travel and language immersion, ESL instruction, community service, academic and enrichment programs. Consultants visit programs while in session, check references and interview directors. Information is available by phone or at camp fairs hosted at private schools in the metropolitan Washington area. Consultants give parents insights not easily found in a brochure.

BIOGRAPHY:
Carey Rivers, B.A. 1964, University of Mississippi. Past President, Parents Council of Washington; Director/consultant Tips on Trips and Camps since 1988.

TLC, THE TREATMENT AND LEARNING CENTERS   301-424-5200
9975 Medical Center Drive, Rockville, MD 20850
WEBSITE: www.ttlc.org
SERVICES:
Contact: Patricia Ritter, Ph.D., CCC-SLP, Assistant Executive Director

TLC offers comprehensive psycho-educational diagnostic evaluations and provides a variety of programs for students with special learning needs. Working one-to-one with experienced tutors, students may improve reading, mathematics, written language and study skills. Speech and language therapy, counseling and occupational and physical therapy are also offered at TLC, using an interdisciplinary team approach to coordinate all services.

FRANCES TURNER LTD.   301-299-2012   FAX 301-299-9404
11137 Hurdle Hill Drive, Potomac, MD 20854
6001 Montrose Avenue, Suite 404, Rockville, MD 20852
E-MAIL: FranLTD@comcast.net
DIRECTOR: Frances Turner, M.Ed.
SERVICES:
Educational Consultant

Frances Turner offers experienced, personalized, educational consulting services built around the philosophy that the student be thoroughly involved in the process and the primary focus of the school selection decision. She provides educational guidance to parents seeking advice about appropriate schools that meet the academic, emotional and social needs of their children in grades Pre-K through High School in public/private day or boarding schools. Educational services provide consultations with parents and schools, screening for readiness, achievement testing, presentations to parent groups, classroom observations and specific recommendations about suitable schools' procedures for admissions.

BIOGRAPHY:
Frances Turner has a Masters Degree in Education and Reading and has dedicated over thirty years to educating young people in public and private schools in New York and Maryland. She was former Assistant Head/Director of Admissions, Dean of Students and Reading Specialist at McLean School, Potomac, Maryland for 10 years. Frances has served on AIMS admissions workshops and has been guest speaker for numerous school/parent organizations. She is currently a member of the Advisory Board of the Bender-Dosik Parenting Center.

TUTORING FOR SUCCESS, INC.   703-390-9220   301-838-7640
13159 Applegrove Lane, Oak Hill, VA 20171
WEBSITE: www.tutoringforsuccess.com
E-MAIL: mail@tutoringforsuccess.com
DIRECTOR: Cheryl Feuer

SERVICES:
Tutoring for Success offers one-to-one tutoring for any age or subject at students' homes. All of the tutors are experienced and hold bachelor's degrees, and many hold higher level degrees; several tutors teach students with special needs such as LD or ADD. We match every student with the most qualified tutor in that area. Tutoring is tailored to meet the needs of each student and adjusted to the student's unique learning style. Monthly evaluations are furnished to track the student's progress. We service the Washington Metropolitan area.

WAKE, KENDALL, SPRINGER, ISENMAN, SCHWEICKERT, WEINTRAUB & ASSOCIATES, PLLC 202-686-7699

5247 Wisconsin Avenue, N.W., Suite 4, Washington, DC 20015

SERVICES:

Wake, Kendall, Springer, Isenman, Schweickert, Weintraub & Associates provides a full range of educational and psychological services to individuals and schools throughout the Washington Metropolitan area. These include assessment, counseling, school admissions testing, and school consultation for clients ranging from preschool age to adult. All services are individualized to meet specific needs and are performed by licensed psychologists and experienced educational diagnosticians.

Index Key for Schools

+   Extended Day or Day Care

*   Ungraded

b   Boarding

&   LD / ED

x   Grades to be added

B   Boys

G   Girls

C   Coed

Northeast Washington, D.C.

	NAME	LOCATION	GRADES		PAGE
	Archbishop Carroll High School	Harewood Road	9–12	C	13
+	Calvary Christian Academy	Rhode Island Avenue	N–8	C	34
&+	City Lights School	T Street	8–12	C	50
	Cornerstone Community School	Maryland Avenue	K–6	C	56
+	Holy Name Catholic School	West Virginia Ave.	N–8	C	110
+	Metropolitan Day School, Inc.	Randolph Street	N–6	C	141
+	Nannie Helen Burroughs School, Inc.	50th Street	N–6	C	150
+	Preparatory School of the District of Columbia	Chillum Place	N–6	C	181
	St. Anselm's Abbey School	South Dakota Ave.	6–12	B	195
+	St. Anthony Catholic School	12th & Lawrence St.	N–8	C	196
+	St. Benedict the Moor School	21st Street	N–8	C	197
+	St. Francis De Sales School	Rhode Island Avenue	N–8	C	200

Northwest Washington, D.C.

	NAME	LOCATION	GRADES		PAGE
&+	Academy for Ideal Education	Gallatin Street	N–5	C	3
&	Academy for Ideal Education Middle/High School	Colorado Avenue	6–12	C	3
+	Aidan Montessori School	27th Street	N–6*	C	6
+	Annunciation School	Klingle Place	K–8	C	11
+	Beauvoir	Woodley Road	N–3	C	20
+	Blessed Sacrament School	Chevy Chase Parkway	K–8	C	25
+	Bridges Academy	Georgia Avenue	N–8	C	29
+	British School of Washington	16th Street	N–12	C	29
	Edmund Burke School	Upton Street	6–12	C	63
	Emerson Preparatory School	18th Street	9–PG	C	65
	The Field School	Foxhall Road	7–12	C	74
+	The Franklin Montessori School, Forest Hills	Connecticut Avenue	N–1*	C	80

Northwest Washington, D.C.

	NAME	LOCATION	GRADES		PAGE
+	Georgetown Day School High School	Davenport Street	N–12	C	87
+	Georgetown Day School Lower/Middle School	MacArthur Boulevard	N–12	C	88
	Georgetown Visitation Preparatory School	35th Street	9–12	G	90
	Gonzaga College High School	Eye Street	9–12	B	93
+	Holy Redeemer School	New Jersey Avenue	N–8	C	110
+	Holy Trinity School	36th Street	N–8	C	111
+	Immaculate Conception School	N Street	N–5 x	C	112
+	Jewish Primary Day School of the Nation's Capital	16th Street	N–6	C	115
& +	Kingsbury Day School	14th Street	* x	C	121
& +	The Lab School of Washington	Reservoir Road	K–12	C	123
+	Lowell School	Kalmia Road	N–6	C	132
+	Maret School	Cathedral Avenue	K–12	C	134
+	National Cathedral School	Mount Saint Alban	4–12	G	151
+	National Presbyterian School	Nebraska Avenue	K–6	C	152
+	Nationhouse Watoto School	Park Road	N–12	C	152
+	Nativity Catholic Academy	Georgia Avenue	N–8	C	153
+	Our Lady of Victory School	Whitehaven Parkway	N–8	C	173
	Parkmont School	16th Street	6–12	C	176
+	The River School	MacArthur Boulevard	N–3*	C	186
+	Rock Creek International School	Foxhall Road	N–8 x	C	187
+	Roots Activity Learning Center	North Capitol Street	N–8	C	188
	Sacred Heart School	Park Road	N–8	C	189
+	San Miguel Middle School	Newton Street	6–8	B	224
+	Sheridan School	36th Street	K–8	C	226
+	Sidwell Friends School	Wisconsin Avenue	N–12	C	227

Northwest Washington, D.C.

NAME	LOCATION	GRADES		PAGE
b + St. Albans School	Wisconsin & Mass.	4–12	B	190
+ St. Ann's Academy	Wisconsin Avenue	N–8	C	193
+ St. Augustine School	V Street	N–8	C	196
+ St. Gabriel School	Webster Street	K–8	C	201
St. John's College High School	Military Road	9–12	C	205
+ St. Patrick's Episcopal Day School	Whitehaven Parkway	N–8	C	217
+ Washington Hebrew Congregation Tyser ECC	Macomb Street	N	C	242
+ Washington International School	Macomb Street	N–12	C	243

Southeast Washington, D.C.

NAME	LOCATION	GRADES		PAGE
+ Anacostia Bible Church Christian School	T Street	K–6	C	10
+ Assumption School	High View Place	N–8	C	15
+ Capitol Hill Day School	South Carolina Ave.	N–8	C	37
+ Clara Muhammad School	M. L. King, Jr. Ave.	N–8	C	51
+ Dupont Park School	Alabama Avenue	N–10	C	62
+ Holy Comforter-St. Cyprian School	East Capitol Street	N–8	C	107
The Learning Academy	16th Street	N–3	C	126
+ Naylor Road School	Naylor Road	N–8	C	154
Our Lady of Perpetual Help	Morris Road	5–8	C	172
+ Our Lady of Perpetual Help	V Street	N–4	C	172
+ St. Francis Xavier School	O Street	N–8	C	201
+ St. Peter's Interparish School	Third Street	N–8	C	218
+ St. Thomas More Catholic School	Fourth Street	N–8	C	221

Anne Arundel / Howard County, Maryland

NAME	LOCATION	GRADES		PAGE
+ Aleph Bet Jewish Day School	Annapolis	K–5	C	8
&+ Annapolis Area Christian School	Annapolis	N–12	C	10

Anne Arundel / Howard County, Maryland

Anne Arundel / Howard County, Maryland

	NAME	LOCATION	GRADES		PAGE
+	Odenton Christian School	Odenton	N–12	C	167
	Old Mill Christian Academy	Millersville	N–12	C	168
	Severn School	Severna Park	6–12	C	226
+	St. Andrew's United Methodist Day School	Edgewater	N–8	C	193
+	St. Anne's Day School	Annapolis	N–8	C	194
+	St. John the Evangelist School	Severna Park	N–8	C	204
+	St. John's Parish Day School	Ellicott City	N–2x	C	207
+	St. Martin's Lutheran School	Annapolis	N–8	C	211
	St. Martin's-in-the-Field Day School	Severna Park	N–5x	C	212
	St. Mary's Elementary School	Annapolis	K–8	C	213
	St. Mary's High School	Annapolis	9–12	C	213
+	St. Paul's Lutheran School	Glen Burnie	N–8	C	218
&	The Summit School	Edgewater	1–8	C	232
+	Tree of Life Christian Academy	Glen Burnie	K–12	C	238
+	Trinity School	Ellicott City	K–8	C	238
+	The Young School	Columbia	K–8	C	251

Calvert / Charles / St. Mary's County, Maryland

+	Archbishop Neale School	LaPlata	N–8	C	13
+	Bay Montessori School	Lexington Park	N–6*	C	19
+	Beddow Montessori School	Waldorf	N–5*	C	21
+	The Calverton School	Huntingtown	N–12	C	36
+	Cardinal Hickey Academy	Owings	N–8	C	38
+	Chesapeake Montessori School	Huntingtown	*	C	44
	Father Andrew White School	Leonardtown	N–8	C	74
+	Grace Lutheran School	LaPlata	N–8	C	98

Calvert / Charles / St. Mary's County, Maryland

	NAME	LOCATION	GRADES		PAGE
	Holy Angels-Sacred Heart	Avenue	K–8	C	107
&	The King's Christian Academy	Lexington Park	K–12	C	120
	Leonard Hall Junior Naval Academy	Leonardtown	6–12	C	128
	Little Flower School	Great Mills	N–8	C	131
+	Mother Catherine Spalding School	Helen	N–8	C	147
+	Our Lady Star of the Sea School	Solomons	K–8	C	173
+	Southern Maryland Christian Academy	White Plains	N–12	C	229
	St. John's School	Hollywood	K–8	C	207
&	St. Mary's Ryken High School	Leonardtown	9–12	C	214
+	St. Mary's School	Bryantown	K–8	C	215
	St. Michael's School	Ridge	K–8	C	216
+	St. Peter's School	Waldorf	K–8	C	218
	The Tidewater School	Huntingtown	N–5	C	236

Frederick / Washington County, Maryland

	NAME	LOCATION	GRADES		PAGE
+	The Banner School	Frederick	K–8	C	17
+	Broadfording Christian Academy	Hagerstown	N–12	C	30
b+	Frederick Academy of the Visitation	Frederick	N–8	G	81
+	Frederick Adventist School	Frederick	K–8	C	82
+	Frederick Christian Academy	Frederick	N–12	C	82
	The Frederick Montessori School	Braddock Heights	N–4*x	C	82
+	Friends Meeting School	Ijamsville	N–8	C	85
+	Heritage Academy Christian School	Hagerstown	N–12	C	104
	New Life Christian School	Frederick	K–12	C	155
b	Saint James School	St. James	8–12	C	202
+	St. John Regional Catholic School	Frederick	K–8	C	204
	St. John's Literary Inst. at Prospect Hall	Frederick	9–12	C	206

Frederick / Washington County, Maryland

	NAME	LOCATION	GRADES		PAGE
	St. Maria Goretti High School	Hagerstown	9–12	C	211
	Truth Christian Academy	Hagerstown	K–12	C	239

Montgomery County, Maryland

	NAME	LOCATION	GRADES		PAGE
+	Academy of the Child Montessori	Germantown	N–6*	C	3
	Academy of the Holy Cross	Kensington	9–12	G	4
+	The Avalon School	Rockville	3–9x	B	16
+	The Barnesville School	Barnesville	N–8	C	18
+	The Barrie School	Silver Spring	N–12	C	18
+	The Bullis School	Potomac	3–12	C	32
+	Butler School	Darnestown	N–8	C	34
+	Calvary Lutheran School	Silver Spring	K–8	C	35
	Charles E. Smith Jewish Day School	Rockville	K–6	C	39
	Charles E. Smith Jewish Day School	Rockville	7–12	C	40
&	Chelsea School	Silver Spring	5–12	C	41
+	The Children's Learning Center	Rockville	N–4	C	46
+	Christ Episcopal School	Rockville	N–8	C	47
	Church of the Redeemer Christian Academy	Gaithersburg	N–7x	C	50
+	Concord Hill School	Chevy Chase	N–3	C	53
	Connelly School of the Holy Child	Potomac	6–12	G	55
	Covenant Life School	Gaithersburg	K–12	C	59
	Ets Chaiyim School	Montgomery Village	K–12	C	67
+	Evergreen School	Wheaton	N–6*	C	67
+	Faith Arts Academy	Silver Spring	N–3	C	72
	Forcey Christian Middle School	Silver Spring	6–8	C	76
	Forcey Christian School	Silver Spring	N–6	C	76
&	Foundation School of Montgomery County	Rockville	7–12	C	78

	NAME	LOCATION	GRADES		PAGE
	Fourth Presbyterian School	Potomac	N–5x	C	79
+	The Franklin Schools	Rockville	N–3*	C	81
	French International School	Bethesda	N–12	C	84
+	Georgetown Hill Early School	Potomac	N	C	88
+	Georgetown Hill Early School	Darnestown	N	C	89
+	Georgetown Hill Early School	Rockville	N–2	C	89
b	Georgetown Preparatory School	North Bethesda	9–12	B	90
	German School	Potomac	N–PG	C	91
+	Good Shepherd Montessori School	Rockville	N–1	C	94
+	Grace Episcopal Day School	Silver Spring	N–6	C	95
	Grace Episcopal Day School	Kensington	N–6	C	96
+	Green Acres School	Rockville	N–8	C	99
+	The Harbor School	Bethesda	N–2	C	101
+	Hebrew Day Institute	Silver Spring	K–6x	C	102
+	Hebrew Day School of Montgomery County	Silver Spring	K–6	C	102
+	The Heights School	Potomac	3–12	B	103
+	Holton-Arms School	Bethesda	3–12	G	106
+	Holy Cross Elementary	Garrett Park	K–8	C	108
+	Holy Redeemer School	Kensington	N–8	C	110
&	Ivymount School	Rockville	*	C	114
+	Jefferson School	Gaithersburg	N–5	C	115
+	John Nevins Andrews School	Takoma Park	N–8	C	116
+	The Julia Brown Montessori Schools	Olney	N–3	C	117
+	The Julia Brown Montessori Schools	Silver Spring	N–3	C	118
&+	Katherine G. Thomas School	Rockville	N–8	C	118
+	Kemp Mill Montessori School Kehilat Montessori	Silver Spring	*	C	119

Montgomery County, Maryland

	NAME	LOCATION	GRADES		PAGE
	Landon School	Bethesda	3–12	B	124
+	Little Flower School	Bethesda	N–8	C	131
+	Lone Oak Montessori School	Potomac	N–6*	C	131
+	Lone Oak Montessori School	Bethesda	N–6*	C	131
+	Manor Montessori School	Potomac	N–3*	C	134
+	Mary of Nazareth Catholic School	Darnestown	K–8	C	135
+	Mater Amoris Montessori School	Ashton	N–6*	C	137
	Mater Dei School	Bethesda	1–8	B	137
&+	McLean School of Maryland	Potomac	K–12	C	138
+	Melvin J. Berman Hebrew Academy	Rockville	N–12	C	139
+	Montrose Christian School	Rockville	N–12	C	146
+	Mother of God School	Gaithersburg	K–8	C	147
	Muslim Community School	Potomac	N–11x	C	150
+	The Newport School	Silver Spring	N–12	C	157
	The Nora School	Silver Spring	9–12	C	158
+	Norwood School	Bethesda	K–8	C	159
+	Oak Chapel School	Silver Spring	N–8	C	162
&	Oakmont School	Gaithersburg	6–12	C	165
+	Olney Adventist Preparatory School	Olney	K–8	C	169
+	Oneness-Family School	Chevy Chase	N–8	C	170
&	Our Lady of Good Counsel High School	Wheaton	9–12	C	170
+	Our Lady of Lourdes School	Bethesda	N–8	C	171
+	Our Lady of Mercy School	Potomac	N–8	C	172
+	Our Lady of Sorrows School	Takoma Park	N–8	C	172
	The Primary Day School	Bethesda	N–2	C	181
+	Primary Montessori Day School	Rockville	N–2	C	182
	Providence Christian School	Burtonsville	K–6	C	182

	NAME	LOCATION	GRADES		PAGE
b+	Sandy Spring Friends School	Sandy Spring	N–12	C	224
+	Seneca Academy/Circle School	Darnestown	N–6x	C	225
+	Sligo Adventist School	Takoma Park	N–8	C	228
+	Spencerville Adventist Academy	Silver Spring	K–12	C	229
+	St. Andrew Apostle School	Silver Spring	N–8	C	191
+	St. Andrew's Episcopal School	Potomac	6–12	C	192
+	St. Bartholomew School	Bethesda	K–8	C	196
+	St. Bernadette School	Silver Spring	K–8	C	197
+	St. Camillus Catholic School	Silver Spring	K–8	C	198
+	St. Catherine Laboure	Wheaton	N–8	C	198
	St. Elizabeth Catholic School	Rockville	K–8	C	200
+	St. Francis Episcopal Day School	Potomac	N–5	C	200
+	St. Jane De Chantal School	Bethesda	K–8	C	203
+	St. John the Baptist Catholic School	Silver Spring	K–8	C	204
+	St. John the Evangelist School	Silver Spring	N–8	C	205
+	St. John's Episcopal School	Olney	K–8	C	206
+	St. Jude Catholic School	Rockville	N–8	C	208
+	St. Martin's School	Gaithersburg	K–8	C	212
+	St. Mary's School	Rockville	N–8	C	215
+	St. Michael School	Silver Spring	K–8	C	216
+	St. Peter's School	Olney	K–8	C	218
+	Stone Ridge School of the Sacred Heart	Bethesda	N–12	G	230
	Takoma Academy	Takoma Park	9–12	C	234
+	Thornton Friends School (Middle School)	Silver Spring	6–8	C	235
	Thornton Friends School (Upper School)	Silver Spring	9–12	C	235
+	Torah School of Greater Washington	Silver Spring	K–6	C	237

Montgomery County, Maryland

NAME	LOCATION	GRADES		PAGE
Village Montessori School	Gaithersburg	N–2*	C	240
+ Washington Christian Academy	Silver Spring	K–12	C	241
+ Washington Episcopal School	Bethesda	N–8	C	241
+ Washington Hebrew Congregation Primary School	Potomac	N–2	C	242
+ Washington Waldorf School	Bethesda	N–12	C	244
+ Washington-McLaughlin Christian School	Takoma Park	N–6	C	245
+ The Winchester School	Silver Spring	N–Kx	C	248
+ The Woods Academy	Bethesda	N–8	C	248
Yeshiva of Greater Washington	Silver Spring	7–12	BG	250

Prince Georges County, Maryland

NAME	LOCATION	GRADES		PAGE
+ Al-Huda School	College Park	K–8	BG	7
+ Ascension Lutheran School	Landover Hills	K–8	C	15
+ Beddow High School and Junior High School	Accokeek	7–12	C	20
+ Beddow Montessori School	Fort Washington	N–7*	C	21
+ Beltsville Adventist School	Beltsville	K–8	C	22
Berwyn Baptist School	College Park	N–6	C	22
+ Bishop McNamara High School	Forestville	9–12	C	24
+ Bowie Montessori Children's House	Bowie	N–8*	C	26
+ Capitol Christian Academy	Upper Marlboro	N–12	C	37
+ Christian Family Montessori School	Mt. Rainier	*x	C	49
+ Clinton Christian School	Upper Marlboro	N–12	C	51
+ Concordia Lutheran School	Hyattsville	N–8	C	54
+ Cornerstone Christian Academy	Bowie	N–8	C	56
Dematha Catholic High School	Hyattsville	9–12	B	59

Prince Georges County, Maryland

	NAME	LOCATION	GRADES		PAGE
	Divine Peace Lutheran School	Largo	1–8	C	60
+	Elizabeth Seton High School	Bladensburg	9–12	G	64
+	Fairhaven School	Upper Marlboro	K–12*	C	71
+	First Baptist School of Laurel	Laurel	N–8	C	75
&	Foundation Intermediate School	Landover	1–8	C	77
&	Foundation School of Prince Georges County	Landover	7–12	C	78
+	Free Gospel Christian Academy	Coral Hills	K–6	C	83
+	Friends Community School	College Park	K–6x	C	84
+	George E. Peters SDA School	Hyattsville	N–8	C	87
&+	Grace Brethren Christian School	Clinton	N–12	C	94
	Grace Christian School	Bowie	K–8	C	95
&+	Henson Valley Montessori School	Temple Hills	N–8*	C	104
+	Holy Family School	Hillcrest Heights	N–8	C	109
+	Holy Redeemer School	College Park	K–8	C	110
+	Holy Trinity Episcopal Day School	Bowie	1–4	C	111
+	Independent Baptist Academy	Clinton	N–12	C	113
	Jericho Christian Academy	Landover	K–12	C	115
+	The Julia Brown Montessori Schools	Laurel	N–3	C	117
+	Lanham Christian School	Lanham	K–12	C	125
&	Leary School of Prince Georges County	Oxon Hill	1–12	C	128
+	The Maryland International Day School	Oxon Hill	N–5	C	135
+	Mitchellville Children's House	Mitchellville	N–4*x	C	142
+	Mount Calvary Catholic School	Forestville	N–8	C	148
+	National Christian Academy	Fort Washington	N–12	C	151
+	New City Montessori School	Hyattsville	N–4*	C	154
	New Covenant Christian Academy	Colmar Manor	N–8	C	154

Prince Georges County, Maryland

	NAME	LOCATION	GRADES		PAGE
+	New Hope Academy	Landover Hills	N–12	C	155
+	Our Savior's School	Forestville	N–7x	C	174
+	Paint Branch Montessori School	Adelphi	N–6*	C	174
+	Patuxent Montessori School	Bowie	N–6*	C	177
+	Potomac Heights Christian Academy	Indian Head	K–8	C	179
+	Progressive Christian Academy	Camp Springs	K–9	C	182
+	Queen Anne School	Upper Marlboro	6–12	C	183
+	Renaissance Christian Academy	Suitland	N–8	C	185
+	Riverdale Baptist School	Upper Marlboro	N–12	C	186
+	St. Ambrose School	Cheverly	N–8	C	191
+	St. Bernard of Clairvaux School	Riverdale Park	K–8	C	197
+	St. Columba School	Oxon Hill	K–8	C	200
+	St. Hugh's School	Greenbelt	K–8	C	202
+	St. Ignatius School	Ft. Washington	N–8	C	202
+	St. Jerome's School	Hyattsville	N–8	C	203
+	St. John the Evangelist School	Clinton	K–8	C	204
+	St. Joseph's School	Beltsville	N–8	C	208
+	St. Margaret of Scotland School	Seat Pleasant	N–8	C	210
+	St. Mark the Evangelist	Hyattsville	N–8	C	211
+	St. Mary of the Assumption School	Upper Marlboro	K–8	C	212
+	St. Mary of the Mills School	Laurel	K–8	C	212
+	St. Mary Star of the Sea School	Indian Head	K–8	C	213
+	St. Mary's Catholic School	Landover Hills	N–8	C	213
+	St. Mary's School of Piscataway	Clinton	K–8	C	216
+	St. Matthias Apostle School	Lanham	N–8	C	216
+	St. Philip the Apostle School	Camp Springs	N–8	C	219
+	St. Pius X Regional School	Bowie	K–8	C	219

Prince Georges County, Maryland

	NAME	LOCATION	GRADES		PAGE
&	St. Vincent Pallotti High School	Laurel	9–12	C	223
	Washington New Church School	Mitchellville	K–10	C	244
+	World View Christian Center	Brandywine	N–6x	C	249

Alexandria / Fairfax County, Virginia

+	Academy of Christian Education	Reston	N–6	C	3
&	Accotink Academy	Springfield	K–PG*	C	5
	Ad Fontes Academy	Fairfax Station	K–12	C	6
+	Agape Christian Academy	Alexandria	N–6	C	6
	Al Fatih Academy	Herndon	N–4	C	7
+	Alexandria Country Day School	Alexandria	K–8	C	8
	Ambleside School	Reston	K–8	C	9
	Angelus Academy	Springfield	K–8	C	10
+	Apple Tree School	Fairfax	N–4	C	12
+	Apple Tree School	Vienna	N–K	C	12
+	Aquinas Montessori School	Alexandria	N–8*	C	12
+	Bishop Ireton High School	Alexandria	9–12	C	23
+	Blessed Sacrament School	Alexandria	N–8	C	25
+	The Boyd School Centreville/Clifton	Centreville	N–6*	C	27
+	The Boyd School Fairfax/Fairfax Station	Fairfax	N–K*	C	27
+	The Boyd School Herndon/Oak Hill	Herndon	N–K*	C	28
+	The Boyd School Reston/Great Falls	Herndon	N–K*	C	28
+	Brentwood Academy	Alexandria	N–2	C	29
+	Brooksfield School	McLean	N–3x	C	30
+	Browne Academy	Alexandria	N–8	C	31
+	Burgundy Farm Country Day School	Alexandria	N–8	C	33
+	Calvary Road Christian School	Alexandria	N–8	C	36

Alexandria / Fairfax County, Virginia

	NAME	LOCATION	GRADES		PAGE
+	Chesapeake Academy of Northern Virginia	Springfield	K–12	C	42
&+	Chesterbrook Academy Elementary	Chantilly	N–6x	C	44
	Christian Assembly Academy	Vienna	K–8	C	48
+	Christian Center School	Alexandria	N–6	C	49
&+	Commonwealth Academy	Alexandria	6–12	C	52
&	Different Drum, Inc.	Chantilly	9–12	C	59
	Dominion Christian School	Oakton	K–7x	C	61
&	Dominion School	Springfield	7–12	C	61
+	Edlin School	Reston	N–8	C	62
+	Embassy School	Herndon	N–3	C	64
+	Engleside Christian School	Alexandria	N–12	C	66
b	Episcopal High School	Alexandria	9–12	C	66
+	Fair Oaks Academy	Fairfax	N–12	C	68
+	Fairfax Baptist Temple Academy	Fairfax Station	K–12	C	69
+	Fairfax Christian School	Vienna	N–12	C	70
+	Fairfax Collegiate School	Annandale	4–9	C	70
	Fairfax SciTech Academy	Herndon	N–6x	C	71
+	Flint Hill School	Oakton	N–12	C	75
&	Foundation School of Alexandria	Alexandria	6–12	C	78
+	Gesher Jewish Day School	Fairfax	K–8	C	92
+	Grace Episcopal School	Alexandria	N–5	C	96
+	Green Hedges School	Vienna	N–8	C	99
	The GW Community School	Springfield	9–12	C	100
&	The High Road School of Northern Virginia	Chantilly	2–12	C	104
&+	Holy Spirit School	Annandale	N–8	C	110
	Hope Montessori School	Annandale	N–2*	C	111

	NAME	LOCATION	GRADES		PAGE
	Immanuel Christian School	Springfield	N–8	C	112
+	Immanuel Lutheran School	Alexandria	K–8	C	112
	Islamic Saudi Academy	Alexandria	2–12	C	114
	Islamic Saudi Academy	Fairfax	N–1	C	114
+	Kenwood School	Annandale	N–6	C	119
+	The Langley School	McLean	N–8	C	124
&	The Learning Community of Northern Virginia	Reston	4–PGx	C	127
&	Leary School of Virginia	Alexandria	1–12	C	128
+	Little Flock Christian School	Fairfax	Nx	C	130
b	The Madeira School	McLean	9–12	G	133
+	Merritt Academy	Fairfax	N–8	C	141
+	Montessori School of Alexandria	Alexandria	N–7*	C	144
+	Montessori School of Herndon	Herndon	N–3*	C	144
	Montessori School of McLean	McLean	N–6*	C	145
+	The Montessori School of Northern Virginia	Annandale	N–4*	C	146
	Montessori School of Oakton	Oakton	N–6*	C	146
+	Mount Pleasant Baptist Church Christian Academy	Herndon	N–3x	C	149
+	Nativity Catholic School	Burke	N–8	C	153
	The New School of Northern Virginia	Fairfax	3–12	C	156
+	Northern Virginia Friends School	Oakton	N–6	C	159
+	Nysmith School for the Gifted	Herndon	N–8	C	161
+	Oak Hill Christian School, Herndon Campus	Oak Hill	N–K	C	162
+	Oak Hill Christian School, Reston Campus	Reston	N–9x	C	163
+	Oakcrest School	McLean	6–12	G	163

Alexandria / Fairfax County, Virginia

	NAME	LOCATION	GRADES		PAGE
&	Oakwood School	Annandale	1–8	C	166
+	Oasis School	Reston	3–8	G	166
	Our Lady of Good Counsel School	Vienna	K–8	C	171
&	Paladin Academy	Chantilly	K–8	C	174
&	Paladin Academy	Vienna	K–8	C	175
&	Paul VI Catholic High School	Fairfax	9–12	C	177
+	Pinecrest School	Annandale	N–5	C	178
+	The Potomac School	McLean	K–12	C	179
+	Queen of Apostles Catholic School	Alexandria	K–8	C	183
+	Reston Montessori School	Reston	N–6*	C	185
+	Springfield Academy	Springfield	N–4	C	230
+	St. Ambrose School	Annandale	K–8	C	191
	St. Andrew the Apostle School	Clifton	N–8	C	192
	St. Bernadette School	Springfield	K–8	C	197
&	St. Coletta School	Alexandria	*	C	199
+	St. John School	McLean	N–8	C	204
	St. Joseph School	Herndon	K–8	C	207
&+	St. Leo the Great Catholic School	Fairfax	N–8	C	208
+	St. Louis Catholic School	Alexandria	K–8	C	209
+	St. Luke School	McLean	K–8	C	209
&+	St. Mary's School	Alexandria	N–8	C	215
	St. Michael Catholic School	Annandale	K–8	C	216
+	St. Rita Elementary School	Alexandria	K–8	C	219
+	St. Stephen's & St. Agnes School	Alexandria	6–8	C	219
+	St. Stephen's & St. Agnes School	Alexandria	N–5	C	219
+	St. Stephen's & St. Agnes School	Alexandria	9–12	C	219
+	St. Timothy School	Chantilly	K–8	C	222

Alexandria / Fairfax County, Virginia

	NAME	LOCATION	GRADES		PAGE
+	Sunset Hills Montessori	Reston	N–6*	C	233
+	Sydenstricker School	Springfield	N–1*	C	233
+	Temple Baptist School	Herndon	N–12	C	234
	Thornton Friends School (Upper School)	Alexandria	9–12	C	236
+	Town and Country School of Vienna	Vienna	N–6	C	237
	Trinity Christian School	Fairfax	1–12x	C	238
	Vienna Adventist Academy	Vienna	K–12	C	239
	Washington Islamic Academy	Springfield	K–6x	C	243
+	Way of Faith Christian Academy	Fairfax	K–12	C	246
+	Westminster School	Annandale	K–8	C	247
+	Word of Life Christian Academy	Springfield	N–12	C	249

Arlington County / Falls Church, Virginia

	NAME	LOCATION	GRADES		PAGE
&	Bishop Denis J. O'Connell High School	Arlington	9–12	C	23
+	The Congressional Schools of Virginia	Falls Church	N–8	C	54
&+	Corpus Christi School	Falls Church	N–8	C	57
+	Early Years Montessori School	Falls Church	N–3*	C	62
+	Fairfax Brewster School	Falls Church	K–6	C	69
+	Falls Church Children's House of Montessori	Falls Church	N–K*	C	73
+	Grace Lutheran School	Falls Church	K–8	C	97
	Khadijah Academy for Girls	Falls Church	5–9	G	120
+	Montessori School of Holmes Run	Falls Church	N–6*	C	145
+	Our Savior Lutheran School	Arlington	K–8	C	173
&	Rivendell School	Arlington	K–8	C	186
+	St. Agnes Catholic School	Arlington	N–8	C	190
&+	St. Ann Elementary School	Arlington	K–8	C	193
+	St. Charles Catholic School	Arlington	K–8	C	199

Arlington County / Falls Church, Virginia

	NAME	LOCATION	GRADES		PAGE
+	St. James School	Falls Church	K–8	C	203
+	St. Thomas More Cathedral School	Arlington	K–8	C	221
	Trinity School at Meadow View	Falls Church	7–12	C	238

Fauquier County / Loudoun County, Virginia

	NAME	LOCATION	GRADES		PAGE
+	Ark Academy	Sterling	K–8	C	15
+	The Boyd School Broadlands	Ashburn	N–6*x	C	27
+	Chesterbrook Academy Elementary School	Sterling	N–8	C	44
+	Christian Fellowship School	Ashburn	N–10x	C	49
+	Dominion Academy	Leesburg	K–8	C	60
&+	Faith Christian School	Sterling	N–12	C	73
b	Foxcroft School	Middleburg	9–12	G	79
+	Highland School	Warrenton	N–12	C	105
	Hill School	Middleburg	K–8	C	106
	Leesburg Christian School	Leesburg	N–12	C	128
&+	Loudoun Country Day School	Leesburg	N–8	C	131
+	Montessori Academy at Belmont Greene	Ashburn	N–4*x	C	143
+	Montessori Children's House of Loudoun	Sterling	N–K*	C	143
+	Munger Academy	Sterling	N–3	C	149
	Notre Dame Academy	Middleburg	9–12	C	160
&	Paladin Academy	Sterling	K–8	C	175
+	St. Theresa School	Ashburn	K–8	C	221
	Wakefield School	The Plains	N–12	C	240

Prince William County, Virginia

	NAME	LOCATION	GRADES		PAGE
+	All Saints Catholic School	Manassas	K–8	C	9
+	Aquinas School	Woodbridge	N–8	C	13
+	Bethel Christian School	Woodbridge	N–6	C	23

Prince William County, Virginia

	NAME	LOCATION	GRADES		PAGE
+	Calvary Christian School	Triangle	N–12	C	35
+	Cardinal Montessori School	Woodbridge	N–7*	C	39
+	Emmanuel Christian School	Manassas	N–12	C	65
+	Evangel Christian School	Dale City	N–12	C	67
	Fairmont Christian Preparatory School	Manassas	K–8	C	72
+	Holy Family Catholic School	Dale City	N–7x	C	109
+	Linton Hall School	Bristow	K–8	C	130
+	Manassas Christian School	Manassas	1–8	C	133
+	The Merit School	Woodbridge	K–3	C	140
+	Prince William Academy/ Early Years Academy	Manassas	N–6x	C	182
	Seton Junior and Senior High School	Manassas	7–12	C	226
+	St. Francis of Assisi School	Triangle	N–8	C	201
	St. John Neumann School	Woodbridge	7–12	C	203
+	Star of Bethlehem Christian Academy	Triangle	N–6	C	230
+	Tabernacle Baptist Academy	Manassas	N–12	C	234
+	Wonders of Wisdom Academy & Daycare	Woodbridge	N–1	C	248

Other Area Schools

b	Chatham Hall	Chatham, VA	9–12	G	40
&	The Children's Guild	Baltimore, MD	1–8x	C	45
&b	Christchurch School	Christchurch, VA	8–PG	B	47
	Colonial Academy	Stafford, VA	N–7	C	52
+	The Country Day School	West Charles Town, WV	N–9	C	58
+	Epiphany School	Culpeper, VA	N–5	C	66
+	Faith Baptist Schools	Fredericksburg, VA	N–12	C	72
b	Fork Union Military Academy	Fork Union, VA	6–PG	B	76
+	Fredericksburg Academy	Fredericksburg, VA	N–12	C	83

Other Area Schools

	NAME	LOCATION	GRADES		PAGE
b+	Garrison Forest School	Owings Mills, MD	N–12	G	86
b	George School	Newtown, PA	9–12	C	87
	Gunston Day School	Centreville, MD	9–12	C	100
+	Holy Cross Academy	Fredericksburg, VA	N–8	C	108
b	The Kiski School	Saltsburg, PA	9–PG	B	121
b	Linden Hall School for Girls	Lititz, PA	6–PG	G	129
b	Massanutten Military Academy	Woodstock, VA	6–PG	C	136
b+	McDonough School	Owings Mills, MD	K–12	C	138
b	Mercersburg Academy	Mercersburg, PA	9–PG	C	139
b	Miller School	Charlottesville, VA	6–12	C	142
&b	Oakland School	Keswick, VA	*	C	164
b	Oldfields School	Glencoe, MD	8–12	G	168
&b	Phelps School	Malvern, PA	7–PG	B	178
	Powhatan School	Boyce, VA	K–8	C	180
b+	Randolph-Macon Academy	Front Royal, VA	6–PG	C	184
+	Ruxton Country School	Owings Mills, MD	K–8	C	188
+	Sacred Heart Academy	Winchester, VA	N–8	C	189
b+	St. Anne's-Belfield School	Charlottesville, VA	N–12	C	194
+	St. John the Evangelist School	Warrenton, VA	N–8	C	205
b	St. Margaret's School	Tappahanock, VA	8–12	G	210
+	St. Patrick Catholic School	Fredericksburg, VA	N–8	C	217
b	St. Timothy's School	Stevenson, MD	9–PG	G	222
+	St. William of York Catholic School	Stafford, VA	N–8	C	224
b	Stuart Hall	Staunton, VA	5–12	G	231
&b	West Nottingham Academy	Colora, MD	6–PG	C	246
b	Woodberry Forest School	Woodberry Forest, VA	9–12	B	248
b	Wyoming Seminary	Kingston, PA	9–PG	C	250